COLLECTOR SERIES™

United States CURRENCY

LARGE SIZE · SMALL SIZE · FRACTIONAL

9th EDITION

Kenneth Bressett

Pricing Editor:
Patrick Ian Perez

Whitman™
SINCE 1934

United States CURRENCY

9th EDITION

Whitman
SINCE 1934

4001 Helton Dr., Florence, AL 35630
whitman.com

Correspondence concerning this book may be directed to the publisher, Attn. Collector Series: United States Currency, at the address above.

ISBN: 978-07948-51897 / WW1761-0325 / Ebook ISBN: 978-07948-52061
Printed in the United States of America.

Disclaimer: No warranty or representation of any kind is made concerning the accuracy or completeness of the information presented, or its usefulness in numismatic purchases or sales. The opinions of others may vary. The author, a professional numismatist, regularly buys, sells, conducts auctions, and may sometimes hold certain of the items discussed in this book.

Caveat: The price estimates given are subject to variation and differences of opinion. Before making decisions to buy or sell, consult the latest information. Past performance of the collectible paper-money market or of any note or series within that market is not necessarily an indication of future performance, as the future is unknown. Such factors as changing demand, popularity, grading interpretations, strength of the overall paper-money market, and economic conditions will continue to be influences.

CONTENTS

FOREWORD

This book will provide the reader with a very good overview and price guide for the entire breadth of United States paper money. It is an excellent stepping-off point if you are just getting started in collecting currency and will be a valuable identification guide to help you understand the various note types that have been issued by the U.S. Treasury.

The collectible paper-money market has seen tremendous growth over the past 10 years, and the prices listed in this volume have been updated using Whitman Brands' industry-leading pricing database across multiple grades (conditions) based on our industry-standard *Greensheet* price guide. Our pricing database is maintained on a monthly basis with the latest transactional data. While all price guides are just that—guides—this book will also help you understand which notes are scarce or rare, and what you can expect to pay when adding notes to your collection.

United States currency has a wide variety of beautiful designs, and there are many ways to collect the notes. Even a collection of a few of them is a joy to look at and can be built on a wide range of budgets. We hope this new volume enhances your collecting experience!

Patrick Ian Perez

Patrick Ian Perez is the pricing and market analyst for the CDN monthly Greensheet *and the* Banknote Book, *and has written the feature articles for the* Greensheet *for the past nine years. A former coin and currency dealer, he has also written articles for the International Banknote Society and has published a book on modern Chinese paper money.*

PREFACE

United States Currency compiles three separate books that have served collectors for many years, plus the work of several authors and many researchers in the field of paper money. The trilogy of books that form its foundation are:

- *United States Large Size Paper Money 1861 to 1923* (sixth ed.), by William P. Donlon, revised by A.M. Kagin and Don Kagin (1979)
- *A Guide Book of United States Fractional Currency,* by Matt Rothert (1963)
- *A Guide Book of Modern United States Currency* (eighth ed.), by Neil Shafer (1979)

It also draws from two more-recent references: *A Guide Book of United States Paper Money,* by Arthur and Ira Friedberg (2024), and the *Whitman Encyclopedia of U.S. Paper Money,* by Q. David Bowers (2009).

The list of contributors to the foundational books above reads like a history of those who have devoted their lives to the study of this fascinating hobby. Their participation is acknowledged here, for without such assistance the original books could not have been compiled. Among those who were most helpful to the original authors and in past editions are:

Thomas C. Baine • A.E. Bebee • Q. David Bowers • Hy Brown • Amon G. Carter • H.K. Crofoot • Tom Denly • Don Fisher • John J. Ford Jr. • Dennis J. Fargue • Harry J. Forman • Arthur Friedberg • Jack Friedberg • Heritage Auctions (HA.com) • Harry E. Jones • Paul S. Kagin • Theodore Kemm • Lyn F. Knight • Michael Kohlman Jr. • Abe Kosoff • Chester L. Krause • Robert H. Lloyd • John H. Morris Jr. • National Numismatic Collection at the Smithsonian Institution • Eric P. Newman • Dean Oakes • V.H. Oswald • M. Perlmutter • Thomas J. Settle • Neil Shafer • Arlie R. Slabaugh • Stack's Bowers Galleries • L.S. Werner

CONDITION: Grades and Terms

Correctly speaking, to merit the distinction of being "Uncirculated" a note would have to be extracted from a pack of unused notes and carefully placed in a protective holder. Present day acetate holders were not available in the last century, and very few notes enjoyed this careful state of preservation.

The term "Uncirculated" rather than "new" is used by most collectors. This description should only be used to describe a note which has all the appearance of having been carefully preserved as above stated. It must be clean, bright, sharp in every detail with no discoloration and no evidence of horizontal or vertical folds. Minor corner creases and very slight evidence of tellers' or collectors' careless handling may be present.

In the early issues, needle holes are often present. These small punctures, sometimes called "pinholes," were frequently caused by sewing together a pack of notes to prevent theft. The most demanding perfectionist should not hesitate to accept early, rare issues because of a few needle holes. Holes of any type in later issues would lower their value.

GEM CRISP UNCIRCULATED (Unc-65)—A nearly perfect new note, well centered and fresh with no signs of aging, fading, handling, or wear.

CHOICE CRISP UNCIRCULATED (Unc-63)—An almost perfect new note, of only slightly less than gem quality. Centering may be just a little off. It may show slight aging or light counting smudges or wrinkles.

CRISP UNCIRCULATED (Unc-60)—No trace of circulation or folding. May not be perfectly centered, and can have a few defects such as pin holes, counting smudges, wrinkles, close margins or a corner tip fold that does not extend into the design.

ABOUT UNCIRCULATED (AU-50)—Only slightly less than the definition of Uncirculated. Close examination will show minor imperfections. Light folds may be noticeable but not sufficient to break the paper or impair the design. May have corner folds, but no fading or mutilation.

EXTREMELY FINE (EF-40)—Note shows light circulation but still has most of its crispness and is bright and attractive. May have some folds and minor imperfections.

VERY FINE (VF-20)—Shows some evidence of circulation and handling but is still bright, not badly soiled and without tears. May show several folds and will have lost some of its crispness and color. Notes that have been cleaned or pressed will grade no higher than Very Fine.

FINE (F-12)—Shows considerable circulation but is still quite clean and has very little crispness left. Edges may be rough or torn, but no portions may be missing. Must not be badly stained or faded.

VERY GOOD (VG-8)—Will be fairly well soiled and may be significantly worn. Edges can be rough and corners rounded. Notes may be lightly stained or faded, with little or no crispness.

GOOD (G-4)—Only the rarest notes are collected in Good condition. These pieces are well worn, may have tears on margins, and even a stain or ink mark. They have generally lost all crispness and may be soiled, limp and somewhat unattractive.

NON-COLLECTIBLE

The term "non-collectible" when used in any listing signifies that if any specimens exist, they are owned by museums or institutions and will not likely be offered for sale.

FACE AND BACK, NOT OBVERSE AND REVERSE

"Face" and "back" are the terms used by the Bureau of Engraving and Printing in referring to what is called "obverse" and "reverse" on coins. These terms do seem more descriptive and are used throughout the text.

VALUATIONS, DEMAND AND SUPPLY

Valuations given in the price section are based upon estimated SUPPLY of the various issues and the DEMAND for those issues. This information has been obtained from many well known suppliers and from actual public offerings during the past few years. Prices have risen considerably since the last edition of this catalog, but that does not necessarily mean that the trend will continue. Values are given as a guide to what the collector might expect to pay. They are not to be construed as an offer to buy or sell on the part of the author or publisher or the prices a collector might hope to obtain when a collection is sold to a dealer who must include a fair margin of profit.

SPECIALIZE!

A word of advice to the neophyte collector—SPECIALIZE!

The collector should specialize, not only because a limited budget might dictate this plan, but also to afford the opportunity to more thoroughly study and assimilate knowledge of the various types or series selected.

Collectors with a limited budget have erroneously believed that a collection of United States paper money is too costly. Facts prove that a prize-winning collection of the large-size or small-size issues may be assembled for less outlay and afford more pleasure and attract more attention if displayed with pertinent information, than a complete collection of Uncirculated Lincoln cents. And it may find a more ready market when the time comes to sell.

United States paper money affords numerous ways to specialize, depending on the imagination and personal preference of the collector. To name just a few:

A Type Collection. A note of each major design of one or more denominations. Strange as it may seem, denominations of $5 or higher might be easier to acquire than $1 and $2.

A Signature Collection. All issues of one or more combination of signatures of Treasury Officials. This is a fascinating endeavor. A signature collection, with a brief commentary on the officials whose signatures appear, makes a prize-winning exhibit.

A Collection of Various Seals. There were many attractive seals used throughout the large size issues. Securing one of each type of each denomination will require some patience and effort, but the chase will be rewarding to the serious collector.

A Collection of Famous Persons. All issues which show a portrait of Washington, Lincoln, Hamilton, Jefferson or any other selected person. This makes a very interesting and attractive exhibit when displayed with a biographical sketch of the person and a description of the notes.

A National Bank Note Collection. National Bank Notes of the First, Second and/or Third Charters offer real opportunities to the collector with imagination. Most popular are the notes of all Charter periods issued by the banks of the collector's own state. Also popular are notes with odd names of banks or places, or industrial or commercial titles such as Traders National Bank, Mechanics National Bank, Brotherhood of Locomotive Engineers, etc. The National Banks of Pennsylvania afford many odd names of points of issue. A note from various state capitols is always interesting.

Historic, Art and Other Special Features. Many notes depict famous paintings and scenes of historic interest. The Coat of Arms of the state are on the backs of most $5 First Charter Nationals and Second Charter Brown Backs. Also a varied collection of eagles is shown on several series.

Only a few suggestions have been given. Numerous other plans of collecting will suggest themselves and will afford the collector hours of pleasure, recognition if exhibited and often financial gain.

HOUSING THE COLLECTION

Collectors of earlier days resorted to the use of envelopes, composition books, scrapbooks and many other forms of housing for their paper money. These makeshifts at times resulted in damage to a prized note.

Demand by thousands of new followers of this fascinating and profitable hobby has developed many forms of protection. Acetate and mylar holders designed for a single note or for two notes back to back seems to be the favorite. These holders allow handling and exhibiting without damage to the notes.

Vinyl pages, which house three notes to each page, are less expensive but notes should be placed in individual acetate holders before placing in vinyl. Experience has shown that notes will absorb oil when placed unprotected in vinyl. This will not occur if notes are first placed in individual holders.

INVENTORY

The serial numbers on U.S. paper money provide a positive means of identification. The inventory system may be a very elaborate card file or as simple as personal choice dictates. It should include catalog number, condition, serial number, date of purchase, from whom and for how much.

The inventory should be kept in a secure place but not with the collection. Such a complete record will prove most helpful if all or part of the collection is lost or eventually sold.

HOW TO DETECT COUNTERFEITS

Counterfeiting has been practiced since coins and currency were first circulated and before the issuance of U.S. coins or currency. In early history it was punishable by death. At the time of the Civil War, counterfeiting was unusually prevalent, with the result that about one-third of the currency in circulation was counterfeit.

On July 5, 1865, the U.S. Secret Service was established to suppress this crime, which had become very lucrative for the forgers but also a potential danger to the nation's economy. This agency was instrumental in materially reducing the number of counterfeit notes in circulation and making attempts at counterfeiting unpopular.

Today, forgeries are again on the increase due to modern photographic, scientific, and electronic equipment. The printing of paper money with no change in design has not proved to be the deterrent which was expected. The new 21st-century United States notes with additional security features and more colorful designs than those in the past are much more difficult to duplicate.

HOW TO DETECT COUNTERFEITS

It is hoped that the illustrations and information will assist new and old collectors in determining whether a note is genuine or counterfeit.

By permission of the Treasury Department, United States Secret Service.

GENUINE

On a GENUINE NOTE the portrait is lifelike and stands out distinctly. Magnification will show hairlines to be sharp and distinct. Points on spiked seals are sharp and even. Scalloped seals and round seals have well defined outlines. Watermarks and security strips are clear and distinct.

COUNTERFEIT

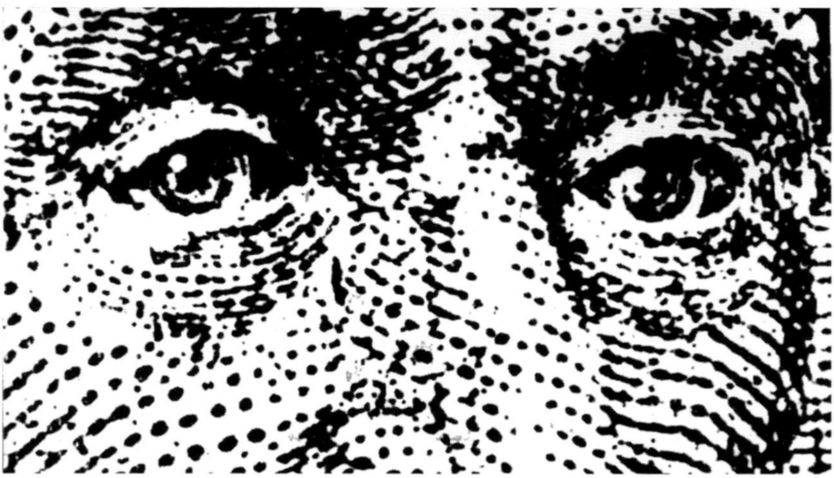

On a COUNTERFEIT NOTE the portrait is lifeless and background probably too dark. Criss-crossed fine lines are not clear or uniform. Points on spiked seals are uneven, blunt or broken. Scalloped seals and round seals usually have thick, "sloppy" outlines. The paper has no colored threads, but some counterfeits have red and blue lines simulating threads. Watermarks and other security features may be missing.

HOW TO DETECT COUNTERFEITS

Comparison of genuine and counterfeit. Note sharpness of genuine note on right side of illustrations.

CHARACTERISTICS AND CHECKPOINTS

Look for these security features, which are present on authentic notes of recent years.

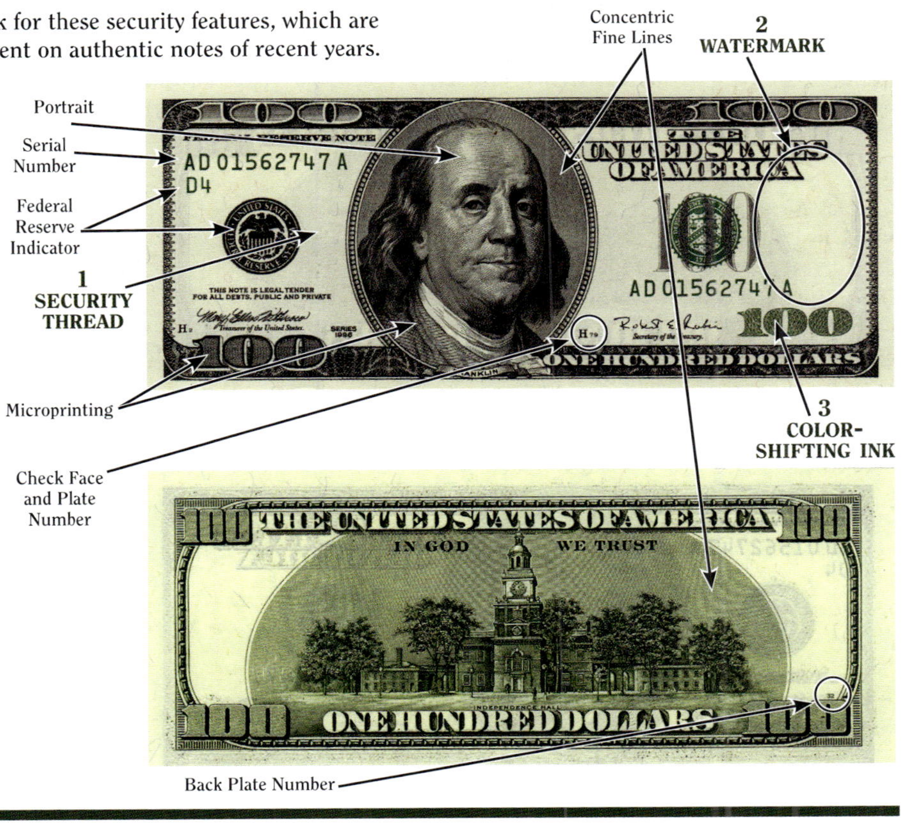

PORTRAITS ON U.S. PAPER MONEY

By law, no living person can be portrayed on U.S. currency or any other obligation of the United States. The reason for this legislation goes back to Civil War days. At that time portraits of President Lincoln and the secretary of the Treasury, Salmon P. Chase, had appeared on U.S. currency while both were still living. No objection had apparently been made.

While Spencer M. Clark was still chief clerk of the National Currency Division of the U.S. Treasury, his portrait appeared on half a million 5-cent Fractional Currency notes. This caused Representative M. Russell Thayer of Pennsylvania to propose an amendment forbidding the practice of showing any living person on U.S. currency or other obligations. The bill passed and became law, and it has not been changed.

Third Issue 5¢ Fractional Currency showing the portrait of Spencer M. Clark on the face.

TREASURY NOTES OF THE WAR OF 1812

It may come as a surprise to some that the first paper money circulated in the United States after the Constitution was issued in 1812—preceding the Demand Notes of 1861 by 49 years. Occasioned by the War of 1812 and the expiration of the charter of the First Bank of the United States, the federal government authorized five Treasury note issues between 1812 and 1815. These notes are considered among the rarest of all issues of American currency.

In total, over $36 million in denominations of $3 to $1,000 were emitted. The last issue included small circulating notes in denominations of less than $100. Because of the shortage of adequate circulating medium and revenue to conduct the War of 1812, these notes proved to be extremely useful as they were transferable by delivery and receivable for duties, taxes, and public use at par plus accrued interest. They also served as interest-bearing reserves for banks since they were convertible into any kind of money and bore interest simultaneously.

The success of the Treasury notes was demonstrated by the fact that they were fully subscribed and accepted by the banks and merchants. In addition, the small Treasury note issues of 1815 indirectly served to increase the circulating medium of the country. They were used to buy goods and services by individuals, pay custom duties by merchants, and acted as cash reserves for banks, preventing bank notes from being discounted.

These Treasury Notes thus became the first circulating currency issued by the United States after ratification of the Constitution.

LISTING OF KNOWN TREASURY NOTES AND THEIR VALUES

Date	Denomination		Signature	Number Known	VF-20	Unc-60
6/30/1812	$1,000		Unsigned	3	$25,000	$40,000
	100		Unsigned	5	17,000	30,000
1/25/1813	1,000			0		
	100			0		
3/4/1814	1,000			0		
	100		Signed	3	20,000	45,000
	20			0		
12/26/1814	100		Unsigned	3	20,000	25,000
	100		Signed	3	15,000	20,000
	20		Unsigned	6	10,000	15,000
	20		Signed	11	8,000	12,000
2/24/1815	100		Unsigned	10	8,000	12,000
	100		Signed	0		
	50		Unsigned	3	8,500	12,500
	50		Signed	15	8,000	12,000
	20		Unsigned	10	7,000	17,000
	20		Signed	0		
	10	Text at right	Unsigned	0		
	10	Text at right	Signed	5	8,000	14,000
	10	No text at right	Unsigned	5	6,000	10,000
	10	No text at right	Signed	25	7,000	10,000
	5		Unsigned	12	7,000	10,000
	5		Signed	2	8,000	12,000
	3		Unsigned	10	8,000	12,000
	3		Signed	5	8,000	12,000

Unsigned notes may be Proofs.

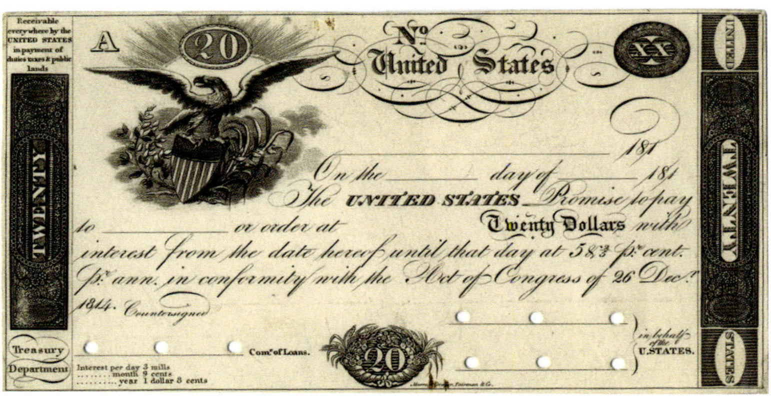

An example of a Treasury Note of the War of 1812.

TERMS OF TREASURY OFFICIALS—LARGE-SIZE NOTES

These signatures appear on United States large-size paper money, with terms of office compiled from information obtained by the Treasury Department.

Register	Treasurer	Term Began	Term Ended
Chittenden	Spinner	April 17, 1861	August 10, 1864
Colby	Spinner	August 11, 1864	September 21, 1867
Jeffries	Spinner	October 5, 1867	March 15, 1869
Allison	Spinner	April 3, 1869	June 30, 1875
Allison	New	June 30, 1875	July 1, 1876
Allison	Wyman	July 1, 1876	June 30, 1877
Allison	Gilfillan	July 1, 1877	March 23, 1878
Scofield	Gilfillan	April 1, 1878	May 20, 1881
Bruce	Gilfillan	May 21, 1881	March 31, 1883
Bruce	Wyman	April 1, 1883	April 30, 1885
Bruce	Jordan	May 1, 1885	June 5, 1885
Rosecrans	Jordan	June 8, 1885	May 23, 1887
Rosecrans	Hyatt	May 24, 1887	May 10, 1889
Rosecrans	Huston	May 11, 1889	April 21, 1891
Rosecrans	Nebeker	April 25, 1891	May 31, 1893
Rosecrans	Morgan	June 1, 1893	June 19, 1893
Tillman	Morgan	July 1, 1893	June 30, 1897
Tillman	Roberts	July 1, 1897	December 2, 1897
Bruce	Roberts	December 3, 1897	March 17, 1898
Lyons	Roberts	April 7, 1898	June 30, 1905
Lyons	Treat	July 1, 1905	April 1, 1906
Vernon	Treat	June 12, 1906	October 30, 1909
Vernon	McClung	November 1, 1909	March 14, 1911
Napier	McClung	March 15, 1911	November 21, 1912
Napier	Thompson	November 22, 1912	March 31, 1913
Napier	Burke	April 1, 1913	October 23, 1913
Parker	Burke	November 1, 1913	December 31, 1914
Teehee	Burke	March 24, 1915	November 20, 1919
Elliott	Burke	November 21, 1919	January 5, 1921
Elliott	White	May 2, 1921	January 24, 1922
Speelman	White	January 25, 1922	September 30, 1927
Woods	White	October 1, 1927	May 1, 1928
Woods	Tate	May 31, 1928	January 17, 1929
Jones	Woods	January 22, 1929	May 31, 1933

FEDERAL RESERVE NOTES, Large Size

Secretary	Treasurer	Term Began	Term Ended
McAdoo	Burke	April 1, 1913	December 15, 1918
Glass	Burke	December 16, 1918	February 1, 1920
Houston	Burke	February 2, 1920	January 5, 1921
Mellon	White	May 2, 1921	May 1, 1928

UNITED STATES OR LEGAL TENDER NOTES

The first Issue of March 10, 1862, was printed in denominations of $5, $10, $20, $50, $100, $500, and $1,000. The Second Issue of August 1, 1862, was printed in denominations of $1 and $2. The face design on these notes indicates that a $3 denomination was also contemplated but never issued. A proof specimen of the $3 design of this series does exist.

The Third Issue, dated March 10, 1863, was almost identical with the First Series, excepting a change in the back design, and was printed in the same denominations, $5 to $1,000.

The Fourth Issue had the greatest number of series, signature and seal changes, and comprised the Series of 1869, 1874, 1875, 1878, 1880, 1907, and 1917. All bear the designation of "United States Note," excepting the Series of 1869 which is designated on the face as "Treasury Note." As a deterrent to counterfeiting, paper with silk threads was used for the first time in all denominations of the 1869 series.

The Fourth Issue was printed in the following denominations:

1869	$1	$2	$5	$10	$20	$50	$100	$500	$1,000
1874	1	2	—	—	—	50	—	500	—
1875	1	2	5	10	20	50	100	500	—
1878	1	2	5	10	20	50	100	500	1,000

Also a $5,000 and a $10,000 denomination in the 1878 series.

1880	$1	$2	$5	$10	$20	$50	$100	$500	$1,000
1907	—	—	5	—	—	—	—	—	—
1917	1	2	—	—	—	—	—	—	—

FACE DESIGNS, First Issue 1862 and Third Issue 1863

$5 On the lower right, Alexander Hamilton, 18th century statesman killed in a duel with Aaron Burr in 1804. On the left, the Washington Capitol statue of Columbia, previously shown on several bank notes.

$10 Portrait of Abraham Lincoln in upper right. On the left, allegorical female portrait representing Art.

$20 Vignette of Library with shield and sword in center.

$50 Alexander Hamilton. Different from that on the $5 note. Engraved by James D. Smillie.

$100 The first note to feature the American Eagle.

$500 Albert Gallatin, secretary of the Treasury, 1801–1813.

$1,000 Robert Morris, a signer of the Declaration of Independence and Superintendent of Finance, 1781 to 1784.

FACE DESIGNS, Second Issue 1862

$1 Vignette of Salmon P. Chase, secretary of the Treasury.

$2 The Capitol Building and Thomas Jefferson, third president of the United States. Portrait of Alexander Hamilton, Jas. D. Smillie engraver.

On all denominations of United States Legal Tender notes, the obligation or promise to pay appears on the FACE of the notes, not on the back as stated in some catalogs. The obligation reads "The United States will pay the Bearer . . . Dollars."

UNITED STATES OR LEGAL TENDER NOTES

BACK DESIGNS, First, Second and Third Issue 1862–1863

First Issue 1862 and Third Issue 1863, denominations $5 to $1,000. Attractive lathe-work designs with two types of inscription.

> Type One inscription reads: "This note is a Legal Tender for all debts public and private, except on duties on Imports and Interest on Public Debt, and is exchangeable for U.S. Six per cent Twenty Year Bonds, redeemable at the pleasure of the U. States after Five Years." Space in the design evidently prevented the word "United" from being spelled out.

> Type Two inscription reads: "This note is a Legal Tender for all debts public and private, except duties on Imports and Interest on the Public Debt, and is receivable in payment for all Loans made to the United States."

Second Issue, $1 and $2 notes, Series 1862, carry the Type Two inscription in the center of the lathe-work design.

FACE DESIGNS, Fourth Issue 1869–1907

The major portion of the face design remained the same throughout the entire Fourth Issue. The obligation on the face reads "United States will pay the Bearer . . . Dollars." The words "At the Treasury in New York" appearing on the first three issues have been removed with the single word "Washington" substituted on the 1869 series, and "Washington D.C." on later series.

The stars following the serial numbers on the 1869 series *do not* indicate replacement notes. Star numbers were not substituted for damaged notes until 1910.

- **$1** 1869 to 1917. Head of Washington facing left and "Columbus Sighting Land". Signature of engraver A. Sealey can be seen at lower edge of Washington portrait on many notes.
- **$2** 1869 to 1917. Capitol Building vignette in center. Thos. Jefferson at left end.
- **$5** 1869 to 1907. The well-known "Pioneer Family" and head of Andrew Jackson. Collectors of designs showing animals should observe that a dog appears prominently in this design.
- **$10** 1869 to 1880. Daniel Webster, secretary of State, and "Presentation of an Indian Princess Representing America to the Old World." Best known as the "Jackass Note," so-called because when the note is inverted, the eagle on the face design appears to be a rather long-eared jackass.
- **$20** 1875 to 1880. Alexander Hamilton and figure of Victory with shield and sword from original sketch by John W. Casilear.
- **$50** 1869. Henry Clay, secretary of State, and a female holding a statue of Mercury.
- **$50** 1874 to 1880. Benjamin Franklin, engraved by Charles Burt after a Duplessis painting, with figure of Liberty.
- **$100** 1869 to 1880. Abraham Lincoln with allegorical figure of Architecture.
- **$500** 1869. John Quincy Adams, sixth president of the United States.
- **$500** 1874 to 1880. Major General Joseph K. Mansfield, mortally wounded in the Civil War Battle of Antietam.
- **$1,000** 1869 to 1880. Dewitt Clinton, governor of New York State; Columbus seated at left.
- **$5,000** 1878. James Madison, fourth president of the United States.
- **$10,000** 1878. Andrew Jackson, "Old Hickory," seventh president of the United States.

UNITED STATES OR LEGAL TENDER NOTES

BACK DESIGNS, Fourth Issue 1869–1907

The words "and is receivable in payment for all Loans made to the United States" have been removed from the Type Two clause of the former issues.

Throughout the entire Fourth Issue the backs of all notes carry the warning against counterfeiting which first appeared on the series of 1869. Counterfeiting had become very prevalent with the issue of paper money backed by the United States and is even more so today.

FACE DESIGNS, Fifth Issue 1901

$10 1901. Bison design with Lewis and Clark, famous explorers. There are nine signature combinations on this popular design.

The note was designed by Ostrander Smith from a sketch of the bison by Charles Knight, noted animal artist, author and publisher. The design was engraved by Marcus N. Baldwin. The portraits of Lewis and Clark and the portraits beside them were engraved by G.G.C. Smillie after Walter Shirlaw.

BACK DESIGN, Fifth Issue 1901

Columbia stands between two pillars and two scrolls which carry the modified inscription appearing on the Fourth Issue.

THE SIXTH ISSUE, 1923

The Series of 1923, comprising only $1 and $10 notes, has always been listed as part of the Fourth Issue. To avoid confusion we are now describing this series as the Sixth Issue, it having followed the designated Fifth Issue of 1901.

The $1 and $10 notes are type designs issued with one set of signatures.

Face design $1—Washington facing right as on small size notes.

Back design $1—Very plain back design, unlike Fourth Series.

Face design $10—Andrew Jackson, seventh president of the United States.

Back design $10—Attractive lathe-work. No inscription.

The words "On Demand" have been added to the obligation to pay on face of notes.

UNITED STATES OR LEGAL TENDER NOTES

ONE DOLLAR—FOUR TYPES

Face Design. See descriptions. Type 1, 2, 3, and 4.

Back Design.

Friedberg No.	Series	Register	Treasurer	Seal at Left	F-12	VF-20	EF-40	AU-50	Unc-60	Unc-63
Red serial numbers. Highlighted numeral in center denotes denomination.										
16	1862	Chittenden	Spinner	Small red	$370	$650	$1,340	$1,620	$2,620	$2,780
National Bank Note Co., twice in lower border. No Monogram.										
16a	1862	Chittenden	Spinner	Small red	360	585	1,750	2,060	3,120	3,750
As above, with monogram ABN Co. upper right.										
17	1862	Chittenden	Spinner	Small red	8,100	25,200	—	—	—	—
National Bank Note Co. American Bank Note Co., lower border. No Monogram. Scarcest of the four types.										
17a	1862	Chittenden	Spinner	Small red	520	650	1,620	1,750	2,120	3,380
As above, with monogram ABN Co. upper right.										

UNITED STATES OR
LEGAL TENDER NOTES—ONE DOLLAR

Face Design. Large red spiked seal.

Back Design, with counterfeit warning.
This back design used only on Series 1869.

Friedberg No.	Series	Register	Treasurer	Seal at Left	F-12	VF-20	EF-40	AU-50	Unc-60	Unc-63
Red serial numbers. First with counterfeit warning and blue end paper.										
18	1869	Allison	Spinner	Large red	$545	$1,020	$2,500	$2,750	$5,000	$6,000
National Bank Note Co., lower portion back design. Suffix star on 1869 series does not indicate a replacement note.										

Robert H. Lloyd in a *Numismatic Scrapbook* article, Nov. 1964, states that there are two types of the $1 1869 notes, the noticeable difference being that Type One was not printed on the blue tint paper of Type Two. There are other minor variations on the face design. Type One is undoubtedly the scarcer but for the present is not given a separate valuation in this catalog.

UNITED STATES OR LEGAL TENDER NOTES—ONE DOLLAR

Series 1874 to 1878—Face Design. Red ornamentation at right.

Series 1874 to 1917—Back Design. Variations are described.

Friedberg No.	Series	Register	Treasurer	Seal at Left	F-12	VF-20	EF-40	AU-50	Unc-60	Unc-63
Red serial numbers. Red ornamentation at right, face design.										
19	1874	Allison	Spinner	Small red	$290	$490	$1,090	$1,380	$1,880	$2,250
Face, micro at right, "Engraved & Printed at the Bureau Engraving & Printing." Back, Columbian Bank Note Co., twice in lower portion.										
20	1875	Allison	New	Small red	160	290	580	780	1,250	1,660
Issued in five additional series, same design excepting Series Letter.										
21	1875 Series "A"				1,150	2,750	4,000	5,000	7,250	8,100
22	1875 Series "B"				1,150	3,750	6,250	7,500	18,000	21,600
23	1875 Series "C"				680	1,750	4,060	4,750	6,250	7,200
24	1875 Series "D"				1,620	3,750	10,250	24,000	—	—
25	1875 Series "E"				1,620	2,250	8,750	11,250	—	—
26	1875	Allison	Wyman	Small red	260	420	845	1,020	1,690	1,880
27	1878	Allison	Gilfillan	Small red	235	455	845	880	1,380	1,690
"Series 1878" top margin, back design. "Printed by Bureau of Engraving & Printing" lower margin, back design.										

UNITED STATES OR LEGAL TENDER NOTES—ONE DOLLAR

Series 1880—Face Design. Red ornamentation replaced by large seal.

Friedberg No.	Series	Register	Treasurer	Seal at Right	F-12	VF-20	EF-40	AU-50	Unc-60	Unc-63
Red serial numbers. Ornamentation removed.										
28	1880	Scofield	Gilfillan	Large brown	$230	$365	$715	$910	$1,250	$1,500
29	1880	Bruce	Gilfillan	Large brown	230	360	780	845	1,060	1,150
30	1880	Bruce	Wyman	Large brown	230	345	750	845	1,090	1,340
Blue serial numbers. Seal at right.										
31	1880	Rosecrans	Huston	Large red	520	890	1,750	2,310	3,000	3,750
32	1880	Rosecrans	Huston	Large brown	520	890	2,000	2,500	3,120	3,750
33	1880	Rosecrans	Nebeker	Large brown	520	960	2,410	2,690	4,310	5,600
Blue serial numbers. Seal at left.										
34	1880	Rosecrans	Nebeker	Small red	145	290	550	650	1,020	1,090
35	1880	Tillman	Morgan	Small red	145	290	550	650	910	960

Series 1917—Face Design. Small scalloped red seal at left.

UNITED STATES OR LEGAL TENDER NOTES—ONE DOLLAR

Friedberg No.	Series	Register	Treasurer	Seal at Left	F-12	VF-20	EF-40	AU-50	Unc-60	Unc-63
36	1917	Teehee	Burke	Small red	$110	$135	$290	$345	$455	$490
37	1917	Elliott	Burke	Small red	110	155	290	325	435	490
37a	1917	Burke	Elliott	Small red	210	360	750	845	1,250	1,620
Signatures transposed on Plate No. 1519 only.										
38	1917	Elliott	White	Small red	110	135	230	345	420	490
39	1917	Speelman	White	Small red	110	135	290	345	420	520

★ Star replacement notes for Series 1917 are valued approximately double these prices.

Series 1923—Face Design. Washington faces right.

Series 1923—Back Design. Counterfeit warning removed.

Friedberg No.	Series	Register	Treasurer	Seal at Left	F-12	VF-20	EF-40	AU-50	Unc-60	Unc-63
40	1923	Speelman	White	Small red	$155	$210	$440	$545	$680	$780

★ Star replacement notes for Series 1923 are valued approximately double these prices.

UNITED STATES OR LEGAL TENDER NOTES—TWO DOLLARS

Face Design.

Back Design.

Friedberg No.	Series	Register	Treasurer	Seal at Right	F-12	VF-20	EF-40	AU-50	Unc-60	Unc-63
Red serial numbers. Vertical numerals in center denote denomination. "Patented April 23, 1860, National Bank Note Co." in lower border, Type Two inscription on back.										
41	1862	Chittenden	Spinner	Small red	$650	$1,250	$2,750	$3,500	$4,880	$5,500
National Bank Note Co., vertically at left, face design and at bottom.										
41a	1862	Chittenden	Spinner	Small red	585	960	2,000	2,250	4,500	5,950
American Bank Note Co., vertically at left, face design, National bottom.										

All uncirculated $2 large size notes are scarce. Plate was engraved for $3 denomination but notes were never issued.

UNITED STATES OR
LEGAL TENDER NOTES—TWO DOLLARS

Face Design. Large red spiked seal.

Back Design, with counterfeit warning.
This design used only on Series 1869.

Friedberg No.	Series	Register	Treasurer	Seal at Right	F-12	VF-20	EF-40	AU-50	Unc-60	Unc-63
Red serial numbers.										
42	1869	Allison	Spinner	Large red	$605	$1,250	$4,500	$5,300	$8,600	$9,400
"Engraved and printed at the Treasury Department," vertically at left, face design. American Bank Note Co. bottom left, face design and twice below back design.										

The suffix star on all Series of 1869 notes does not indicate a replacement note.

UNITED STATES OR LEGAL TENDER NOTES—TWO DOLLARS

Face Design. Seal replaced by red ornamentation. Minor changes.

Back Design. Minor variations.

Friedberg No.	Series	Register	Treasurer	Seal at Left	F-12	VF-20	EF-40	AU-50	Unc-60	Unc-63
Red serial numbers. Red ornamentation at right.										
43	1874	Allison	Spinner	Small red	$420	$750	$1,280	$1,880	$2,500	$3,000
Face engraved and printed at the Bureau of Engraving & Printing. Back, Columbian Bank Note Co., Washington, D.C.										
44	1875	Allison	New	Small red	390	650	1,220	1,500	2,380	3,620
Issued in two additional series, same design.										
45	1875 Series A, lower right of face design				1,500	3,750	5,250	6,550	8,750	10,000
46	1875 Series B, lower right of face design				910	1,500	2,620	3,120	5,450	5,600
47	1875	Allison	Wyman	Small red	520	845	1,500	1,750	2,750	6,000
48	1878	Allison	Gilfillan	Small red	395	620	1,020	1,150	2,250	2,410
49	1878	Scofield	Gilfillan	Small red	8,100	12,000	22,800	36,000	—	—

UNITED STATES OR LEGAL TENDER NOTES—TWO DOLLARS

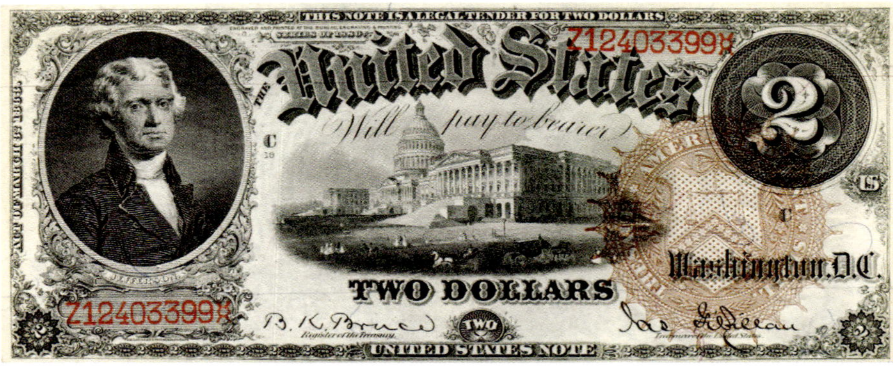

Face Design. Red ornamentation replaced by large seal.

Back Design.

Friedberg No.	Series	Register	Treasurer	Seal at Right	F-12	VF-20	EF-40	AU-50	Unc-60	Unc-63
Red serial numbers. Ornamentation removed.										
50	1880	Scofield	Gilfillan	Large brown	$215	$360	$780	$990	$1,500	$1,940
51	1880	Bruce	Gilfillan	Large brown	215	420	845	1,020	1,500	1,750
52	1880	Bruce	Wyman	Large brown	195	390	760	910	1,310	1,970
Blue serial numbers. Large seal.										
53	1880	Rosecrans	Huston	Large red	1,180	1,810	4,750	5,800	8,750	10,400
54	1880	Rosecrans	Huston	Large brown	3,940	5,500	13,200	16,800	21,600	24,000
Blue serial numbers. Small seal.										
55	1880	Rosecrans	Nebeker	Small red	215	325	715	880	1,500	1,750
56	1880	Tillman	Morgan	Small red	215	285	520	750	940	1,180

UNITED STATES OR LEGAL TENDER NOTES—TWO DOLLARS

Face Design.

Back Design. Series date added.

Friedberg No.	Series	Register	Treasurer	Seal at Right	F-12	VF-20	EF-40	AU-50	Unc-60	Unc-63
Red serial numbers.										
57	1917	Teehee	Burke	Small red	$110	$155	$305	$360	$520	$620
58	1917	Elliott	Burke	Small red	110	155	285	345	420	520
59	1917	Elliott	White	Small red	110	155	260	290	455	585
60	1917	Speelman	White	Small red	110	215	360	390	535	585

★ Star replacement notes for Series 1917 are valued at over double these prices.

UNITED STATES OR LEGAL TENDER NOTES—FIVE DOLLARS

Face Design. Type One.

Back Design. Type One inscription.

Back Design. Type Two inscription.

UNITED STATES OR LEGAL TENDER NOTES—FIVE DOLLARS

Friedberg No.	Series	Register	Treasurer	Seal at Right	F-12	VF-20	EF-40	AU-50	Unc-60	Unc-63
Type One inscription on back. Red serial numbers.										
61a	1862	Chittenden	Spinner	Small red	$585	$780	$1,250	$1,660	$2,560	$4,250
American Bank Note Co. in top border face design, Series and Patented.										
Type Two inscription. Red serial numbers.										
62	1862	Chittenden	Spinner	Small red	520	1,090	1,500	2,190	3,500	6,000
American Bank Note Co.-National Bank Note Co. lower border face design.										
63	1863	Obverse of 1862, without "Series"			520	910	1,380	1,560	2,620	3,440
American Bank Note Co. and National Bank Note Co.										
63a	1863	Chittenden	Spinner	Small red	520	960	1,250	1,880	3,750	4,500
American Bank Note Co., twice in lower border face design. One serial number.										
63b	1863	Chittenden	Spinner	Small red	455	845	1,690	1,940	3,000	3,120
American Bank Note Co., twice in lower border. Two serial numbers.										

Face Design. Large red spiked seal.

Back Design. Used only on Series 1869.

UNITED STATES OR LEGAL TENDER NOTES—FIVE DOLLARS

Friedberg No.	Series	Register	Treasurer	Seal at Right	F-12	VF-20	EF-40	AU-50	Unc-60	Unc-63
Red serial numbers.										
64	1869	Allison	Spinner	Large red	$520	$1,310	$2,440	$2,750	$3,750	$4,620

Face Design. Red ornamentation with "V."

Back Design. Variations as described.

Friedberg No.	Series	Register	Treasurer	Seal at Left	F-12	VF-20	EF-40	AU-50	Unc-60	Unc-63
Red serial numbers. Large "V" in red ornamentation at right.										
65	1875	Allison	New	Small red	$390	$550	$990	$1,150	$1,750	$2,000
Face printed at Bureau, back by Columbian Bank Note Co.										
Issued in two additional series, same design.										
66	1875 Series A in lower right of face design.				1,020	1,690	4,940	5,250	—	—
67	1875 Series B in lower right of face design.				260	520	750	910	1,500	1,780
68	1875	Allison	Wyman	Small red	390	520	910	1,060	1,500	2,000
69	1878	Allison	Gilfillan	Small red	325	455	910	1,020	1,500	1,660

The Bureau assumed the complete printing of all notes October 1877.

UNITED STATES OR LEGAL TENDER NOTES—FIVE DOLLARS

Face Design. Ornamentation replaced by large seal.

Friedberg No.	Series	Register	Treasurer	Seal at Right	F-12	VF-20	EF-40	AU-50	Unc-60	Unc-63
Red serial numbers.										
70	1880	Scofield	Gilfillan	Large brown	$455	$780	$1,310	$1,500	$2,190	$2,380
71	1880	Bruce	Gilfillan	Large brown	390	490	845	910	1,310	1,440
72	1880	Bruce	Wyman	Large brown	325	455	910	1,090	1,440	1,590
Blue serial numbers.										
73	1880	Bruce	Wyman	Large red, plain	345	420	680	780	1,250	1,620
74	1880	Rosecrans	Jordan	Large red	260	390	810	910	1,250	1,440
75	1880	Rosecrans	Hyatt	Large red	585	1,220	3,000	6,250	—	21,600
76	1880	Rosecrans	Huston	Large red, spikes	390	650	1,620	2,160	3,120	3,810
Similar, with large brown seal.										
77	1880	Rosecrans	Huston	Large brown	390	780	2,250	2,620	3,750	5,250
78	1880	Rosecrans	Nebeker	Large brown	600	910	1,810	2,120	3,750	4,750

Face Design. Small scalloped red seal.

Friedberg No.	Series	Register	Treasurer	Seal at Right	F-12	VF-20	EF-40	AU-50	Unc-60	Unc-63
79	1880	Rosecrans	Nebeker	Small red	$160	$240	$455	$620	$1,150	$1,250
80	1880	Tillman	Morgan	Small red	195	260	520	585	990	1,090
81	1880	Bruce	Roberts	Small red	160	260	455	650	1,090	1,250
82	1880	Lyons	Roberts	Small red	160	240	455	585	910	960

UNITED STATES OR LEGAL TENDER NOTES—FIVE DOLLARS

Face Design. Ornamental "V" added over "FIVE" at left.

Friedberg No.	Series	Register	Treasurer	Seal at Right	F-12	VF-20	EF-40	AU-50	Unc-60	Unc-63
Red serial numbers. Ornamental "V" at left.										
83	1907	Vernon	Treat	Small red	$160	$235	$390	$475	$680	$780
84	1907	Vernon	McClung	Small red	160	235	420	455	680	845
85	1907	Napier	McClung	Small red	160	235	490	550	780	845
86	1907	Napier	Thompson	Small red	325	455	1,020	1,560	3,120	3,750
87	1907	Parker	Burke	Small red	160	235	420	520	650	715
88	1907	Teehee	Burke	Small red	160	230	420	490	620	715
89	1907	Elliott	Burke	Small red	160	210	390	520	1,880	2,120
90	1907	Elliott	White	Small red	160	230	370	420	585	650
91	1907	Speelman	White	Small red	160	235	500	520	620	715
92	1907	Woods	White	Small red	210	235	390	490	625	940

★ Star replacement notes for Series 1907 are valued at approximately three times these prices.

Early issues of U.S. paper money were printed by Columbian, National or American Bank Note Cos., only the seals and serial numbering being added at the Treasury Dept. Later notes were partially printed at the Bureau which assumed more and more of the operation. On October 1, 1877, the Bureau took over the entire printing job.

The design below shows the elimination of the name of the private company, and the addition of "Bureau of Engraving & Printing" in the upper and lower border of the back design.

UNITED STATES OR LEGAL TENDER NOTES—TEN DOLLARS

Face Design. Three types described.

Back Design. Type One inscription.

Back Design. Type Two inscription.

UNITED STATES OR LEGAL TENDER NOTES—TEN DOLLARS

Friedberg No.	Series	Register	Treasurer	Seal at Right	F-12	VF-20	EF-40	AU-50	Unc-60	Unc-63
Type One inscription on back. One red serial number.										
93	1862	Chittenden	Spinner	Small red	$1,620	$2,380	$4,690	$6,250	$10,000	$21,600
American Bank Note Co. upper border.										
Type Two inscription on back. One red serial number.										
94	1862	Chittenden	Spinner	Small red	1,500	2,380	5,000	5,950	—	48,000
American Bank Note Co. upper border.										
Type Two inscription on back. One red serial number.										
95	1863	Chittenden	Spinner	Small red	1,380	1,940	4,750	6,000	—	—
National Bank Note Co. lower border.										
95a	1863	Chittenden	Spinner	Small red	1,250	2,190	5,000	6,250	8,750	11,250
American Bank Note Co. upper and lower borders.										
Type Two inscription on back. Two red serial numbers.										
95b	1863	Chittenden	Spinner	Small red	1,250	1,880	4,380	5,000	11,250	12,000
American Bank Note Co. upper and lower borders.										

Face Design. Large spiked red seal.

Back Design. Inscription and counterfeit warning.

UNITED STATES OR
LEGAL TENDER NOTES—TEN DOLLARS

Friedberg No.	Series	Register	Treasurer	Seal at Right	F-12	VF-20	EF-40	AU-50	Unc-60	Unc-63
Red serial numbers.										
96	1869	Allison	Spinner	Large red	$880	$1,750	$3,000	$3,310	$6,250	$7,500
Face: Bureau of Engraving and Printing. Back: National Bank Note Co.										

Face Design. "TEN" in red ornamentation.

Back Design, with minor variations.

Friedberg No.	Series	Register	Treasurer	Seal at Right	F-12	VF-20	EF-40	AU-50	Unc-60	Unc-63
97	1875	Allison	New	Small red	$5,600	$11,250	$28,800	$36,000	—	—
Issued in one additional series, same design.										
98	1875 Series A, lower right of face design				1,220	2,250	5,000	6,900	$11,250	$20,400
99	1878	Allison	Gilfillan	Small red	940	1,180	2,750	3,250	5,000	6,250
	1878	Allison	Gilfillan	Similar, with pink background						

UNITED STATES OR LEGAL TENDER NOTES—TEN DOLLARS

Face Design. Large "TEN" replaced by seal.

Back Design by Columbian Bank Note Co.

Friedberg No.	Series	Register	Treasurer	Seal at Right	F-12	VF-20	EF-40	AU-50	Unc-60	Unc-63
Red serial numbers.										
100	1880	Scofield	Gilfillan	Large brown	$570	$845	$1,250	$1,530	$2,000	$2,190
101	1880	Bruce	Gilfillan	Large brown	570	780	1,250	1,530	1,810	2,190
102	1880	Bruce	Wyman	Large brown	570	780	1,500	2,000	2,500	2,690
Blue serial numbers.										
103	1880	Bruce	Wyman	Large red	500	700	1,180	1,470	1,750	1,880
104	1880	Rosecrans	Jordan	Large red	500	700	1,440	1,620	2,500	3,500
105	1880	Rosecrans	Hyatt	Large red	500	700	1,180	1,470	1,660	1,880
106	1880	Rosecrans	Hyatt	Red spikes	500	700	1,180	1,470	1,660	1,880
107	1880	Rosecrans	Huston	Red spikes	520	715	1,250	1,470	1,810	2,160
108	1880	Rosecrans	Huston	Large brown	500	750	1,250	1,500	2,380	2,880
109	1880	Rosecrans	Nebeker	Large brown 2 known	—	—	100,800	—	—	—
110	1880	Rosecrans	Nebeker	Small red	415	715	1,150	1,310	1,750	1,940
111	1880	Tillman	Morgan	Small red	490	750	1,250	1,500	1,750	1,880
112	1880	Bruce	Roberts	Small red	520	845	2,380	3,500	5,000	6,500
113	1880	Lyons	Roberts	Small red	415	620	1,250	1,380	1,690	1,810

UNITED STATES OR LEGAL TENDER NOTES—TEN DOLLARS

Face Design. The Bison note.

Back Design.

Friedberg No.	Series	Register	Treasurer	Seal at Right	F-12	VF-20	EF-40	AU-50	Unc-60	Unc-63
Red serial numbers. Large "X" at left.										
114	1901	Lyons	Roberts	Small red	$845	$1,310	$3,250	$3,750	$4,620	$5,000
115	1901	Lyons	Treat	Small red	845	1,250	3,250	3,750	4,620	5,000
116	1901	Vernon	Treat	Small red	845	1,250	3,250	3,750	4,620	5,000
117	1901	Vernon	McClung	Small red	845	1,250	3,250	3,750	4,620	6,250
118	1901	Napier	McClung	Small red	845	1,310	3,250	3,750	4,620	5,000
119	1901	Parker	Burke	Small red	845	1,250	3,250	3,750	4,620	5,000
120	1901	Teehee	Burke	Small red	845	1,250	3,250	3,750	4,620	5,000
121	1901	Elliott	White	Small red	845	1,380	3,250	3,750	5,000	6,550
122	1901	Speelman	White	Small red	845	1,250	3,250	3,750	4,620	5,000

★ Star replacement notes for Series 1901 are valued at over double these prices.

UNITED STATES OR LEGAL TENDER NOTES—TEN DOLLARS

Face Design. Andrew Jackson. A type note.

Back Design. Issued in Series 1923 only.

Friedberg No.	Series	Register	Treasurer	Seal at Right	F-12	VF-20	EF-40	AU-50	Unc-60	Unc-63
Red serial numbers. Large "X" at right.										
123	1923	Speelman	White	Small red	$1,380	$3,000	$5,750	$6,250	$8,600	$9,900

★ Star replacement notes for Series 1923 are extremely rare.

The Series of 1923 $10 United States note, by reason of being of especially attractive design, as well as a type note, has always been popular with collectors. In recent years very few have been offered in strictly Uncirculated condition. The above evaluation is believed to be conservative. Only 696,000 were issued. Many were converted by the public to the current small-size issues.

UNITED STATES OR LEGAL TENDER NOTES—TWENTY DOLLARS

Face Design. Three types described. Above, Type One.

Back Design. Type One inscription.

Back Design. Type Two inscription.

UNITED STATES OR LEGAL TENDER NOTES—TWENTY DOLLARS

Friedberg No.	Series	Register	Treasurer	Seal at Right	F-12	VF-20	EF-40	AU-50	Unc-60	Unc-63
Type One inscription on back. One red serial number.										
124	1862	Chittenden	Spinner	Small red	$2,380	$6,250	$12,000	$14,400	—	—
American Bank Note Co. lower border. Reportedly fewer than ten known in Uncirculated condition.										
Type Two inscription on back. One red serial number.										
125	1862	Chittenden	Spinner	Small red	2,500	4,380	7,200	9,700	—	—
National Bank Note Co. and American Bank Note Co. at bottom.										
Type Two inscription on back. One red serial number.										
126	1863	Chittenden	Spinner	Small red	2,190	4,060	13,200	—	—	—
ABN and NBN, as above.										
126a	1863	Chittenden	Spinner	Small red	3,750	15,000	—	—	—	—
ABN at bottom.										
Type Two inscription on back. Two red serial numbers.										
126b	1863	Chittenden	Spinner	Small red	2,190	3,500	7,500	8,750	$12,000	$13,800
ABN at bottom.										

Face Design. Large spiked red seal at left.

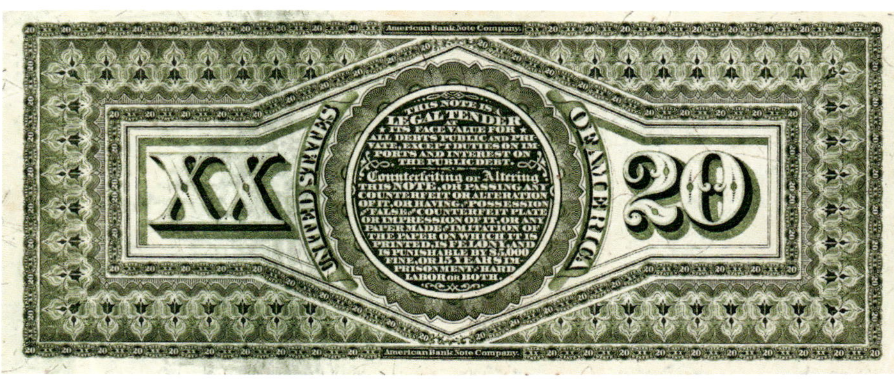

Back Design. Numeral “20” repeated 105 times. “XX” repeated 103 times.

UNITED STATES OR LEGAL TENDER NOTES—TWENTY DOLLARS

Friedberg No.	Series	Register	Treasurer	Seal at Right	F-12	VF-20	EF-40	AU-50	Unc-60	Unc-63
Blue serial numbers.										
127	1869	Allison	Spinner	Large red	$2,410	$5,000	$12,000	$18,000	$22,800	$25,200
Face printed by the Bureau. Back, American Bank Note Co.										

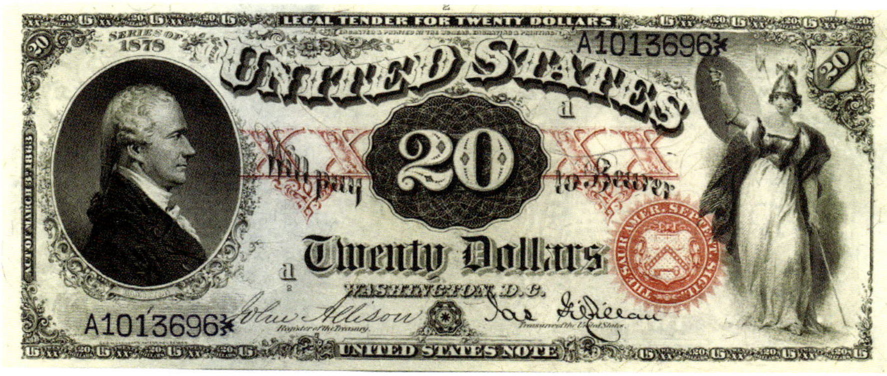

Face Design. "XX" twice. Red seal.

Back Design. Variations described.

Friedberg No.	Series	Register	Treasurer	Seal at Right	F-12	VF-20	EF-40	AU-50	Unc-60	Unc-63
Blue serial numbers. "XX" twice on face of note.										
128	1875	Allison	New	Small red	$1,250	$1,900	$2,700	$3,850	$4,750	$5,000
Face printed by the Bureau. Back, Columbian Bank Note Co.										
129	1878	Allison	Gilfillan	Small red	1,220	1,410	1,940	2,440	3,250	4,810
Printed by the Bureau of Engraving and Printing, as were all subsequent issues.										

UNITED STATES OR LEGAL TENDER NOTES—TWENTY DOLLARS

Face Design. Twin "XX" removed.

Friedberg No.	Series	Register	Treasurer	Seal at Right	F-12	VF-20	EF-40	AU-50	Unc-60	Unc-63
Blue serial numbers. "XX" removed.										
130	1880	Scofield	Gilfillan	Large brown	$5,000	$10,000	$24,000	—	—	—
131	1880	Bruce	Gilfillan	Large brown	1,500	3,120	4,000	$6,000	$7,500	$14,400
132	1880	Bruce	Wyman	Large brown	960	1,440	2,810	3,750	5,300	8,750
133	1880	Bruce	Wyman	Large red	1,150	2,560	3,000	5,000	6,250	12,000
134	1880	Rosecrans	Jordan	Large red	550	910	2,120	2,500	5,600	8,750
135	1880	Rosecrans	Hyatt	Large red	550	715	1,500	1,620	2,380	2,500
136	1880	Rosecrans	Hyatt	Red spikes	550	780	1,750	1,880	2,250	2,440
137	1880	Rosecrans	Huston	Red spikes	475	715	1,810	2,000	2,310	2,560
138	1880	Rosecrans	Huston	Large brown	715	1,020	1,690	2,750	3,750	4,750
139	1880	Rosecrans	Nebeker	Large brown	1,750	2,690	6,900	11,250	14,400	—
140	1880	Rosecrans	Nebeker	Small red	365	520	1,310	1,470	1,750	2,000
141	1880	Tillman	Morgan	Small red	405	520	1,020	1,470	1,750	2,000
142	1880	Bruce	Roberts	Small red	405	520	1,020	1,470	1,750	2,000
143	1880	Lyons	Roberts	Small red	405	520	1,250	1,500	3,120	—
144	1880	Vernon	Treat	Small red	405	480	1,090	1,470	1,750	2,000
145	1880	Vernon	McClung	Small red	440	585	1,560	1,810	4,000	6,250
Red serial numbers.										
146	1880	Teehee	Burke	Small red	365	470	1,150	1,620	2,500	3,500
147	1880	Elliott	White	Small red	390	680	1,310	1,500	2,310	2,500

UNITED STATES OR LEGAL TENDER NOTES—FIFTY DOLLARS

Face Design. Three types described.

Back Design. Two types. Type Two inscription shown.

Friedberg No.	Series	Register	Treasurer	Seal in Center	F-12	VF-20	EF-40	AU-50	Unc-60	Unc-63
Type One inscription on back. Red serial numbers.										
148	1862	Chittenden	Spinner	Small red	$30,000	$48,000	$120,000	—	—	—
American Bank Note Co.										
Type Two inscription on back. Red serial numbers.										
150	1863	Chittenden	Spinner	Small red	—	72,000	210,000	$240,000	—	—
National Bank Note Co.										
150a	1863	Chittenden	Spinner	Small red	42,000	60,000	—	150,000	—	—
National Bank Note Co. and American Bank Note Co. at top.										

Many counterfeits of the above series were made in the 19th century.

UNITED STATES OR LEGAL TENDER NOTES—FIFTY DOLLARS

Face Design. Large red seal in center.

Back Design. Used only on Series 1869.

Friedberg No.	Series	Register	Treasurer	Seal in Center	F-12	VF-20	EF-40	AU-50	Unc-60	Unc-63
Blue serial numbers.										
151	1869	Allison	Spinner	Large red	$21,600	$46,200	$96,000	$138,000	$264,000	—
Face printed by the Bureau. Back, American Bank Note Co.										

The above is a type note, design used on Series 1869 only. It well qualifies for the description "rare."

Counterfeits were made of the above shortly after release in the 1870s.

UNITED STATES OR LEGAL TENDER NOTES—FIFTY DOLLARS

Face Design. Position of signatures transposed.

Back Design by Columbian Bank Note Co.

Friedberg No.	Series	Signatures		F-12	VF-20	EF-40	AU-50	Unc-60	Unc-63
Signatures transposed. Small red seal center. Blue serial numbers. Ornate "L" twice on face.									
152	1874	Spinner-Allison		$5,950	$8,450	$20,400	$25,800	$45,600	$54,000
Face engraved and printed by the Bureau of Engraving and Printing. Back, Columbian Bank Note Co.									
153	1875	Wyman-Allison	4 known	114,000	126,000	—	—	—	—
154	1878	Gilfillan-Allison		6,250	11,250	26,400	42,000	—	—

All later issues were printed at the Bureau of Engraving and Printing.

Transposed signatures are the rule, not the exception, as sometimes emphasized. This applies to all Series of 1874, 1875, 1878, and all Series of 1880 excepting Bruce-Roberts and Lyons-Roberts.

UNITED STATES OR LEGAL TENDER NOTES—FIFTY DOLLARS

Face Design. Without ornate "L" left and right.

Back Design. Printed at the Bureau.

Friedberg No.	Series	Signatures		Seal at Right	F-12	VF-20	EF-40	AU-50	Unc-60	Unc-63
Blue serial numbers in center, unlike any other series.										
Signatures transposed until Tillman-Morgan.										
155	1880	Gilfillan	Bruce	Large brown	$14,400	$24,000	$36,000	$48,000	—	—
156	1880	Wyman	Bruce	Large brown	6,250	12,000	36,000	—	—	—
157	1880	Jordan	Rosecrans	Large red	8,100	10,950	—	—	—	—
158	1880	Hyatt	Rosecrans	Large red	5,600	8,750	36,000	—	—	—
159	1880	Hyatt	Rosecrans	Red spikes	5,600	8,750	—	—	—	—
160	1880	Huston	Rosecrans	Red spikes	5,000	12,000	36,000	—	—	—
161	1880	Huston	Rosecrans	Large brown	4,560	7,200	9,400	10,300	$13,200	$16,500
162	1880	Tillman	Morgan	Small red	2,940	5,000	10,000	11,900	13,500	16,500
163	1880	Bruce	Roberts	Small red	42,000	60,000	90,000	—	—	—
164	1880	Lyons	Roberts	Small red	2,940	4,750	9,750	11,900	21,600	21,600

UNITED STATES OR LEGAL TENDER NOTES—ONE HUNDRED DOLLARS

Face Design. Three types described.

Back Design. Type One inscription.

Back Design. Type Two inscription.

UNITED STATES OR LEGAL TENDER NOTES—ONE HUNDRED DOLLARS

Friedberg No.	Series	Register	Treasurer	Seal at Right	F-12	VF-20	EF-40	AU-50	Unc-60	Unc-63
Type One inscription on back. Red serial numbers.										
165	1862	Chittenden	Spinner	Small red	$33,000	$62,400	—	—	—	—
American Bank Note Co. or National Bank Note Co.										
Type Two inscription on back. Red serial numbers.										
167	1863	Chittenden	Spinner	Small red			2 known			
National Bank Note Co. and American Bank Note Co. at top.										
Type Two inscription on back. Red serial numbers.										
167a	1863	Chittenden	Spinner	Small red	78,000	108,000	$180,000	$240,000	$312,000	$360,000
National Bank Note Co. at top										

The above series were counterfeited soon after issue. Genuine notes show the small "100" design in the right reverse. Counterfeits show "001" instead of "100."

Face Design. Large red seal, right.

Back Design. Used only on Series 1869.

UNITED STATES OR LEGAL TENDER NOTES—ONE HUNDRED DOLLARS

Friedberg No.	Series	Register	Treasurer	Seal at Right	F-12	VF-20	EF-40	AU-50	Unc-60	Unc-63
Blue serial numbers.										
168	1869	Allison	Spinner	Large red	$21,600	$45,000	$102,000	$144,000	$180,000	$210,000

Face printed by the Bureau. Back by American Bank Note Co.

The back design used on the Series 1869 $100 United States notes was changed on subsequent issues. The face design, with minor changes, remained the same throughout all later series of United States notes of this denomination.

Very rare and popular.

Face Design.

Back Design.

Friedberg No.	Series	Register	Treasurer	Seal at Right	F-12	VF-20	EF-40	AU-50	Unc-60	Unc-63
169	1875	Allison	New (Series A)	Small red	$24,000	$31,800	$60,000	—	—	—
170	1875	Allison	Wyman	Small red	26,400	36,000	—	—	—	—
171	1878	Allison	Gilfillan	Small red	12,000	28,800	—	$48,000	—	—

Printed by the Bureau, as were all subsequent issues. All scarce. Series "A" 1875 rare.

UNITED STATES OR LEGAL TENDER NOTES—ONE HUNDRED DOLLARS

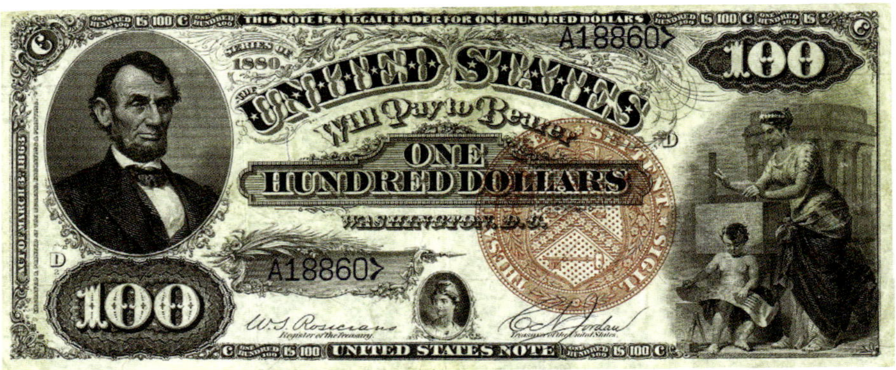

Face Design. Various seals.

Back Design.

Friedberg No.	Series	Register	Treasurer	Seal at Right	F-12	VF-20	EF-40	AU-50	Unc-60	Unc-63
172	1880	Bruce	Gilfillan	Large brown	$11,900	$18,000	$32,400	$42,000	$66,000	$72,000
173	1880	Bruce	Wyman	Large brown	13,200	20,400	—	—	—	—
174	1880	Rosecrans	Jordan	Large red	11,900	22,800	42,000	—	—	—
175	1880	Rosecrans	Hyatt	Large red				Very Rare		
176	1880	Rosecrans	Hyatt	Red spikes	21,000	26,400	54,000	78,000	—	—
177	1880	Rosecrans	Huston	Red spikes	11,900	16,800	48,000	60,000	—	—
178	1880	Rosecrans	Huston	Large brown	18,000	24,000	42,000	60,000	—	—
179	1880	Tillman	Morgan	Small red	12,000	15,600	36,000	54,000	84,000	96,000
180	1880	Bruce	Roberts	Small red	24,000	42,000	—	—	—	—
181	1880	Lyons	Roberts	Small red	10,600	16,200	30,000	38,400	48,000	—

UNITED STATES OR LEGAL TENDER NOTES—FIVE HUNDRED DOLLARS

Friedberg No.	Series	Register	Treasurer	Seal at Left
Type One inscription on back. Red serial numbers.				
183a	1862	Chittenden	Spinner	Small red
Type Two inscription on back.				
183b	1862	Chittenden	Spinner	Small red
183c	1863	Chittenden	Spinner	Small red
184	1869	Allison	Spinner	Large red
185a	1874	Allison	Spinner	Small red
185b	1875	Allison	New	Small red
185c	1875	Allison	Wyman	Small red
185d	1878	Allison	Gilfillan	Small red
185e–n	1880	*		

* This series was issued with ten different signature combinations, with small red, large red, and large brown seals. All are extremely rare.

ONE THOUSAND DOLLARS

Issues of this denomination are extremely scarce. It would be presumptuous to evaluate these high denominations. No confirmed records are available as to number issued or known to exist.

Face Design.

Back Design.

FIVE THOUSAND and TEN THOUSAND DOLLARS

Legal Tender notes of $5,000 and $10,000 were issued. All have been redeemed.

SILVER CERTIFICATES

ACTS OF CONGRESS, FEBRUARY 28, 1878, AND AUGUST 4, 1886

Large-size Silver Certificates of all issues are very popular with collectors, and afford a variety of designs, seals and signatures. There were five issues from Series 1878 to Series 1923.

FIRST ISSUE, 1878 and 1880

The First Issue, series 1878 and 1880, included denominations from $10 to $100. The face of the notes certifies: "There have been deposited with the Treasurer of the United States at Washington, D.C." (or the Assistant Treasurer at New York or San Francisco. See illustrations) "payable at his office to the bearer on demand (amount) Silver Dollars." The notes were inscribed "Certificate of Deposit."

FACE DESIGNS, Series 1878 and 1880

- **$10** Robert Morris, a signer of the Declaration of Independence and U.S. senator, 1789–1795.
- **$20** Stephen Decatur, commodore in the U.S. Navy, killed in a duel in 1820.
- **$50** Edward Everett, governor of Massachusetts, U.S. senator, and secretary of State under President Millard Fillmore.
- **$100** James Monroe, fifth president of the U.S. and founder of the Monroe Doctrine.
- **$500** Charles Sumner, U.S. senator. Leader in the abolishment of slavery.
- **$1,000** William L. Marcy, New York state governor, secretary of War under President James K. Polk, and secretary of State under President Franklin Pierce.

The Treasury seal on the countersigned certificates of 1878, through error in designing, has the key in the red seal pointing to the right instead of the left. This error was corrected on the Series of 1880.

BACK DESIGNS, Series 1878–1880

This is the only series of United States paper money with backs printed in black ink. The word SILVER in large letters stands out on the very striking black scrollwork design. The inscription in the back design is "This Certificate is Receivable for Customs, Taxes, and all Public Dues and When so received May be Reissued."

SECOND ISSUE, 1886, 1891, and 1908

The Second Issue of Silver Certificates comprises the series of 1886, 1891, and 1908. Series 1886 was issued in $1, $2, $5, $10, and $20 denominations. Series 1891 included these denominations and also $50, $100, and $1,000 certificates. Series 1908 was issued in $10 denomination only, with three combinations of signatures and a blue seal in contrast to the red or brown seals of earlier series.

The certification on the face of series of the second issue reads: "This certifies that there have been deposited in the Treasury of the United States . . . Silver Dollars payable to the Bearer on Demand."

FACE DESIGNS, Series 1886, 1891, and 1908

- **$1** Series 1886 and 1891, Martha Washington.
- **$2** Series 1886, General Winfield Scott Hancock, died February 1886.
- **$2** Series 1891, William Windom, secretary of the Treasury from 1881–1884 and again from 1889 until his death in 1891.

Both $2 certificates commemorate the passing of great Americans.

- **$5** Series 1886 and 1891, Ulysses S. Grant, Civil War general and 18th U.S. president.
- **$10** Series 1886 and 1908, Thomas A. Hendricks, vice president with Grover Cleveland, serving only nine months until his death in November 1885. This design may also be said to commemorate the passing of an American statesman.

SILVER CERTIFICATES

$20 Series 1886 and 1891, Daniel Manning, born in Albany, New York, 1831. Secretary of the Treasury, 1885–1887.

$50 Series 1891, Edward Everett, portrait to right as on Series 1878 and 1880, with modified design.

$100 Series 1891, James Monroe, design modified, with portrait as on Series 1878 and 1880.

$1,000 Series 1891, William L. Marcy, same portrait as Series 1878 and 1880, but now at right in small oval.

BACK DESIGN, Series 1886

The attractive green all-over lathe-work designs used throughout the 1886 series should be examined with a glass to properly appreciate the intricacies of these designs and the skill of the designer and engraver. Large numerals denoting the denomination are featured, and the certification is the same as that of Series 1878 and 1880.

The back design of the $5 certificate is unique. It features in actual size five facsimile silver dollars, the obverse of one showing the date "1886." Being a type design, this note is in great demand. The National Gold Bank Notes of California and this $5 certificate are the only issues featuring designs of United States coins.

BACK DESIGNS, Series 1891 and 1908

On certificates of Series 1891 and 1908, the lathe-work designs of Series 1890 were changed to a more open design intended to prevent counterfeiting which prevailed on many early issues. Large numerals, and on some denominations, Roman numerals indicate the denomination. The certification remains the same as on previous series.

THIRD ISSUE, Series 1896

Thomas F. Morris, designer and chief of the Engraving Division of the Bureau of Engraving and Printing, Nov. 1, 1893, to June 30, 1897, designed and/or re-designed the three denominations of this well known and popular "Educational Series." Thomas F. Morris II, artist and numismatist, is the son of the former chief, and has contributed many factual articles to the various numismatic media.

Other designers of this series included Will H. Low, $1; Edwin H. Blashfield, $2; and Walter Shirlaw, $5. Known engravers of the series were Charles Schlecht and Geo. F.C. Smillie.

Claude M. Johnson, chief of the Bureau of Engraving and Printing, is credited with advocating the printing of more artistic and representative designs in currency. The original plan was to eventually have this type of artistic and educational design used on all denominations of silver certificates $1 to $1,000.

The $1, $2, and $5 denominations were printed and released. The plates for a $10 note were engraved but notes were never issued. The higher denominations apparently were not designed. The three denominations released enjoyed a very short life, much to the regret of present-day collectors.

FACE DESIGNS, Series 1896

Beautiful allegorical scenes are depicted in the face designs, as follows:

$1 "History Instructing Youth." A background of the Washington Monument and Capitol. The Constitution of the United States is shown in an open book. Names of 23 great American statesmen are shown in an attractive border design.

$2 "Steam and Electricity," represented by two youthful figures, are presented to "Commerce and Manufacture," mature female figures, by "Science," also a mature female.

$5 This beautiful allegorical scene depicts "Electricity," represented by a winged female, as a powerful controlling factor in world history.

SILVER CERTIFICATES

The obligation to redeem in silver dollars is on the face of each of the three denominations. It reads: "This certifies that there have been deposited in the Treasury of the United States . . . Silver Dollars, payable to the Bearer on demand."

BACK DESIGNS, Series 1896

The green back designs of all three denominations are also eye-catching:

- **$1** Portraits of Martha and George Washington in center double ovals.
- **$2** Two great inventors, Samuel F.B. Morse and Robert Fulton.
- **$5** Generals Ulysses S. Grant and Phillip Henry Sheridan.

FOURTH ISSUE, Series 1899

The Fourth Issue of Silver Certificates comprising only one series, 1899, in three denominations, is notable for the number of signature combinations. Eleven combinations on $1, ten on $2, and eleven on $5 certificates. The scarcest signature combination in this series is that of James C. Napier and Carmi A. Thompson, in office only four and a half months.

FACE DESIGNS, Series 1899

- **$1** The well-known American eagle design with portraits of Lincoln and Grant; all three engraved by Geo. F.C. Smillie.
- **$2** George Washington between figures representing Mechanics and Agriculture, also engraved by Geo. F.C. Smillie. Two figures from sculptured group by D.C. French.
- **$5** "Running Antelope," a Sioux Indian, best known as "Chief Oncpapa" or "Onepapa." The most popular of the many versions of how the Indian chief design was created seems to be that the Chief of the Uncpapa or Hunkpapa Sioux tribe wore a headdress with three feathers, which projected too high to look good. A Pawnee warbonnet was procured, but as it belonged to a rival tribe, the Sioux Indian refused to pose with it. The bonnet was photographed on an employee of the Engraving Division, cut out and super-imposed on the photograph of the Sioux. The design was engraved by Geo. F. C. Smillie in November 1899.

BACK DESIGNS, Series 1899

The green back designs were modified considerably from those of earlier issues. The denomination is indicated by large numerals. The Roman numeral "V" is featured in the center design of the $5 certificate. The inscription in the back design is the same as on earlier issues.

FIFTH ISSUE, Series 1923

The Fifth Issue of Silver Certificates consists of a single series, 1923, with only two denominations, $1 and $5. There were three signature combinations on the $1 Series 1923 certificate, and only one signature combination on the $5 denomination. The latter is therefore a type note.

FACE DESIGNS, Series 1923

- **$1** George Washington, as on Series 1923, $1 Legal Tender note.
- **$5** Abraham Lincoln in center of circular design. Sometimes referred to as the "porthole" note.

The certification that silver dollars have been deposited with the Treasurer of the United States, and the obligation to pay in silver dollars on demand, is the same as on earlier issues. The inscription, formerly in the back design, is on the face at left with seal.

BACK DESIGNS, Series 1923

- **$1** Open design, "The United States of America, One Dollar" prominent in center.
- **$5** Attractive design features the front or obverse of "The Great Seal of the United States." There is no legend or inscription other than "The United States of America" and the denomination.

SILVER CERTIFICATES—ONE DOLLAR

Face Design. Various small and large seals.

Back Design. Series 1886.

Back Design. Series 1891.

SILVER CERTIFICATES—ONE DOLLAR

Friedberg No.	Series	Register	Treasurer	Seal at Right	F-12	VF-20	EF-40	AU-50	Unc-60	Unc-63
Blue serial numbers on all Silver Certificates, all denominations.										
215	1886	Rosecrans	Jordan	Small red	$290	$490	$1,250	$1,380	$1,620	$2,310
216	1886	Rosecrans	Hyatt	Small red	300	390	1,120	1,500	1,690	1,940
217	1886	Rosecrans	Hyatt	Large red	300	455	1,150	1,380	2,190	2,560
218	1886	Rosecrans	Huston	Large red	325	455	1,150	1,310	2,000	2,120
219	1886	Rosecrans	Huston	Large brown	325	420	1,500	1,880	2,620	3,250
220	1886	Rosecrans	Nebeker	Large brown	325	455	1,250	1,880	2,620	2,750
221	1886	Rosecrans	Nebeker	Small red	325	420	1,020	1,380	1,750	1,880
222	1891	Rosecrans	Nebeker	Small red	245	440	1,020	1,150	1,590	1,810
223	1891	Tillman	Morgan	Small red	245	455	1,220	1,500	1,720	1,880

Face Design. History Instructing Youth.

Back Design. Martha and George Washington.

Friedberg No.	Series	Register	Treasurer	Seal at Right	F-12	VF-20	EF-40	AU-50	Unc-60	Unc-63
224	1896	Tillman	Morgan	Small red	$310	$550	$1,500	$1,810	$2,560	$2,750
225	1896	Bruce	Roberts	Small red	310	520	1,380	1,750	2,560	2,880

SILVER CERTIFICATES—ONE DOLLAR

Face Design.

Back Design. Modified design.

Friedberg No.	Series	Register	Treasurer	Seal at Right	F-12	VF-20	EF-40	AU-50	Unc-60	Unc-63
Series date above serial number.										
226	1899	Lyons	Roberts	Small blue	$135	$210	$275	$310	$520	$620
Series date below serial number.										
226a	1899	Lyons	Roberts	Small blue	130	170	290	325	565	585
227	1899	Lyons	Treat	Small blue	130	170	360	390	500	550
228	1899	Vernon	Treat	Small blue	130	170	325	370	520	585
229	1899	Vernon	McClung	Small blue	130	170	290	325	490	585
Series date vertically at right.										
229a	1899	Vernon	McClung	Small blue	325	520	1,500	3,000	3,750	4,500
230	1899	Napier	McClung	Small blue	130	155	290	370	475	520
231	1899	Napier	Thompson	Small blue	170	495	910	1,090	1,690	1,880
232	1899	Parker	Burke	Small blue	130	155	325	390	500	570
233	1899	Teehee	Burke	Small blue	130	155	290	360	520	650
234	1899	Elliott	Burke	Small blue	130	155	290	325	520	620
235	1899	Elliott	White	Small blue	130	155	325	390	520	550
236	1899	Speelman	White	Small blue	130	155	360	420	550	620

★ Star replacement notes for Series 1899 are valued at approximately double these prices.

SILVER CERTIFICATES—ONE DOLLAR

Face Design. Washington, as on small size notes.

Back Design.

Friedberg No.	Series	Register	Treasurer	Seal at Left	F-12	VF-20	EF-40	AU-50	Unc-60	Unc-63
237	1923	Speelman	White	Small blue	$43	$54	$81	$94	$160	$190
238	1923	Woods	White	Small blue	47	54	88	94	160	230
239	1923	Woods	Tate	Small blue	100	180	360	455	520	605

★ Star replacement notes for Series 1923 are valued at approximately double these prices.

SILVER CERTIFICATES—TWO DOLLARS

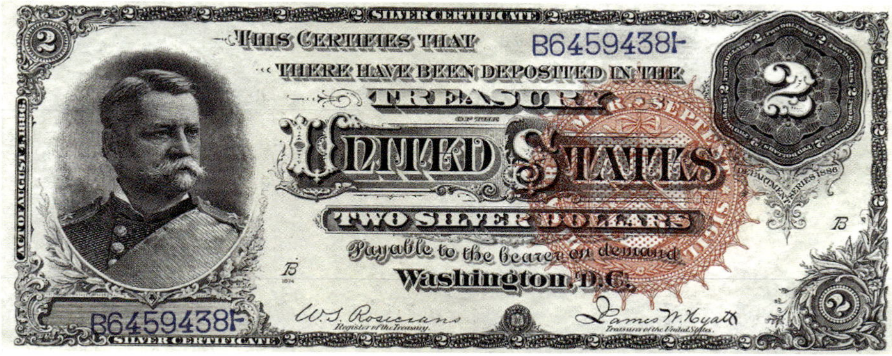

Face Design. Three types of seals.

Back Design. Unusual lathe work in green.

Friedberg No.	Series	Register	Treasurer	Seal at Right	F-12	VF-20	EF-40	AU-50	Unc-60	Unc-63
240	1886	Rosecrans	Jordan	Small red	$585	$780	$1,690	$2,190	$2,620	$2,810
241	1886	Rosecrans	Hyatt	Small red	585	780	1,810	2,250	2,750	3,120
242	1886	Rosecrans	Hyatt	Large red	585	910	1,750	2,250	2,500	3,750
243	1886	Rosecrans	Huston	Large red	585	780	1,690	2,190	2,750	2,940
244	1886	Rosecrans	Huston	Large brown	585	1,060	2,380	2,750	3,620	3,940

The above is a type design used only on Series 1886. It commemorates the passing of Winfield Scott Hancock in 1886 following his long career. He participated in the Mexican War and the Civil War in which he was shot but recovered. He was Democratic candidate for the U.S. presidency in 1880, but was defeated by James A. Garfield.

SILVER CERTIFICATES—TWO DOLLARS

Face Design. Wm. Windom, Small Issue.

Back Design. This issue only.

Friedberg No.	Series	Register	Treasurer	Seal at Right	F-12	VF-20	EF-40	AU-50	Unc-60	Unc-63
245	1891	Rosecrans	Nebeker	Small red	$520	$940	$1,940	$2,690	$4,380	$5,400
246	1891	Tillman	Morgan	Small red	520	910	2,120	2,940	4,250	4,810

The above design used only on Series 1891 honors William Windom, American financier and statesman who died in January 1891. He enjoyed a brilliant political career during which he served in the U.S. Congress and U.S. Senate. Windom was an early advocate of the gold standard.

SILVER CERTIFICATES—TWO DOLLARS

Face Design. Educational series.

Back Design. Inventors Morse and Fulton.

Friedberg No.	Series	Register	Treasurer	Seal at Right	F-12	VF-20	EF-40	AU-50	Unc-60	Unc-63
247	1896	Tillman	Morgan	Small red	$780	$1,560	$3,500	$4,500	$5,600	$6,250
248	1896	Bruce	Roberts	Small red	780	1,500	3,500	4,120	5,200	5,550

Face Design. Washington, Mechanics, Agriculture.

SILVER CERTIFICATES—TWO DOLLARS

Back Design.

Friedberg No.	Series	Register	Treasurer	Seal at Right	F-12	VF-20	EF-40	AU-50	Unc-60	Unc-63
249	1899	Lyons	Roberts	Small blue	$180	$260	$780	$1,020	$1,250	$1,500
250	1899	Lyons	Treat	Small blue	180	260	585	845	1,020	1,150
251	1899	Vernon	Treat	Small blue	180	290	585	845	1,020	1,380
252	1899	Vernon	McClung	Small blue	180	260	750	910	1,150	1,250
253	1899	Napier	McClung	Small blue	195	345	780	960	1,250	1,380
254	1899	Napier	Thompson	Small blue	520	910	1,750	2,250	3,750	4,880
255	1899	Parker	Burke	Small blue	180	260	520	845	1,020	1,250
256	1899	Teehee	Burke	Small blue	195	325	845	1,020	1,380	1,720
257	1899	Elliott	Burke	Small blue	200	475	880	1,250	2,060	2,500
258	1899	Speelman	White	Small blue	285	390	650	910	1,250	1,380

★ Star replacement notes for Series 1899 are valued at from two to three times prices shown here. None are known for the Napier-Thompson issue.

Face Design. Ulysses S. Grant.

SILVER CERTIFICATES—FIVE DOLLARS

Back Design. The "Silver Dollar" back.

Friedberg No.	Series	Register	Treasurer	Seal at Left	F-12	VF-20	EF-40	AU-50	Unc-60	Unc-63
Blue serial numbers.										
259	1886	Rosecrans	Jordan	Small red	$1,220	$1,880	$5,000	$7,500	$13,200	—
260	1886	Rosecrans	Hyatt	Small red	1,020	1,880	5,000	7,250	9,000	$10,000
261	1886	Rosecrans	Hyatt	Large red	1,020	1,880	5,250	7,250	10,300	11,250
262	1886	Rosecrans	Huston	Large red	1,020	1,880	5,000	7,500	9,000	10,000
263	1886	Rosecrans	Huston	Large brown	1,020	1,880	5,000	6,250	8,500	9,050
264	1886	Rosecrans	Nebeker	Large brown	1,020	1,880	5,000	7,250	9,000	10,000
265	1886	Rosecrans	Nebeker	Small red	1,560	3,560	11,900	14,400	16,800	19,200

All very scarce, especially in Uncirculated condition. A very popular series in all conditions.

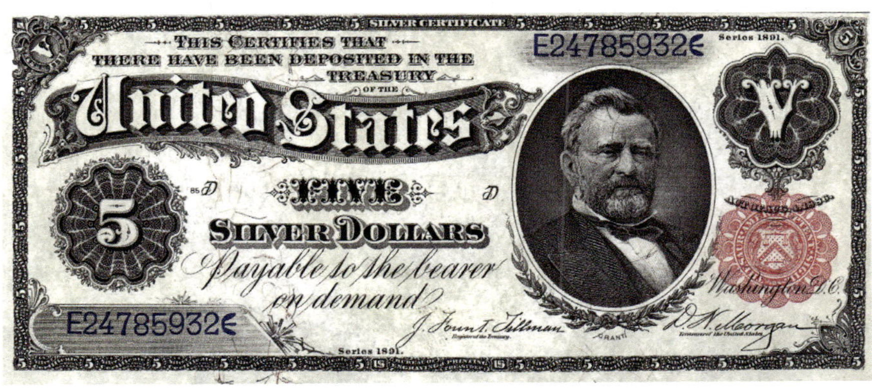

Face Design. Only two signature combinations. Red scalloped seals.

SILVER CERTIFICATES—FIVE DOLLARS

Back Design. Silver dollars eliminated.

Friedberg No.	Series	Register	Treasurer	Seal at Right	F-12	VF-20	EF-40	AU-50	Unc-60	Unc-63
Blue serial numbers.										
266	1891	Rosecrans	Nebeker	Small red	$495	$940	$1,500	$2,120	$3,190	$3,750
267	1891	Tillman	Morgan	Small red	495	940	1,810	2,500	3,500	3,750

First used on Series 1886 $5 silver certificates, the above design honors the former Civil War general and our 18th president. Named "Hiram Simpson Grant" at birth in 1822, Grant's name was entered as "Ulysses Simpson Grant" when he entered West Point Military Academy in 1839. Grant continued to use this name until his death in July 1885.

Face Design. Vignette depicts "Electricity" enlightening the world.

SILVER CERTIFICATES—FIVE DOLLARS

Back Design. Grant and Sheridan.

Friedberg No.	Series	Register	Treasurer	Seal at Right	F-12	VF-20	EF-40	AU-50	Unc-60	Unc-63
The Educational series.										
268	1896	Tillman	Morgan	Small red	$1,220	$3,060	$7,750	$8,750	$12,000	$12,900
269	1896	Bruce	Roberts	Small red	1,380	2,810	6,000	8,750	11,250	12,600
270	1896	Lyons	Roberts	Small red	1,020	2,500	7,500	8,750	12,000	12,900

Face Design. Running Antelope, Lakota Chief. A composite design.

Through common usage, the chief of the Oncpapa or Hunkpapa tribe of Lakota (Sioux) Indians is widely known to collectors as "Onepapa."

SILVER CERTIFICATES—FIVE DOLLARS

Back Design. Featuring Roman "V."

Friedberg No.	Series	Register	Treasurer	Seal at Right	F-12	VF-20	EF-40	AU-50	Unc-60	Unc-63
271	1899	Lyons	Roberts	Small blue	$620	$845	$1,500	$2,060	$2,750	$3,250
272	1899	Lyons	Treat	Small blue	620	845	1,500	2,060	2,620	2,810
273	1899	Vernon	Treat	Small blue	620	845	1,500	2,060	2,620	2,810
274	1899	Vernon	McClung	Small blue	620	845	1,500	2,060	2,620	2,810
275	1899	Napier	McClung	Small blue	620	845	1,500	2,060	2,620	3,000
276	1899	Napier	Thompson	Small blue	650	1,500	3,750	5,300	6,900	8,750
277	1899	Parker	Burke	Small blue	620	845	1,500	2,060	2,620	2,810
278	1899	Teehee	Burke	Small blue	620	845	1,500	2,060	2,750	3,310
279	1899	Elliott	Burke	Small blue	620	845	1,500	2,060	2,620	2,880
280	1899	Elliott	White	Small blue	620	845	1,500	2,060	2,750	3,000
281	1899	Speelman	White	Small blue	620	845	1,500	2,060	2,620	3,000

★ Star replacement notes for Series 1899 are valued at from two to three times the prices shown here.

Face Design. A type note of small issue.

SILVER CERTIFICATES—FIVE DOLLARS

Back Design. Features Great Seal in attractive setting.

Friedberg No.	Series	Register	Treasurer	Seal at Left	F-12	VF-20	EF-40	AU-50	Unc-60	Unc-63
Lincoln design. A type note.										
282	1923	Speelman	White	Small blue	$880	$1,250	$3,000	$3,500	$5,050	$5,600

★ Star replacement notes for Series 1923 are valued at approximately double the prices shown here.

Issued only in Series 1923, the Lincoln "porthole" design is very popular with collectors. Its value has steadily increased. The Lincoln pose continued to be used on small-size notes.

TEN DOLLARS

Face Design. Five types in the $10 denomination.
Above, Type Three, with three signatures.

A large suffix "X" with serial number appears only on the three signature notes. The key in the seal points RIGHT on the 1878 series. It was corrected on the 1880 series.

No series date appears on the 1878 series.

SILVER CERTIFICATES—TEN DOLLARS

Back Design. Attractive black on white "SILVER."

Friedberg No.	Series	Countersigned by		G-4	VG-8	F-12	VF-20
Scofield-Gilfillan signatures. Blue serial numbers.							
Countersigned by Assistant Treasurers.							
283	1878	W.G. White	Unique	$318,000	—	—	—
284	1878	J.C. Hopper	4 known	—	—	$360,000	—
284a	1878	T. Hillhouse	Unknown				
285	1878	A.U. Wyman	2 known	—	—	—	—
286	1880	T. Hillhouse		10,600	$16,800	—	—

Types 1, 2, and 5, place of deposit: New York. Type 3 place of deposit: Washington, D.C. Series 1878: Large red center seal and large red "TEN" below seal. Series 1880: Large brown center seal and large "X" below seal.

Face Design. Two signatures.

Friedberg No.	Series	Register	Treasurer	Seal in Center	F-12	VF-20	EF-40	AU-50	Unc-60	Unc-63
Blue serial numbers. Large "X" below center seal.										
287	1880	Scofield	Gilfillan	Large brown	$2,250	$3,500	$8,750	$10,600	$14,400	$18,600
288	1880	Bruce	Gilfillan	Large brown	2,250	3,500	8,750	10,600	14,400	15,600
289	1880	Bruce	Wyman	Large brown	2,250	3,500	8,750	10,600	13,200	16,800

SILVER CERTIFICATES—TEN DOLLARS

Face Design. Without large "X." Seal position lowered.

Friedberg No.	Series	Register	Treasurer	Seal in Center	F-12	VF-20	EF-40	AU-50	Unc-60	Unc-63
Blue serial numbers, without large "X" below center seal.										
290	1880	Bruce	Wyman	Large red	$3,500	$6,900	$28,800	$43,200	—	—

Face Design. Three different seals.

Back Design. Attractive green lathe-work.

SILVER CERTIFICATES—TEN DOLLARS

Friedberg No.	Series	Register	Treasurer	Seal at Right	F-12	VF-20	EF-40	AU-50	Unc-60	Unc-63
291	1886	Rosecrans	Jordan	Small red	$1,020	$1,940	$5,600	$10,000	$12,000	$14,400
292	1886	Rosecrans	Hyatt	Small red	1,020	1,940	5,600	9,400	12,000	14,400
293	1886	Rosecrans	Hyatt	Large red	1,020	1,940	5,600	9,400	13,200	15,600
294	1886	Rosecrans	Huston	Large red	1,020	1,940	5,600	9,400	14,400	26,400
295	1886	Rosecrans	Huston	Large brown	1,020	1,940	5,600	9,400	12,000	14,400
296	1886	Rosecrans	Nebeker	Large brown	1,020	2,250	5,600	9,400	12,000	14,400
297	1886	Rosecrans	Nebeker	Small red	1,020	1,940	5,600	9,400	12,000	14,400

Face Design. Hendricks, with changed series date.

Back Design. More open than previous series.

Friedberg No.	Series	Register	Treasurer	Seal at Right	F-12	VF-20	EF-40	AU-50	Unc-60	Unc-63
298	1891	Rosecrans	Nebeker	Small red	$650	$960	$2,380	$3,000	$4,380	$5,600
299	1891	Tillman	Morgan	Small red	810	1,060	2,120	2,750	4,000	4,810
300	1891	Bruce	Roberts	Small red	650	1,090	2,440	3,000	4,250	4,810
301	1891	Lyons	Roberts	Small red	680	960	2,060	2,560	4,250	5,000

SILVER CERTIFICATES—TEN DOLLARS

Face Design. Hendricks with blue seals.

Back Design. Same as Series 1891.

Friedberg No.	Series	Register	Treasurer	Seal at Right	F-12	VF-20	EF-40	AU-50	Unc-60	Unc-63
302	1908	Vernon	Treat	Small blue	$845	$1,150	$3,750	$4,250	$5,950	$9,400
303	1908	Vernon	McClung	Small blue	845	1,150	3,190	3,750	5,600	9,400
304	1908	Parker	Burke	Small blue	845	1,250	3,190	3,750	5,600	9,400

★ A unique star replacement note exists for the Series 1908, Parker-Burke issue.

SILVER CERTIFICATES—TWENTY DOLLARS

Face Design, four types described. Type One, shown above, has three signatures

Back Design. Black ink on white back.

Friedberg No.	Series	Countersigned by		G-4	VG-8	F-12	VF-20
Scofield-Gilfillan signatures. Blue serial numbers.							
Countersigned by Assistant Treasurers.							
305	1878	J.C. Hopper	3 known				
306	1878	T. Hillhouse	3 known				
307	1878	A.U. Wyman		$19,200	$33,600	—	—
308	1880	T. Hillhouse		19,200	36,000	—	—

All are rare. Type One (1878) with brown seal and XX, and Type Two (1880) with large TWENTY and brown seal, were issued at New York. All others show place of deposit as Washington.

SILVER CERTIFICATES—TWENTY DOLLARS

Face Design. Not countersigned. Large "XX" below seal.

Friedberg No.	Series	Register	Treasurer	Seal in Center	F-12	VF-20	EF-40	AU-50	Unc-60	Unc-63
309	1880	Scofield	Gilfillan	Large brown	$4,000	$7,500	$19,200	$36,000	$46,800	$54,000
310	1880	Bruce	Gilfillan	Large brown	4,000	7,500	16,200	26,400	42,000	48,000
311	1880	Bruce	Wyman	Large brown	4,000	7,500	16,200	26,400	42,000	48,000

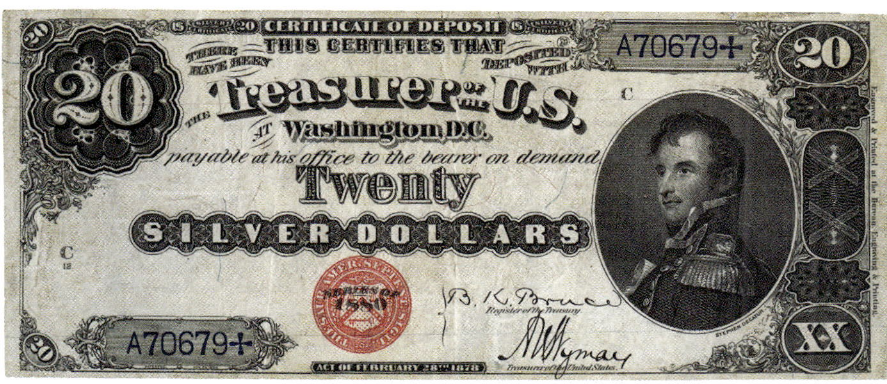

Face Design. "XX" removed. Small red seal.

Friedberg No.	Series	Register	Treasurer	Seal in Center	F-12	VF-20	EF-40	AU-50	Unc-60	Unc-63
Large "XX" removed.										
312	1880	Bruce	Wyman	Small red, left	$5,000	$12,000	$33,600	$60,000	—	—

SILVER CERTIFICATES—TWENTY DOLLARS

Face Design. Large seal left.

Back Design. Overall green lathe-work.

Friedberg No.	Series	Register	Treasurer	F-12	VF-20	EF-40	AU-50	Unc-60	Unc-63
Large red seal, left.									
313	1886	Rosecrans	Hyatt	$3,750	$8,750	$24,000	$54,000	$60,000	$66,000
Large brown seal, left.									
314	1886	Rosecrans	Huston	3,750	8,750	24,000	48,000	60,000	66,000
315	1886	Rosecrans	Nebeker	3,750	8,750	24,000	54,000	81,600	—
Small red seal, right.									
316	1886	Rosecrans	Nebeker	4,750	13,200	45,600	69,000	74,400	—

SILVER CERTIFICATES—TWENTY DOLLARS

Face Design. Daniel Manning is on all Series 1886. Small red seal.

Face Design. Blue seal. Large blue XX at left.

Back Design. Open back, to discourage counterfeiting.

SILVER CERTIFICATES—TWENTY DOLLARS

Friedberg No.	Series	Register	Treasurer	Seal at Right	F-12	VF-20	EF-40	AU-50	Unc-60	Unc-63
"Series 1891" upper right and lower left.										
317	1891	Rosecrans	Nebeker	Small red	$910	$1,250	$3,250	$5,000	$6,250	$7,200
318	1891	Tillman	Morgan	Small red	910	1,380	3,500	5,000	6,250	7,200
319	1891	Bruce	Roberts	Small red	910	1,250	3,250	5,000	6,250	7,200
320	1891	Lyons	Roberts	Small red	910	1,500	3,620	5,600	10,600	11,250
Large blue "XX" at left.										
321	1891	Parker	Burke	Small blue	910	1,250	3,750	5,000	6,250	7,500
322	1891	Teehee	Burke	Small blue	910	1,380	3,750	5,600	8,750	15,000

★ Star replacement notes for Series 1891 are extremely rare.

FIFTY DOLLARS

First of the face designs. Countersigned note shown here has three signatures.

Back Design.

Friedberg No.	Series	Countersigned by		G-4	VG-8	F-12
Scofield-Gilfillan signatures. Blue serial numbers. Countersigned by Assistant Treasurers. Large "FIFTY" below center seal.						
324	1878	T. Hillhouse	2 known	—	—	—
324a	1878	R.M. Anthony	Unique	—	—	—
324c	1878	A.U. Wyman	3 known	—	—	—

Type 3 payable at Washington, D.C. Type 4 payable in New York. Type 6 payable at San Francisco—unknown.

SILVER CERTIFICATES—FIFTY DOLLARS

Face Design. Edward Everett. Minor variations and two signatures.

Back Design. Black on white.

Friedberg No.	Series	Register	Treasurer	Seal		F-12	VF-20	EF-40	AU-50
Large "L" in center.									
325	1880	Scofield	Gilfillan	Large brown, center	Unique	—	—	—	—
326	1880	Bruce	Gilfillan	Large brown, center		$36,000	$48,000	—	—
327	1880	Bruce	Wyman	Large brown, center		32,400	48,000	$156,000	—
Large "L" removed.									
328	1880	Rosecrans	Huston	Large brown, spikes		14,400	31,200	84,000	$108,000
329	1880	Rosecrans	Nebeker	Small red, right		13,800	19,200	74,400	96,000

SILVER CERTIFICATES—FIFTY DOLLARS

Face Design. Minor variations.

Back Design. Open back, to discourage counterfeiting.

Friedberg No.	Series	Register	Treasurer	Seal at Right	F-12	VF-20	EF-40	AU-50	Unc-60	Unc-63
330	1891	Rosecrans	Nebeker	Small red	$12,000	$18,000	$48,000	$60,000	—	—
331	1891	Tillman	Morgan	Small red	2,810	5,250	12,600	18,000	—	—
332	1891	Bruce	Roberts	Small red	3,310	4,380	—	—	—	—
333	1891	Lyons	Roberts	Small red	2,810	5,000	13,200	16,800	$30,000	$42,000
334	1891	Vernon	Treat	Small red	2,810	4,060	9,400	11,250	15,600	20,400
335	1891	Parker	Burke	Blue	2,810	4,440	8,750	11,250	18,000	20,400

SILVER CERTIFICATES—ONE HUNDRED DOLLARS
THE COUNTERSIGNED SERIES

Type 3 place of deposit: Washington, D.C. Type 6 place of deposit: San Francisco. Type 7 place of deposit: New York.

Face Design. President James Monroe. Three types. Above, Type Three.

Face Design. Type Six, San Francisco.

Back Design. Black on white.

SILVER CERTIFICATES—ONE HUNDRED DOLLARS

Friedberg No.	Series	Countersigned by		VG-8	VF-20
Scofield-Gilfillan signatures. Blue serial numbers.					
336	1878	W.G. White	Unique	—	—
337	1878	R.M. Anthony	Unique	—	—
337b	1878	A.U. Wyman	4 known	—	—

All have large red "100" below center seal.

Face Design. President James Monroe, two signatures.

Back Design. Black ink.

Friedberg No.	Series	Register	Treasurer	Seal		F-12	VF-20	EF-40	AU-50
Large "C" below center seal.									
338	1880	Scofield	Gilfillan	Large brown, center	Unknown				
339	1880	Bruce	Gilfillan	Large brown, center	4 known				
340	1880	Bruce	Wyman	Large brown, center		$30,000	$66,000	$246,000	—
No "C" below center seal.									
341	1880	Rosecrans	Huston	Large brown, spikes		30,000	60,000	132,000	$192,000
342	1880	Rosecrans	Nebeker	Small red, right		30,000	60,000	96,000	162,000

SILVER CERTIFICATES—ONE HUNDRED DOLLARS

Face Design. Minor change.

Back Design. Green ink.

Friedberg No.	Series	Register	Treasurer	Seal at Right	VG-8	F-12	VF-20	EF-40	AU-50
343	1891	Rosecrans	Nebeker	Small red	$8,750	$12,600	$30,000	$60,000	$90,000
344	1891	Tillman	Morgan	Small red	5,100	8,750	24,000	66,000	90,000

The above series were extensively counterfeited. Genuine notes have fibers on the back of the note. Counterfeits have "ink drawn" threads, or none.

SILVER CERTIFICATES—FIVE HUNDRED DOLLARS

Countersigned Series. One only, Type Three, payable at Washington, D.C. Scofield-Gilfillan signatures. Blue serial numbers.

Friedberg No.	Series	Countersigned by	Seal in Center	
345a	1878	A.U. Wyman	Large red	Unique

SILVER CERTIFICATES—FIVE HUNDRED DOLLARS

Face Design.

Back Design. Black ink.

Friedberg No.	Series	Register	Treasurer	Seal in Center	
345b	1880	Scofield	Gilfillan	Large brown	Unknown
345c	1880	Bruce	Gilfillan	Large brown	5 known
345d	1880	Bruce	Wyman	Large brown	2 known

There have been no recent public sales. All are extremely rare. Some might not exist. Reportedly fewer than 15 have not been redeemed of all the above.

SILVER CERTIFICATES—ONE THOUSAND DOLLARS

Friedberg No.	Series	Countersigned by	Seal in Center	
346a	1878	A.U. Wyman	Large red	Unknown

SILVER CERTIFICATES—ONE THOUSAND DOLLARS

Face Design. Series of 1891.

Back Design.

Friedberg No.	Series	Register	Treasurer	Seal	
346b	1880	Scofield	Gilfillan	Large brown, center	Unknown
346c	1880	Bruce	Gilfillan	Large brown, center	Unknown
346d	1880	Bruce	Wyman	Large brown, center	5 known
346e	1891	Tillman	Morgan	Small red, right	2 known

Reportedly fewer than 10 notes of this denomination, all series, have not been redeemed.

As with the $500 denomination, only Type Three was issued in the countersigned series, Scofield-Gilfillan signatures and blue serial numbers.

The Silver Certificates Series 1878 to 1923 include some of the finest engravings and most attractive designs used in the printing of United States paper money. The memory of many great Americans has been perpetuated in the face designs: Martha Washington, General Winfield Scott, William Windom, Thos. A. Hendricks, Daniel Manning, Edward Everett, Wm. L. Marcy, and former U.S. presidents Washington, Lincoln, Grant, and Monroe. The Silver Dollar back design of Series 1886 is exceptionally attractive. The well known and much sought after Educational Series 1896 is outstanding for the designs and engraving on the face of the notes and the back designs honoring Martha and George Washington, inventors Robert Fulton and Samuel Morse and generals U.S. Grant and Philip Henry Sheridan. Our American Indians are honored by the face design of the Series 1899 $5 certificate, commonly known as the "Onepapa" design.

NATIONAL BANK NOTES

Authorized by the National Currency Act, February 25, 1863, and June 3, 1864, National Bank Notes were issued by Chartered Banks from 1863 to 1928 in large size. During the Civil War, coins of gold and silver were hoarded and practically disappeared from circulation. The unsecured Legal Tender Notes, commonly known as "Greenbacks," were not popular and not readily accepted by skeptical persons having no confidence in the government's promise to pay.

Although the National Currency Act was not passed until February 26, 1863, as early as April 1862 Spencer M. Clark, Chief of Construction of the Treasury Department conceived the plan to have National Banks issue their own currency. The plan was endorsed by the then-secretary of the Treasury, Salmon P. Chase, who directed Clark to invite artists and engravers to submit proposals and designs. Clark had previously suggested that historic pictures be used as back designs for the "Greenbacks" of 1862, claiming that these designs offered greater protection against counterfeiting. His proposed designs were not adopted for the Legal Tender notes, but were adopted for the National Bank Notes issued under secretary of the Treasury W.P. Fessenden. Clark suggested that these designs cover the entire back of the notes, but while the designs were adopted, the size of each was reduced to allow space for denomination and legends.

Spencer M. Clark later became chief of the Division and was largely responsible for the establishment of the Bureau of Engraving and Printing.

Under the original Act of February 25, 1863, National Banks qualifying under the terms of the Act were granted 20-year charters to date from the enactment of the Act. The Act of June 1864 changed this procedure and permitted granting of charters for 20 years from the date of the charter. Changes in the original Act through the years provided for renewal of charters for 20-year periods. Banks so chartered were permitted to issue National Currency not to exceed 90 percent of the total of the U.S. Government Bonds deposited with the Treasurer of the United States.

The Act of 1863 provided for the issuance of denominations from $5 to $1,000. The Act of 1864 added $1, $2, and $3 notes. The $3 note was never issued although a plate was engraved.

Early issues will be found with the imprint of American, Continental and National Bank Note Companies. These companies supplied the paper and delivered the printed notes to the Treasury. The Treasury number and Treasury seal were then imprinted by the Bureau.

The *History of the Bureau of Engraving and Printing* supplies this information: "National Bank Notes were printed exclusively by private contractors until Sept. 1875. Thereafter this type of currency was partially printed by the Bureau of Engraving and Printing. Beginning in October 1877, the Bureau executed all work in connection with the printing of national currency."

Notes will be found bearing the imprint of one of the three bank note companies in the design and in very small type in the margin of the note the notation: "Printed at the Bureau of Engraving & Printing."

The dates appearing on National Bank Notes do not always indicate the date the charter was granted nor the date the notes were issued. Nor do these dates denote the term of office of the Treasury officials whose signatures appear on the notes. Plates engraved with the names of the U.S. Treasurer and Register of the Treasury were frequently used after the officials left office. The date appearing on the note is usually later than the granting of the charter. Some banks, organized late in the First Charter period, continued to issue Series 1875 notes until February 1902.

At the close of 1928, 13,269 banks had been chartered but many did not issue bank notes. Notes issued by banks in small communities are usually scarcer than those of large city banks. This thinking has at times been upset when a small town bank released a stock of notes which had been held in their reserve funds.

In addition to the engraved signatures of the two Treasury officials, National Bank Notes have the signatures of two bank officers, usually the president and cashier. Early issues did not carry the plate number on face or back.

NATIONAL BANK NOTES

The first charter notes of $1 and $2 denominations were usually printed in sheets of three $1 notes and one $2 note. Check letters on notes so printed are A, B, and C on the $1 notes and A on the $2 note. Known exceptions to "three ones and a two" are:

The Westchester County National Bank, Peekskill, New York, Charter No. 1422.
The Merchants National Bank, Bangor, Maine. Charter No. 1437.
The City National Bank, Manchester, New Hampshire. Charter No. 1530.

The above three banks were supplied with sheets of two $1 notes, check letters A and B, and two $2 notes, check letters A and B.

The other known exception is the First National Bank of Philadelphia, with sheets of four $1 and sheets of four $2 notes.

The word "National" by law, must appear in the title of all chartered banks. The exception is the Bank of North America, Philadelphia, Pennsylvania, which during its term of operation was allowed to retain the title used as a state bank.

REGIONAL LETTERS ON NATIONAL CURRENCY

To assist in sorting notes presented for redemption, a large letter was printed with the charter numbers on National Currency for a period of about 25 years, approximately 1901–1925. These regional letters indicated the geographical area or region in which the issuing bank was located and may be found on Second and Third Charter Period notes. Six letters were used as follows:

E	Eastern Region	**P**	Pacific Region, including Hawaii and Alaska
M	Middle States Region	**S**	Southern Region
N	New England Region	**W**	Western Region

Many collectors endeavor to obtain at least one bank note from each of the six areas; also a note with a regional letter and a note without the letter, issued by the same bank. Other collectors seek to obtain as many notes as are available with their own regional letter.

CHARTER NUMBERS

Bank charter numbers were overprinted on Series 1875 and all later series and may also be found on some notes of the Original Series. The exact position varies on the face of the notes. These numbers on the First Issue are in red with the exception of a very few banks which were supplied with notes bearing BLACK charter numbers.

Reported "Black Charters" are $5 notes of the following banks:

No. 1830 Minneapolis, Minnesota. Merchants National Bank. Allison-Spinner.
No. 2129 Central City, Colorado Territory, First National Bank. Allison-New.
No. 2130 Red Oak, Iowa. First National Bank. Allison-Spinner.
No. 2132 Green Bay, Wisconsin. Kellogg National Bank. Allison-Gilfillan.
No. 2137 Boyertown, Pennsylvania. First National Bank. Allison-Wyman.
No. 2138 Rochester, New Hampshire. National Bank. Allison-New.
No. 2141 Pontiac, Illinois. The National Bank. Allison-Wyman.
No. 2131 Possibly issued to the National Bank, Green Lane, Pennsylvania.

All the above are very rare and are valued conservatively at ten times the valuation of notes from the same states issued with red charter numbers.

66-YEAR RECORD OF CHARTERED NATIONAL BANKS

The following chart indicating the last charter number granted in each year from 1863 to the close of 1928 will be found helpful in determining the year in which any charter was granted.

NATIONAL BANK NOTES

Year	No.	Year	No.	Year	No.	Year	No.	Year	No.	Year	No.	Year	No.
1863	179	1873	2131	1883	3101	1893	4934	1903	7081	1913	10472	1923	12481
1864	682	1874	2214	1884	3281	1894	4983	1904	7541	1914	10672	1924	12615
1865	1626	1875	2315	1885	3427	1895	5029	1905	8027	1915	10810	1925	12866
1866	1665	1876	2344	1886	3612	1896	5054	1906	8489	1916	10932	1926	13022
1867	1675	1877	2375	1887	3832	1897	5108	1907	8979	1917	11126	1927	13159
1868	1688	1878	2405	1888	3954	1898	5165	1908	9302	1918	11282	1928	13269
1869	1696	1879	2445	1889	4190	1899	5240	1909	9622	1919	11570		
1870	1759	1880	2498	1890	4494	1900	5662	1910	9913	1920	11903		
1871	1912	1881	2606	1891	4673	1901	6074	1911	10119	1921	12082		
1872	2073	1882	2849	1892	4832	1902	6566	1912	10305	1922	12287		

The record is not available as to the number of banks chartered early in 1929 before the issuance of small-size notes in July of that year.

COMPARATIVE RARITY TABLE

The following Rarity Table has been compiled after consultation with several ardent followers of this interesting series, plus the writer's experience in endeavoring to assemble a collection of National Bank Notes. *One hundred percent accuracy is not to be expected* and changes will be made as new factual information is received. As with California notes, relative rarity for many states changes with the Charters.

Rarity 1	**Rarity 2**	**Rarity 3**	**Rarity 4**	**Rarity 5**
California, 3rd Ch.	Indiana	Kansas	Alabama	California, 2nd Ch.
Illinois	Iowa	Kentucky	Connecticut	Colorado
New York	Massachusetts	Michigan	Maryland	District of Columbia
Ohio	New Jersey	Minnesota	Nebraska	New Hampshire
Pennsylvania	Texas	Missouri	Tennessee	North Carolina
		Wisconsin	Virginia	Oklahoma
				Washington
				West Virginia

Rarity 6	**Rarity 7**	**Rarity 8**	**Rarity 9**	**Rarity 10**
Georgia	Arkansas	Arizona	California, 1st Ch.	Puerto Rico
Louisiana	Delaware	Idaho	District of Alaska	
Maine	Florida	Hawaii	Territorial Notes	
North Dakota	Montana	Mississippi		
Oregon	Rhode Island	Nevada		
South Carolina	Utah	New Mexico		
Vermont	Wyoming	South Dakota		

Values listed for the various signature combinations throughout the three charter periods are for notes of RARITY ONE. No set rule can be given for every denomination of each charter period for each state. Valuations for Rarity One may be increased for the various degree of rarity, approximately as follows:

Rarity 2	20%	**Rarity 5**	60%	**Rarity 8**	Four to five times.
Rarity 3	30%	**Rarity 6**	70%	**Rarity 9**	Five to ten times.
Rarity 4	50%	**Rarity 7**	Three to four times.	**Rarity 10**	Ten or more times.

Notes of the high rarity groups are seldom offered and prices are largely a matter between buyer and seller.

NATIONAL BANK NOTES
THE FIRST CHARTER PERIOD
ORIGINAL SERIES AND SERIES 1875

First issue of National Bank Notes is known as the "Original Series." This was followed by Series 1875. The two series comprise the issue of First Charter notes, denominations of $1 to $1,000. Only two banks are known to have issued First Charter notes in denominations higher than $100.

The obligation to pay is by the issuing bank printed on the face of the notes and reads: "This note is secured by Bonds of the United States, deposited with the United States Treasurer at Washington. The . . . (Bank) . . . will pay the Bearer on Demand . . . Dollars."

FACE DESIGNS, First Charter Notes

$1 "Concordia." Two maidens clasping hands before an altar of earlier times which bears the coat of arms of the United States. The design represents the new Union brought about by the aid of Heaven, and the eventual return to peace. The vignette was designed by T.A. Liebler and engraved by Charles Burt.

$2 "Stars and Stripes" depicts a maiden unfurling the American flag. Engraved by James Smillie for the National Bank Note Co. Bank serial number at upper right. Treasury number at lower left in vertical position.

Known as the "Lazy 2" because of the large numeral "2" reclining on its side with the certification that bonds have been deposited with the Treasurer of the U.S. at Washington. Similar large numerals were used on obsolete notes.

$5 "Columbus Sighting Land" shows the discoverer with some of his crew on the deck of the caravel. The scene at lower right depicts Columbus introducing America, represented by an Indian princess, to the Old World, Africa, Asia, and Europe. Continental Bank Note Co. designer Fenton produced the design for engraving by Charles Burt.

$10 "Franklin and the Lightning" is the historical scene at left, symbolic of Benjamin Franklin experimenting with electrical energy and his assistant seated near him with a Leyden jar placed nearby. The year is marked by the figures "1752" in the corner. Eagle in flight bearing Liberty is shown at right, symbolizing "America Grasping the Lightning." Engraving by Alfred Jones.

$20 "Battle of Lexington 1775" depicts colonists in action, nurses attending the wounded and at right a symbolic design of "Loyalty." A procession for defense and preservation of the Union is led by Columbia with flag. The design is by Felix O.C. Darley. Engravings by Louis Delnoce and Alfred Jones.

$50 "Washington Crossing the Delaware" before his victorious battle at Princeton is the symbolical vignette at left. Engraved by Alfred Jones. "A Prayer for Victory" is depicted at right. Engraved by Louis Delnoce.

$100 Powell's painting "The Battle of Lake Erie" was the inspiration for the vignette at left engraved by Louis Delnoce. This shows Commodore Perry leaving his burning ship, the *Lawrence*. At right, Columbia is seated with a fasces, a bundle of rods with projecting ax handle. Inscribed are the words "The Union" and to the right "Maintain it." Engraving by James Bannister.

$500 "Genius of the American Navy," left, and arrival of the *Sirius,* 1838, right. James MacDonough, designer.

$1,000 "General Scott entering the City of Mexico" is shown at left, after the painting by John Trumbull. It was engraved by James Smillie and possibly Alfred Jones and A. Sealey. At right, the Capitol Building, Washington, D.C. This note is believed to be non-existent.

NATIONAL BANK NOTES—FIRST CHARTER PERIOD

BACK DESIGNS, First Charter Notes

The coat of arms of the state of issue appears in oval at left with the exception of notes issued by banks in the territories of Arizona, Nebraska, New Mexico, Oklahoma, Utah, and Washington. The American eagle is shown in the oval at right. A rather lengthy inscription qualifying the acceptance of the note and the warning against counterfeiting "Punishable by $1,000 fine, or fifteen years' imprisonment at hard labor, or both" is also part of the back design. The border designs are green with center illustrations in black.

$1 "Landing of the Pilgrims" in center of back design depicts one of the memorable events in United States history. It is framed by the legend giving the legal value of the note, the purpose for which the note was intended, and the warning to counterfeiters. Engraved by Elisha Hobart.

$2 "Sir Walter Raleigh Presenting Tobacco From America." Sir Walter Raleigh, with a long stem smoking pipe, demonstrates the use of tobacco brought from America, and displays corn from the New World. The king of England looks on with interest. Engraved by Louis Delnoce.

$5 "The Landing of Columbus," from the well-known mural by John Vanderlyn. Louis Delnoce, engraver.

$10 "DeSoto Discovering the Mississippi, 1541." The beautiful mural by W.H. Powell shows a group of natives, soldiers, and monks. A crucifix is being erected on the spot. Engraved by Girsch.

$20 "The Baptism of Pocahontas at Jamestown, Virginia, 1613." The impressive scene shows Pocahontas kneeling, with John Smith and spectators, some of whom express interest and surprise. The painting is by John G. Chapman.

$50 "Embarkation of the Pilgrims," a reproduction of Robert W. Weir's mural which depicts the Pilgrims, before departing for America, kneeling to ask the Divine blessing. Engraved by W.W. Rice.

$100 "The Signing of the Declaration of Independence, July 4, 1776." One of John Trumbull's masterpieces showing Washington, Jefferson, Franklin, and a dignified group assembled for the acceptance and signing of the historic document. Engraved by Girsch.

$500 "The Surrender of Burgoyne." Another mural by artist John Trumbull vividly portraying the surrender of the general to General Gates of the American Army at Saratoga, New York, October 17, 1777. Engraved by Girsch.

$1,000 "Washington Resigning His Commission, December 23, 1783, at Annapolis, Maryland." John Trumbull's mural shows the commander-in-chief presenting his written resignation to the Congress. Engraved by Girsch and Louis Delnoce.

NATIONAL BANK NOTES—FIRST CHARTER PERIOD

ONE DOLLAR

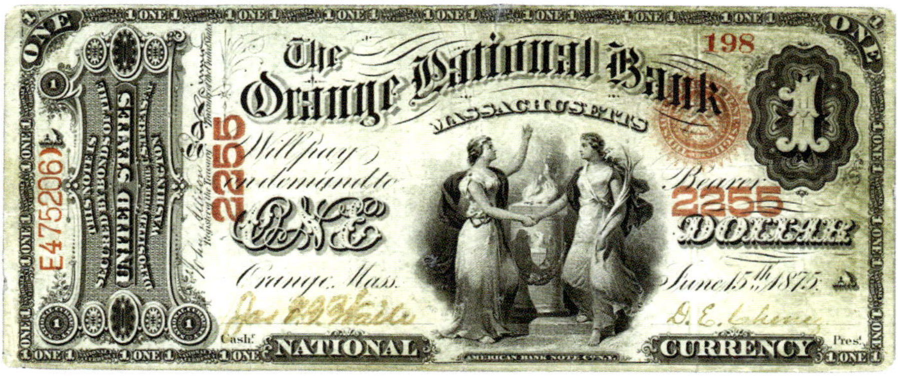

Face Design. Original Series with Bank Charter number and small red seal.

Back Design. "Landing of Pilgrims."

The early issues known as Original Series, with a few exceptions, bore no charter number and no series date. Additional information is given in the descriptive text in the preceding pages.

Friedberg No.	Series	Register	Treasurer	Seal at Right	VG-8	F-12	VF-20	EF-40
380	Original	Colby	Spinner	Small red	$600	$850	$1,200	$2,000
381	Original	Jeffries	Spinner	Small red	2,250	3,500	4,500	—
382	Original	Allison	Spinner	Small red	600	850	1,200	2,000
Charter number and "Series 1875" added. Shield with scallops.								
383	1875	Allison	New	Red	625	900	1,250	2,100
384	1875	Allison	Wyman	Red	625	900	1,250	2,100
385	1875	Allison	Gilfillan	Red	625	900	1,250	2,100
386	1875	Scofield	Gilfillan	Red	700	1,000	1,350	2,200

Signature combination Chittenden-Spinner not issued.

Gem, well-centered early Charters are difficult to find. Uncut sheets were cut apart by shear-happy tellers. Many New England notes were trimmed right down to the design.

NATIONAL BANK NOTES—FIRST CHARTER PERIOD

TWO DOLLARS ("THE LAZY 2")

Face Design. Original Series without Bank Charter number.

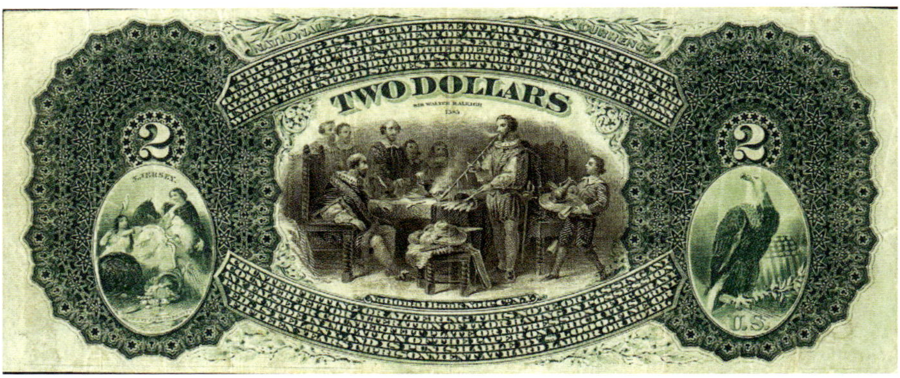

Back Design. "Sir Walter Raleigh Presenting Tobacco From America."

Friedberg No.	Series	Register	Treasurer	Seal at Right	VG-8	F-12	VF-20	EF-40
387	Original	Colby	Spinner	Small red	$2,750	$4,000	$5,000	$6,500
388	Original	Jeffries	Spinner	Small red	10,000	11,200	24,000	
389	Original	Allison	Spinner	Small red	2,750	4,000	5,000	6,500
Charter number and "Series 1875" added. Shield with scallops.								
390	1875	Allison	New	Red	2,750	4,000	5,250	6,750
391	1875	Allison	Wyman	Red	2,750	4,000	5,250	6,750
392	1875	Allison	Gilfillan	Red	2,750	4,000	5,250	6,750
393	1875	Scofield	Gilfillan	Red	2,750	4,000	5,250	6,750

Issuance of $1 and $2 National Bank Notes was discontinued in 1878. The latest date observed is July 30, 1878. First Charter denominations of $5 and higher continued to be issued as late as 1909.

NATIONAL BANK NOTES—FIRST CHARTER PERIOD

FIVE DOLLARS

Face Design. Original Series with Bank Charter number.

Back Design. "The Landing of Columbus."

Printed in sheets of four $5 notes from 1863 to 1909.

Friedberg No.	Series	Register	Treasurer	Seal at Right	VG-8	F-12	VF-20	EF-40
394	Original	Chittenden	Spinner	Small red	$1,200	$1,500	$2,000	$2,800
397	Original	Colby	Spinner	Small red	1,200	1,500	2,000	2,800
398	Original	Jeffries	Spinner	Small red	5,500	7,500	8,750	12,000
399	Original	Allison	Spinner	Small red	1,200	1,500	2,000	2,800
Charter number and "Series 1875" added.								
401	1875	Allison	New	Red	1,200	1,500	2,000	2,800
402	1875	Allison	Wyman	Red	1,200	1,500	2,000	2,800
403	1875	Allison	Gilfillan	Red	1,200	1,500	2,000	2,800
404	1875	Scofield	Gilfillan	Red	1,200	1,500	2,000	2,800
405	1875	Bruce	Gilfillan	Red	1,200	1,500	2,000	2,800
406	1875	Bruce	Wyman	Red	—	—	—	—
406a	1875	Bruce	Jordan	Red	—	—	—	—
407	1875	Rosecrans	Jordan	Red	1,200	1,500	2,000	2,800
408	1875	Rosecrans	Huston	Red	—	—	—	—

Signature combination Rosecrans-Hyatt not issued.

NATIONAL BANK NOTES—FIRST CHARTER PERIOD

TEN DOLLARS

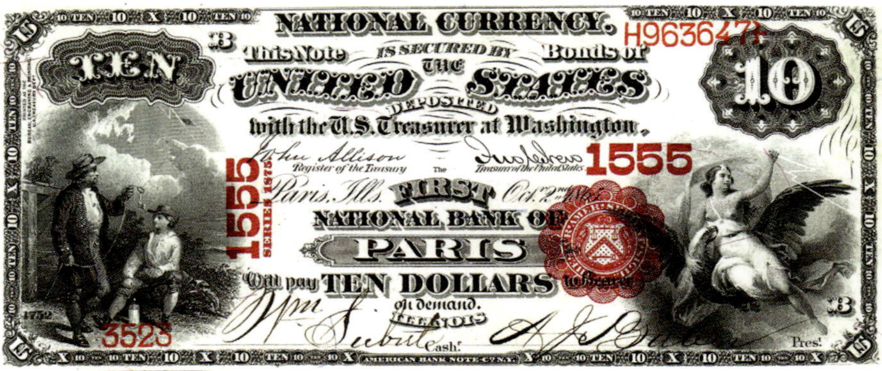

Face Design. Series 1875 with Bank Charter number.

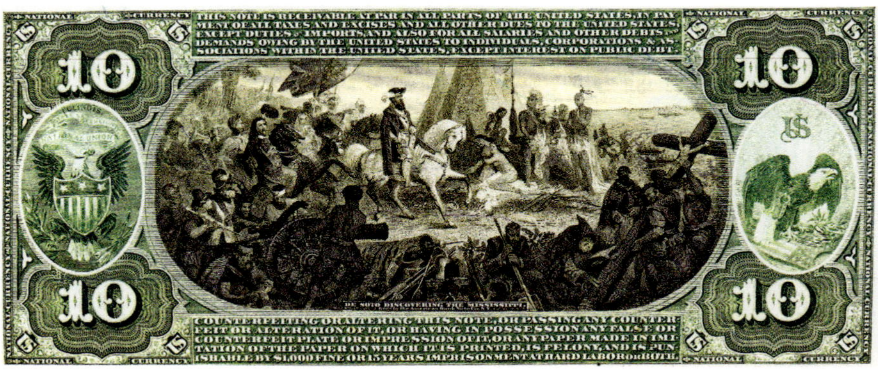

Back Design. "DeSoto Discovering the Mississippi, 1541."

Sheets of four $10, three $10 / one $20, and other combinations 1863 to 1909. Early issues have Continental Bank Note Co. in lower border. Later issues printed at Bureau.

Friedberg No.	Series	Register	Treasurer	Seal at Right		VG-8	F-12	VF-20	EF-40
409	Original	Chittenden	Spinner	Small red		$1,200	$1,500	$2,400	$3,000
412	Original	Colby	Spinner	Small red		1,200	1,500	2,400	3,000
413	Original	Jeffries	Spinner	Small red	Unique	—	—	—	—
414	Original	Allison	Spinner	Red		1,200	1,500	2,400	3,000
416	1875	Allison	New	Red		1,200	1,500	2,400	3,000
417	1875	Allison	Wyman	Red		1,200	1,500	2,400	3,000
418	1875	Allison	Gilfillan	Red		1,200	1,500	2,400	3,000
419	1875	Scofield	Gilfillan	Red		1,200	1,500	2,400	3,000
420	1875	Bruce	Gilfillan	Red		1,200	1,500	2,400	3,000
421	1875	Bruce	Wyman	Red		1,200	1,500	2,400	3,000
422	1875	Rosecrans	Huston	Red		2,000	3,000	4,500	
423	1875	Rosecrans	Nebeker	Red		1,200	1,500	2,400	3,000
423a	1875	Tillman	Morgan	Red	Unique	—	—	—	—

See page 72 for suggested valuations for all states.

NATIONAL BANK NOTES—FIRST CHARTER PERIOD

TWENTY DOLLARS

Face Design. Original Series without Bank Charter number.

Back Design. "The Baptism of Pocahontas at Jamestown, Virginia, 1613."

Printed in sheets of several combinations, including three $10 / one $20 and four $20 bills, from 1863 to 1902.

Friedberg No.	Series	Register	Treasurer	Seal at Right		VG-8	F-12	VF-20	EF-40
424	Original	Chittenden	Spinner	Small red		$2,300	$3,000	$4,000	$4,800
427	Original	Colby	Spinner	Small red		2,300	3,000	4,000	4,800
428	Original	Jeffries	Spinner	Small red	Unique				
429	Original	Allison	Spinner	Red		2,300	3,000	4,000	4,800
431	1875	Allison	New	Red		2,300	3,000	4,000	4,800
432	1875	Allison	Wyman	Red		2,300	3,000	4,000	4,800
433	1875	Allison	Gilfillan	Red		2,300	3,000	4,000	4,800
434	1875	Scofield	Gilfillan	Red		2,300	3,000	4,000	4,800
435	1875	Bruce	Gilfillan	Red		2,300	3,000	4,000	4,800
436	1875	Bruce	Wyman	Red	2 known				
437	1875	Rosecrans	Huston	Red	Rare				
438	1875	Rosecrans	Nebeker	Red	Rare				
439	1875	Tillman	Morgan	Red	Unique				

NATIONAL BANK NOTES—FIRST CHARTER PERIOD

FIFTY DOLLARS

Face Design. Series 1875 with Bank Charter number.

Back Design. "Embarkation of the Pilgrims."

Printed in sheets of three $50 and one $100 or sheets of two $50, plus other combinations, including one $50 and one $100 on a sheet of two, from 1863 to 1902.

Friedberg No.	Series	Register	Treasurer	Seal at Right		G-4	VG-8	F-12	VF-20
440	Original	Chittenden	Spinner	Small red		$13,000	$17,500	$20,000	$24,000
442	Original	Colby	Spinner	Small red		13,000	17,500	20,000	24,000
443	Original	Allison	Spinner	Small red	3 known				
444	1875	Allison	New	Scalloped red		13,000	17,500	20,000	24,000
444a	1875	Allison	Wyman	Scalloped red	4 known				
445	1875	Allison	Gilfillan	Scalloped red	5 known				
446	1875	Scofield	Gilfillan	Scalloped red		13,000	17,500	20,000	24,000
447	1875	Bruce	Gilfillan	Scalloped red		13,000	17,500	20,000	24,000
448	1875	Bruce	Wyman	Scalloped red		13,000	17,500	20,000	24,000
449	1875	Rosecrans	Huston	Scalloped red	1 known			—	—
450	1875	Rosecrans	Nebeker	Scalloped red	1 known			—	—
451	1875	Tillman	Morgan	Scalloped red	2 known			—	—

NATIONAL BANK NOTES—FIRST CHARTER PERIOD

ONE HUNDRED DOLLARS

Face Design. Series 1875 with Bank Charter number.

Back Design. "The Signing of the Declaration of Independence, July 4, 1776."

Printed in sheets of one $100 and three $50, and sheets of two $100 or one $50 and one $100, and other combinations.

Friedberg No.	Series	Register	Treasurer	Seal at Right		G-4	VG-8	F-12	VF-20
452	Original	Chittenden	Spinner	Small red	Rare				
454	Original	Colby	Spinner	Small red		$14,000	$18,000	$25,000	$30,000
455	Original	Allison	Spinner	Small red	Rare				
456	1875	Allison	New	Red		14,000	18,000	25,000	30,000
457	1875	Allison	Wyman	Red		14,000	18,000	25,000	30,000
458	1875	Allison	Gilfillan	Red	Rare				
459	1875	Scofield	Gilfillan	Red		14,000	18,000	25,000	30,000
460	1875	Bruce	Gilfillan	Red		14,000	18,000	25,000	30,000
461	1875	Bruce	Wyman	Red		14,000	18,000	25,000	30,000
462	1875	Rosecrans	Huston	Red	Rare				
462a	1875	Rosecrans	Nebeker	Red	Rare				
463	1875	Tillman	Morgan	Red	Rare				

All above are very scarce in any condition. It is doubtful that notes with some of the signature combinations issued still exist.

NATIONAL BANK NOTES—FIRST CHARTER PERIOD

FIVE HUNDRED DOLLARS

Issued in the Original Series and some in Series 1875. Although over 150 notes remain unredeemed, only three have been reported. Possibly unique in private hands.

ONE THOUSAND DOLLARS

This denomination is unknown, although about 20 notes have not been redeemed.

Attractive tableau scenes are illustrated on the back designs of all notes of the First Charter period. The original murals decorated the rotunda of the Capitol Building in Washington and were the work of early American artists.

THE SECOND CHARTER PERIOD

SERIES 1882 BROWN BACKS, SERIES 1882–1908 AND SERIES 1882 WITH DENOMINATION SPELLED OUT ON BACK OF NOTE

First Issue: Series 1882. The well known and very popular Brown Backs.

Second Issue: Series 1882–1908 emergency issue. Whereas banks had previously been required to deposit United States Government bonds with the Treasurer, by Act of Congress on May 30, 1908, they were permitted to deposit other types of securities, thus enabling the banks to place a larger number of notes into circulation.

Third Issue: Series 1882. Denomination spelled out on back. Scarcest of the three Series of 1882 Nationals. Not all banks issued this series.

FACE DESIGNS, First, Second and Third Issues

The face designs of the three Second Charter issues are the same as the First Charter issues with the exception of the $5 notes. The bank obligation to pay is also the same.

The face design of the $5 denomination of all three issues of 1882 is distinctly different from the higher denominations of this series or the $5 First Charter notes. Portrait of James A. Garfield, 20th president, is in oval at left and possibly used to immortalize the statesman following his assassination in 1881, the same year in which he assumed office. The design is by Geo. W. Casilear and engraved by Alonzo C. Hatch.

BACK DESIGNS, First Issue—1882 Brown Backs

"Brown Back" is the well known description of the First Series of Second Charter notes. The state seals are in ovals at left in the back design, as on the First Charter notes, and the American eagle is again shown in oval at right.

The striking change in the "Brown Backs" is in the center design, which prominently features the Bank Charter number in large numerals against a green background surrounded by a brown lathe-work design.

The legend appears in the top margin and the rather lengthy counterfeiting warning extends across bottom of the back design.

GREEN BACK DESIGNS, Second Issue—1882–1908 Series

The back design of the Emergency Series, 1882–1908, shows various personages and designs in the small oval at left instead of the state seals as used on the Brown Backs and First Charter notes. Various subjects are shown in the oval at right. Featured are the following:

$5 Washington at left; Capitol Building, Washington, D.C., at right.
$10 William P. Fessenden at left; right, Mechanics represented by seated workmen.
$20 American eagle, two different poses, left and right ovals.
$50 Eagle with shield left and right.
$100 Eagle with flag at left and with shield at right.

NATIONAL BANK NOTES—SECOND CHARTER PERIOD

GREEN BACK DESIGNS, Third Issue—"Denomination Back"

The center design spells out in large letters the denomination of the notes. Vignettes in small ovals at left and right remain the same as the Second Issue, also legend at top and the counterfeiting warning at bottom.

FIRST ISSUE—"THE BROWN BACKS"

All "Brown Backs" are Series 1882. Many shades of brown seals in various positions, usually at right.

TYPE 1 FIVE DOLLARS – BLUE SERIAL NUMBERS

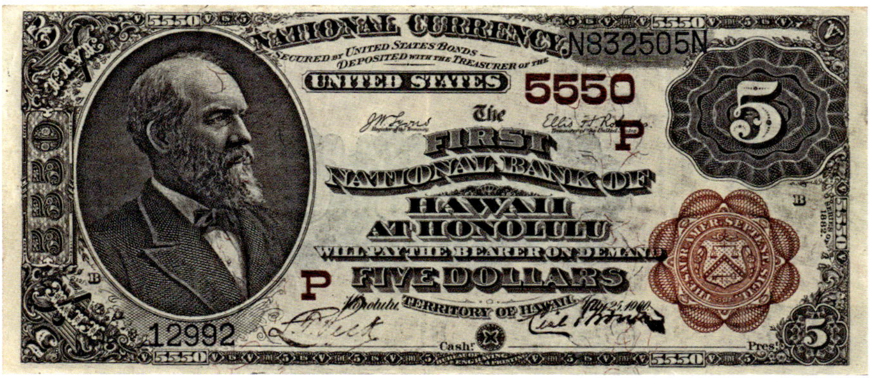

Face Design. Bank charter number with regional letter.

Back Design. Bank charter number in center.

Issued 1882–1909. Printed in sheets of four $5 notes.

Friedberg No.	Register	Treasurer	VG-8	VF-20	AU-50	Unc-60	Unc-63
466	Bruce	Gilfillan	$450	$750	$1,500	$1,850	$2,200
467	Bruce	Wyman	450	750	1,500	1,850	2,200
468	Bruce	Jordan	450	750	1,500	1,850	2,200
469	Rosecrans	Jordan	450	750	1,500	1,850	2,200
470	Rosecrans	Hyatt	450	750	1,500	1,850	2,200
471	Rosecrans	Huston	450	750	1,500	1,850	2,200
472	Rosecrans	Nebeker	450	750	1,500	1,850	2,200

See page 72 for suggested valuations for all states.

NATIONAL BANK NOTES—SECOND CHARTER PERIOD

TYPE 1 FIVE DOLLARS – BLUE SERIAL NUMBERS

Friedberg No.	Register	Treasurer		VG-8	VF-20	AU-50	Unc-60	Unc-63
473	Rosecrans	Morgan		$700	$1,750	$3,000	$3,750	$4,500
474	Tillman	Morgan		450	750	1,500	1,850	2,200
475	Tillman	Roberts		500	800	1,800	2,200	3,000
476	Bruce	Roberts		450	850	1,650	2,000	2,800
477	Lyons	Roberts		450	750	1,500	1,850	2,200
477a	Lyons	Treat	Possibly exists				—	—
478	Vernon	Treat					—	—

See page 72 for suggested valuations for all states.

TYPE 1 TEN DOLLARS – RED SERIAL NUMBERS

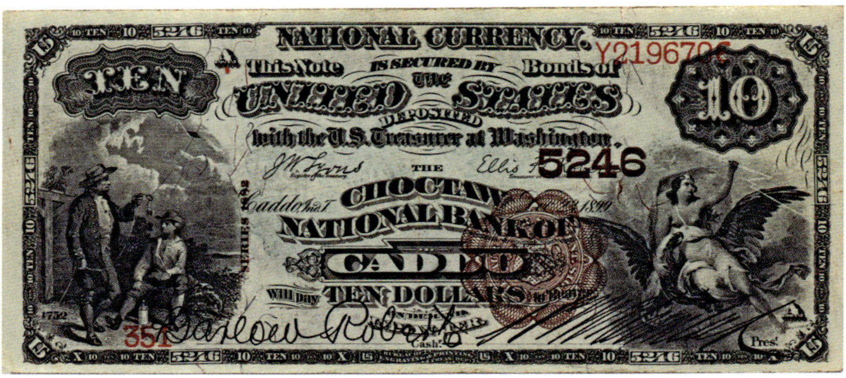

Face Design. Bank charter number without regional letter.

Back Design. Territorial note. American eagle instead of state seal.

Issued 1882–1909. Printed in sheets of three $10 and one $20, and a few sheets of four $10.

Friedberg No.	Register	Treasurer	VG-8	VF-20	AU-50	Unc-60	Unc-63
Series 1882. Brown seal at right of center.							
479	Bruce	Gilfillan	$500	$800	$1,600	$2,200	$2,850
480	Bruce	Wyman	500	800	1,600	2,200	2,850

NATIONAL BANK NOTES—SECOND CHARTER PERIOD

TYPE 1 TEN DOLLARS – RED SERIAL NUMBERS

Friedberg No.	Register	Treasurer	VG-8	VF-20	AU-50	Unc-60	Unc-63
Series 1882. Brown seal at right of center.							
481	Bruce	Jordan	$500	$800	$1,600	$2,200	$2,850
482	Rosecrans	Jordan	500	800	1,600	2,200	2,850
483	Rosecrans	Hyatt	500	800	1,600	2,200	2,850
484	Rosecrans	Huston	500	800	1,600	2,200	2,850
485	Rosecrans	Nebeker	500	800	1,600	2,200	2,850
486	Rosecrans	Morgan	1,800	3,500	5,000	6,250	7,500
487	Tillman	Morgan	500	800	1,600	2,200	2,850
488	Tillman	Roberts	500	800	1,600	2,200	2,850
489	Bruce	Roberts	500	800	1,600	2,200	2,850
490	Lyons	Roberts	500	800	1,600	2,200	2,850
491	Lyons	Treat	850	3,500	4,500	5,500	6,500
492	Vernon	Treat	850	3,500	4,500	5,500	6,500

TYPE 1 TWENTY DOLLARS – RED SERIAL NUMBERS

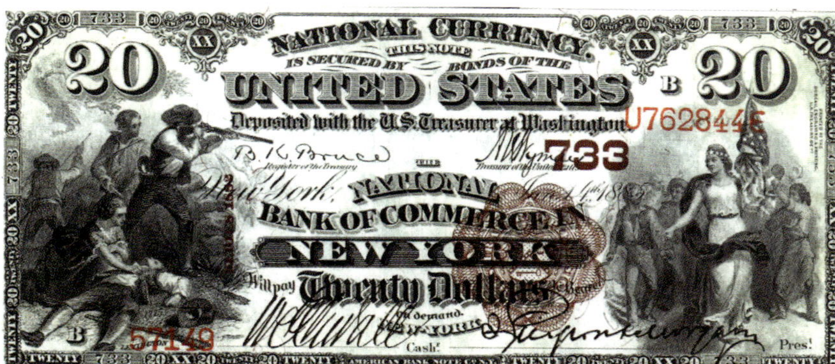

Face Design. Bank charter number without regional letter.

Back Design. Bank charter number in large numerals. State seal at left.

Issued 1882–1909. Printed in sheets of one $20 and three $10.

NATIONAL BANK NOTES—SECOND CHARTER PERIOD

TYPE 1 TWENTY DOLLARS – RED SERIAL NUMBERS

Friedberg No.	Register	Treasurer		VG-8	VF-20	AU-50	Unc-60	Unc-63
Series 1882. Brown seal at right of center.								
493	Bruce	Gilfillan		$600	$1,000	$2,500	$3,000	$3,500
494	Bruce	Wyman		600	1,000	2,500	3,000	3,500
495	Bruce	Jordan		600	1,000	2,500	3,000	3,500
496	Rosecrans	Jordan		600	1,000	2,500	3,000	3,500
497	Rosecrans	Hyatt		600	1,000	2,500	3,000	3,500
498	Rosecrans	Huston		600	1,000	2,500	3,000	3,500
499	Rosecrans	Nebeker		600	1,000	2,500	3,000	3,500
500	Rosecrans	Morgan	3 known					
501	Tillman	Morgan		600	1,000	2,500	3,000	3,500
502	Tillman	Roberts		600	1,000	2,500	3,000	3,500
503	Bruce	Roberts		600	1,000	2,500	3,000	3,500
504	Lyons	Roberts		600	1,000	2,500	3,000	3,500
505	Lyons	Treat		1,800	4,800	7,500	8,500	—
506	Vernon	Treat		1,800	4,800	7,500	8,500	—

$10 and $20 "brown backs" have been found with charter numbers just to the right of the series date printed vertically.

TYPE 1 FIFTY DOLLARS – RED SERIAL NUMBERS

Face Design. Bank charter number without regional letter.

Back Design. Bank charter number in large numerals. State seal at left.

NATIONAL BANK NOTES—SECOND CHARTER PERIOD

TYPE 1 FIFTY DOLLARS – RED SERIAL NUMBERS

Issued 1882–1909. Printed in sheets of three $50 and one $100.

Friedberg No.	Register	Treasurer		VG-8	VF-20	AU-50	Unc-60
Series 1882. Brown seal at right of center.							
507	Bruce	Gilfillan		$4,250	$6,750	$10,000	$15,000
508	Bruce	Wyman		4,250	6,750	10,000	15,000
509	Bruce	Jordan	6 known				
510	Rosecrans	Jordan		4,250	6,750	10,000	15,000
511	Rosecrans	Hyatt		4,250	6,750	10,000	15,000
512	Rosecrans	Huston		4,250	6,750	10,000	15,000
513	Rosecrans	Nebeker		4,250	6,750	10,000	15,000
514	Rosecrans	Morgan		4,250	6,750	10,000	15,000
515	Tillman	Morgan		4,250	6,750	10,000	15,000
516	Tillman	Roberts	4 known				
517	Bruce	Roberts		4,250	6,750	10,000	15,000
518	Lyons	Roberts		4,250	6,750	10,000	15,000
518a	Vernon	Treat	2 known				

Signature combination Lyons-Treat not issued.

TYPE 1 ONE HUNDRED DOLLARS – RED SERIAL NUMBERS

Face Design. Bank charter number with regional letter.

NATIONAL BANK NOTES—SECOND CHARTER PERIOD
TYPE 1 ONE HUNDRED DOLLARS – RED SERIAL NUMBERS

Back Design. Bank charter number in large numerals. State seal at left.

Issued 1882–1909. Printed in sheets of one $100 and three $50.

Friedberg No.	Register	Treasurer	VG-8	VF-20	AU-50	Unc-60
Series 1882. Brown seal, red serial numbers.						
519	Bruce	Gilfillan	$4,500	$7,500	$14,500	$18,000
520	Bruce	Wyman	4,500	7,500	14,500	18,000
521	Bruce	Jordan	4,500	7,500	14,500	18,000
522	Rosecrans	Jordan	4,500	7,500	14,500	18,000
523	Rosecrans	Hyatt	4,500	7,500	14,500	18,000
524	Rosecrans	Huston	4,500	7,500	14,500	18,000
525	Rosecrans	Nebeker	4,500	7,500	14,500	18,000
526	Rosecrans	Morgan	4,500	7,500	14,500	18,000
527	Tillman	Morgan	4,500	7,500	14,500	18,000
528	Tillman	Roberts	4,500	7,500	14,500	18,000
529	Bruce	Roberts	4,500	7,500	14,500	18,000
530	Lyons	Roberts	4,500	7,500	14,500	18,000
531	Vernon	Treat	4,500	7,500	14,500	18,000

Signature combination Lyons-Treat not issued.

NATIONAL BANK NOTES—SECOND CHARTER PERIOD
SECOND ISSUE—1882–1908 DATE BACKS
TYPE 2 FIVE DOLLARS

Face Design. Very similar to Type One.

Back Design. The "Date Back" in green ink.

Issued 1908–1916. Printed in sheets of four $5 notes.

Friedberg No.	Register	Treasurer		VG-8	VF-20	AU-50	Unc-60	Unc-63
Series 1882–1908. Blue seal, blue charter and serial numbers.								
532	Rosecrans	Huston		$500	$700	$1,500	$1,850	$2,500
533	Rosecrans	Nebeker		500	700	1,500	1,850	2,500
533a	Rosecrans	Morgan	3 known		—			
534	Tillman	Morgan		500	700	1,500	1,850	2,500
535	Tillman	Roberts		500	700	1,500	1,850	2,500
536	Bruce	Roberts		500	700	1,500	1,850	2,500
537	Lyons	Roberts		500	700	1,500	1,850	2,500
538	Vernon	Treat		550	700	1,500	2,000	2,750
538a	Vernon	McClung	Unknown					
538b	Napier	McClung	7 known	1,500	3,000	4,800	5,700	6,500

Signature combination Lyons-Treat not issued. See page 72 for suggested valuations for all states.

NATIONAL BANK NOTES—SECOND CHARTER PERIOD

TYPE 2 TEN DOLLARS

Back Design. The "Date Back."

Issued 1908–1916. Printed in sheets of four $10; also three $10 and one $20.

Friedberg No.	Register	Treasurer		VG-8	VF-20	AU-50	Unc-60	Unc-63
Series 1882–1908. Blue seal, blue charter and serial numbers.								
539	Rosecrans	Huston		$500	$800	$1,600	$2,200	$2,750
540	Rosecrans	Nebeker		500	800	1,600	2,200	2,750
541	Rosecrans	Morgan	Extremely Rare (2 known)					
542	Tillman	Morgan		500	800	1,600	2,200	2,750
543	Tillman	Roberts		500	800	1,600	2,200	2,750
544	Bruce	Roberts		500	800	1,600	2,200	2,750
545	Lyons	Roberts		500	1,000	1,800	2,500	3,100
546	Vernon	Treat		500	800	1,600	2,200	2,750
547	Vernon	McClung		600	1,000	2,000	2,800	3,500
548	Napier	McClung		1,000	1,800	3,800	4,750	

Signature combination Lyons-Treat not issued.

TYPE 2 TWENTY DOLLARS

Issued 1908–1916. Printed in sheets of one $20 and three $10.

Friedberg No.	Register	Treasurer		VG-8	VF-20	AU-50	Unc-60	Unc-63
Series 1882–1908. Blue seal, blue charter and serial numbers.								
549	Rosecrans	Huston		$800	$1,200	$1,850	$2,750	$3,200
550	Rosecrans	Nebeker		750	1,500	1,850	2,750	3,200
551	Rosecrans	Morgan	2 known					
552	Tillman	Morgan		650	1,200	1,850	2,750	3,200
553	Tillman	Roberts		650	1,200	1,850	2,750	3,200
554	Bruce	Roberts		650	1,500	2,500	3,200	4,500
555	Lyons	Roberts		650	1,200	1,850	2,750	3,200
556	Vernon	Treat		650	1,200	1,850	2,750	3,200
556a	Vernon	McClung	1 known					
557	Napier	McClung		900	1,800	3,000	3,500	4,500

Signature combination Lyons-Treat not issued.

NATIONAL BANK NOTES—SECOND CHARTER PERIOD

TYPE 2 FIFTY DOLLARS

Back Design. The "Date Back."

Issued 1908–1922. Printed in sheets of three $50 and one $100.

Friedberg No.	Register	Treasurer	VG-8	VF-20	AU-50	Unc-60
Series 1882–1908. Blue seal, blue charter and serial numbers.						
558	Rosecrans	Huston	$5,000	$7,000	$10,000	$15,000
559	Rosecrans	Nebeker	5,000	7,000	10,000	15,000
560	Tillman	Morgan	5,000	7,000	10,000	15,000
561	Tillman	Roberts	5,000	7,000	10,000	15,000
562	Bruce	Roberts	5,000	7,000	10,000	15,000
563	Lyons	Roberts	5,000	7,000	10,000	15,000
564	Vernon	Treat	5,000	7,000	10,000	15,000
565	Napier	McClung	5,000	7,000	10,000	15,000

Signature combinations 16, 21, and 23 not issued.

TYPE 2 ONE HUNDRED DOLLARS

Issued 1908–1922. Printed in sheets of one $100 and three $50.

Friedberg No.	Register	Treasurer	VG-8	VF-20	AU-50	Unc-60
Series 1882–1908. Blue seal, blue charter and serial numbers.						
566	Rosecrans	Huston	$5,500	$7,500	$13,000	$17,000
567	Rosecrans	Nebeker	5,500	7,500	13,000	17,000
568	Tillman	Morgan	5,500	7,500	13,000	17,000
569	Tillman	Roberts	5,500	7,500	13,000	17,000
570	Bruce	Roberts	5,500	7,500	13,000	17,000
571	Lyons	Roberts	5,500	7,500	13,000	17,000
572	Vernon	Treat Rare				
572a	Napier	McClung	6,000	8,500	14,000	18,000

NATIONAL BANK NOTES—SECOND CHARTER PERIOD
THIRD ISSUE—GREEN BACK WITH VALUE
TYPE 3 FIVE DOLLARS

Back Design. The "Value Back."

Issued 1916–1922. Printed in sheets of four $5 notes. All are scarce.

Friedberg No.	Register	Treasurer		VG-8	VF-20	AU-50	Unc-60	Unc-63
Series 1882. Blue seal, blue charter and serial numbers.								
573	Tillman	Morgan		$550	$950	—	—	—
573a	Tillman	Roberts		850	1,300	$2,500	$3,250	—
574a	Bruce	Roberts	Rare				—	—
574	Lyons	Roberts	8 known	550	950	2,000	2,600	$3,100
575	Vernon	Treat		550	950	2,400	3,100	3,600
575a	Napier	McClung	11 known	800	1,250	—	—	—
575b	Teehee	Burke	6 known	—	—	—	—	—

TYPE 3 TEN DOLLARS

Back Design. The "Value Back."

NATIONAL BANK NOTES—SECOND CHARTER PERIOD

TYPE 3 TEN DOLLARS

Issued 1916–1922. Printed in sheets of four $10; also three $10 and one $20.

Friedberg No.	Register	Treasurer		VG-8	VF-20	AU-50	Unc-60
Series 1882. Blue seal, blue charter and serial numbers.							
576	Tillman	Morgan		$1,000	$1,850	$3,800	$4,500
576a	Tillman	Roberts		1,200	2,500	4,500	6,000
576b	Bruce	Roberts		1,200	2,500	4,500	6,000
577	Lyons	Roberts		725	1,500	2,000	3,000
577a	Lyons	Treat	Unknown				
578	Vernon	Treat		825	1,400	3,100	3,675
579	Napier	McClung		825	1,400	3,100	3,675
579b	Teehee	Burke		875	1,500	3,200	3,750

TYPE 3 TWENTY DOLLARS

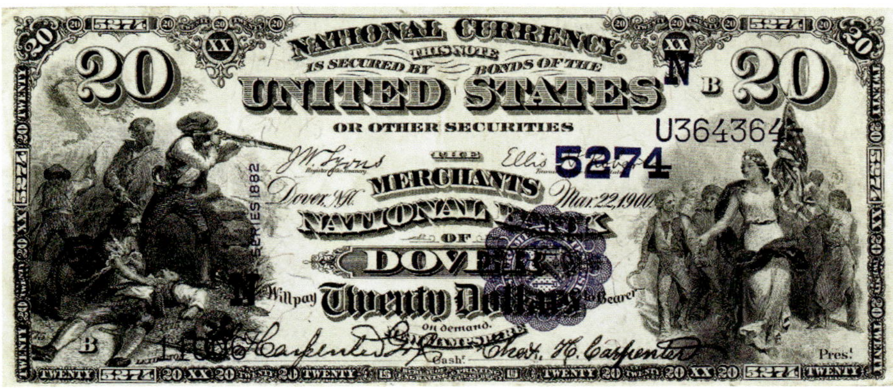

Face Design.

Issued 1916–1922. Printed in sheets of one $20 and three $10 notes.

Friedberg No.	Register	Treasurer		VG-8	VF-20	AU-50	Unc-60
Series 1882. Blue seal, blue charter and serial numbers.							
580	Tillman	Morgan	6 known				
580a	Tillman	Roberts	4 known				
580b	Bruce	Roberts	3 known				
581	Lyons	Roberts		$1,000	$1,800	$3,000	$4,000
582	Lyons	Treat	Unique				
583	Vernon	Treat		1,000	1,800	3,000	4,000
584	Napier	McClung		1,000	1,800	3,000	4,000
585	Teehee	Burke	5 known				

TYPE 3 FIFTY DOLLARS

Only eight known. Four New Orleans, Louisiana, four Dayton, Ohio. Only one signature combination, Lyons-Roberts.

TYPE 3 ONE HUNDRED DOLLARS

Only five now known. Three New Orleans, Louisiana, two Dayton, Ohio. One signature combination, Lyons-Roberts.

THE THIRD CHARTER PERIOD

First Issue, Series 1902—Red Seal and Charter Numbers. Blue Serial Numbers
Notes of this issue are scarce, having been issued by comparatively few chartered banks. Red seals were printed with only three signature combinations of Treasury Officials. Reference to the table of Terms of Office will explain why the Lyons-Treat and Vernon-Treat signatures are less frequently found than those of Lyons-Roberts.

Second Issue, 1902–1908—Blue Seal, Emergency Series, Dates on back
Authorized under Act of May 30, 1908, as were the Series 1882–1908 Second Charter Notes. They were first issued in 1908 and with two exceptions discontinued in 1916. The $50 and $100 denominations were issued through 1925.

Third Issue, 1902—Blue Seal, No dates on back
First issued in 1916 and most common of the three issues of Third Charter notes. There were 15 signature combinations, the scarcest being the Jones-Woods signatures. Edward E. Jones assumed the office of Register and Walter O. Woods the office of Treasurer in 1929, the same year in which large size notes were discontinued.

FACE DESIGNS, Third Charter Notes
The Treasury seal is at right on all denominations of the three issues. Prominent statesmen are featured in the oval, at left.

- **$5** Benjamin Harrison, 23rd president of the United States.
- **$10** William McKinley, 25th president of the United States, assassinated in Buffalo, 1901.
- **$20** Hugh McCulloch, secretary of Treasury, 1865–1869 and 1884–1885.
- **$50** John Sherman, secretary of the Treasury, 1877–1881; secretary of State, 1897–1898.
- **$100** John J. Knox, comptroller of Currency, 1872–1884. Later, president of the National Bank of the Republic, New York City.

Ostrander Smith designed all of the above. The $20 note was engraved by Charles Burt, all others by Geo. F.C. Smillie.

BACK DESIGNS, Third Charter Notes
Back designs of the three issues of Third Charter Notes feature:

- **$5** "Landing of the Pilgrims."
- **$10** Female figure with ships in background.
- **$20** Columbia and Capitol in Washington.
- **$50** Allegorical scene. Train and female figure at right. Primitive man reclining at left is a Walter Shirlaw design. Engraved by Geo. F.C. Smillie.
- **$100** American eagle on shield, with two male figures.

The back design of all denominations bears a rather lengthy inscription:

"This note is receivable at par in all parts of the United States in payment of all taxes and excises and all other dues to the United States except duties on imports and also for all salaries and other debts and demands owing by the United States to individuals, corporations and associations within the United States except interest on public debt."

NATIONAL BANK NOTES—THIRD CHARTER PERIOD
FIRST ISSUE—RED SEAL
SERIES 1902. RED CHARTER NUMBERS. BLUE SERIAL NUMBERS. ONLY THREE SIGNATURE COMBINATIONS.

TYPE 1 FIVE DOLLARS

Issued 1902–1922. Printed in sheets of four $5 notes.

Friedberg No.	Register	Treasurer	VG-8	VF-20	AU-50	Unc-60	Unc-63
587	Lyons	Roberts	$550	$800	$1,600	$2,050	$2,350
588	Lyons	Treat	600	900	1,800	2,150	2,500
589	Vernon	Treat	600	900	1,800	2,150	2,500

Designs on Red Seal notes are the same as Type 3, Blue Seal, Third Charter.

TYPE 1 TEN DOLLARS

Issued 1902–1908. Printed in sheets of three $10 and one $20; also four $10 for some banks.

Friedberg No.	Register	Treasurer	VG-8	VF-20	AU-50	Unc-60	Unc-63
613	Lyons	Roberts	$700	$1,000	$2,200	$2,800	$3,800
614	Lyons	Treat	700	1,000	2,200	2,800	3,800
615	Vernon	Treat	700	1,000	2,200	2,800	3,800

TYPE 1 TWENTY DOLLARS

Issued 1902–1908. Printed in sheets of three $10 and one $20.

Friedberg No.	Register	Treasurer	VG-8	VF-20	AU-50	Unc-60	Unc-63
639	Lyons	Roberts	$850	$1,250	$3,100	$3,650	$4,500
640	Lyons	Treat	850	1,250	3,100	3,650	4,500
641	Vernon	Treat	850	1,250	3,100	3,650	4,500

TYPE 1 FIFTY DOLLARS

Issued 1902–1908. Printed in sheets of three $50 and one $100.

Friedberg No.	Register	Treasurer	VG-8	VF-20	AU-50	Unc-60	Unc-63
664	Lyons	Roberts	$6,000	$7,000	$12,000	$16,500	$20,000
665	Lyons	Treat	7,000	8,000	13,000	17,000	22,000
666	Vernon	Treat	7,000	8,000	13,000	17,000	22,000

The $50 Red Seals are very rare in acceptable condition. See page 72 for suggested valuations for all states.

NATIONAL BANK NOTES—THIRD CHARTER PERIOD

TYPE 1 ONE HUNDRED DOLLARS

Issued 1902–1908. Printed in sheets of one $100 and three $50.

Friedberg No.	Register	Treasurer	VG-8	VF-20	AU-50	Unc-60	Unc-63
686	Lyons	Roberts	$7,500	$11,000	$16,000	$20,000	$23,500
687	Lyons	Treat	7,500	11,000	16,000	20,000	23,500
688	Vernon	Treat	7,500	11,000	16,000	20,000	23,500

The $100 Red Seals are very rare in acceptable condition. See page 72 for suggested valuations for all states.

SECOND ISSUE—BLUE SEAL, 1902–1908 DATE BACK

TYPE 2 FIVE DOLLARS

Back Design. The "Date Back."

Issued 1908–1916. Printed in sheets of four $5 notes.

Friedberg No.	Register	Treasurer	VG-8	VF-20	AU-50	Unc-60	Unc-63
Series 1902. Blue seal right. Blue serial and charter numbers.							
590	Lyons	Roberts	$160	$250	$525	$635	$800
591	Lyons	Treat	160	250	525	635	800
592	Vernon	Treat	160	250	525	635	800
593	Vernon	McClung	160	250	525	635	800
594	Napier	McClung	160	250	525	635	800
595	Napier	Thompson	225	475	675	800	1,000
596	Napier	Burke	160	250	525	635	800
597	Parker	Burke	160	250	525	635	800
597a	Teehee	Burke Unique					

See page 72 for suggested valuations for all states.

NATIONAL BANK NOTES—THIRD CHARTER PERIOD

TYPE 2 TEN DOLLARS

Back Design. The "Date Back." Face Design same as Type Three.

Issued 1908–1916. Printed in sheets of four $10; also three $10 and one $20.

Friedberg No.	Register	Treasurer	VG-8	VF-20	AU-50	Unc-60	Unc-63
Series 1902. Blue seal right. Blue serial and charter numbers.							
616	Lyons	Roberts	$160	$250	$550	$700	$875
617	Lyons	Treat	160	250	550	700	875
618	Vernon	Treat	160	250	550	700	875
619	Vernon	McClung	160	250	550	700	875
620	Napier	McClung	160	250	550	700	875
621	Napier	Thompson	215	450	875	1,100	1,350
622	Napier	Burke	185	285	650	775	900
623	Parker	Burke	185	285	650	775	900
623a	Teehee	Burke	200	350	1,050	1,300	1,500

TYPE 2 TWENTY DOLLARS

Back Design. The "Date Back." Face Design same as Type Three.

Issued 1902–1908. Printed in sheets of one $20 and three $10.

NATIONAL BANK NOTES—THIRD CHARTER PERIOD

TYPE 2 TWENTY DOLLARS

Friedberg No.	Register	Treasurer		VG-8	VF-20	AU-50	Unc-60	Unc-63
Series 1902. Blue seal right. Blue serial and charter numbers.								
642	Lyons	Roberts		$180	$375	$550	$700	$900
643	Lyons	Treat		180	375	550	700	900
644	Vernon	Treat		180	375	550	700	900
645	Vernon	McClung		180	375	550	700	900
646	Napier	McClung		180	375	550	700	900
647	Napier	Thompson		275	475	775	925	1,200
648	Napier	Burke		200	400	625	775	975
649	Parker	Burke		200	400	625	775	975
649a	Teehee	Burke	4 known					

TYPE 2 FIFTY DOLLARS

Issued 1908–1929. Printed in sheets of three $50 and one $100; also a limited number of sheets with one $50 and one $100.

Friedberg No.	Register	Treasurer	VG-8	VF-20	AU-50	Unc-60	Unc-63
Series 1902. Blue seal right. Blue serial and charter numbers.							
667	Lyons	Roberts	$800	$1,200	$3,200	$4,800	$6,000
668	Lyons	Treat	800	1,200	3,200	4,800	6,000
669	Vernon	Treat	800	1,200	3,200	4,800	6,000
670	Vernon	McClung	800	1,200	3,200	4,800	6,000
671	Napier	McClung	800	1,200	3,200	4,800	6,000
672	Napier	Thompson	1,200	2,400	4,500	6,500	7,500
673	Napier	Burke	800	1,200	3,200	4,800	6,000
674	Parker	Burke	800	1,200	3,200	4,800	6,000
674a	Teehee	Burke	800	1,200	3,200	4,800	6,000

TYPE 2 ONE HUNDRED DOLLARS

Back Design. The "Date Back." Face Design same as Type Three.

Issued 1908–1929. Printed in sheets of one $100 and three $50; also a limited number of sheets with one $100 and one $50.

NATIONAL BANK NOTES—THIRD CHARTER PERIOD

TYPE 2 ONE HUNDRED DOLLARS

Friedberg No.	Register	Treasurer	VG-8	VF-20	AU-50	Unc-60
Series 1902. Blue seal right. Blue serial and charter numbers.						
689	Lyons	Roberts	$1,500	$2,200	$5,000	$6,200
690	Lyons	Treat	1,500	2,200	5,000	6,200
691	Vernon	Treat	1,500	2,200	5,000	6,200
692	Vernon	McClung	1,500	2,200	5,000	6,200
693	Napier	McClung	1,500	2,200	5,000	6,200
694	Napier	Thompson	2,250	3,500	6,500	7,500
695	Napier	Burke	1,500	2,200	5,000	6,200
696	Parker	Burke	1,500	2,200	5,000	6,200
697	Teehee	Burke	1,500	2,200	5,000	6,200

THIRD ISSUE—BLUE SEAL, NO 1902–1908 ON BACK

TYPE 3 FIVE DOLLARS

Face Design. Used on Type One, Type Two, and Type Three, Third Charter.

Back Design. No date shown.

NATIONAL BANK NOTES–THIRD CHARTER PERIOD

TYPE 3 FIVE DOLLARS

Issued 1916–1929. Printed in sheets of four $5 notes.

Friedberg No.	Register	Treasurer	VG-8	VF-20	AU-50	Unc-60	Unc-63
Series 1902. Blue seal right. Blue serial and charter numbers.							
598	Lyons	Roberts	$125	$200	$375	$500	$625
599	Lyons	Treat	125	200	375	500	625
600	Vernon	Treat	125	200	375	500	625
601	Vernon	McClung	125	200	375	500	625
602	Napier	McClung	125	200	375	500	625
603	Napier	Thompson	175	225	500	650	825
604	Napier	Burke	125	200	375	500	625
605	Parker	Burke	125	200	375	500	625
606	Teehee	Burke	125	200	375	500	625
607	Elliott	Burke	125	200	375	500	625
608	Elliott	White	125	200	375	500	625
609	Speelman	White	125	200	375	500	625
610	Woods	White	125	200	375	500	625
611	Woods	Tate	125	200	375	500	625
612	Jones	Woods	400	750	1,850	2,500	3,500

TYPE 3 TEN DOLLARS

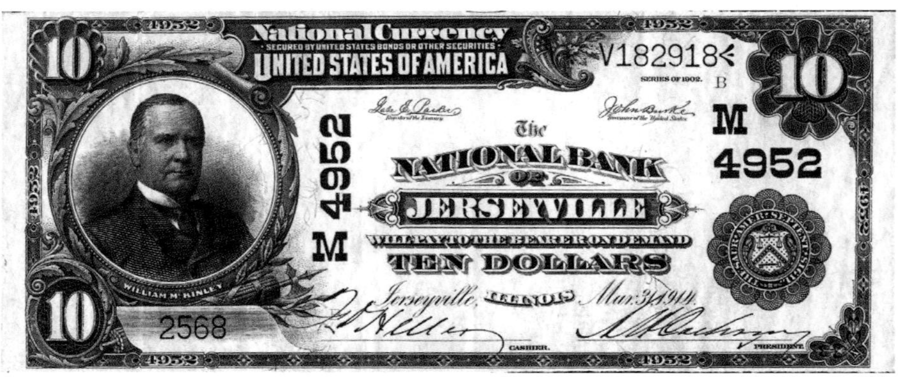

Face Design. Used on Type One, Type Two, and Type Three, Third Charter.

NATIONAL BANK NOTES–THIRD CHARTER PERIOD

TYPE 3 TEN DOLLARS

Back Design. No date shown.

Issued 1916–1929. Printed in sheets of four $10; also three $10 and one $20.

Friedberg No.	Register	Treasurer	VG-8	VF-20	AU-50	Unc-60	Unc-63
624	Lyons	Roberts	$150	$200	$475	$550	$650
625	Lyons	Treat	150	200	475	550	650
626	Vernon	Treat	150	200	475	550	650
627	Vernon	McClung	150	200	475	550	650
628	Napier	McClung	150	200	475	550	650
629	Napier	Thompson	275	450	950	1,100	1,350
630	Napier	Burke	150	200	475	550	650
631	Parker	Burke	150	200	475	550	650
632	Teehee	Burke	150	200	475	550	650
633	Elliott	Burke	150	200	475	550	650
634	Elliott	White	150	200	475	550	650
635	Speelman	White	150	200	475	550	650
636	Woods	White	150	200	475	550	650
637	Woods	Tate	150	200	475	550	650
638	Jones	Woods	650	900	1,250	1,400	—

Register Edward E. Jones and Treasurer Walter O. Woods did not assume office until January 22, 1929. Only a few banks received large-size National Currency with this signature combination.

NATIONAL BANK NOTES–THIRD CHARTER PERIOD

TYPE 3 TWENTY DOLLARS

Face Design. Used on Type One, Type Two, and Type Three, Third Charter.

Back Design. No date shown.

Issued 1916–1929. Printed in sheets of one $20 and three $10.

Friedberg No.	Register	Treasurer	VG-8	VF-20	AU-50	Unc-60	Unc-63
650	Lyons	Roberts	$170	$250	$500	$650	$800
651	Lyons	Treat	170	250	500	650	800
652	Vernon	Treat	170	250	500	650	800
653	Vernon	McClung	170	250	500	650	800
654	Napier	McClung	170	250	500	650	800
655	Napier	Thompson	175	275	625	750	900
656	Napier	Burke	170	250	500	650	800
657	Parker	Burke	170	250	500	650	800
658	Teehee	Burke	170	250	500	650	800
659	Elliott	Burke	170	250	500	650	800
660	Elliott	White	170	250	500	650	800
661	Speelman	White	170	250	500	650	800
662	Woods	White	350	500	900	1,000	1,500
663	Woods	Tate	400	575	1,750	2,150	2,500
663a	Jones	Woods	—	—	—	—	—

NATIONAL BANK NOTES—THIRD CHARTER PERIOD
TYPE 3 FIFTY DOLLARS

Face Design. Used on Type One, Type Two, and Type Three, Third Charter.

Back Design. No date shown.

Issued 1916–1929. Printed in sheets of three $50 and one $100.

Friedberg No.	Register	Treasurer		VG-8	VF-20	AU-50	Unc-60
675	Lyons	Roberts		$850	$1,200	$3,500	$4,150
676	Lyons	Treat		850	1,200	3,500	4,150
677	Vernon	Treat		850	1,200	3,500	4,150
678	Vernon	McClung		850	1,200	3,500	4,150
679	Napier	McClung		850	1,200	3,500	4,150
679a	Napier	Thompson		1,200	2,000	3,750	4,250
680	Napier	Burke	7 known				
681	Parker	Burke		850	1,200	3,500	4,150
682	Teehee	Burke		850	1,200	3,500	4,150
683	Elliott	Burke		850	1,200	3,500	4,150
684	Elliott	White		850	1,200	3,500	4,150
685	Speelman	White		850	1,200	3,500	4,150
685a	Woods	White	2 known				

NATIONAL BANK NOTES—THIRD CHARTER PERIOD
TYPE 3 ONE HUNDRED DOLLARS

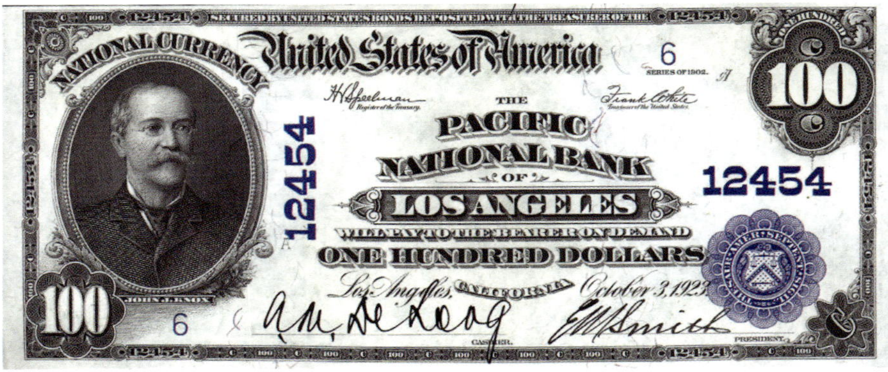

Face Design. Used on Type One, Type Two, and Type Three, Third Charter.

Back Design. No date shown.

Issued 1916–1929. Printed in sheets of one $100 and three $50.

Friedberg No.	Register	Treasurer	VG-8	VF-20	AU-50	Unc-60
698	Lyons	Roberts	$1,200	$2,500	$4,750	$5,700
699	Lyons	Treat	1,200	2,500	4,750	5,700
700	Vernon	Treat	1,200	2,500	4,750	5,700
701	Vernon	McClung	1,200	2,500	4,750	5,700
702	Napier	McClung	1,200	2,500	4,750	5,700
702a	Napier	Thompson	1,800	2,850	4,850	6,000
703	Parker	Burke	1,200	2,500	4,750	5,700
704	Teehee	Burke	1,200	2,500	4,750	5,700
705	Elliott	Burke	1,200	2,500	4,750	5,700
706	Elliott	White	1,200	2,500	4,750	5,700
707	Speelman	White	1,200	2,500	4,750	5,700

Signature combination Woods-White, two notes known. Signature combination Woods-Tate, if issued, not reported. Signature combination Jones-Woods not issued.

NATIONAL GOLD BANK NOTES

ISSUED 1870–1884 IN DENOMINATIONS OF $5 TO $1,000
SERIES 1870–1872 AND 1874, BY NINE CALIFORNIA BANKS

Approximately $3,500,000 was issued in various denominations. About half of the total amount was issued by the National Gold Bank of San Francisco.

Charter	Bank	Charter Date
1741	First National Gold Bank, San Francisco	November 30, 1870
1994	National Gold Bank & Trust Co., San Francisco	June 3, 1872
2014	National Gold Bank of D.O. Mills, Sacramento	July 19, 1872
2077	First National Gold Bank, Stockton	January 27, 1873
2104	First National Gold Bank, Santa Barbara	May 7, 1873
2158	Farmers' National Gold Bank, San Jose	July 21, 1874
2193	First National Gold Bank, Petaluma	October 12, 1874
2248	First National Gold Bank, Oakland	April 10, 1875
2266	Union National Gold Bank, Oakland	May 20, 1875

Although the National Currency Act was enacted in 1863 and over 1,700 banks had been organized by 1870, no California bank had been chartered during that period. Hard money was preferred by Californians who did not readily accept National Bank notes of other states or Legal Tender notes then in circulation.

On July 12, 1870, Congress passed an amendment to the Act of 1863 which created the National Gold Banks and authorized them to issue currency redeemable in gold coin, up to 80 percent of the amount of bonds deposited with the U.S. Treasurer. The First National Gold Bank of San Francisco became the first bank in California to be chartered as a National Bank or National Gold Bank.

Gold Bank Notes were issued from 1870 to 1884 in denominations of $5 to $1,000 in series 1870, 1872, and 1874. Records of redemption were maintained until October 1914. After that date redemption of Gold Bank notes was not separated from redemption records of other National Currency.

The following table shows the total issue for all National Gold Banks and the number of notes outstanding as of October 31, 1914, after which date no separate record of redemption was maintained.

Denomination	Number Issued	Number Outstanding, October 14, 1914
$5.00	72,828	3,451
$10.00	74,649	2,481
$20.00	38,129	806
$50.00	8,097	113
$100.00	8,097	84
$500.00	685	4
$1,000.00	75	None

FACE DESIGNS, National Gold Bank Notes

The face designs of this series are the same as those of the First Issue of National Bank Notes. The inscription reads: "Redeemable in Gold Coin. This note is secured by Bonds of the United States deposited with the U.S. Treasurer at Washington." The obligation to pay is by the issuing bank and states that the bank "will pay to the Bearer on Demand . . . Dollars in Gold Coin."

BACK DESIGNS, National Gold Bank Notes

The back design of this series is very unusual. Printed in black, it features a liberal assortment of gold coins with a total face value of $211.00. Shown very prominently is a double eagle of 1871. The metallic appearance of the coins was produced by using extremely fine cut lines engraved by James Smillie for the American Bank Note Co. The border design is the same as First Charter notes with a warning against counterfeiting and lengthy legend.

All National Gold Bank Notes are extremely scarce and very seldom found in new condition.

NATIONAL GOLD BANK NOTES

The Kidder National Gold Bank of Boston

Records indicate that the Kidder National Gold Bank of Boston was the first National Gold Bank authorized under the new Act of 1870. Also that this bank received notes of $50, $100, $500, and $1,000 denomination, and that these Gold Bank notes were never placed in circulation, the entire issue having been returned for cancellation. This bank was liquidated in 1872.

Included in the listing of notes issued to the Kidder National Gold Bank were 75 $1,000 notes. Records show that only 75 notes of the $1,000 denomination were issued for all banks authorized to issue these notes backed by gold. It is therefore logical to assume that no Gold Bank notes of $1,000 denomination were ever placed in circulation. The comptroller report of October 31, 1914, shows no $1,000 Gold Bank notes outstanding.

Allison-Spinner signatures appear on all issues, except the following:

Scofield-Gilfillan on Series 1875, $10 notes of Stockton and Petaluma.

Scofield-Gilfillan on Series 1875, $20 notes of Oakland.

Bruce-Gilfillan on Series 1875, $20 and $100 notes of First National Gold Bank, San Francisco.

FIVE DOLLARS

Face Design. Similar to early issues of National Bank Notes.

Back Design, all denominations. California state seal and gold coins.

NATIONAL GOLD BANK NOTES—FIVE DOLLARS

Friedberg No.	Series	Issuing Bank	Location	G-4	VG-8	F-12
1136	1870	First National Gold Bank	San Francisco	$2,000	$3,200	$8,500
1137	1872	National Gold Bank & Trust Co.	San Francisco	3,000	5,250	15,000
1138	1872	National Gold Bank of D.O. Mills	Sacramento	3,000	5,250	15,000
1139	1873	First National Gold Bank	Santa Barbara	5,500	8,500	—
1140	1873	First National Gold Bank	Stockton	5,750	9,000	—
1141	1874	Farmers' National Gold Bank	San Jose	2,850	4,000	10,000

This denomination was not issued by the National Gold Banks in Petaluma and Oakland.

TEN DOLLARS

Face Design. Charter numbers left and right.

Friedberg No.	Series	Issuing Bank	Location	G-4	VG-8	F-12
1142	1870	First National Gold Bank	San Francisco	$3,250	$7,500	$12,500
1143	1872	National Gold Bank & Trust Co.	San Francisco	4,750	11,000	19,500
1144	1872	National Gold Bank of D.O. Mills	Sacramento	5,500	11,500	22,500
1145	1873	First National Gold Bank	Santa Barbara	11,000	25,000	65,000
1146	1873	First National Gold Bank	Stockton	4,000	10,000	16,500
1147	1875	First National Gold Bank	Stockton	5,500	12,000	22,500
1148	1874	Farmers' National Gold Bank	San Jose	4,500	11,500	25,000
1149	1874	First National Gold Bank	Petaluma	4,500	11,500	25,000
1150	1875	First National Gold Bank	Petaluma	8,000	16,000	37,500
1151	1875	First National Gold Bank	Oakland	5,500	11,500	25,000
1151a	1875	Union National Gold Bank	Oakland	45,000	80,000	—

National Gold Bank Notes are seldom found in better than Fine condition. Above values should be increased for notes in better condition and decreased if the note is only About Good or in Poor or Fair condition.

NATIONAL GOLD BANK NOTES—TWENTY DOLLARS

Face Design. Redeemable in gold coin clause.

Back Design.

Friedberg No.	Series	Issuing Bank	Location		G-4	VG-8	F-12
1152	1870	First National Gold Bank	San Francisco		$9,500	$16,500	$40,000
1153	1875	First National Gold Bank	San Francisco		18,000	24,000	50,000
1159b	1872	National Gold Bank & Trust Co.	San Francisco	Unknown			
1154	1872	National Gold Bank of D.O. Mills	Sacramento	3 known	20,000	27,000	50,000
1155	1873	First National Gold Bank	Stockton		18,000	24,000	50,000
1159a	1873	First National Gold Bank	Santa Barbara	Unique			
1156	1874	Farmers' National Gold Bank	San Jose	8 known	21,500	30,000	65,000
1157	1875	First National Gold Bank	Petaluma	2 known			
1158	1875	First National Gold Bank	Oakland	8 known	22,500	30,000	65,000
1159	1875	Union National Gold Bank	Oakland	2 known			

See remarks on page 107 regarding condition and values.

NATIONAL GOLD BANK NOTES—FIFTY DOLLARS

Notes of this denomination were possibly issued by several National Gold Banks, although notes from only two banks are known. Allison-Gilfillan and Bruce-Gilfillan signatures appear on the known issues. Only five notes are known.

Friedberg No.	Series	Issuing Bank	Location		G-4	VG-8
1160	1870	First National Gold Bank	San Francisco	4 known	—	—
1161	1874	National Gold Bank	San Jose	Unique	—	—

ONE HUNDRED DOLLARS

Face Design.

Friedberg No.	Series	Issuing Bank	Location		G-4	VG-8
1162	1870	First National Gold Bank	San Francisco	3 known	—	—
1163	1875	First National Gold Bank	San Francisco	2 known	—	—
1164	1873	First National Gold Bank	Santa Barbara	Unique	—	—
1165	1874	First National Gold Bank	Petaluma	2 known	—	—
1166	1875	Union National Gold Bank	Oakland	Unique	—	—

As with the $50 denomination of this series, the $100 notes were possibly issued by National Gold Banks other than the above. A Conservative valuation of $10,000 or more is justified for notes of $100 denomination from any issuing bank in this series. Fewer than 10 notes are known to exist.

FIVE HUNDRED DOLLARS

Records indicate that $500 notes were issued by three National Gold Banks: First National Gold Bank and the National Gold & Trust Co. of San Francisco and the National Gold Bank of D.O. Mills, Sacramento.

Four notes have not been redeemed, but to date none have been reported.

FEDERAL RESERVE BANK NOTES, SERIES 1915 AND 1918

Designated as National Currency on the face and back of notes, this series had a very limited issue. Total face value from the 12 Federal Reserve Banks, $1 to $50, amounted to $761,944,000. Of this total issue only $29,068 was reported outstanding on January 30, 1970.

The $50 denomination was issued by St. Louis only. Only 29 of these are known to exist today. See list of known serial numbers on page 116.

$1	1918	12 Federal Reserve Banks
$2	1918	12 Federal Reserve Banks
$5	1915	Atlanta, Chicago, Kansas City, Dallas, San Francisco
$5	1918	All Federal Reserve Banks, except Richmond
$10	1915	Atlanta, Chicago, Kansas City, Dallas
$10	1918	New York, Chicago, Atlanta, St. Louis
$20	1915	Atlanta, Chicago, Kansas City, Dallas
$20	1918	Atlanta, St. Louis
$50	1918	St. Louis only

The latter is a very scarce note, seldom found in Uncirculated condition.

All bear the signature of the United States Treasurer, John Burke, and either Houston B. Teehee or Wm. S. Elliott, as Register of the Treasury. There are also signatures of two Federal Reserve officers.

FACE DESIGNS, Federal Reserve Bank Notes, Series 1915 and 1918

Presidents of the United States are featured on the left of the face design of these series. The blue seal is prominent on the right. Serial numbers have the prefix letter indicating bank of issue.

$1	George Washington	**$5**	Abraham Lincoln	**$20**	Grover Cleveland
$2	Thomas Jefferson	**$10**	Andrew Jackson	**$50**	Ulysses Grant

The inscription of the face of the note, Series 1918, reads: "Secured by United States Certificates of indebtedness or United States one-year Gold Notes, deposited with the Treasurer of the United States of America." There is a minor difference in the wording on Series 1915.

The obligation to pay is by the issuing bank and reads: "The Federal Reserve Bank of . . . will pay to the Bearer on Demand (amount)."

BACK DESIGNS, Federal Reserve Bank Notes, Series 1915 and 1918

- **$1** The American flag in talons of large flying eagle, Series 1918 only.
- **$2** American battleship, Series 1918 only.
- **$5** "Columbus in Sight of Land," at left. At right, the "Landing of the Pilgrims" as on the $1 First Charter Note, but a different engraving.
- **$10** Agriculture and Commerce. A reaper drawn by four horses and smoke from factory smokestacks indicate prosperity.
- **$20** Transportation. Various methods of sea and land travel.
- **$50** Female figure representing Panama shown between two oceans.

The rather lengthy inscription printed in a panel in the border at bottom of back designs reads: "This note is receivable at par in all parts of the United States in payment of all taxes and excises and all other dues to the United States except duties on imports and also for all salaries and other debts and demands owing by the United States to individuals, corporations and associations within the United States except interest on public debt."

FEDERAL RESERVE BANK NOTES—SERIES 1915

Act of December 23, 1913, authorized $5, $10, and $20 notes. Act of April 23, 1918, authorized $1 to $50 notes.

FEDERAL RESERVE BANK NOTES—SERIES 1915

FIVE DOLLARS

Friedberg No.	Bank	Register	Treasurer	Bank Officers		F-12	VF-20	EF-40	Unc-60
788	Atlanta	Teehee	Burke	Bell	Wellborn	$650	$1,090	$2,750	$5,000
789	Atlanta	Teehee	Burke	Pike	McCord	240	325	545	1,120
793	Chicago	Teehee	Burke	McLallen	McDougal	240	325	545	1,120
800	Kansas City	Teehee	Burke	Anderson	Miller	290	490	960	1,500
801	Kansas City	Teehee	Burke	Cross	Miller	2,190	2,500	6,250	—
802	Kansas City	Teehee	Burke	Helm	Miller	2,500	4,380	7,500	—
805	Dallas	Teehee	Burke	Hoopes	Van Zandt	1,020	1,220	2,380	7,500
806	Dallas	Teehee	Burke	Talley	Van Zandt	2,250	2,810	10,000	—
808	San Francisco	Teehee	Burke	Clerk	Lynch	845	1,380	2,690	6,450

TEN DOLLARS

Friedberg No.	Bank	Register	Treasurer	Bank Officers		F-12	VF-20	EF-40	Unc-60
811	Atlanta	Teehee	Burke	Bell	Wellborn	$4,380	$7,500	$24,000	—
813	Chicago	Teehee	Burke	McLallen	McDougal	1,150	1,810	3,500	$5,100
816	Kansas City	Teehee	Burke	Anderson	Miller	1,150	1,810	3,500	5,100
817	Kansas City	Teehee	Burke	Cross	Miller	1,150	1,810	3,500	5,000
818	Kansas City	Teehee	Burke	Helm	Miller	—	24,000	54,000	—
819	Dallas	Teehee	Burke	Hoopes	Van Zandt	1,150	1,810	3,500	8,750
820	Dallas	Teehee	Burke	Gilbert	Van Zandt	8,100	16,800	—	—
821	Dallas	Teehee	Burke	Talley	Van Zandt	7,500	12,000	24,000	—

TWENTY DOLLARS

Friedberg No.	Bank	Register	Treasurer	Bank Officers		F-12	VF-20	EF-40	Unc-60
822	Atlanta	Teehee	Burke	Bell	Wellborn	$2,620	$12,000	$19,800	—
822a	Atlanta	Teehee	Burke	Pike	McCord	—	—	84,000	—
824	Chicago	Teehee	Burke	McLallen	McDougal	1,970	3,120	6,100	$10,000
826	Kansas City	Teehee	Burke	Anderson	Miller	1,970	3,120	10,600	—
827	Kansas City	Teehee	Burke	Cross	Miller	1,970	3,120	9,400	—
828	Dallas	Teehee	Burke	Hoopes	Van Zandt	2,250	3,880	9,750	—
829	Dallas	Teehee	Burke	Gilbert	Van Zandt	8,100	12,000	—	—
830	Dallas	Teehee	Burke	Talley	Van Zandt	24,000	36,000	—	—

The signature of M.W. Bell appears as Cashier on one issue of Atlanta notes and as Secretary on a later issue of this same bank. Values are about the same.

FEDERAL RESERVE BANK NOTES—SERIES 1918

ONE DOLLAR

Face Design. Issued by all 12 Federal Reserve Banks.

FEDERAL RESERVE BANK NOTES—SERIES 1918

ONE DOLLAR

Back Design. American eagle with flag.

Friedberg No.	Bank	Register	Treasurer	Bank Officers		VF-20	EF-40	Unc-60	Unc-63
708	Boston	Teehee	Burke	Bullen	Morss	$230	$285	$455	$520
709	Boston	Teehee	Burke	Willett	Morss	230	265	520	585
710	Boston	Elliott	Burke	Willett	Morss	230	290	455	520
711	New York	Teehee	Burke	Sailer	Strong	230	260	390	455
712	New York	Teehee	Burke	Hendricks	Strong	230	290	420	455
713	New York	Elliott	Burke	Hendricks	Strong	230	290	440	490
714	Philadelphia	Teehee	Burke	Hardt	Passmore	230	260	415	495
715	Philadelphia	Teehee	Burke	Dyer	Passmore	230	290	390	455
716	Philadelphia	Elliott	Burke	Dyer	Passmore	230	260	415	500
717	Philadelphia	Elliott	Burke	Dyer	Norris	230	290	390	490
718	Cleveland	Teehee	Burke	Baxter	Fancher	230	260	390	520
719	Cleveland	Teehee	Burke	Davis	Fancher	230	260	455	490
720	Cleveland	Elliott	Burke	Davis	Fancher	230	260	415	455
721	Richmond	Teehee	Burke	Keesee	Seay	230	310	455	550
722	Richmond	Elliott	Burke	Keesee	Seay	230	290	520	550
723	Atlanta	Teehee	Burke	Pike	McCord	230	290	455	910
724	Atlanta	Teehee	Burke	Bell	McCord	260	520	2,500	—
725	Atlanta	Teehee	Burke	Bell	Wellborn	230	370	960	1,380
726	Atlanta	Elliott	Burke	Bell	Wellborn	230	325	490	715
727	Chicago	Teehee	Burke	McCloud	McDougal	230	260	435	490
728	Chicago	Teehee	Burke	Cramer	McDougal	230	325	420	520
729	Chicago	Elliott	Burke	Cramer	McDougal	230	260	490	550
730	St. Louis	Teehee	Burke	Attebery	Wells	230	260	420	520
731	St. Louis	Teehee	Burke	Attebery	Biggs	230	310	1,250	—
732	St. Louis	Elliott	Burke	Attebery	Biggs	230	390	1,090	1,250
733	St. Louis	Elliott	Burke	White	Biggs	230	260	455	520
734	Minneapolis	Teehee	Burke	Cook	Wold	230	260	650	715
735	Minneapolis	Teehee	Burke	Cook	Young	290	715	2,620	3,000
736	Minneapolis	Elliott	Burke	Cook	Young	230	285	490	550
737	Kansas City	Teehee	Burke	Anderson	Miller	230	260	390	455
738	Kansas City	Elliott	Burke	Anderson	Miller	230	260	390	490
739	Kansas City	Elliott	Burke	Helm	Miller	230	260	390	490
740	Dallas	Teehee	Burke	Talley	Van Zandt	230	325	715	880
741	Dallas	Elliott	Burke	Talley	Van Zandt	240	520	1,250	4,190

FEDERAL RESERVE BANK NOTES—SERIES 1918

ONE DOLLAR

Friedberg No.	Bank	Register	Treasurer	Bank Officers		VF-20	EF-40	Unc-60	Unc-63
742	Dallas	Elliott	Burke	Lawder	Van Zandt	$230	$310	$490	$585
743	San Francisco	Teehee	Burke	Clerk	Lynch	230	285	415	520
744	San Francisco	Teehee	Burke	Clerk	Calkins	230	340	845	1,020
745	San Francisco	Elliott	Burke	Clerk	Calkins	230	325	780	1,020
746	San Francisco	Elliott	Burke	Ambrose	Calkins	230	260	520	650

★ Star replacement notes for this series are valued at approximately double these prices.

TWO DOLLARS

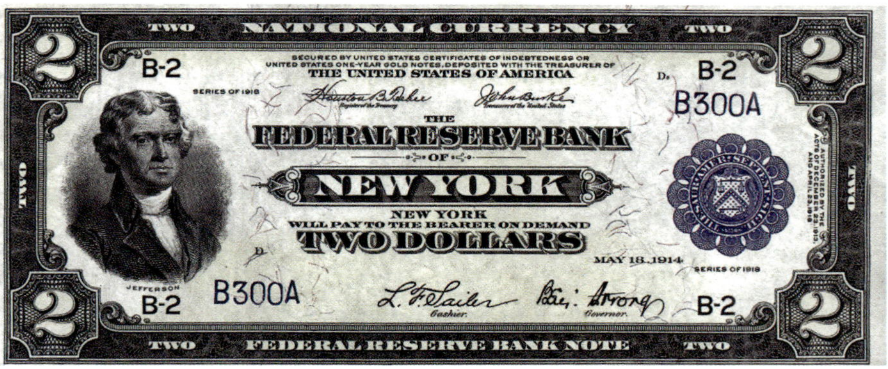

Face Design. Issued by all 12 Federal Reserve Banks.

Back Design. World War I battleship.

Friedberg No.	Bank	Register	Treasurer	Bank Officers		VF-20	EF-40	Unc-60	Unc-63
747	Boston	Teehee	Burke	Bullen	Morss	$680	$1,310	$2,190	$2,380
748	Boston	Teehee	Burke	Willett	Morss	750	1,250	2,500	3,750
749	Boston	Elliott	Burke	Willett	Morss	750	1,180	1,940	2,190
750	New York	Teehee	Burke	Sailer	Strong	750	990	2,120	2,380
751	New York	Teehee	Burke	Hendricks	Strong	750	1,310	2,120	2,250
752	New York	Elliott	Burke	Hendricks	Strong	750	1,120	1,690	1,810
753	Philadelphia	Teehee	Burke	Hardt	Passmore	750	960	1,690	1,940
754	Philadelphia	Teehee	Burke	Dyer	Passmore	750	1,060	2,500	3,120

FEDERAL RESERVE BANK NOTES—SERIES 1918

TWO DOLLARS

Friedberg No.	Bank	Register	Treasurer	Bank Officers		VF-20	EF-40	Unc-60	Unc-63
755	Philadelphia	Elliott	Burke	Dyer	Passmore	$780	$2,190	$12,000	—
756	Philadelphia	Elliott	Burke	Dyer	Norris	750	1,250	2,120	$2,380
757	Cleveland	Teehee	Burke	Baxter	Fancher	750	1,090	1,750	2,310
758	Cleveland	Teehee	Burke	Davis	Fancher	750	1,020	2,380	3,120
759	Cleveland	Elliott	Burke	Davis	Fancher	750	910	2,380	2,560
760	Richmond	Teehee	Burke	Keesee	Seay	750	1,250	3,500	4,120
761	Richmond	Elliott	Burke	Keesee	Seay	750	1,310	3,310	3,750
762	Atlanta	Teehee	Burke	Pike	McCord	750	1,280	2,750	3,440
763	Atlanta	Teehee	Burke	Bell	McCord	1,880	5,000	—	—
764	Atlanta	Elliott	Burke	Bell	Wellborn	750	1,250	3,750	6,900
765	Chicago	Teehee	Burke	McCloud	McDougal	750	1,150	2,060	2,500
766	Chicago	Teehee	Burke	Cramer	McDougal	750	1,150	2,440	2,750
767	Chicago	Elliott	Burke	Cramer	McDougal	750	1,250	1,690	2,000
768	St. Louis	Teehee	Burke	Attebery	Wells	750	1,380	2,500	3,750
769	St. Louis	Teehee	Burke	Attebery	Biggs	1,250	3,120	—	—
770	St. Louis	Elliott	Burke	Attebery	Biggs	750	1,810	—	—
771	St. Louis	Elliott	Burke	White	Biggs	750	1,500	4,750	5,000
772	Minneapolis	Teehee	Burke	Cook	Wold	750	1,220	1,750	2,250
773	Minneapolis	Elliott	Burke	Cook	Young	780	1,500	—	—
774	Kansas City	Teehee	Burke	Anderson	Miller	750	1,150	2,120	2,250
775	Kansas City	Elliott	Burke	Helm	Miller	750	1,500	2,250	2,500
776	Dallas	Teehee	Burke	Talley	Van Zandt	750	1,150	2,500	2,880
777	Dallas	Elliott	Burke	Talley	Van Zandt	750	910	2,620	2,880
778	San Francisco	Teehee	Burke	Clerk	Lynch	750	1,500	2,500	3,060
779	San Francisco	Elliott	Burke	Clerk	Calkins	750	1,090	2,500	—
780	San Francisco	Elliott	Burke	Ambrose	Calkins	750	2,060	—	—

★ Star replacement notes for this series are valued at approximately three times these prices.

FIVE DOLLARS

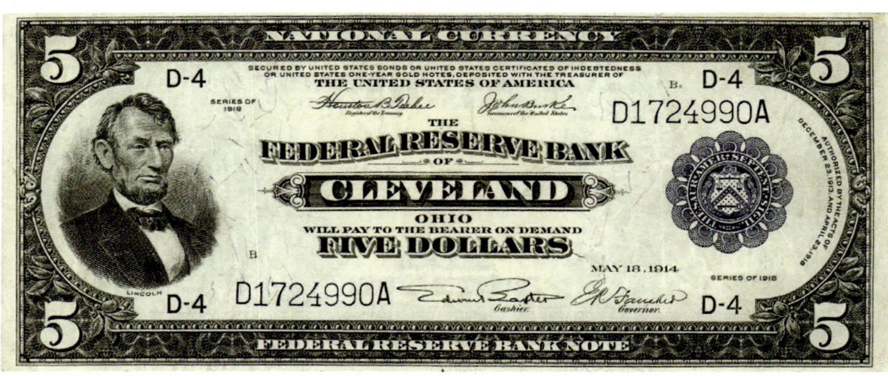

Face Design. Series 1915 and 1918. Issued all districts except Richmond.

Friedberg No.	Bank	Register	Treasurer	Bank Officers		VF-20	EF-40	Unc-60	Unc-63
781	Boston	Teehee	Burke	Bullen	Morss	$325	$545	$1,120	$1,220
782	New York	Teehee	Burke	Hendricks	Strong	325	620	1,310	1,500
783	Philadelphia	Teehee	Burke	Hardt	Passmore	360	910	2,500	2,940

FEDERAL RESERVE BANK NOTES—SERIES 1918

FIVE DOLLARS

Friedberg No.	Bank	Register	Treasurer	Bank Officers		VF-20	EF-40	Unc-60	Unc-63
784	Philadelphia	Teehee	Burke	Dyer	Passmore	$490	$1,500	—	—
785	Cleveland	Teehee	Burke	Baxter	Fancher	325	545	$1,120	$1,220
786	Cleveland	Teehee	Burke	Davis	Fancher	325	545	1,120	1,220
787	Cleveland	Elliott	Burke	Davis	Fancher	390	650	1,380	1,500
790	Atlanta	Teehee	Burke	Pike	McCord	360	880	2,250	—
791	Atlanta	Teehee	Burke	Bell	Wellborn	1,150	2,500	4,380	8,750
792	Atlanta	Elliott	Burke	Bell	Wellborn	1,150	3,750	—	—
794	Chicago	Teehee	Burke	McCloud	McDougal	325	585	1,250	1,690
795	Chicago	Teehee	Burke	Cramer	McDougal	3,750	6,250	—	—
796	St. Louis	Teehee	Burke	Attebery	Wells	390	845	1,690	2,620
797	St. Louis	Teehee	Burke	Attebery	Biggs	550	1,750	3,750	—
798	St. Louis	Elliott	Burke	White	Biggs	325	545	1,120	1,220
799	Minneapolis	Teehee	Burke	Anderson	Wold	490	1,090	2,620	2,880
803	Kansas City	Teehee	Burke	Miller	Cook	325	780	1,750	—
804	Kansas City	Elliott	Burke	Talley	Miller	390	960	1,880	—
807	Dallas	Teehee	Burke	Helm	Van Zandt	780	3,750	—	—
809	San Francisco	Teehee	Burke	Clerk	Lynch	3,000	5,000	—	—

★ Star replacement notes in this series are all very rare. Most San Francisco notes are dated May 20, 1914. One issue dated May 18, 1914, is scarce.

TEN DOLLARS

Face Design. Series date 1915 or 1918 at upper right and left border.

Friedberg No.	Bank	Register	Treasurer	Bank Officers		VF-20	EF-40	Unc-60
810	New York	Teehee	Burke	Hendricks	Strong	$2,060	$4,620	$6,250
812	Atlanta	Elliott	Burke	Bell	Wellborn	1,880	5,100	—
814	Chicago	Teehee	Burke	McCloud	McDougal	1,810	4,120	5,300
815	St. Louis	Teehee	Burke	Attebery	Wells	2,250	4,750	—

★ Star replacement notes in this series are all extremely rare. Boston, Philadelphia, Cleveland, Richmond, Minneapolis, and San Francisco did not issue notes of $10 denomination. Kansas City and Dallas issued this denomination in Series 1915 only. See 1915 listing on page 111.

FEDERAL RESERVE BANK NOTES—SERIES 1918

TWENTY DOLLARS

Friedberg No.	Bank	Register	Treasurer	Bank Officers		VF-20	EF-40	Unc-60
823	Atlanta	Elliott	Burke	Bell	Wellborn	$3,120	$7,200	—
825	St. Louis	Teehee	Burke	Attebery	Wells	5,000	20,400	—

★ Star replacement notes of this denomination are unknown. Boston, New York, Philadelphia, Cleveland, Richmond, Minneapolis, and San Francisco did not issue notes of $20 denomination. Kansas City and Dallas issued this denomination in Series 1915 only. See page 111.

Face Design. Issued by St. Louis bank only.

FIFTY DOLLARS

Friedberg No.	Bank	Register	Treasurer	Bank Officers		VG-8	F-12	VF-20	EF-40	Unc-60
831	St. Louis	Teehee	Burke	Attebery	Wells	$4,380	$11,250	$15,000	$26,400	$45,600

The following serial numbers have been reported with condition ranging from Very Good to strictly Uncirculated. Known existence of other serial numbers and condition will be appreciated.

103	118	153	656	683	768	2128	3402
110	122	168	671	689	774	2923	3800
115	138	608	674	741	821	3213	
117	151	649	682	751	898	3299	

Four thousand $50 St. Louis Federal Reserve Bank Notes were reportedly issued.

FEDERAL RESERVE NOTES, SERIES 1914 AND 1918

FEDERAL RESERVE ACT, DEC. 23, 1913

Red Seal Series 1914 $5 to $100

Red Seal Signatures: John Burke, Treasurer of the United States; Wm. G. McAdoo, Secretary of the Treasury.

Blue Seal Series 1914 $5 to $100 and Series 1918 $500 to $10,000

Blue Seal signatures: John Burke-Wm. G. McAdoo; Burke-Carter Glass; Burke-D.F. Houston; Frank White-A.W. Mellon.

There are three types of Blue Seal notes with White-Mellon signatures.

FEDERAL RESERVE NOTES, SERIES 1914 AND 1918

Type One: District numeral and letter, rather large, lower left and upper right. Most common of the three types.

Type Two: Smaller letters and numerals at lower left, larger letters and numerals at upper right same as Type One.

Type Three: Larger numerals and letters, slightly to the left and higher. Seals closer to center of note. Scarcest of the three types.

These issues are designated as a-b-c, or a-b, next to the city.

Unlike the Federal Reserve *Bank* Notes, the obligation to pay is by the United States and reads: "The United States of America will pay the Bearer on Demand (amount) . . . Dollars."

FACE DESIGNS, Series 1914—Red and Blue Seals
Portraits of presidents as on Federal Reserve Bank notes are featured in center oval on denominations $5 to $50. The $100 note has a portrait of Benjamin Franklin. The seal with number and letter of issuing bank is at left. Treasury seal is at right.

FACE DESIGNS, Series 1918—Blue Seals

$500 John Marshall, secretary of State and jurist.
$1,000 Alexander Hamilton, first secretary of the Treasury.
$5,000 James Madison, fourth president of the United States.
$10,000 Salmon P. Chase, secretary of Treasury under Lincoln.

BACK DESIGNS, Series 1914 and 1918—Red and Blue Seals
Series 1914 $5 to $50 have the same overall back designs as the Federal Reserve Bank notes with the designation National Currency removed. The back design of the $100 notes features five allegorical figures.

BACK DESIGNS, Series 1918—Blue Seals

$500 "DeSoto Discovering the Mississippi, 1541" as on the $10 First Charter National Currency note.
$1,000 American eagle with flag. A beautiful design.
$5,000 "Washington Resigning His Commission," as on the $1,000 First Charter note.
$10,000 "Embarkation of the Pilgrims," as on the $50 First Charter note.

The lengthy inscription in the lower border of the back design differs from that on the Federal Reserve *Bank* Notes. It stipulates that the note is payable in gold, and reads:

> This note is receivable by all national and member banks and the Federal Reserve Banks, and for all taxes, customs and other public dues. It is redeemable in gold on demand at the Treasury Department of the United States in the city of Washington, District of Columbia, or in gold or lawful money at any Federal Reserve Bank.

FEDERAL RESERVE NOTES—SERIES 1914, RED SEAL

Face and back designs the same as Blue Seal Federal Reserve Notes. All with signature combination Treasurer John Burke. Secretary Wm. G. McAdoo.

It would require a little patience and time to acquire a complete set of 12 banks in any one denomination. Catalog values do not indicate the actual scarcity of Red Seal Federal Reserve Notes issued for a period of about one year, 1914–1915.

FEDERAL RESERVE NOTES—SERIES 1914, RED SEAL

FIVE DOLLARS

Friedberg No.	Bank	F-12	VF-20	EF-40	AU-50	Unc-60	Unc-63
832	Boston	$180	$390	$1,250	$1,620	$2,120	$2,500
833	New York	180	390	990	1,250	1,750	1,880
834	Philadelphia	210	390	960	1,250	2,310	2,500
835	Cleveland	180	345	780	1,250	2,120	2,250
836	Richmond	210	390	1,090	1,500	2,380	2,560
837	Atlanta	180	345	960	1,250	1,750	1,780
838	Chicago	180	345	780	1,380	2,000	2,120
839	St. Louis	180	345	780	1,250	1,750	1,780
840	Minneapolis	180	345	780	1,250	1,880	2,000
841	Kansas City	290	585	1,280	2,500	3,750	4,000
842	Dallas	290	520	1,250	1,560	6,250	9,700
843	San Francisco	390	715	2,750	3,750	—	—

TEN DOLLARS

Friedberg No.	Bank	F-12	VF-20	EF-40	AU-50	Unc-60	Unc-63
892	Boston	$275	$585	$1,150	$1,690	$2,440	$3,440
893	New York	240	390	780	1,500	3,000	—
894	Philadelphia	275	535	1,020	1,690	2,440	2,810
895	Cleveland	275	535	1,020	1,690	2,440	2,810
896	Richmond	560	1,250	2,250	—	—	—
897	Atlanta	275	535	1,020	1,690	2,810	3,750
898	Chicago	275	535	1,020	1,690	2,440	2,810
899	St. Louis	275	535	1,560	2,060	2,810	3,750
900	Minneapolis	275	535	1,150	1,690	2,500	—
901	Kansas City	275	535	1,020	1,690	2,440	2,810
902	Dallas	275	535	1,020	1,690	2,440	2,810
903	San Francisco	455	715	1,880	3,120	—	—

TWENTY DOLLARS

Friedberg No.	Bank	F-12	VF-20	EF-40	AU-50	Unc-60	Unc-63
952	Boston	$910	$1,880	$5,600	—	—	—
953	New York	390	715	1,560	$2,250	$3,750	$4,750
954	Philadelphia	420	715	1,560	2,250	2,880	4,750
955	Cleveland	420	715	1,560	2,250	2,880	4,750
956	Richmond	420	715	1,560	2,250	2,880	4,750
957	Atlanta	420	715	1,560	2,250	2,880	4,750
958	Chicago	420	650	1,560	2,250	2,880	4,750
959	St. Louis	420	960	2,500	3,250	4,380	—
960	Minneapolis	420	1,020	3,000	3,750	6,250	—
961	Kansas City	420	715	1,560	2,250	2,880	4,750
962	Dallas	520	780	6,250	—	—	—
963	San Francisco	910	2,120	6,250	—	—	—

FIFTY DOLLARS

Friedberg No.	Bank	F-12	VF-20	EF-40	AU-50	Unc-60	Unc-63
1012	Boston	$6,500	$12,000	—	—	—	—
1013	New York	3,000	3,750	$6,900	—	—	—
1014	Philadelphia	1,880	2,750	7,500	$10,000	$18,000	$20,400
1015	Cleveland	2,620	3,750	8,100	—	—	30,000
1016	Richmond	2,750	4,380	12,000	15,600	—	—

FEDERAL RESERVE NOTES—SERIES 1914, RED SEAL

FIFTY DOLLARS

Friedberg No.	Bank	F-12	VF-20	EF-40	AU-50	Unc-60	Unc-63
1017	Atlanta	$2,750	$4,810	—	—	—	—
1018	Chicago	1,880	3,120	$6,900	$11,250	—	—
1019	St. Louis	2,500	3,750	5,950	8,750	—	$24,000
1020	Minneapolis	3,120	5,000	15,600	—	—	—
1021	Kansas City	6,050	8,100	24,000	—	—	—
1022	Dallas	2,500	3,500	—	—	—	—
1023	San Francisco	3,120	6,250	12,000	—	—	—

ONE HUNDRED DOLLARS

Friedberg No.	Bank	F-12	VF-20	EF-40	AU-50	Unc-60	Unc-63
1072	Boston	$2,750	$4,750	—	$11,250	$14,400	$30,000
1073	New York	3,750	8,100	—	—	—	—
1074	Philadelphia	2,380	3,750	$5,450	7,500	8,750	36,000
1075	Cleveland	4,380	—	24,000	36,000	—	—
1076	Richmond	2,810	5,000	10,600	—	—	—
1077	Atlanta	2,250	5,000	8,750	12,000	—	—
1078	Chicago	3,120	6,250	14,400	25,200	—	—
1079	St. Louis	2,880	8,100	11,250	12,000	—	—
1080	Minneapolis	14,400	24,000	—	—	—	—
1081	Kansas City	3,120	6,250	21,000	24,000	—	—
1082	Dallas	5,250	8,100	26,400	—	—	—
1083	San Francisco	4,000	6,900	11,250	—	24,000	—

FEDERAL RESERVE NOTES—SERIES 1914, BLUE SEAL

Face Design. Back Designs same as Federal Reserve Bank Notes.
The designation "NATIONAL CURRENCY" has been removed from face and back.

Four signature combinations issued by each of the 12 Federal Reserve Banks

FIVE DOLLARS

Friedberg No.	Bank	Treasurer	Secretary	VF-20	EF-40	Unc-60	Unc-63
844	Boston	Burke	McAdoo	$94	$260	$650	$910
845	Boston	Burke	Glass	94	220	620	715
846	Boston	Burke	Houston	94	115	180	210

FEDERAL RESERVE NOTES—SERIES 1914, BLUE SEAL

FIVE DOLLARS

Friedberg No.	Bank	Treasurer	Secretary	VF-20	EF-40	Unc-60	Unc-63
847A	Boston	White	Mellon Type One	$94	$230	$390	$490
847B	Boston	White	Mellon Type Two	130	160	355	450
848	New York	Burke	McAdoo	94	115	260	360
849	New York	Burke	Glass	94	215	520	585
850	New York	Burke	Houston	94	155	260	325
851A	New York	White	Mellon Type One	94	195	325	435
851B	New York	White	Mellon Type Two	90	150	375	485
851C	New York	White	Mellon Type Three	90	135	275	350
852	Philadelphia	Burke	McAdoo	94	115	180	210
853	Philadelphia	Burke	Glass	94	115	180	210
854	Philadelphia	Burke	Houston	94	175	325	390
855A	Philadelphia	White	Mellon Type One	94	195	325	390
855B	Philadelphia	White	Mellon Type Two	90	135	345	450
855C	Philadelphia	White	Mellon Type Three	90	135	275	350
856	Cleveland	Burke	McAdoo	100	195	455	715
857	Cleveland	Burke	Glass	94	115	180	210
858	Cleveland	Burke	Houston	110	195	325	545
859A	Cleveland	White	Mellon Type One	94	195	290	390
859B	Cleveland	White	Mellon Type Two	110	150	365	475
859C	Cleveland	White	Mellon Type Three	90	135	275	350
860	Richmond	Burke	McAdoo	94	155	325	390
861	Richmond	Burke	Glass	94	115	180	210
862	Richmond	Burke	Houston	94	130	195	260
863A	Richmond	White	Mellon Type One	110	215	420	585
863B	Richmond	White	Mellon Type Two	1,250	2,000	3,200	—
864	Atlanta	Burke	McAdoo	94	115	180	210
865	Atlanta	Burke	Glass	145	390	1,500	2,500
866	Atlanta	Burke	Houston	94	175	325	390
867A	Atlanta	White	Mellon Type One	94	130	325	455
868	Chicago	Burke	McAdoo	94	180	325	420
869	Chicago	Burke	Glass	94	130	260	325
870	Chicago	Burke	Houston	94	130	215	325
871A	Chicago	White	Mellon Type One	94	260	390	455
871B	Chicago	White	Mellon Type Two	100	155	310	415
871C	Chicago	White	Mellon Type Three	100	170	350	475
872	St. Louis	Burke	McAdoo	94	115	180	210
873	St. Louis	Burke	Glass	94	115	180	210
874	St. Louis	Burke	Houston	130	195	325	390
875A	St. Louis	White	Mellon Type One	94	115	180	210
875B	St. Louis	White	Mellon Type Two	110	170	375	515
876	Minneapolis	Burke	McAdoo	120	195	490	650
877	Minneapolis	Burke	Glass	115	370	650	—
878	Minneapolis	Burke	Houston	94	230	390	520
879A	Minneapolis	White	Mellon Type One	94	115	180	210
880	Kansas City	Burke	McAdoo	94	115	260	290
881	Kansas City	Burke	Glass	145	260	490	845
882	Kansas City	Burke	Houston	94	115	180	210
883A	Kansas City	White	Mellon Type One	100	175	325	390
883B	Kansas City	White	Mellon Type Two	325	500	750	1,250
884	Dallas	Burke	McAdoo	195	455	1,250	1,500

FEDERAL RESERVE NOTES—SERIES 1914, BLUE SEAL

FIVE DOLLARS

Friedberg No.	Bank	Treasurer	Secretary	VF-20	EF-40	Unc-60	Unc-63
885	Dallas	Burke	Glass	$230	$715	—	—
886	Dallas	Burke	Houston	115	220	—	—
887A	Dallas	White	Mellon Type One	94	195	$360	$520
887B	Dallas	White	Mellon Type Two	180	315	550	850
888	San Francisco	Burke	McAdoo	94	115	180	210
889	San Francisco	Burke	Glass	94	115	180	210
890	San Francisco	Burke	Houston	115	230	520	—
891A	San Francisco	White	Mellon Type One	110	210	390	490
891B	San Francisco	White	Mellon Type Two	110	170	350	525
891C	San Francisco	White	Mellon Type Three	400	900	1,800	2,500

★ Star replacement notes for this series are valued at approximately three times these prices. See text on pages 116 and 117 describing three types of notes with White-Mellon signatures.

TEN DOLLARS

Face Design. Andrew Jackson, seventh president of the United States

Back Design. Agriculture and Commerce.

Friedberg No.	Bank	Treasurer	Secretary	VF-20	EF-40	Unc-60	Unc-63
904	Boston	Burke	McAdoo	$110	$135	$195	$255
905	Boston	Burke	Glass	110	135	195	255
906	Boston	Burke	Houston	110	135	195	255

FEDERAL RESERVE NOTES—SERIES 1914, BLUE SEAL

TEN DOLLARS

Friedberg No.	Bank	Treasurer	Secretary	VF-20	EF-40	Unc-60	Unc-63
907A	Boston	White	Mellon Type One	$160	$260	$455	$520
907B	Boston	White	Mellon Type Two	110	160	335	425
908	New York	Burke	McAdoo	110	195	455	585
909	New York	Burke	Glass	110	135	195	255
910	New York	Burke	Houston	110	260	390	455
911A	New York	White	Mellon Type One	130	290	420	455
911B	New York	White	Mellon Type Two	110	230	520	550
911C	New York	White	Mellon Type Three	130	260	585	650
912A	Philadelphia	Burke	McAdoo	110	135	195	255
913	Philadelphia	Burke	Glass	145	235	1,150	1,500
914	Philadelphia	Burke	Houston	130	235	650	715
915A	Philadelphia	White	Mellon Type One	110	325	455	550
915C	Philadelphia	White	Mellon Type Three	115	325	455	550
916	Cleveland	Burke	McAdoo	155	260	1,090	2,190
917	Cleveland	Burke	Glass	160	290	1,150	2,500
918	Cleveland	Burke	Houston	110	135	325	390
919A	Cleveland	White	Mellon Type One	110	180	390	455
919B	Cleveland	White	Mellon Type Two	110	170	475	875
919C	Cleveland	White	Mellon Type Three	100	150	425	950
920	Richmond	Burke	McAdoo	110	135	195	255
921	Richmond	Burke	Glass	110	135	195	255
922	Richmond	Burke	Houston	110	195	550	—
923	Richmond	White	Mellon Type One	110	195	325	390
924	Atlanta	Burke	McAdoo	120	325	780	—
925	Atlanta	Burke	Glass	110	135	195	255
926	Atlanta	Burke	Houston	130	180	910	—
927A	Atlanta	White	Mellon Type One	110	135	230	260
927B	Atlanta	White	Mellon Type Two	145	215	500	800
928	Chicago	Burke	McAdoo	110	160	290	455
929	Chicago	Burke	Glass	155	235	325	455
930	Chicago	Burke	Houston	130	215	420	455
931A	Chicago	White	Mellon Type One	110	230	455	520
931B	Chicago	White	Mellon Type Two	110	230	390	455
931C	Chicago	White	Mellon Type Three	130	360	520	650
932	St. Louis	Burke	McAdoo	110	135	195	255
933	St. Louis	Burke	Glass	110	135	195	255
934	St. Louis	Burke	Houston	110	160	325	390
935	St. Louis	White	Mellon Type One	130	240	910	—
936	Minneapolis	Burke	McAdoo	130	390	—	—
937	Minneapolis	Burke	Glass	110	135	195	255
938	Minneapolis	Burke	Houston	110	135	195	255
939	Minneapolis	White	Mellon Type One	120	305	455	520
940	Kansas City	Burke	McAdoo	110	210	310	390
941	Kansas City	Burke	Glass	520	780	1,250	—
942	Kansas City	Burke	Houston	130	160	910	—
943	Kansas City	White	Mellon Type One	130	290	435	650
944	Dallas	Burke	McAdoo	110	135	455	520
945	Dallas	Burke	Glass	110	135	195	255
946	Dallas	Burke	Houston	110	135	195	255
947	Dallas	White	Mellon Type One	110	160	390	455

FEDERAL RESERVE NOTES—SERIES 1914, BLUE SEAL

TEN DOLLARS

Friedberg No.	Bank	Treasurer	Secretary	VF-20	EF-40	Unc-60	Unc-63
948	San Francisco	Burke	McAdoo	$110	$135	$195	$255
949	San Francisco	Burke	Glass	260	650	1,500	3,120
950	San Francisco	Burke	Houston	110	135	195	255
951A	San Francisco	White	Mellon Type One	130	260	455	520
951B	San Francisco	White	Mellon Type Two	110	290	780	1,500
951C	San Francisco	White	Mellon Type Three	180	260	1,020	1,750

★ Star replacement notes for this series are valued at approximately three times these prices. See text on pages 116 and 117 describing three types of notes with White-Mellon signatures.

TWENTY DOLLARS

Face Design. Stephen Grover Cleveland.

Back Design. Various means of transportation.

Friedberg No.	Bank	Treasurer	Secretary	VF-20	EF-40	Unc-60	Unc-63
964	Boston	Burke	McAdoo	$215	$585	—	—
965	Boston	Burke	Glass	180	715	—	—
966	Boston	Burke	Houston	145	390	$1,250	—
967	Boston	White	Mellon Type One	155	390	1,020	—
968	New York	Burke	McAdoo	145	260	1,380	—
969	New York	Burke	Glass	155	360	—	—
970	New York	Burke	Houston	130	350	—	—
971A	New York	White	Mellon Type One	160	325	650	$910

FEDERAL RESERVE NOTES—SERIES 1914, BLUE SEAL

TWENTY DOLLARS

Friedberg No.	Bank	Treasurer	Secretary		VF-20	EF-40	Unc-60	Unc-63
971B	New York	White	Mellon Type Two		$130	$390	$650	$1,250
972	Philadelphia	Burke	McAdoo		155	475	1,880	—
973	Philadelphia	Burke	Glass		195	390	—	—
974	Philadelphia	Burke	Houston		130	325	—	960
975	Philadelphia	White	Mellon Type One		145	360	550	650
976	Cleveland	Burke	McAdoo		130	260	420	520
977	Cleveland	Burke	Glass		130	370	910	—
978	Cleveland	Burke	Houston		130	310	960	1,150
979A	Cleveland	White	Mellon Type One		145	490	1,150	1,500
979B	Cleveland	White	Mellon Type Two		225	500	950	1,250
980	Richmond	Burke	McAdoo		150	290	—	—
981	Richmond	Burke	Glass		290	845	—	—
982	Richmond	Burke	Houston		130	290	—	—
983	Richmond	White	Mellon Type One		130	290	—	—
984	Atlanta	Burke	McAdoo		130	325	585	780
985	Atlanta	Burke	Glass	None printed				
986	Atlanta	Burke	Houston		130	240	520	650
987	Atlanta	White	Mellon Type One		130	195	390	585
988	Chicago	Burke	McAdoo		130	325	910	—
989	Chicago	Burke	Glass		145	345	650	1,090
990	Chicago	Burke	Houston		130	285	780	960
991A	Chicago	White	Mellon Type One		130	390	585	780
991B	Chicago	White	Mellon Type Two		145	260	520	650
991C	Chicago	White	Mellon Type Three		750	1,000	1,750	—
992	St. Louis	Burke	McAdoo		130	195	455	520
993	St. Louis	Burke	Glass		520	2,880	—	—
994	St. Louis	Burke	Houston		130	195	325	650
995	St. Louis	White	Mellon Type One		130	325	585	680
996	Minneapolis	Burke	McAdoo		130	360	1,880	2,250
997	Minneapolis	Burke	Glass		715	3,120	—	—
998	Minneapolis	Burke	Houston		130	290	520	585
999	Minneapolis	White	Mellon Type One		130	325	650	715
1000	Kansas City	Burke	McAdoo		130	290	520	845
1001	Kansas City	Burke	Glass	None printed				
1002	Kansas City	Burke	Houston		130	230	390	475
1003	Kansas City	White	Mellon Type One		130	310	455	620
1004	Dallas	Burke	McAdoo		130	260	490	650
1005	Dallas	Burke	Glass		650	1,150	—	—
1006	Dallas	Burke	Houston		155	390	1,750	2,250
1007	Dallas	White	Mellon Type One		130	260	585	715
1008	San Francisco	Burke	McAdoo		130	195	310	390
1009	San Francisco	Burke	Glass		325	960	2,500	4,750
1010	San Francisco	Burke	Houston		130	195	310	390
1011A	San Francisco	White	Mellon Type One		260	455	780	1,020
1011B	San Francisco	White	Mellon Type Two		230	455	650	780
1011C	San Francisco	White	Mellon Type Three		230	455	650	780

★ Star replacement notes for this series are valued at from three to four times these prices. See text on pages 116 and 117 describing three types of notes with White-Mellon signatures.

FEDERAL RESERVE NOTES—SERIES 1914, BLUE SEAL

FIFTY DOLLARS

Face Design. Ulysses S. Grant, general and president.

Back Design. Panama represented by female figure, with two oceans.

Friedberg No.	Bank	Treasurer	Secretary	VF-20	EF-40	Unc-60	Unc-63
1024	Boston	Burke	McAdoo	$390	$1,090	—	—
1025	Boston	Burke	Glass	455	910	$2,500	$3,120
1026	Boston	Burke	Houston	520	1,750	4,380	6,250
1027	Boston	White	Mellon Type One	910	—	—	—
1028	New York	Burke	McAdoo	455	845	2,500	3,440
1029	New York	Burke	Glass	520	2,500	—	—
1030	New York	Burke	Houston	420	845	—	—
1031A	New York	White	Mellon Type One	520	1,250	—	—
1031B	New York	White	Mellon Type Two	—	—	—	—
1032	Philadelphia	Burke	McAdoo	475	880	3,750	—
1033	Philadelphia	Burke	Glass	910	—	—	—
1034	Philadelphia	Burke	Houston	390	845	—	—
1035	Philadelphia	White	Mellon Type One	390	1,090	2,310	2,500
1036	Cleveland	Burke	McAdoo	370	960	—	—
1037	Cleveland	Burke	Glass	520	1,880	—	—
1038	Cleveland	Burke	Houston	390	845	2,500	—
1039A	Cleveland	White	Mellon Type One	420	780	3,310	4,380
1039B	Cleveland	White	Mellon Type Two	455	910	—	—

FEDERAL RESERVE NOTES—SERIES 1914, BLUE SEAL

FIFTY DOLLARS

Friedberg No.	Bank	Treasurer	Secretary		VF-20	EF-40	Unc-60	Unc-63
1040	Richmond	Burke	McAdoo		$390	$910	$1,880	$2,500
1041	Richmond	Burke	Glass		550	1,250	—	—
1042	Richmond	Burke	Houston		390	1,020	—	—
1043	Richmond	White	Mellon Type One		390	780	2,120	2,500
1044	Atlanta	Burke	McAdoo		455	910	2,250	4,380
1045	Atlanta	Burke	Glass		2,000	—	—	—
1046	Atlanta	Burke	Houston		390	715	2,000	2,620
1047	Atlanta	White	Mellon Type One		390	1,020	2,250	2,500
1048	Chicago	Burke	McAdoo		390	1,090	1,880	2,500
1049	Chicago	Burke	Glass		390	715	1,500	1,940
1050	Chicago	Burke	Houston		390	715	1,500	1,940
1051	Chicago	White	Mellon Type One		390	1,020	2,500	3,120
1052	St. Louis	Burke	McAdoo		390	715	1,500	1,940
1053	St. Louis	Burke	Glass		390	715	1,500	1,940
1054	St. Louis	Burke	Houston		390	715	1,500	1,940
1055	St. Louis	White	Mellon Type One	None reported				
1056	Minneapolis	Burke	McAdoo		500	1,150	3,310	3,620
1057	Minneapolis	Burke	Glass	None printed				
1058	Minneapolis	Burke	Houston		390	715	1,500	1,940
1059	Minneapolis	White	Mellon Type One		7,500	—	—	—
1060	Kansas City	Burke	McAdoo		390	1,020	2,620	3,750
1061	Kansas City	Burke	Glass	None printed				
1062	Kansas City	Burke	Houston	None printed				
1063	Kansas City	White	Mellon Type One		1,750	—	—	—
1064	Dallas	Burke	McAdoo		455	1,500	2,500	3,120
1065	Dallas	Burke	Glass	None reported				
1066	Dallas	Burke	Houston	3 known				
1067	Dallas	White	Mellon Type One	None reported				
1068	San Francisco	Burke	McAdoo		390	1,180	2,750	3,120
1069	San Francisco	Burke	Glass	None printed				
1070	San Francisco	Burke	Houston		455	990	2,500	—
1071	San Francisco	White	Mellon Type One		520	1,750	—	—

★ Star replacement notes for this series are very rare. See text on pages 116 and 117 describing three types of notes with White-Mellon signatures.

ONE HUNDRED DOLLARS

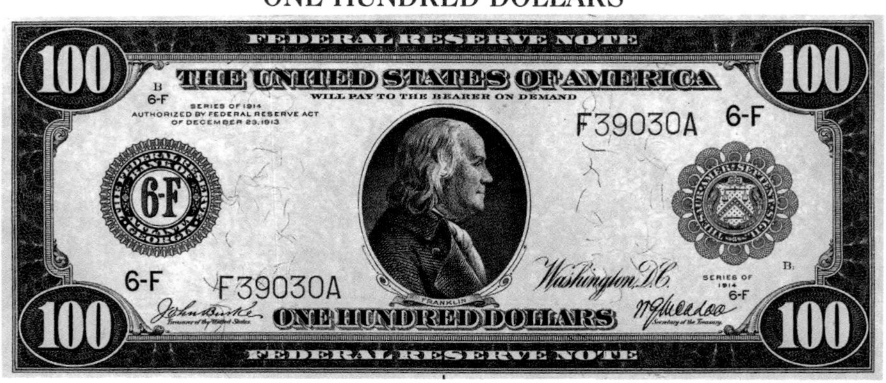

Face Design. Benjamin Franklin.

FEDERAL RESERVE NOTES—SERIES 1914, BLUE SEAL

ONE HUNDRED DOLLARS

Back Design. Not issued in Federal Reserve Bank Notes.

All of this denomination are Type One.

Friedberg No.	Bank	Treasurer	Secretary		VF-20	EF-40	Unc-60	Unc-63
1084	Boston	Burke	McAdoo		$1,150	$2,250	$6,900	—
1085	Boston	Burke	Glass		1,150	4,380	—	—
1086	Boston	Burke	Houston	None printed				
1087	Boston	White	Mellon		1,150	1,880	4,380	$5,600
1088	New York	Burke	McAdoo		940	1,880	2,500	3,000
1089	New York	Burke	Glass		1,020	2,500	—	—
1090	New York	Burke	Houston		960	2,000	3,000	—
1091	New York	White	Mellon		1,020	1,500	3,560	4,380
1092	Philadelphia	Burke	McAdoo		960	1,690	2,500	2,750
1093	Philadelphia	Burke	Glass	None printed				
1094	Philadelphia	Burke	Houston	None printed				
1095	Philadelphia	White	Mellon		1,090	2,000	—	—
1096	Cleveland	Burke	McAdoo		1,060	1,880	—	—
1097	Cleveland	Burke	Glass		1,150	1,880	—	—
1098	Cleveland	Burke	Houston		960	2,250	3,750	4,380
1099	Cleveland	White	Mellon		990	1,880	4,000	—
1100	Richmond	Burke	McAdoo		880	1,250	2,620	2,750
1101	Richmond	Burke	Glass		1,020	3,750	—	7,500
1102	Richmond	Burke	Houston	None printed				
1103	Richmond	White	Mellon	1 known				
1104	Atlanta	Burke	McAdoo		1,020	1,750	2,880	3,750
1105	Atlanta	Burke	Glass	None printed				
1106	Atlanta	Burke	Houston		2,120	5,950	—	—
1107	Atlanta	White	Mellon		910	1,500	2,940	—
1108	Chicago	Burke	McAdoo		1,090	1,750	3,120	3,500
1109	Chicago	Burke	Glass	None printed				
1110	Chicago	Burke	Houston		1,090	2,250	3,000	3,440
1111	Chicago	White	Mellon	None printed				
1112	St. Louis	Burke	McAdoo		940	1,560	3,310	3,750
1113	St. Louis	Burke	Glass	None printed				
1114	St. Louis	Burke	Houston	None printed				
1115	St. Louis	White	Mellon					
1116	Minneapolis	Burke	McAdoo		910	1,750	3,750	—
1117	Minneapolis	Burke	Glass	None printed				

FEDERAL RESERVE NOTES—SERIES 1914, BLUE SEAL

ONE HUNDRED DOLLARS

Friedberg No.	Bank	Treasurer	Secretary		VF-20	EF-40	Unc-60	Unc-63
1118	Minneapolis	Burke	Houston	None printed				
1119	Minneapolis	White	Mellon		$1,500	$2,190	$5,600	—
1120	Kansas City	Burke	McAdoo		1,020	2,000	4,750	$5,600
1121	Kansas City	Burke	Glass	None printed				
1122	Kansas City	Burke	Houston	None printed				
1123	Kansas City	White	Mellon		940	1,720	2,620	—
1124	Dallas	Burke	McAdoo		1,220	2,000	2,750	4,380
1125	Dallas	Burke	Glass	None printed				
1126	Dallas	Burke	Houston	None printed				
1127	Dallas	White	Mellon		1,880	10,000	—	—
1128	San Francisco	Burke	McAdoo		910	1,690	3,120	3,500
1129	San Francisco	Burke	Glass	None printed				
1130	San Francisco	Burke	Houston		1,150	1,880	2,940	3,560
1131	San Francisco	White	Mellon		960	2,250	6,250	—

FEDERAL RESERVE NOTES—SERIES 1918, BLUE SEAL

FIVE HUNDRED DOLLARS

Face Design. John Marshall, chief justice of the Supreme Court.

Back Design. "DeSoto Discovering the Mississippi, 1541."

Issued by Federal Reserve Banks in all districts except Richmond.

FEDERAL RESERVE NOTES—SERIES 1918, BLUE SEAL

FIVE HUNDRED DOLLARS

Friedberg No.	Bank	F-12	VF-20	EF-40	Unc-60
1132	New York, Chicago, San Francisco – Others are rare	$11,250	$16,800	$42,000	—

ONE THOUSAND DOLLARS

Face Design. Alexander Hamilton, first secretary of the Treasury.

Back Design. American eagle with flag. A much admired design.

Issued by Federal Reserve Banks in all districts except Richmond. Values shown are for the more common notes of New York, Chicago, Cleveland, Philadelphia, and San Francisco.

Friedberg No.	Bank	F-12	VF-20	EF-40	Unc-60
1133	Common Banks	$12,000	$22,000	$45,000	—

FIVE THOUSAND DOLLARS

Face Design: James Madison, fourth president of the United States.
Back Design: "Washington Resigning His Commission."

TEN THOUSAND DOLLARS

Face Design: Salmon P. Chase, secretary of the Treasury under Lincoln.
Back Design: "Embarkation of the Pilgrims," as on the $50 First Charter.

GOLD CERTIFICATES

ACTS OF MARCH 3, 1863; JULY 12, 1882; MARCH 14, 1900; DECEMBER 24, 1919

FIRST, SECOND, and THIRD ISSUES

The above issues may be considered to be non-collectible, having been used principally in transactions between banks. Some of these issues were uniface. In the First Issue, denominations ranged from $20 to $10,000; in later issues, $100 to $10,000. The $20 and $100 certificates of these issues are extremely rare. The higher denominations have not been discovered. Dates of issue were filled in with pen and ink on these three issues. Two $20 first issue certificates are known.

FOURTH ISSUE, Series 1882

$20 to $10,000 denomination. As with the first three issues, denominations higher than $100 are extremely rare, practically unknown.

The obligation to pay in gold is on the face of the note. It reads: "This certifies that there have been deposited in the Treasury of the United States . . . Dollars in Gold Coin, payable to the Bearer on Demand." This issue is indicated as "Department Series" on the face of the certificates.

FACE DESIGNS, Series 1882

$20 James A. Garfield, 20th president of the United States. Assassinated six months after his inauguration in 1881. Portrait at right.
$50 Silar Wright, U.S. senator, 1833–1834. New York State governor, 1845–1846. Portrait at left.
$100 Thomas H. Benton, left. U.S. senator for over 30 years.
$500 Abraham Lincoln. Portrait at left.
$1,000 Alexander Hamilton, at right.
$5,000 James Madison, at left, engraved by A. Sealey.
$10,000 Andrew Jackson, at left.

Some notes of the 1882 series, bearing Bruce-Gilfillan signatures and a brown seal, were countersigned by Thomas C. Acton, Assistant Treasurer, and were payable in New York. Notes so countersigned are rare.

BACK DESIGNS, Series 1882

The American eagle in various poses is featured on the back design of all denominations of this series. There is no legend or inscription. Large Roman numerals "C," "D," and "M" in the back design indicate the $100, $500, and $1,000 denominations. "United States" without "of America" is used on all back designs of this series.

FIFTH ISSUE, Series 1888

Two denominations only:

$5,000 James Madison, portrait at left. Back design: "5,000" and eagle.
$10,000 Andrew Jackson, portrait at left. Back design: "10,000" and eagle with flag.

SIXTH ISSUE, Series 1900

$10,000 only. Andrew Jackson, as on Series 1888. Back design same as 1888.

GOLD CERTIFICATES

SEVENTH ISSUE, Series 1905, 1906, and 1907

$10 Series 1907. Center, Michael Hillegas, treasurer of the United States, 1777–1789. Large "X" Roman equivalent of "10" at left.

$20 Series 1905, George Washington. The beautiful blending of gold, red, black, and white has caused this note to be known as the "Technicolor Note."

$20 Series 1906, George Washington. Gold and black design with Roman numeral "XX."

The back design of gold for this series carries no inscription. Simply the designation "Gold Certificate," the denomination, and the seal.

EIGHTH ISSUE, Series 1907

$1,000 Alexander Hamilton. One denomination.

NINTH ISSUE, Series 1913

$50 Series 1913. Portrait of Grant. Issued with two signature combinations, both of which were offered in the Grinnell sale in 1945. Series 1913 and Series 1922 were the only two issues of the $50 denomination.

LAST ISSUE, Series 1922

$10 to $1,000 denominations. All bear signature combination 31, Speelman-White.

A legend was added to the face of the notes: "This certificate is a Legal Tender in the amount thereof, in payment of all debts and dues public and private. Acts of March 14, 1900, as amended, and December 24, 1919."

$10 Michael Hillegas, first U.S. Treasurer.
$20 George Washington.
$50 Ulysses Grant.
$100 Thomas H. Benton.
$500 Abraham Lincoln.
$1,000 Alexander Hamilton.

The back designs in gold feature the seal, the denomination and United States of America. There is no legend or inscription.

ACT OF MARCH 3, 1863—ISSUED 1865 TO 1876

Signatures Colby-Spinner or Allison-Spinner—countersignature and date added with pen and ink.

FIRST ISSUE

$20 and $100 Extremely rare.
$500 to $5,000 Non-collectible.

SECOND ISSUE

$100 to $10,000 Non-collectible.

THIRD ISSUE

$100 Series 1875, Allison-New Extremely rare.
$500 to $10,000 Non-collectible.

GOLD CERTIFICATES

TWENTY DOLLARS – SERIES 1882, RED SEAL

Face Design. Fourth Issue. James A. Garfield.

Back Design. American eagle.

Friedberg No.	Register	Treasurer	Seal at Right	F-12	VF-20	EF-40	Unc-60
1174	Bruce	Gilfillan	Brown	$5,300	$10,000	$25,200	—
	Countersigned Thos. C. Acton, Asst. Treas.						
1175a	Bruce	Gilfillan	Brown	5,600	10,000	24,000	—
1176	Bruce	Wyman	Brown	5,300	9,400	22,800	$66,000
1177	Rosecrans	Huston	Large brown	5,300	9,400	22,800	84,000
1178	Lyons	Roberts	Small red	735	1,250	4,500	9,600

GOLD CERTIFICATES

FIFTY DOLLARS – SERIES 1882, RED SEAL

Friedberg No.	Register	Treasurer	Seal at Right		F-12	VF-20	EF-40	Unc-60
Countersigned notes of this issue are very rare.								
1188	Bruce	Gilfillan	Brown	8 known	$6,250	—	—	—
1189	Bruce	Wyman	Brown	5 known	14,400	—	—	—
1191	Rosecrans	Hyatt	Large red	4 known				
1192	Rosecrans	Huston	Large brown	Rare	—	$14,400	—	—
1193	Lyons	Roberts	Small red		1,380	1,780	$5,600	$11,250
1194	Lyons	Treat	Small red		1,440	2,000	11,250	—
1195	Vernon	Treat	Small red		1,590	1,880	8,100	27,600
1196	Vernon	McClung	Small red		1,880	3,000	13,800	—
1197	Napier	McClung	Small red		1,380	2,000	5,600	12,600

ONE HUNDRED DOLLARS – SERIES 1882, RED SEAL

Face Design. Fourth Issue. Thomas H. Benton.

Friedberg No.	Register	Treasurer	Seal at Right		F-12	VF-20	EF-40	Unc-60
Countersigned notes of this issue are very rare.								
1201	Bruce	Gilfillan	Brown	7 known	—	$78,000		
1203	Bruce	Wyman	Brown	3 known	$300,000			
1204	Rosecrans	Hyatt	Large red	4 known				
1205	Rosecrans	Huston	Large brown	8 known				
1206	Lyons	Roberts	Small red		960	1,560	$3,620	$8,000
1207	Lyons	Treat	Small red		2,500	3,750	10,450	—
1208	Vernon	Treat	Small red		1,090	2,500	3,880	—
1209	Vernon	McClung	Small red		960	1,560	3,620	8,000
1210	Napier	McClung	Small red		1,880	3,380	11,250	—
1211	Napier	Thompson	Small red		1,500	2,120	5,250	—
1212	Napier	Burke	Small red		1,500	2,000	6,000	—
1213	Parker	Burke	Small red		1,220	2,620	7,250	—
1214	Teehee	Burke	Small red		960	1,880	4,620	9,400

FIVE HUNDRED TO TEN THOUSAND DOLLARS – SERIES 1882, RED SEAL

Series 1882 $500, $1,000, $5,000, and $10,000 were issued but are considered non-collectible, although notes of each denomination do exist.

GOLD CERTIFICATES

FIVE THOUSAND DOLLARS – SERIES 1888, RED SEAL

TEN THOUSAND DOLLARS – SERIES 1888 AND 1900, RED SEALS

As with the Series 1882 Gold Certificates, high denomination notes of Series 1888 and 1900 reportedly exist, but may be considered to be non-collectible. See page 130 for a description of these notes.

TEN DOLLARS – SERIES 1907 AND 1922, GOLD SEALS

Face Design. Series 1907 and 1922, with minor addition.

Back Design. Series 1907 and 1922.

Friedberg No.	Series	Register	Treasurer	VF-20	EF-40	AU-50	Unc-60	Unc-63
1167	1907	Vernon	Treat	$235	$845	$1,090	$2,500	$3,120
1168	1907	Vernon	McClung	325	715	910	1,620	2,250
1169	1907	Napier	McClung	235	650	960	1,250	2,220
1170	1907	Napier	Thompson	910	3,000	3,750	6,250	—
1171	1907	Parker	Burke	285	750	1,090	1,750	1,940
1172	1907	Teehee	Burke	285	630	1,020	1,500	2,160
1173	1922	Speelman	White	290	715	940	1,500	1,620

★ Star replacement notes for Series 1907 are very scarce. Those for Series 1922 are valued at approximately double the prices shown here.

GOLD CERTIFICATES

TWENTY DOLLARS – SERIES 1905, 1906, AND 1922

Face Design. Series 1905, 1906, and 1922. Legend added to Series 1922.

Back Design. Series 1905, 1906, and 1922.

Series 1905 have red seals, others have gold seals, and a few orange seals.

Friedberg No.	Series	Register	Treasurer	VF-20	EF-40	AU-50	Unc-60	Unc-63
1179	1905	Lyons	Roberts	$3,500	$11,250	$19,200	$24,000	$31,200
1180	1905	Lyons	Treat	4,810	12,000	13,800	19,200	26,400
1181	1906	Vernon	Treat	360	960	1,250	2,000	3,000
1182	1906	Vernon	McClung	360	880	1,250	2,500	3,000
1183	1906	Napier	McClung	390	940	1,750	2,500	3,000
1184	1906	Napier	Thompson	410	1,500	3,250	4,000	4,500
1185	1906	Parker	Burke	360	1,020	1,560	2,380	2,620
1186	1906	Teehee	Burke	360	910	1,250	1,560	1,880
1187	1922	Speelman	White	340	990	1,310	1,880	2,380

★ Star replacement notes for Series 1906 are rare. Those for Series 1922 are valued at approximately three times the prices shown here.

GOLD CERTIFICATES

FIFTY DOLLARS – SERIES 1913 AND 1922, GOLD SEALS

Face Design. Series 1913 and 1922. Minor change on Series 1922.

Friedberg No.	Series	Register	Treasurer	VF-20	EF-40	AU-50	Unc-60
1198	1913	Parker	Burke	$1,220	$4,380	$5,500	$10,000
1199	1913	Teehee	Burke	1,150	4,380	4,880	8,750
1200	1922	Speelman	White	1,020	2,880	4,060	6,250

★ Star replacement notes for this series are rare.

ONE HUNDRED DOLLARS – SERIES 1922, RED SEAL

Face Design. With legend added as on all Series 1922.

Friedberg No.	Series	Register	Treasurer	VF-20	EF-40	AU-50	Unc-60
1215	1922	Speelman	White	$1,620	$3,750	$4,750	$8,100

★ Star replacement notes for this series are rare.

Notes in denominations of $500 and $1,000 were also issued in Series 1922. All are rare.

TREASURY OR COIN NOTES

ACT OF JULY 14, 1890

Under the above Act, Congress authorized the secretary of the Treasury to issue notes which would be payable in coin on demand. Although backed by deposits of silver bullion, redemption in either silver or gold was left to the discretion of the secretary of the Treasury.

Two series were issued, 1890 and 1891, in denominations from $1 to $1,000, the $50 note being issued only, in Series 1891. The issue is characterized as having the smallest number of signatures, seals and varieties in design of any other type of United States currency.

It is important to note that all serial numbers of both series were followed by a star. This star does not indicate a replacement note. It is merely a printing embellishment as on Series 1869 Legal Tender notes.

FACE DESIGNS, Series 1890–1891

- **$1** Edwin M. Stanton, secretary of War, 1862–1868, serving under Presidents Lincoln and Andrew Johnson.
- **$2** General James D. McPherson, killed in action, 1864.
- **$5** General George H. Thomas, Civil War hero.
- **$10** General Philip H. Sheridan, Civil War and later in Indian Wars.
- **$20** John Marshall, secretary of State under President John Adams, 1800–1801. Chief Justice of the Supreme Court for 30 years.
- **$50** 1891 only. William H. Seward, admitted to the bar in Utica, New York, in 1822. Secretary of State, 1860–1869. Negotiated purchase of Alaska from Russia, at the time called "Seward's Folly," for the sum of $7,200,000.
- **$100** David Glasgow Farragut, first admiral of the U.S. Navy.
- **$500** General Wm. T. Sherman. Designed for Series 1891 but probably never printed. There are no known specimens. A proof exists and is illustrated on page 146.
- **$1,000** General George Gordon Meade, active in the Seminole Indian War, the War with Mexico, and the Civil War.

The obligation to pay on the face of the notes, both series, reads very simply: "The United States will Pay to the Bearer on Demand . . . Dollars in Coin."

BACK DESIGNS, Series 1890–1891

The brilliant green lathe-work back design of the 1890 series is most attractive. It was changed to a more open design on the 1891 series due to the belief that the first design was more easily counterfeited by means of photography.

The inscription on both back designs reads: "This Note is Legal Tender at its Face Value in Payment of Debts Public and Private Except When Otherwise Expressly Stipulated in the Contract."

The large zeros in the back design of Series 1890 $100 note have caused it to be known as the "watermelon note." It ranks high in the rarity tables of United States currency.

Treasury Notes of all denominations are very scarce. This is especially true of Series 1890, with the brilliant green lathe-work back designs. The 1890 series was printed for less than two years, quickly being replaced by Series 1891, which also had a comparatively short life.

Series 1890 notes have large brown or small red seals; the seals on Series 1891 notes are small and red.

TREASURY OR COIN NOTES

ONE DOLLAR

Face Design. Series 1890 and 1891.

Back Design. Series 1890.

Friedberg No.	Series	Register	Treasurer	Seal at Right	F-12	VF-20	EF-40	AU-50	Unc-60
347	1890	Rosecrans	Huston	Large brown	$390	$750	$2,500	$3,250	$4,620
348	1890	Rosecrans	Nebeker	Large brown	520	1,090	2,000	3,120	6,250
349	1890	Rosecrans	Nebeker	Small red	390	620	1,810	2,880	3,750

TREASURY OR COIN NOTES

ONE DOLLAR

Back Design. Series 1891.

Friedberg No.	Series	Register	Treasurer	Seal at Right	F-12	VF-20	EF-40	AU-50	Unc-60
350	1891	Rosecrans	Nebeker	Small red	$210	$360	$585	$845	$1,020
351	1891	Tillman	Morgan	Small red	230	390	650	845	1,220
352	1891	Bruce	Roberts	Small red	195	360	650	845	1,090

TWO DOLLARS

Face Design. Series 1890 and 1891.

TREASURY OR COIN NOTES
TWO DOLLARS

Back Design. Series 1890.

Friedberg No.	Series	Register	Treasurer	Seal at Right	F-12	VF-20	EF-40	AU-50	Unc-60
353	1890	Rosecrans	Huston	Large brown	$960	$1,720	$6,250	$8,100	$16,800
354	1890	Rosecrans	Nebeker	Large brown	1,880	2,500	6,900	12,000	31,200
355	1890	Rosecrans	Nebeker	Small red	910	1,720	6,050	7,500	9,400

Back Designs. Series 1891.

Friedberg No.	Series	Register	Treasurer	Seal at Right	F-12	VF-20	EF-40	AU-50	Unc-60
356	1891	Rosecrans	Nebeker	Small red	$550	$950	$1,880	$2,380	$2,880
357	1891	Tillman	Morgan	Small red	550	910	1,880	2,250	3,000
358	1891	Bruce	Roberts	Small red	520	910	1,880	2,250	2,690

TREASURY OR COIN NOTES

FIVE DOLLARS

Face Design. Series 1890 and 1891.

Back Design. Series 1890.

Friedberg No.	Series	Register	Treasurer	Seal at Right	F-12	VF-20	EF-40	AU-50	Unc-60
359	1890	Rosecrans	Huston	Large brown	$520	$1,120	$3,940	$4,560	$5,100
360	1890	Rosecrans	Nebeker	Large brown	7,500	12,000	38,400	48,000	132,000
361	1890	Rosecrans	Nebeker	Small red	520	1,180	2,500	4,560	5,000

TREASURY OR COIN NOTES

FIVE DOLLARS

Back Design. Series 1891.

Friedberg No.	Series	Register	Treasurer	Seal at Right	F-12	VF-20	EF-40	AU-50	Unc-60
362	1891	Rosecrans	Nebeker	Small red	$520	$960	$1,620	$1,810	$2,620
363	1891	Tillman	Morgan	Small red	450	940	1,750	2,000	2,750
364	1891	Bruce	Roberts	Small red	450	940	1,250	1,500	2,560
365	1891	Lyons	Roberts	Small red	1,020	1,880	5,300	8,750	14,400

TEN DOLLARS

Face Design. Series 1890 and 1891.

TREASURY OR COIN NOTES

TEN DOLLARS

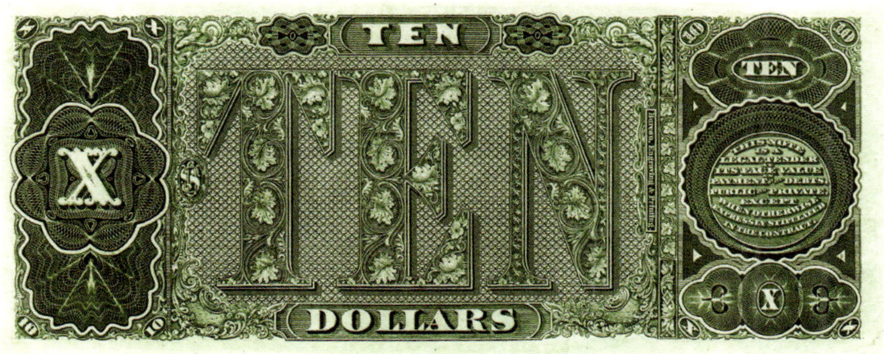

Back Design. Series 1890.

Friedberg No.	Series	Register	Treasurer	Seal at Right	F-12	VF-20	EF-40	AU-50	Unc-60
366	1890	Rosecrans	Huston	Large brown	$1,620	$1,880	$5,300	$7,500	$14,400
367	1890	Rosecrans	Nebeker	Large brown	1,620	2,810	3,750	7,500	14,400
368	1890	Rosecrans	Nebeker	Small red	975	1,690	3,560	3,750	4,940

Back Design. Series 1891.

Friedberg No.	Series	Register	Treasurer	Seal at Right	F-12	VF-20	EF-40	AU-50	Unc-60
369	1891	Rosecrans	Nebeker	Small red	$695	$1,150	$1,660	$1,940	$3,120
370	1891	Tillman	Morgan	Small red	695	1,120	1,940	2,310	3,120
371	1891	Bruce	Roberts	Small red	1,090	1,880	3,440	3,940	4,560

TREASURY OR COIN NOTES

TWENTY DOLLARS

Face Design. Series 1890 and 1891.

Back Design. Series 1890.

Friedberg No.	Series	Register	Treasurer	Seal at Right	F-12	VF-20	EF-40	AU-50	Unc-60
372	1890	Rosecrans	Huston	Large brown	$4,380	$7,100	$21,600	$31,200	$36,000
373	1890	Rosecrans	Nebeker	Large brown	8,750	24,000	42,000	—	—
374	1890	Rosecrans	Nebeker	Small red	3,000	5,300	9,400	12,250	19,200
Series 1891 with modified back design.									
375	1891	Tillman	Morgan	Small red	3,020	4,380	6,500	7,500	8,550
375a	1891	Bruce	Roberts	Small red	138,000	—	—	—	—

TREASURY OR COIN NOTES

FIFTY DOLLARS

Face Design. Series 1891.

Friedberg No.	Series	Register	Treasurer	Seal at Right	VG-8	F-12	VF-20	EF-40	AU-50
376	1891	Rosecrans	Nebeker	Small red	$30,000	$72,000	$132,000	$144,000	$162,000

Only one signature combination issued.

ONE HUNDRED DOLLARS

Face Design. Series 1890 and 1891.

TREASURY NOTES

ONE HUNDRED DOLLARS

Back Design. Series 1890. The "Watermelon Back."

Friedberg No.	Series	Register	Treasurer	Seal at Right	VG-8	F-12	VF-20	EF-40	AU-50
377	1890	Rosecrans	Huston	Large brown	$42,000	$84,000	$168,000	$234,000	$300,000
Series 1891 with modified back design.									
378	1891	Rosecrans	Nebeker	Small red	72,000	108,000	144,000	—	—

Records indicate 120,000 Series 1890 issued and only 16,000 Series 1891. Only one signature combination was issued in each series.

FIVE HUNDRED DOLLARS

It is believed that the above note was designed as a memorial to General William T. Sherman, who died in 1891. For some reason it was never issued. General Sherman is best known for his "march to the sea" in 1864 and for originating the saying "War is Hell," which is still in use.

TREASURY NOTES

ONE THOUSAND DOLLARS, SERIES 1890–1891

Friedberg No.	Series	Register	Treasurer	Seal at Right	
379a	1890	Rosecrans	Huston	Large brown	Extremely rare; an AU was the first note to sell in auction for over $1,000,000
379b	1890	Rosecrans	Nebeker	Small red	2 known
379c	1891	Rosecrans	Nebeker	Small red	Unique; reportedly sold privately for over $2,000,000
379d	1891	Tillman	Morgan	Small red	Unique

The above denomination may be considered non-collectible. Reportedly, fewer than 25 notes have not been redeemed.

DEMAND NOTES OF 1861

ISSUED UNDER ACTS OF CONGRESS, JULY 17 AND AUGUST 5, 1861

Denominations $5, $10, and $20 only. All bear the date of the first authorization and also the date of issue, August 10, 1861. These notes were not originally legal tender, but later were so specified and were the first notes authorized by Congress to circulate as money.

With the exception of early issues of Fractional Currency, this is the only issue of United States paper money that does not bear the Treasury seal. The names of the United States Treasurer and the Register of the Treasury were not engraved or printed on Demand Notes. Clerks in the Treasury Department signed the notes with the added notation "for the" Register and "for the" Treasurer. Subsequently the words "for the" were engraved on the plates. Notes with "for the" handwritten are quite rare.

The major portion of the face designs are the same as the Legal Tender notes of the $5, $10, and $20 denominations. See description under "United States Legal Tender Notes."

Notes were payable on demand by the Assistant Treasurer of the United States, at Boston, New York, Philadelphia, St. Louis, and Cincinnati. All bear the following obligation to pay: "The United States Promise to pay the Bearer . . . Dollars on Demand." In the border design on the face of the notes, is the inscription: "Receivable in Payment of all Public Dues."

The term "greenback" originated from the back design of the Demand Notes which have an all-over lathe work design in vivid green. The denomination is shown in large letters and numerals. There is no other legend.

All-over back designs were used on the three denominations.

DEMAND NOTES OF 1861

FIVE DOLLARS

Face Design. Type One shown, with "For the" handwritten.

No Treasury Seal. No signatures of Register and Treasurer. Type One has "for the" handwritten. On Type Two, "for the" is printed.

Friedberg No.	Payable at	Type		G-4	VG-8	F-12
1a	New York	Type One	Rare	$30,000	$42,000	$48,000
1	New York	Type Two		1,000	1,880	3,120
2a	Philadelphia	Type One	Not issued			
2	Philadelphia	Type Two		1,200	1,880	2,500
3a	Boston	Type One	Unique	—	—	—
3	Boston	Type Two		1,200	1,880	3,000
4a	Cincinnati	Type One	Unknown		—	—
4	Cincinnati	Type Two	5 known	—	12,000	16,800
5a	St. Louis	Type One	Unique		—	—
5	St. Louis	Type Two	9 known	—	10,000	14,400

TEN DOLLARS

Face Design. Type Two shown, with "For the" printed.

DEMAND NOTES OF 1861

TEN DOLLARS

Friedberg No.	Payable at	Type		G-4	VG-8	F-12
6a	New York	Type One	5 known		—	
6	New York	Type Two		$1,500	$3,750	$6,550
7a	Philadelphia	Type One	3 known		—	—
7	Philadelphia	Type Two		1,600	3,750	6,250
8a	Boston	Type One	2 known	—	—	
8	Boston	Type Two		1,800	3,750	7,500
9a	Cincinnati	Type One	Unique		—	—
9	Cincinnati	Type Two	7 known		—	26,400
10a	St. Louis	Type One	Unique		—	—
10	St. Louis	Type Two	4 known		60,000	—

TWENTY DOLLARS

Face Design. Type Two shown, with "For the" printed.

Friedberg No.	Payable at	Type		G-4	VG-8	F-12
11a	New York	Type One	Unique		—	—
11	New York	Type Two		$12,500	$36,000	$54,000
12a	Philadelphia	Type One	Unknown		—	—
12	Philadelphia	Type Two		13,000	36,000	54,000
13a	Boston	Type One	Unknown		—	—
13	Boston	Type Two		13,500	36,000	54,000
14a	Cincinnati	Type One	Unknown		—	—
14	Cincinnati	Type Two	Unique		—	—
15a	St. Louis	Type One	None reported			
15	St. Louis	Type Two	Unknown			

INTEREST-BEARING NOTES

As an emergency measure to alleviate the financial condition of the U.S. Treasury caused by the Civil War, Congress, by Acts of July 17, 1861, June 30, 1864, and March 3, 1865, authorized various issues of paper money which would bear interest and would also circulate as legal tender.

INTEREST-BEARING NOTES

THREE-YEAR 7 AND 3/10% INTEREST-BEARING NOTES
ACT OF CONGRESS, JULY 17, 1861

The first Interest Bearing Notes and now the rarest were the Three Year Notes first authorized by the above act. This issue paid the highest rate of interest, a very attractive 7-3/10 percent.

Only the higher denominations of $50 to $5,000 were issued in this series. Five coupons were attached to each note which could be presented for payment as the interest became due, with final interest payment upon redemption of the note itself. Due to this factor and the tight money situation, it is understandable that very few notes of this issue were preserved, with coupons or minus coupons, to be handed down to present-day collectors.

By Act of August 5, 1861, the Three-Year Notes were convertible into 20-year government bonds with interest at 6 percent, in units of $500 and $1,000.

SIGNATURES: CHITTENDEN-SPINNER OR COLBY-SPINNER

All Extremely Rare, Unique or Non-Collectible.

Friedberg No.	Denomination	Design	G-4
207	$50	American Eagle with Shield in center.	Unique
208	$100	General Winfield Scott.	
209	$500	George Washington.	2 known
210	$1,000	Salmon P. Chase.	Unknown
211	$5,000	Justice and Indian Maid with Shield and Eagle.	Unknown

ISSUED UNDER THE ACT OF JUNE 30, 1864

Friedberg No.	Denomination	Design	G-4
212	$50	Eagle with Shield.	7 known

Convertible into 6% Bonds at option of Bearer.

ISSUED UNDER ACT OF MARCH 3, 1865

Friedberg No.	Denomination	Design	G-4
212d	$50	Eagle with Shield.	8 known
212e	$100	General Winfield Scott.	3 known
212f	$500	Alexander Hamilton.	1 known
212g	$1,000	Justice Seated with Shield.	3 known

At left end on face of this issue was the inscription: "The Government reserves the right of paying in coin the interest on this note at the rate of 6% per annum."

Printed by American Bank Note Co., three notes to each sheet.

TWO-YEAR 5% INTEREST-BEARING NOTES
ACT OF CONGRESS, MARCH 3, 1863

The $500 note of this issue had three coupons attached which could be presented for 5% interest payment in six month periods. Interest on other denominations was payable upon redemption of the notes.

Friedberg No.	Denomination	Design	VG-8	F-12	VF-20
203	$50	Three female figures, Justice in center.		7 known	
204	$100	Vignettes representing Farming and Mechanics.		2 known	
205	$500	American Eagle and Liberty with flag and anchor.		Unknown	
206	$1,000	"DeSoto Discovering the Mississippi, 1541" and ships *Constitution* and *Guerriere*.	—	—	—

All of the above are extremely rare, unknown, or non-collectible.

INTEREST-BEARING NOTES

ONE-YEAR 5% INTEREST-BEARING NOTES
ACT OF CONGRESS, MARCH 3, 1863

The $10 and $20 denominations were added to this issue undoubtedly to attract investors with limited funds. The $5,000 denomination was also added and probably was not too popular. No coupons were attached to the One-Year Notes.

Friedberg No.	Denomination	Design	VG-8	F-12	VF-20
196a	$10	Eagle with Flag, center. Salmon P. Chase at left. Peace holding sheaf of wheat at right.	$3,250	$8,500	—
197a	$20	Mortar firing, center. Figure of Victory at left. Abraham Lincoln at right.	7,500	18,500	—
198	$50	Alexander Hamilton, right. Allegorical Loyalty at left.	Extremely Rare		
199	$100	George Washington, center. "The Guardian" at left. Justice with shield right.	3 known		
200	$500	Vignette "Standard Bearer" and the ship *New Ironsides*.	Unknown		
201	$1,000	Eagles and Shield, center. Justice, left. Liberty at right.	Unknown		
202	$5,000	"The Altar of Liberty" represented by vignette of female figure.	Unknown		

There are no recent records of any of this series being offered. The $10 note sold in the Grinnell sale, November 1944, for $65 and more recently at $500 to $1,000. Condition was stated to be Fine to Very Fine. The $20 note sold in same Grinnell sale for $145 Extra Fine, and later at $750 and up. The $50 denomination brought $125 in the Grinnell sale. It was described as "good, re-inforced."

6% COMPOUND INTEREST TREASURY NOTES
ISSUED UNDER ACTS OF MARCH 3, 1863, AND JUNE 30, 1864

SIGNATURES: CHITTENDEN-SPINNER OR COLBY-SPINNER

This issue, as with other Interest-Bearing issues, freely circulated as legal tender. Interest was compounded semi-annually and the accumulated interest for each six-month period was indicated in a table in the center of the green lathe-work design on the back of the note.

Denomination	Interest	Redemption Value
$10	1.94	11.94
$20	3.88	23.88
$50	9.70	59.70
$100	19.40	119.40
$500	97.03	597.03
$1,000	194.06	1,194.06

The Treasury seal was in red. The obligation to pay, with interest, appeared on the face of the note, which also bore in prominent gold letters the surcharge "Compound Interest Note." On some existing specimens the gold surcharge has eaten through the paper, possibly caused by oxidation.

With interest at 6 percent payable only upon redemption of the notes, very few escaped redemption. Interest-Bearing Notes of all issues are still redeemable at face value plus interest for the period stated on the note. Due to the present numismatic value, it is doubtful that many will be redeemed. Six percent Compound Interest notes were issued as follows:

Friedberg No.	Denomination	Design	VG-8	F-12	VF-20
190	$10	Salmon P. Chase, usually found Fair to Very Fine.	$2,380	$3,250	$10,000
191	$20	Abraham Lincoln, seldom found better than Fine.	—	—	36,000
192	$50	Alexander Hamilton, extremely rare, any condition. Two varieties exist, one with Chittenden-Spinner, the other Colby-Spinner.	108,000	—	—
193	$100	George Washington, extremely rare, any condition.	Rare	—	—
194	$500	*New Ironsides*, believed non-collectible.	—	—	—
195	$1,000	Liberty and Justice, believed non-collectible.	—	—	

INTEREST-BEARING NOTES

Face Design. Lincoln, as on One-Year Interest-Bearing Note.

4% REFUNDING CERTIFICATES
ACT OF CONGRESS, FEBRUARY 26, 1879

$10 denomination only. Signatures: G.W. Scofield and James Gilfillan.

Issued in the low denomination to attract investors with lower incomes. Two types were issued, both earning 4% interest and originally with no time limit set for redemption. By Act of Congress, April 1907, interest was discontinued as of July 1, 1907. On that date the total redemption value was $21.30 and remains at that figure.

Type One was payable to order with name of person to whom issued on the face of the note. The certifications read: "This certifies that (name) . . . has deposited with the Treasurer of the United States the sum of Ten Dollars under Act of Feb. 26th 1879." Space was provided for endorsement by the purchaser. This was printed in black, vertically across the back of the note, with lengthy inscription.

Type Two provided no name space and was payable to bearer. The certification was changed to read: "This certifies the sum of Ten Dollars has been deposited under Act of Feb. 26th, 1879."

The three-line inscription across the lower portion of the face of both types reads: "Convertible with accrued interest of 4% per annum into 4% bonds of the United States, issued under the Acts of July 14, 1870 and January 20, 1871, upon presentation properly endorsed, at the Office of the Treasurer of the U.S., Washington, D.C. in sums of $50 or multiples thereof." The words "properly endorsed" were eliminated on Type Two.

Type Two back design was in black and was printed horizontally as are most notes. The denomination "TEN" was prominent, and an explanatory table showed earned interest:

Interest on this note will accrue as follows:

For each 9 days, or 1/10 of a quarter . . . . 1 cent
For each quarter year . . . . 10 cents
For each entire year. . . . . 40 cents

INTEREST-BEARING NOTES

	VG-8	F-12	VF-20	AU-50
Type Two notes	$1,350	$2,250	$3,350	$7,500

Only two of the Type One notes are known.

ERRORS OR MISPRINTED NOTES

Probably no branch of manufacturing or printing has such rigid rules and inspection methods as the printing of United States paper money. When one considers the millions of notes coming off the presses at the Bureau of Engraving and Printing, it is understandable that misprints and errors do occur. The infrequency in which these misprints escape into circulation is a tribute to the efficiency of the "check and double check" system in the Bureau.

In the printing of U.S. large-size paper money, more operations were involved and perhaps imperfections were more readily detected by pressmen and inspectors. Possibly this is the explanation for comparatively few errors or misprinted notes being found in our large-size paper money. When found and offered for sale, the valuation is largely a matter between buyer and seller. A sufficient number do exist to make possible the acquisition of some interesting and possibly unique varieties.

THE "DOUBLE DENOMINATION" NOTE

The error most coveted and which is now valued well into four figures is the double denomination note, with the face of one denomination and the back of another.

Large-size National Bank Notes were printed customarily in sheets of three "tens" and a "twenty," or three "fifties" and one "one hundred." If a sheet of printed backs were turned end for end before printing the face, the $20 back would be imprinted with the $10 face and the $10 back would also become a double denomination with a $20 face design.

On this same sheet of four notes the second and third notes would have inverted faces. Notes so misprinted have been called "Inverted Backs," however, this is a misnomer as it is the face of the note which was actually inverted. Perhaps the term "Inverted Design" would be more appropriate.

When double denomination notes are found in series other than National Bank Notes, the error was probably caused by a sheet of one denomination with previously printed back being removed for inspection and then through error replaced in a rack of another denomination. To this writer's knowledge a complete uncut or cut sheet of large-size double denomination notes is unknown.

ERRORS OR MISPRINTED NOTES

Other misprints include notes with white streaks on face or back caused by a fold in the paper at time of printing. Also notes to which a piece of paper adhered during printing caused a blank white space and notes with seals and signatures well out of position was caused by improper alignment of the sheet before the addition of seals and signatures. Inverted seals and signatures were caused by a sheet being turned end for end before these imprints were added.

Double Denomination, National Bank Note, Third Charter Period, Type 2. Chicago.
$20 Face / $10 Back. The back is also inverted in relation to the front.

Double Denomination, National Bank Note, Second Charter Period, Type 1.
Middlebury, VT. $20 Face / $10 Back. The back is not inverted.

ERRORS OR MISPRINTED NOTES

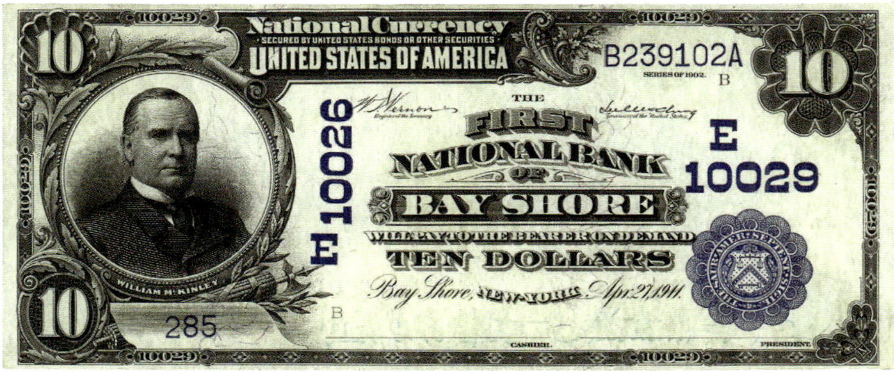

Misprint, National Bank Note, Third Charter Period, Type 2. Bay Shore, NY.
The Bank Charter numbers do not match.

Double Denomination, Federal Reserve Bank Note, Series 1918. Chicago.
$2 Face / $1 Back. The back is not inverted in relation to the front.

ERRORS OR MISPRINTED NOTES

Double Denomination, Federal Reserve Note, Series 1914. Boston.
$20 Face / $10 Back. The back is not inverted in relation to the front.

STAR NUMBERED NOTES

Star numbered notes were not substituted for misprinted or damaged notes prior to 1910. Defective notes of earlier issues were either replaced by notes of an entirely different sequence of numbers, which caused confusion in record keeping, or they were replaced by a specially-numbered note which duplicated the number of the spoiled note.

Starting around the beginning of this century entirely separate printings were made of star notes that utilize independent sets of serial numbers that are entirely different than those found on the regular production notes. A supply of these is provided to inspectors so that when they find misprints, they simply substitute star notes for the misprints in order to maintain total counts in the orders. There is no relationship between a number on a star note and the number on the note it replaced.

With each new issue a supply of star notes is serial numbered so that a reserve of star notes is available of each of the Federal Reserve districts. No attempt is made to match the Federal Reserve Districts on star notes with the notes being replaced. For instance, when inspecting Minneapolis production notes, the inspector may be inserting New York district star notes.

Inspectors randomly fan packs of 100 notes as they come out of the overprinting and cutting machinery but before they are packaged. If they spot an error, they discard the entire pack even though the rest of the notes are perfect, and replace the pack with a pack of star notes, because to replace individual notes would be time consuming. There may be circumstances where individual errors get replaced, but that appears to be atypical.

FRACTIONAL CURRENCY

United States Fractional Currency, by Matt Rothert

INTRODUCTION

The general public is usually surprised to know that we Americans used paper for such small amounts as three cents, five cents, and 10 cents, and that it is still redeemable at full face value today. In the 14 years of issue (1862–1876) about 369 million dollars of Fractional Currency was printed, yet very little exists today and the average person has never seen any of it. It is estimated that $1.8 million is now in existence.

Collectors like Fractional Currency because it is a short yet varied series. A denominational collection consists of only six notes. A type collection can be made with only 25 notes and a collection of about 140 notes and 50 Specimens would be practically complete. Fractional Currency has its error notes, too. In addition one can collect sheets, pairs, strips, blocks and a Fractional Currency Shield. This series also has many unusual varieties and was printed on many types of paper as part of the experimentation to discourage counterfeiting.

Fractional Currency is a most important and vital part of numismatics—a bridge between the all-metal "hard money" period before 1861 and the metal and paper money combination period after 1862. It is an interesting series to collect because it is the product of a period of our history full of important events—the years 1862 to 1876. It exemplifies the need for small change, the "Necessity" money born of the scarcity of hard money in these troubled times.

It is said that there are no large stocks of Fractional Currency. A letter from the Treasury Department in February 1962, disclosed that there is less than one half of one percent of the amount issued still outstanding. There are undoubtedly many "sleepers," many rare notes, in this series. The history and romance that could be connected with every single note should stir the spirit of the thoughtful collector. These notes are easy to keep in albums or individual holders, and when displayed they obtain the attention and invite the interest of non-collectors with that same indefinable intrigue that holds the admiration of the most advanced numismatist.

The author became interested in United States Fractional Currency many years ago and has made an extensive study of this subject. A small collection was obtained in one purchase from the relative of a man who had worked in the "Department" at the time it was printed. These uncirculated notes were the nucleus of an exciting search for others.

Matt Rothert, 1963

SPECIMEN NOTES

The term "Specimen" as used generally in this book refers to a note other than one issued for general circulation and may include "Proof," "Essay," and "Specimen" notes as well as experimental pieces. These should come only in new condition.

The Specimen notes listed in the catalog section consist specifically of separately printed fronts or backs with plain margins on all four sides. The backs are blank, or they may have the word "SPECIMEN" on them.

Some of the Specimen notes are on paper watermarked CSA. This paper, made in England for the Confederate States of America, was captured on a blockade runner by a Union ship. No single Specimen note is known with all three of these letters, though many have two.

Values shown in the catalog section are for wide margin notes. Those with close margins are worth less than the listed prices.

FRACTIONAL CURRENCY

Typical Specimen Note, Wide Margin.

Typical Back of a Specimen Note.

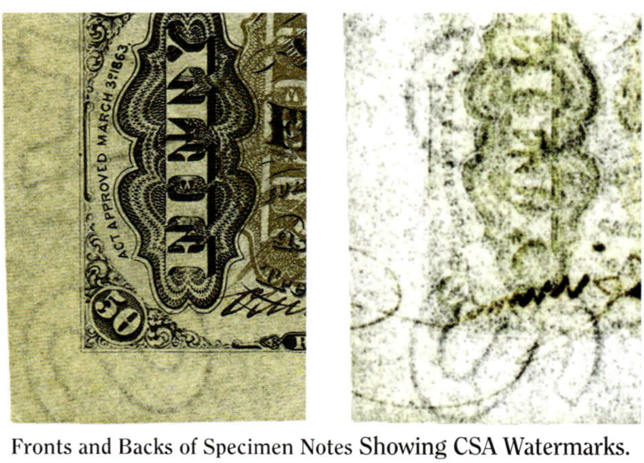

Fronts and Backs of Specimen Notes Showing CSA Watermarks.

FRACTIONAL CURRENCY

VALUATIONS

The valuations in this book are based on the realistic retail value of these notes as obtained from auction sales, from dealers, and from actual sales when and if the dealers have them in stock. Perfectly centered, bright new specimens are worth an extra premium, while closely cut edges and off-centered notes are worth slightly less. Many of these notes were destroyed by fire or simply worn out in the pockets of past generations. Thus, some of them may be "sleepers" and the prices shown may be low on those particular notes.

The notes that are known to be extremely rare are not priced because they come up for sale so seldom that their price is an individual matter between buyer and seller.

HISTORY

On the eve of the Civil War in 1861, trade and commerce seemed to be coming to a sudden stop, for almost overnight all the gold, silver, and copper money in the United States had disappeared.

The prospect of a long struggle between the North and South caused the hoarding of coins. Large amounts of silver coins were sent to Canada, and a premium of from 10 to 12 percent was offered by businessmen for them. It was reported that one building in New York had so many copper coins stored in it that the floors collapsed!

Even the heavy discounting of the "wild cat" notes and the state bank notes then in circulation failed to bring the coins out of their hiding places. Throughout the country it was a serious problem to make change. In fact, if a person had a five-dollar gold piece, he would probably have had to take change for a purchase in potatoes, corn, or some other commodity.

Merchants' "tickets," metal tokens, or anything having any apparent value were pressed into service to make change. Many firms and individual merchants issued their own notes of small value, generally less than one dollar, redeemable at their place of business. These were often called "shinplasters," a term said to have originated during the Revolutionary War when Continental Currency had become almost worthless. (These bills were supposedly used in the absence of bandages to protect minor cuts and bruises on the shins. The name came into early use in the United States for notes without legal security.)

Private notes were practically worthless to most people because they could be redeemed only by the firm or person that issued them. They were prohibited by law on July 17, 1862, but were nevertheless issued as the need arose through 1863.

5¢ Note of Newport, Rhode Island.

FRACTIONAL CURRENCY

Postage stamps were next turned to as a form of relief from the severe dearth of small coins. Some firms put various amounts of stamps in small envelopes and issued them as change. Henry Russell Drowne, an early collector of Fractional Currency, published an important article on these postage stamp envelopes in the *American Journal of Numismatics,* Volume LII, 1918, page 63. He records 90 separate issues of different designs with the names and addresses of 60 of the business firms, stationers, printers, etc. printed on these envelopes.

Photos of some of the envelopes are shown below:

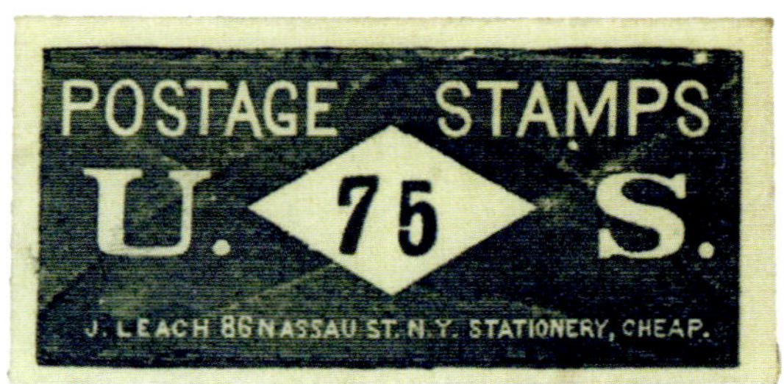

The stamps soon stuck to each other inside the envelopes and the envelopes themselves became torn, so this substitute for coins proved unsatisfactory.

Stamps were also enclosed in brass holders with mica fronts. This idea, patented by J. Gault in 1862, was used by firms as a convenient means of advertising. The name of the business or the product was embossed on the back of the holder. Their denominations were 1¢, 3¢, 5¢, 10¢, 12¢, 24¢, 30¢, and 90¢. Since this was a relatively expensive undertaking, plus the fact that the mica front was easily cracked, the encased postage stamps did not see very wide circulation.

Obverse and Reverse of Encased Postage Stamp.

FRACTIONAL CURRENCY

Typical Examples of Casings Used for Encased Postage Stamps.

Out of this confusion was born one of the most interesting types of paper money—United States Fractional Currency. These beautiful little bills, ranging in denominations from 3¢ to 50¢, played their part to help carry on commerce during and after the Civil War.

The first of the five issues was known as "Postage Currency," and was issued in 1862 and 1863. The next four issues, 1863 to 1876, were called "Fractional Currency." As the term Fractional Currency has been widely used to refer to all U.S. issues of less than one dollar, the author will continue its use for both Postage Currency and Fractional Currency.

FIRST GENERAL ISSUE—DENOMINATIONS: 5¢, 10¢, 25¢, 50¢

The country was really hard put to carry on even the simplest commercial activities by early 1862. On July 14 of that year, Treasury Secretary Salmon P. Chase finally got around to suggesting two alternative proposals to Congress. The first outlined a plan for the reduction in size of silver coins, and the second asked for the authority to issue and use ordinary postage stamps as circulating change. Incredibly enough, Chase himself favored the proposal that would legalize the circulation of small squares of gummed paper as a national medium of exchange!

Congress went ahead and adopted the postage stamp idea, and it actually became law when President Lincoln signed it on July 17, 1862. The immediate effect of the law was a run on stamps at the post offices, since they were needed everywhere and no way had been provided for the Treasury Department to acquire and release the stamps as money. The volume of stamp purchases was very greatly increased. In New York, for example, stamp sales jumped from a daily normal of $3,000 to over $20,000 soon after the new law was announced.

The supply of stamps was soon exhausted. Postmaster General Blair was understandably irritated, since he had not been consulted beforehand. He therefore refused to permit further sale of stamps to be used as money. The Treasury Department then called on Commissioner of Internal Revenue Boutwell to settle things with Blair. In short, Boutwell's suggestions were that specially marked stamps be made, that the Treasury sell and redeem them, that post offices accept them as postage, and that either party be free to withdraw from such an agreement. Blair accepted these proposals and went ahead with arrangements to print these special stamps for the Treasury.

Meanwhile, a great many stamps had been placed in circulation, and almost immediately they became unfit for further use either as a substitute for coin or as postage. Blair refused to allow their redemption at first. The Treasury was also unwilling to redeem them since it had never sold any stamps to the public in the first place. Blair then gave in, announcing that in the public interest he would redeem the crumpled, sticky messes that were held by so many people.

FRACTIONAL CURRENCY

FIRST GENERAL ISSUE—DENOMINATIONS: 5¢, 10¢, 25¢, 50¢

As previously noted, a special issue of ordinary stamps was agreed upon by Boutwell and Blair to be distributed by the Treasury. This was in accordance with the law of July 17. Just before their manufacture, it was happily decided to issue them in sizes more convenient to handle than the diminutive postage stamps, and the backs were to be left ungummed. Thus they ceased to be stamps altogether, for in this form they were no less than fractional federal promissory notes. They bore the authorization date of July 17, 1862, but this was not true. That law referred only to stamps and not to notes; therefore, these small notes were made and issued without any legal authorization whatsoever! (It was not until the law of March 3, 1863, which provided for the government to print fractional notes that the Postage Currency already in use was legally recognized and sanctioned.)

The original format for the Postage Currency was conceived by General F.E. Spinner, then U.S. Treasurer, who pasted unused U.S. postage stamps on bits of Treasury paper cut to uniform size for convenience in handling.

The purpose of Spinner's pasted stamps was primarily to develop the idea of what "Postage Currency" might actually look like. It is doubtful whether his pieces ever circulated. All known specimens are unique.

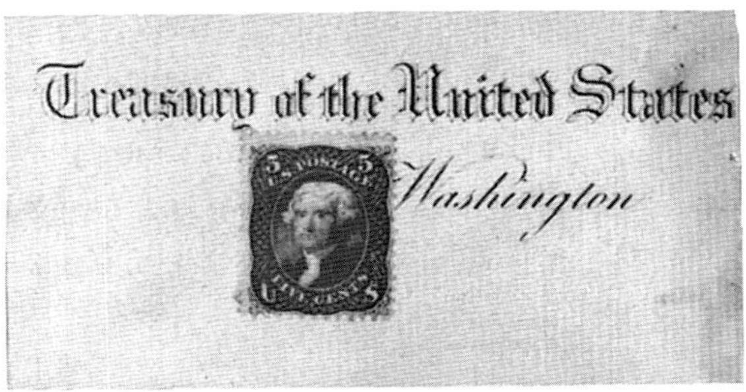

FRACTIONAL CURRENCY

FIRST GENERAL ISSUE—DENOMINATIONS: 5¢, 10¢, 25¢, 50¢

Stamps pasted on Treasury paper, made by General Spinner.
Photos Courtesy H.K. Crofoot Collection.

An article in the *Washington Star* of this period states:

> In 1862 small change became very scarce . . . It was more than a day's search to find a five-cent silver piece . . . General Spinner was then Treasurer of the United States. He was constantly appealed to from all quarters to do something to supply the demand for small change. In his dilemma he bethought him of the postage stamp. He sent down to the Post Office Department and purchased a quantity of stamps. He then ordered up a package of the paper upon which Government Securities were printed. He cut this into various sizes and on the pieces he pasted stamps to represent different amounts. He thus invented a substitute for fractional silver.

The *Savannah Republican,* Savannah, Georgia, March 27, 1863, contained this article:

> The Yankee Post Office Department is having postage stamps printed . . . on ungummed paper, to be used for general circulation as a substitute for specie.

It is interesting to observe that early trial designs carry the heading "Postage Stamps" at the top. This was changed on the actual notes to read "Postage Currency," another step farther from the original law which had called for stamps.

The following illustrations are the artist's models or designs, with corrections, from which the first plates were engraved. They were made "in the similitude" of General Spinner's original pasted bills, and are unique.

FRACTIONAL CURRENCY

FIRST GENERAL ISSUE—DENOMINATIONS: 5¢, 10¢, 25¢, 50¢

Artist's models labeled "Postage Stamps."
Photos Courtesy H.K. Crofoot Collection.

FRACTIONAL CURRENCY

FIRST GENERAL ISSUE—DENOMINATIONS: 5¢, 10¢, 25¢, 50¢

Artist's model labeled "Postage Stamps."

The fronts of the First Issue were designed under the direction of James MacDonough, a master in bank note designing who was then secretary of the National Bank Note Company at 1 Wall Street. The lettering was probably engraved by W.D. Nichols, who at an earlier period did similar work for Danforth, Perkins and Company.

The portraits were engraved by W. Marshall, one of the best in the business. The transfer rolls for the postage stamps of the 1861 issue were used to lay down the multiple values on the fronts of the Postage Currency. The lathe work was done by Cyrus Durand.

The backs were designed under the direction of James P. Major, head of the Designing and Engraving Department of the American Bank Note Company, then at 55 Wall Street. Mr. Major was assisted by Nathaniel Jocelyn, formerly of N. & S.S. Jocelyn, a firm which consolidated with the American Bank Note Company in 1858.

The lettering for the back of the five-cent note was engraved by J.E. Van Houten, American Bank Note Company, as shown by the records of Thomas F. Morris Sr.

The National Currency Bureau was a new department of the government when the First Issue appeared on August 21, 1862. The notes themselves were printed by two bank note companies. The American Bank Note Company printed the back side and the National Bank Note Company printed the front. (It is thought that when the National Bank Note Company printed both the front and the back, the monogram of the American Bank Note Company was removed from the back.) These two concerns were closely related, and contracts were given to both of them in this manner not to prevent the fraudulent issue of money but to prevent possible wrongdoing by individual employees. As notes were needed quickly and time was short, it was desirable that both companies work on this project at the same time. (The New York Bank Note Company, another firm, was busy printing the Demand Notes of 1861 and postage stamps for the government.)

D.W. Valentine in his book *Fractional Currency* states that Mrs. Whitman, daughter of Thomas Cunningham, neighbor of General F.E. Spinner, recalled conversations between her father and Spinner regarding objections raised against the perforated edges of the First Issue. This situation was soon rectified when the edges were made straight.

There are no signatures and no Treasury seals on the First Issue. A few sheets made for the government were stamped "Treasury Dept." on the upper right hand corner of the front.

FRACTIONAL CURRENCY

SECOND GENERAL ISSUE—DENOMINATIONS: 5¢, 10¢, 25¢, 50¢

The Second Issue was authorized by Congress on March 3, 1863, and the name was officially changed to "Fractional Currency." The many counterfeits that had so quickly appeared dictated changes in the design, size and paper.

The cost of producing the First Issue under the contracts with the bank note companies was excessive as compared with the plans for production of the Second Issue by the Treasury Department. Secretary Chase said the price paid for the postal currency to the companies was much greater than their actual cost of production. In his own language—"though bearing no interest, it was the dearest loan."

When the Second Issue was being considered, therefore, we find the following correspondence dated October 7, 1862, from S.M. Clark, then chief clerk of the Treasury Department Bureau of Construction to the Honorable S.P. Chase, secretary of the Treasury:

> Sir: I have the honor to report that I have matured the details for carrying out the Secretary's plan of supplying the place of the present Postage Currency, with a currency based on the issue of revenue stamps, as follows:
>
> Upon the Secretary's suggestion that the size of all denominations shall be the same as the present 10-cent Postage Currency, I respectfully recommend that —

A sheet of 5 cent stamps contain	50 or	$2.50
A sheet of 10 cent stamps contain	50 or	5.00
A sheet of 25 cent stamps contain	40 or	10.00
A sheet of 50 cent stamps contain	40 or	20.00

> and that the proposed issue of $100,000 per day be divided as follows:

8,000 sheets, 14 x 19 inches, of 5 cents	$20,000
4,000 sheets, 14 x 19 inches, of 10 cents	20,000
2,000 sheets, 14-1/2 x 16 inches, of 25 cents	20,000
2,000 sheets, 14-1/2 x 16 inches, of 50 cents	40,000
16,000	$100,000

> The obverse of all denominations I would print in black, and the reverse in four different colors; say 50's red, 25's purple, 10's green, and 5's tan color.
>
> To print 16,000 sheets per day, (if the obverse is of plate-printing, and the reverse of surface-printing, which I very decidedly recommend) there would be required —
>
> Thirty 22-inch copper-plate presses.
> Ten 18-inch copper-plate presses.
> Four Gordon presses for surface-printing, similar to those now in use for Bonds.
>
> To trim and separate 16,000 sheets per day, there would be required five trimmers and ten separators.
>
> The power presses, with the trimmers and separators, could be moved by the same power, and in the same room, now used for the small note machinery, without disturbing the present arrangements, except that the present work would require to be suspended for a few days, while the additional machinery was being put in place.
>
> The plate presses, which would be worked by hand, (and for which I do not think machinery can be substituted, as it requires the varied action of the brain as well as the hand at each printing,) could be placed in a portion of the new attic, designed for the west

wing, to and from which the paper could be elevated, and the printed sheets lowered, by a dumbwaiter, constructed in the southeast corner, on the extreme courtyard side.

The engraving of the bed-plates could all be done in the Department by three artists, and would take about 30 days. After the bed-plates were made, 84 plates would be required; these could be made by one transfer press, to be worked day and night, which would make one plate by day and one by night; taking 42 days in all; but in view of possible failures, I should think it safe to say it would take three months.

I have a design prepared for the Secretary's inspection, whenever he has the time to examine it.

The trimmers and separators, with the paper, etc., could all be prepared within the same period.

The cost of the whole, presses, cutters, separators, etc., with fixtures, I estimate, will be less than $20,000. The machinery I make about $16,000, and allow $4,000 for fixtures and contingencies. Making the paper would be in addition to this.

I respectfully suggest that the product be packed in neat paper boxes, in packages of $10, $20, and $50 each, which boxes, for transmission could be packed in hermetically sealed tin boxes, in such quantities as may be required, and then enclosed in wooden cases for transportation.

If these details meet the Secretary's approval, I respectfully recommend that Mr. Neale be placed in charge of the printing department, at a proper compensation, to be under my general direction, and that he be immediately detailed to go to Philadelphia and New York, etc., to secure the necessary plate presses and workmen. The press workmen would be hired "by the piece," probably at not over 75¢ to $1 per 100 sheets. (The Secretary can compare this price with the price paid for printing to the Bank Note Companies.)

I further respectfully recommend, as it is impossible for me to get away from Washington until the small-note room is more perfectly systematized, and operatives more experienced than now, that I be authorized to send for such parties to confer with as may be necessary, or to send parties to them if desirable.

I respectfully suggest to the Secretary, if these details are to be carried out, that he should give me some title—(not to carry any pay—but) to give more of an air of official authority, than a naked signature will carry.

If the Secretary approves this project, and endorses it, I will take immediate steps for its prosecution. How soon Mr. Rogers will get his new roof ready, so that the attic can be occupied, I can only conjecture; he will, doubtless, anticipate finishing it before it will be needed, but I have much fear that he will be disappointed.

I have the honor to be, very respectfully, your obedient servant,

S.M. Clark,
Chief Clerk, Bureau of Construction.

The Secretary adopted the report on the 10th of October, 1862, and approved the design.

By October 1, 1864, the Division had printed and finished 3,529,064 sheets of the Second Issue of Fractional Currency, amounting to $13,851,859, issued under act of March 3, 1863.

To give some idea of the amount of fiber paper notes of the Second Issue that was printed to October 1, 1864, S.M. Clark gives these figures:

FRACTIONAL CURRENCY

SECOND GENERAL ISSUE—DENOMINATIONS: 5¢, 10¢, 25¢, 50¢

Fractional Currency on Membrane Paper, printed dry:

5¢	$14,821.25
10¢	42,745.00
25¢	293,445.00
50¢	623,000.00
Total on membrane paper	$974,011.25

Printed on Regular Bank Note Paper:

	Printed Dry	Printed Wet
5¢	$8,125.00	$1,245,005.50
10¢	22,500.00	3,123,237.50
25¢	325,000.00	2,379,230.00
50¢	41,000.00	5,733,750.00
	$396,625.00	12,481,223.00
		396,625.00
Total on regular paper		$12,877,848.00

The cost of printing for the First Issue of Postage Currency by the bank note companies as compared with the Second Issue was noted in 1864 by Clark as follows: "The cost of the issues produced in the department has generally been about one-fourth the amount which the same issues would cost under the former contracts with the New York Bank Note Companies. The amount paid these companies for printing the United States notes, for 14,245,552 impressions, was $1,516,297.38. The cost of the same work, if done in the department, as ascertained and made record of on the 13th of November, 1863, would have been $413,899.93."

THIRD GENERAL ISSUE—DENOMINATIONS: 3¢, 5¢, 10¢, 25¢, 50¢

The Third General Issue of Fractional Currency came about through provisions of the law of June 30, 1864. S.M. Clark in his report stated that "To protect that portion of the public which will not protect itself by the exercise of ordinary diligence in scrutinizing paper money, the only course of my judgment when a counterfeit gets into the channels of circulation is therefore to make a new issue and withdraw the latter from circulation."

Valentine has this to say regarding the Third General Issue: "Counterfeits of the Second General Issue were more numerous than those of the First Issue and of much better workmanship; this and the increased demand for Fractional Currency necessitated the change of type and created two additional denominations, though one of these, the 15-cent denomination, was only made as an 'essay,' the other, the three-cent denomination, is the first and the only one of such denomination in all issues, and was only printed with the green back. It is the only variety of this issue that has no signature, though none has a seal. The need of this denomination was afterwards eliminated by an Act of Congress March 3, 1865, providing for the coinage of a three-cent coin of nickel."

An Act of Congress May 17, 1866, provided for the coinage of the five-cent nickel and prohibited the issue of any bill with a denomination of less than 10 cents.

Valentine and others cannot understand why notes with the likeness of a living person could be issued after the act of April 7, 1866 was passed. However, a careful reading of this act passed by the first session of the 39th Congress gives the answer. It states:

> Section 12. And be it further enacted, that the following sums be, and the same are hereby appropriated to supply deficiencies in the appropriations for the fiscal year ending the thirtieth of June, eighteen hundred and sixty-five, out of any money in the treasury not otherwise appropriated:

FRACTIONAL CURRENCY

THIRD GENERAL ISSUE—DENOMINATIONS: 3¢, 5¢, 10¢, 25¢, 50¢

> For plates, engraving, printing, and paper for national currency notes, two hundred and fifty thousand dollars: Provided, That no portrait or likeness of any living person hereafter engraved, shall be placed upon any of the bonds, securities, notes, Fractional or Postal Currency of the United States.

In other words, if the plates had already been prepared, then the notes could be issued.

The portrait of the controversial S.M. Clark was not eliminated by this act. (See page 183.) It was only upon the abolishment of the manufacture of all denominations under 10 cents that Clark's portrait was permanently removed from U.S. Currency.

All notes of the Third Issue were made by the Treasury Department.

FOURTH GENERAL ISSUE—DENOMINATIONS: 10¢, 15¢, 25¢, 50¢

There are further improvements in the Fourth General Issue. For the first time the Treasury seal appears on all varieties, bronze surcharges are left off, and the paper is more artistic.

The American Bank Note Company made plates for the fronts of the 10- and the "50-Cent Lincoln," and the plates for the backs of the 15-cent, 25-cent, and "50-Cent Stanton." The National Bank Note Company made the plates for the fronts of the 15- and 25-cent notes and the plates for the backs of the 10-cent note, the "50-Cent Lincoln," and the "50-Cent Dexter." The Bureau of Engraving and Printing made the plates for the fronts of the "50-Cent Stanton" and the "50-Cent Dexter." Mr. C. Burt engraved the portrait of Lincoln. The Columbia and the portrait of Washington were engraved by Douglas C. Romerson.

The bust of Liberty on the 10-cent note is said to be the portrait of a girl named Mary Hull, engraved by C. Burt.

FIFTH GENERAL ISSUE—DENOMINATIONS: 10¢, 25¢, 50¢

The fifth and last General Issue was the simplest. Appropriations to print more were about exhausted, and an Act of Congress of April 17, 1876, called for the issuance of fractional silver coins to redeem Fractional Currency.

The few varieties include the green seal 10 cents, and the "long key" and "short key" 10- and 25-cent notes.

All front plates were made at the Bureau of Engraving and Printing. Plates for the backs of the 10- and 25-cent notes were made by the Columbian Bank Note Company of Washington, D.C., and the back of the 50-cent note came from the firm of Joseph R. Carpenter of Philadelphia.

The retirement of Fractional Currency has been carried on since 1876. It is estimated that less than one-half of one percent of the total amount issued of all series is outstanding.

POSTAGE CURRENCY

FIRST ISSUE—AUGUST 21, 1862, TO MAY 27, 1863

Illegally issued under the Act of Congress of July 17, 1862, the notes were made by privately operated bank note companies while the new National Currency Bureau was getting organized. Both perforated and unperforated, or straight edge, notes were issued, the straight edge with monogram being the most common, although all are scarce. The monogram ABNCo stands for the American Bank Note Company. Notes of this issue without the monogram are believed to have been printed solely by the National Bank Note Company.

No signatures appear on notes of the First Issue.

POSTAGE CURRENCY

FIRST ISSUE – FIVE CENTS

Face, brown.

Back, black. ABNCo monogram.

This note comes in various shades of brown and tan on pale yellow, bright yellow, grayish-yellow, orange, and buff-colored paper. Collectors do not set different values on these shades, but the brightest, cleanest notes are most valuable. It was printed in sheets of 20 notes. These notes have been found with inverted backs, which are, of course, rare.

Friedberg No.	Description	F-12	VF-20	AU-50	Unc-60	Unc-63
1228	Perforated edges, with ABNCo on back	$34	$40	$88	$155	$275
1229	Perforated edges, without monogram on back	40	54	145	210	390
1230	Straight edges, with ABNCo on back	34	40	68	115	130
1231	Straight edges, without monogram on back	38	47	110	195	260

Specimen notes of 5 cents, face and back. White or buff paper.

POSTAGE CURRENCY

FIRST ISSUE – FIVE CENTS

Values are for narrow margin specimens	AU-50	Unc-60	Unc-63
Specimen of face	$50	$90	$125
Specimen of back	60	80	100

FIRST ISSUE – TEN CENTS

Face, green.

Back, black.

This denomination comes in various shades of green on shades of white and grayish-white paper. It was printed in sheets of 20 notes. Inverted backs are known and are very rare.

Friedberg No.	Description	F-12	VF-20	AU-50	Unc-60	Unc-63
1240	Perforated edges, with ABNCo on back	$34	$47	$110	$195	$285
1241	Perforated edges, without monogram on back	68	88	120	180	310
1242	Straight edges, with ABNCo on back	34	40	68	100	150
1243	Straight edges, without monogram on back	47	57	88	145	215

Specimen note of 10 cents, face.
White or gray paper.

POSTAGE CURRENCY

FIRST ISSUE – TEN CENTS

Specimen note of 10 cents, back.
White or gray paper.
Note the engraver's ruling marks.

Values are for narrow margin specimens	AU-50	Unc-60	Unc-63
Specimen of face	$60	$75	$110
Specimen of back	50	65	100

FIRST ISSUE – TWENTY-FIVE CENTS

Face, brown.

Back, black.

POSTAGE CURRENCY

FIRST ISSUE – TWENTY-FIVE CENTS

This note comes in various shades of brown and on various shades of paper similar to the five-cent denomination. It was printed in sheets of 16 notes. Inverted backs are known and are rare.

Friedberg No.	Description	F-12	VF-20	AU-50	Unc-60	Unc-63
1279	Perforated edges, with ABNCo on back	$34	$40	$130	$290	$325
1280	Perforated edges, without monogram on back	88	120	195	390	550
1281	Straight edges, with ABNCo on back	34	40	68	130	155
1282	Straight edges, without monogram on back	47	81	130	235	455

Specimen notes of 25 cents, face and back.
White or buff paper.

Values are for narrow margin specimens	AU-50	Unc-60	Unc-63
Specimen of face	$60	$100	$150
Specimen of back	50	80	110

POSTAGE CURRENCY
FIRST ISSUE – FIFTY CENTS

Face, green.

Back, black.

This denomination comes in various shades of green on white, cream, and grayish-white paper. It was printed in sheets of 16 notes. Inverted backs are rare.

Friedberg No.	Description	F-12	VF-20	AU-50	Unc-60	Unc-63
1310	Perforated edges, with ABNCo on back	$36	$43	$160	$260	$440
1311	Perforated edges, without monogram on back	81	94	285	390	780
1312	Straight edges, with ABNCo on back	34	51	120	195	240
1313	Straight edges, without monogram on back	81	145	325	520	960

POSTAGE CURRENCY

FIRST ISSUE – FIFTY CENTS

Specimen notes of 50 cents, face and back.
White or gray paper.

Values are for narrow margin specimens	AU-50	Unc-60	Unc-63
Specimen of face	$60	$100	$125
Specimen of back	50	80	100

FRACTIONAL CURRENCY

SECOND ISSUE—OCTOBER 10, 1863, TO FEBRUARY 23, 1867

The Act of March 3, 1863, authorized this issue of Fractional Currency and provided that the Treasury Department print its own notes. In line with the suggestion made by S.M. Clark, Superintendent of the National Currency Bureau, all notes of this issue have the same design, the head of Washington in a bronze oval frame, and each denomination has a different color on the back. This bronze overprint sometimes turns green with age, making the notes less valuable than bright ones. Various ideas were incorporated to discourage counterfeiting and to test different kinds of paper. This issue was printed in sheets of 20 notes. Inverted backs and inverted back surcharges are known, but are rare.

Some Specimen notes of the Second Issue are found on paper watermarked CSA.

There are no signatures on notes of the Second Issue.

FRACTIONAL CURRENCY

SECOND ISSUE – FIVE CENTS

Face, slate color with bronze oval frame.

Back, brown with bronze overprint.

The surcharges on the reverse place the figure 18 in the lower left corner, the figure 63 in the lower right corner, the letter in upper left corner, and the 1 in the upper right corner. Some back surcharges are blurred, and some even seem to be missing.

Friedberg No.	Description	F-12	VF-20	AU-50	Unc-60	Unc-63
1232	Without small surcharge on corners of back	$31	$32	$68	$100	$130
1233	With surcharge 18-63	34	38	68	130	150
1234	With surcharge S-18-63	34	40	74	130	180
1235	With surcharge R-1-18-63. Fiber paper	40	68	260	390	780

This note is found with surcharge "18" only or surcharge "63" only. A double-denomination note with 5¢ face and 50¢ back has been found.

Specimen notes of five cents, face and back. White or parchment paper.

FRACTIONAL CURRENCY

SECOND ISSUE – FIVE CENTS

Values are for narrow margin specimens	AU-50	Unc-60	Unc-63
Specimen of face	$60	$90	$125
Specimen of back	50	75	200

SECOND ISSUE – TEN CENTS

Face, slate color with bronze oval frame.

Back, green with bronze overprint.

Friedberg No.	Description	F-12	VF-20	AU-50	Unc-60	Unc-63
1244	Without small surcharge on corners of back	$27	$30	$65	$94	$120
1245	With surcharge 18-63	27	30	68	120	150
1246	With surcharge S-18-63	27	30	65	100	155
1247	With surcharge 1-18-63. Rare. Only one or two sheets issued.	47	54	88	155	390

Back, with surcharge 0-63

Friedberg No.	Description	F-12	VF-20	AU-50	Unc-60	Unc-63
1248	With surcharge 0 in upper left, 63 in upper right	$520	$960	$1,750	$3,000	$4,310
1249	With surcharge T-1-18-63. Fiber paper	74	88	195	390	585

This denomination is known with surcharge "18" only and "63" only. It is also found surcharged 63-63, with individual surcharge figures and letters inverted and with the back printing inverted. These are classed as misprints and not priced, as they are rare and appear so seldom that the price is determined on an individual basis.

FRACTIONAL CURRENCY
SECOND ISSUE – TEN CENTS

Specimen notes of 10 cents, face and back. White or cream paper.

Values are for narrow margin specimens	AU-50	Unc-60	Unc-63
Specimen of face	$40	$80	$110
Specimen of back	35	75	100

A few of these Specimens are printed on fiber paper.

SECOND ISSUE – TWENTY-FIVE CENTS

Face, slate color with bronze oval frame.

Back, purple with bronze overprint. A few are found with a steel-colored back.

FRACTIONAL CURRENCY

SECOND ISSUE – TWENTY-FIVE CENTS

Friedberg No.	Description	F-12	VF-20	AU-50	Unc-60	Unc-63
1283	Without small surcharge on corners of back	$27	$28	$68	$110	$145
1284	With surcharge 18-63	27	28	61	130	180
1285	With surcharge A-18-63	27	28	61	180	260
1286	With surcharge S-18-63	27	28	61	110	145
1288	With surcharge 2-18-63	27	28	88	130	260
1289	With surcharge T-1-18-63. Fiber paper	60	80	210	290	650
1290	With surcharge T-2-18-63. Fiber paper	60	80	230	345	680

This issue is also found surcharged 1-S-63, "18" only, and "63" only. These are rare and are not considered regular issues. S-18-63 comes with inverted "S" only, the balance of the surcharge not being inverted.

Specimen notes of 25 cents. White or cream paper.

Values are for narrow margin specimens	AU-50	Unc-60	Unc-63
Specimen of face	$45	$70	$100
Specimen of back	40	60	80

FRACTIONAL CURRENCY
SECOND ISSUE – FIFTY CENTS

Face, slate color with bronze oval frame.

Back, red with bronze overprint. Some are reddish-orange.

Friedberg No.	Description	F-12	VF-20	AU-50	Unc-60	Unc-63
1314	Without small surcharge on corners of back. Beware of forgeries or notes with the surcharge removed. Here is one case where the Specimen note is not as valuable as the regular note.			Unconfirmed		
1316	With surcharge 18-63. (Also comes with 18 only or 63 only)	$34	$45	$94	$155	$230
1317	With surcharge A-18-63	34	45	110	160	230
1318	With surcharge 1-18-63	34	45	94	145	230

Back, with surcharge R-2-18-63.

Back, with surcharge T-1-18-63.

Friedberg No.	Description	F-12	VF-20	AU-50	Unc-60	Unc-63
1320	With surcharge O-1-18-63. Fiber paper	$34	$54	$145	$325	$390
1321	With surcharge R-2-18-63. Fiber paper	61	88	290	620	910
1322	With surcharge T-1-18-63. Fiber paper	34	47	145	310	390
	Also known with T-18-63 (no 1). Fiber paper			Rare		

FRACTIONAL CURRENCY
SECOND ISSUE – FIFTY CENTS

Specimen notes of 50 cents, face and back. White or cream paper.

Values are for narrow margin specimens	AU-50	Unc-60	Unc-63
Specimen of face	$45	$70	$100
Specimen of back (no surcharge)	40	60	90

FRACTIONAL CURRENCY

THIRD ISSUE—DECEMBER 5, 1864, TO AUGUST 16, 1869

The Third Issue includes the first three-cent note. The designs of this issue are different for each denomination. They are more intricate than the first two issues. The five-cent notes and higher denominations have the signatures of the Register and the Treasurer, and also have sheet position check letters and numbers. Those with green backs have printed signatures but the red back notes of 10, 15 and 50 cents have both printed and autographed signatures. This is one of the rare instances of autographed signatures appearing on United States regular issue notes.

Though the larger U.S. notes carried some form of signature from their inception in 1861, it was not until the Third Issue of Fractional Currency that signatures were placed on the smaller notes. All denominations except the three-cent note carry either printed or autographed signatures, as indicated in the listings for each type and denomination. The names of the officials whose signatures appear on the notes are S.B. Colby, N.L. Jeffries, or John Allison as Register, and F.E. Spinner or John C. New as Treasurer.

Some of the Specimens of this series are on paper watermarked CSA.

THIRD ISSUE – THREE CENTS

Face, light background.

Back, green.

These were printed in sheets of 25 notes. These notes are made on thick or thin paper and are occasionally found with inverted backs.

Friedberg No.	Description	F-12	VF-20	AU-50	Unc-60	Unc-63
1226	With light background to Washington's portrait	$54	$61	$81	$130	$160
1227	With dark background to Washington's portrait	61	74	94	115	245

FRACTIONAL CURRENCY

THIRD ISSUE – THREE CENTS

Specimen notes of 3 cents, face and back. White or cream paper.

Values are for narrow margin specimens	AU-50	Unc-60	Unc-63
Specimen of face with dark background	$60	$150	$200
Specimen of face with light background	—	—	—
Specimen of back	50	100	125

THIRD ISSUE – FIVE CENTS

Face, black.

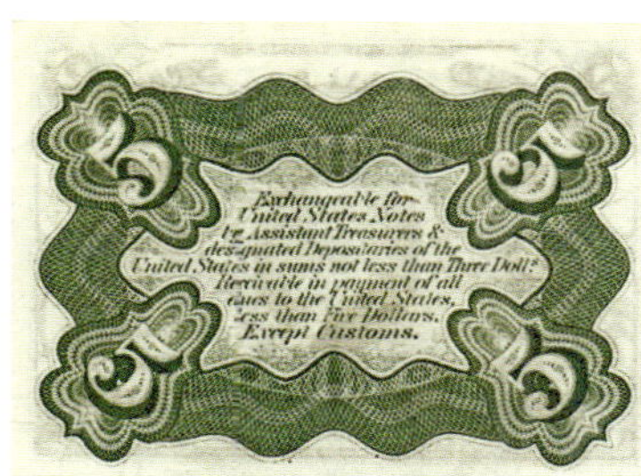

Back, red or green.

FRACTIONAL CURRENCY

THIRD ISSUE – FIVE CENTS

Five-cent notes were printed in sheets of 20. Spencer M. Clark (1810–1890) was superintendent of the National Currency Bureau and had his likeness put on this note without authority from his superiors. This action caused a law to be passed forbidding the unauthorized portrait of a living person to appear on United States currency. (See History, pages 168 and 169.)

Friedberg No.	Description	F-12	VF-20	AU-50	Unc-60	Unc-63
1236	With red back	$31	$34	$115	$175	$215
1237	Same, with position letter "a" on face	31	34	110	180	360
1238	With green back	31	32	68	130	170
1239	Same, with position letter "a" on face	31	32	59	115	160

a				
a				
a				
a				

Location of position letter "a."

The letter "a" is not always the same size, nor in exactly the same position.

FRACTIONAL CURRENCY

THIRD ISSUE – FIVE CENTS

Specimen note of 5 cents, face. White or cream paper.

Values are for narrow margin specimens	AU-50	Unc-60	Unc-63
Specimen of face	$50	$90	$100
Specimen of red back	50	80	110
Specimen of green back	40	75	90

THIRD ISSUE – TEN CENTS

Face, black with bronze overprint.

Back, red or green with bronze overprint.

FRACTIONAL CURRENCY

THIRD ISSUE – TEN CENTS

These were printed in sheets of 16. Through an inexcusable error, the word "CENTS" does not appear anywhere on this note. The numeral 1 comes in both large and small size, and its position varies slightly.

Friedberg No.	Description	F-12	VF-20	AU-50	Unc-60	Unc-63
1251	Red back with printed signatures	$27	$32	$68	$145	$190
1252	Same, with position numeral "1" on face	27	32	68	155	260
1253	Red back with autographed signatures "Colby" and "Spinner"	47	68	110	215	230
1254	Same, with autographed signatures "Jeffries" and "Spinner"	88	100	195	285	390
1255	Green back with printed signatures	27	30	68	110	130
1256	Same, with position numeral "1" on face	27	30	68	110	130

Location of position numeral "1."

The numeral "1" comes in both large and small sizes, and its position varies slightly.

FRACTIONAL CURRENCY

THIRD ISSUE – TEN CENTS

Specimen notes of 10 cents, face and back.

Values are for narrow margin specimens	AU-50	Unc-60	Unc-63
Specimen of face with printed signatures "Colby" and "Spinner"	$80	$100	$125
Specimen of face with autographed signatures "Colby" and "Spinner"	100	120	150
Same, with autographed signatures "Jeffries" and "Spinner"	150	250	280
Specimen of red back	70	120	150
Specimen of green back	70	95	110

THIRD ISSUE – FIFTEEN CENTS

Face, black, wide margin.

FRACTIONAL CURRENCY
THIRD ISSUE – FIFTEEN CENTS

Back, red or green, wide margin.

This denomination was made only in uniface Specimens and was not placed in actual circulation. As previously mentioned under the five-cent note of this issue, a law was passed making it illegal to place the likeness of a living person on currency before this note had been produced in quantity for circulation, and while Grant and Sherman were alive. The notes produced with wide margins are the first Specimens or essays. Those with narrow margins were printed or cut for the Fractional Currency Shields which were being assembled at this same time. They were probably cut from the wide margin notes. (See Fractional Shields, page 208.) Many of the wide margin Specimens show engraver's ruling marks. Prices are for the narrow margin notes. Wide margin notes are considerably more valuable.

Values are for narrow margin specimens	AU-50	Unc-60	Unc-63
Specimen of face with autographed signatures "Colby" and "Spinner"	$1,500	$2,750	$4,000
Same, with autographed signatures "Jeffries" and "Spinner"	350	450	500
Same, with autographed signatures "Allison" and "Spinner"	375	500	550

Face, narrow margins, printed signatures.

Values are for narrow margin specimens	AU-50	Unc-60	Unc-63
Same, without any signatures	Rare	—	—
Specimen of red back	$70	$100	$140
Specimen of face with printed signatures "Colby" and "Spinner"	250	350	500
Specimen of green back	70	95	125

The Allison signature is found as "Allison" or "Alleson." Jeffries is written "Jeffus" or "Jeffries."

FRACTIONAL CURRENCY
THIRD ISSUE – TWENTY-FIVE CENTS

Face, black with open bronze overprint.

William Pitt Fessenden (1806–1869) was secretary of the Treasury in 1864–1865. He was a United States senator from Maine.

Back, red or green with bronze overprint.

These were printed in sheets of 12 notes.

Friedberg No.	Description	F-12	VF-20	AU-50	Unc-60	Unc-63
1291	Red back with printed signatures	$27	$30	$100	$195	$260
1292	Same, with position letter "a" on face	27	30	100	195	260
1294	Green back with printed signatures	27	36	81	115	170
1295	Same, with position letter "a" on face	27	36	81	145	195
1297	Green back with surcharge M-2-6-5. Fiber paper	32	61	130	290	420
1298	Same, with position letter "a" on face	32	61	180	360	495

Face, black with filled bronze overprint and position letter "a."

Friedberg No.	Description	F-12	VF-20	AU-50	Unc-60	Unc-63
1299	Same as above, the two ornamental designs on the face surcharged in heavy solid bronze instead of outlined. Fiber paper	$260	$455	$715	$1,880	$4,000
1300	Same as above, with position letter "a" on face	910	1,500	4,380	6,900	—

FRACTIONAL CURRENCY

THIRD ISSUE – TWENTY-FIVE CENTS

a		
a		
a		
a		

Location of position letter "a" on face.

The letter "a" comes in both large and small sizes.

FRACTIONAL CURRENCY

THIRD ISSUE – TWENTY-FIVE CENTS

Specimen notes of 25 cents, face and back.

Values are for narrow margin specimens	AU-50	Unc-60	Unc-63
Specimen of face	$80	$150	$250
Specimen of red back	70	125	150
Specimen of green back	70	90	120

THIRD ISSUE – FIFTY CENTS, TYPE 1

Face, black with bronze overprint. Justice Seated.

FRACTIONAL CURRENCY
THIRD ISSUE – FIFTY CENTS, TYPE 1

Back, red or green with bronze overprint.

These were printed in sheets of 12 notes.

Friedberg No.	Description	F-12	VF-20	AU-50	Unc-60	Unc-63
1343	Red back with printed signatures and no surcharge	$70	$88	$195	$290	$405
1344	Same, with position figures "1" and "a" on face	180	910	1,250	1,750	2,250
1345	Same, with position figure "1" only	70	88	230	370	520
1346	Same, with position letter "a" only	70	88	195	390	650
1347	Red back, printed signatures, with surcharge A-2-6-5 on back. Plain paper. These surcharge letters come in two slightly different sizes	70	88	195	290	420
1348	Same, with position figures "1" and "a" on face. Plain paper	390	780	1,020	2,500	4,250
1349	Same, with position figure "1" only. Plain paper	70	88	195	325	650
1350	Same, with position letter "a" only. Plain paper	70	88	240	520	940
1351	Red back, printed signatures with surcharge S-2-6-4 on back. Fiber paper. 13 known	2,500	7,500	13,000	17,500	—
1352	Same, with position figures "1" and "a" on face. Fiber paper	36,000	—	120,000	—	—
1353	Same, with position figure "1" only. Fiber paper	4,000	10,000	16,000	19,000	—
1354	Same, with position letter "a" only. Fiber paper	4,200	13,000	17,000	20,000	—
1355	Red back without surcharge or position figures, with autographed signatures of "Colby" and "Spinner"	68	74	195	285	390
1356	Red back with surcharge A-2-6-5, with autographed signatures of "Colby" and "Spinner." Plain paper	68	74	325	390	455
1357	Red back with surcharge S-2-6-4, with autographed signatures of "Colby" and "Spinner." Fiber paper	180	310	650	1,280	1,880
1358	Green back (all green back notes have printed signatures). No surcharge or position figures	61	94	180	260	370

FRACTIONAL CURRENCY

THIRD ISSUE – FIFTY CENTS, TYPE 1

Friedberg No.	Description	F-12	VF-20	AU-50	Unc-60	Unc-63
1359	Same, with position figures "1" and "a" on face	$420	$620	$1,020	$2,120	$2,500
1360	Same, with position figure "1" only on face	60	94	180	285	420
1361	Same, with position letter "a" only on face	60	94	180	325	490
1362	Green back with surcharge A-2-6-5 on back, compactly spaced	60	94	180	290	455

Back, with surcharge A-2-6-5 compactly spaced.

Friedberg No.	Description	F-12	VF-20	AU-50	Unc-60	Unc-63
1363	Same, with position figures "1" and "a" on face	$60	$94	$180	$260	$325
1364	Same, with position figure "1" only on face	60	94	180	285	365
1365	Same, with position letter "a" only on face	60	94	195	370	520

Back, with surcharge A-2-6-5 widely spaced.

Friedberg No.	Description	F-12	VF-20	AU-50	Unc-60	Unc-63
1366	Green reverse with surcharge A-2-6-5 on back, widely spaced	$80	$115	$235	$325	$520
1367	Same, with position figures "1" and "a" on face	780	1,250	5,000	6,250	7,500
1368	Same, with position figure "1" only on face	61	94	290	550	845
1369	Same, with position letter "a" only on face	60	94	360	1,250	1,750

FRACTIONAL CURRENCY

THIRD ISSUE – FIFTY CENTS, TYPE 1

Back, with surcharge S-2-6-4.

Friedberg No.	Description	F-12	VF-20	AU-50	Unc-60	Unc-63
1370	Green back with surcharge A-2-6-5. Fiber paper	$70	$100	$260	$650	$715
1371	Same, with position figures "1" and "a" on face. Fiber paper	520	780	2,250	3,000	5,000
1372	Same, with position figure "1" only. Fiber paper	70	100	290	1,150	1,310
1373	Same, with position letter "a" only. Fiber paper	70	100	455	910	1,020
1373a	Green back with surcharge S-2-6-4. Fiber paper. Extremely Rare	9,000	20,000	30,000	—	—

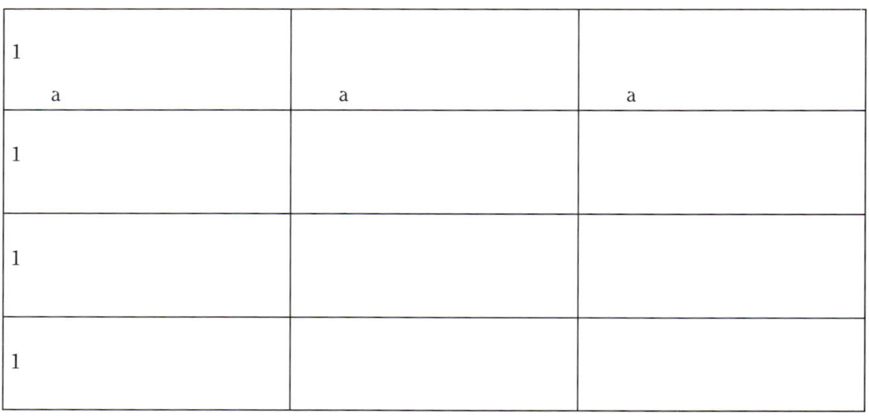

Location of position figures "1" and "a."

FRACTIONAL CURRENCY

THIRD ISSUE – FIFTY CENTS, TYPE 1

The "1" and "a" come large and small; their position may vary slightly.

Specimen note of 50 cents, face, Type 1.

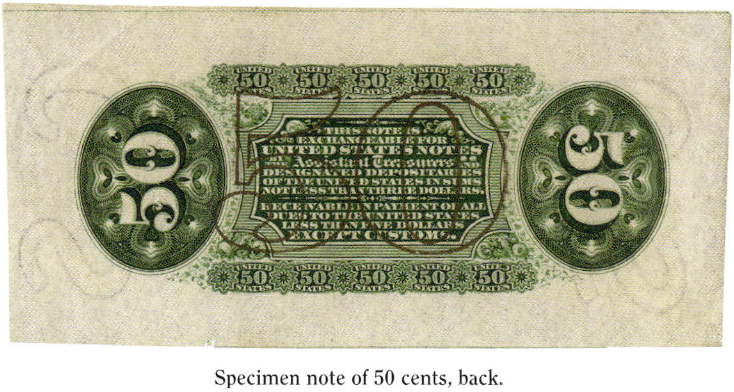

Specimen note of 50 cents, back.

FRACTIONAL CURRENCY

THIRD ISSUE – FIFTY CENTS, TYPE 1

Values are for narrow margin specimens	AU-50	Unc-60	Unc-63
Specimen of face with autographed signatures of "Colby" and "Spinner"	$160	$175	$200
Same, with autographed signatures "Jeffries" and "Spinner"	250	500	850
Specimen of red back	100	125	170
Specimen of face with printed signatures	60	105	150
Specimen of green back	60	105	150

THIRD ISSUE – FIFTY CENTS, TYPE 2

Face, black, with bronze overprint. General F.E. Spinner.

General F.E. Spinner (1802–1890), the "father of Fractional Currency," is portrayed on this note. He was treasurer of the United States from 1861 to 1875. (See History, pages 168 and 169.)

Back, red or green with bronze overprint.

These were printed in sheets of 12 notes. The location of position figures and letters is the same as the previous note. Some of the autographed notes come with only one signature.

FRACTIONAL CURRENCY

THIRD ISSUE – FIFTY CENTS, TYPE 2

Friedberg No.	Description	F-12	VF-20	AU-50	Unc-60	Unc-63
1324	Red back with printed signatures and with surcharge A-2-6-5 on back	$65	$77	$145	$240	$325
1325	Same, with position figures "1" and "a" on face	80	145	340	650	780
1326	Same, with position figure "1" only on face	65	77	145	255	325
1327	Same, with position letter "a" only on face	65	77	145	230	325
1328	Red back with surcharge A-2-6-5, with autographed signatures of "Colby" and "Spinner." This note is also found with one signature	60	74	155	260	310

Face, black, with bronze overprint. General F.E. Spinner.
Signatures of Allison and Spinner. Rare.

Friedberg No.	Description	F-12	VF-20	AU-50	Unc-60	Unc-63
1329	Red back with surcharge A-2-6-5, with autographed signatures of "Allison" and "Spinner"	$60	$74	$155	$360	$455

FRACTIONAL CURRENCY
THIRD ISSUE – FIFTY CENTS, TYPE 2

Face, black. General F.E. Spinner.
Signatures of Allison and New.

Friedberg No.	Description	F-12	VF-20	AU-50	Unc-60	Unc-63
1330	Red back with surcharge A-2-6-5, with autographed signatures of "Allison" and "New." This is another rare note; only about 20 are known, possibly only 24 issued	—	$1,880	$2,750	$4,120	$4,810
1331	Green back without surcharge or position figures	$59	81	155	235	260
1332	Same, with position figures "1" and "a" on face	59	88	175	285	365
1333	Same, with position figure "1" only	59	81	130	215	290
1334	Same, with position letter "a" only	59	81	130	195	290
1335	Green back with surcharge A-2-6-5 on back	59	81	130	260	325
1336	Same, with position figures "1" and "a" on face	160	260	1,150	2,190	2,500
1337	Same, with position figure "1" only	100	160	325	455	585
1338	Same, with position letter "a" only	68	100	455	1,220	1,560

FRACTIONAL CURRENCY

THIRD ISSUE – FIFTY CENTS, TYPE 2

Specimen notes of 50 cents, face and back.

Values are for narrow margin specimens	AU-50	Unc-60	Unc-63
Specimen of face with autographed signatures of "Colby" and "Spinner"	$150	$200	$300
Same, with autographed signatures of "Jeffries" and "Spinner"	4,250	7,800	10,000
Specimen of red back	60	100	125
Specimen of face with printed signatures	80	150	175
Specimen of green back	50	90	115

THIRD ISSUE – FIFTY CENTS, TYPE 3

Face, black with bronze overprint.

FRACTIONAL CURRENCY

THIRD ISSUE – FIFTY CENTS, TYPE 3

Back, green with bronze overprint.

These were printed in sheets of 12 notes. The notes are found on regular paper or heavier cream paper.

Friedberg No.	Description	F-12	VF-20	AU-50	Unc-60	Unc-63
1339	Green back without surcharge or position figures	$70	$81	$130	$260	$360
1340	Same, with position figures "1" and "a" on face	70	81	130	290	585
1341	Same, with position figure "1" only	70	81	130	235	360
1342	Same, with position letter "a" only	70	81	130	260	360

Values are for narrow margin specimens	AU-50	Unc-60	Unc-63
Specimen of face with printed signatures	$120	$200	$250
Specimen of green back	60	150	200

FOURTH ISSUE—JULY 14, 1869, TO FEBRUARY 16, 1875

Each of the notes of this issue is of a different design. The United States Treasury seal was added to the faces for the first time. A new, improved type of bank note paper containing silk fibers was used. All backs and most faces of these notes were printed by the American Bank Note Company and the National Bank Note Company, both of New York.

Some notes were issued without the seal, through error. No Specimen notes of the Fourth Issue were printed.

All notes of this issue carry printed signatures of John Allison, Register, and F.E. Spinner, Treasurer. Some notes of the Fourth and Fifth Issues come with a bright pink color over the entire face. These are worth a premium.

FOURTH ISSUE – TEN CENTS

Face, black.

FRACTIONAL CURRENCY

FOURTH ISSUE – TEN CENTS

Back, green.

These were printed in sheets of 16 notes. The face design shows a bust of Liberty. "Allison" is spelled with an "i," an "e" with a dot over it or with a closed "e."

Friedberg No.	Description	F-12	VF-20	AU-50	Unc-60	Unc-63
1257	Large red seal (40 millimeters), watermarked	$27	$32	$54	$81	$115
1258	Same large seal, paper with pink silk fibers	27	32	68	110	155
1259	Same large seal, paper with violet fibers and blue ends	27	32	61	130	155
1261	Smaller red seal (38 millimeters), paper with violet fibers and blue ends	27	32	54	120	155

The lines making up the design of the large seal are finer and closer together than those of the small seal, especially noticeable in the border of the shield inside the seal. The color of these seals varies from red to pink. Some have an orange tinge.

FOURTH ISSUE – FIFTEEN CENTS

Face, black. Bust of Columbia.

Back, green.

FRACTIONAL CURRENCY

FOURTH ISSUE – FIFTEEN CENTS

These were printed in sheets of 12 notes. Allison spelled as before.

Friedberg No.	Description	F-12	VF-20	AU-50	Unc-60	Unc-63
1267	Large red seal (40 millimeters), watermarked	$85	$90	$120	$135	$195
1268	Same large seal, paper with pink fibers	230	325	1,150	1,500	1,880
1269	Same, paper with violet fibers and blue ends	85	88	130	160	190
1271	Smaller red seal (38 millimeters), paper with violet fibers and blue ends	80	88	130	150	170

On a few notes Columbia seems to have a hairpin in her hair under the third star.

FOURTH ISSUE – TWENTY-FIVE CENTS

Face, black. Bust of Washington.

Back, green.

These were printed in sheets of 12 notes.

Friedberg No.	Description	F-12	VF-20	AU-50	Unc-60	Unc-63
1301	Large red seal (40 millimeters), watermarked	$27	$38	$100	$150	$210
1302	Same seal, paper with pink fibers	27	38	100	155	195
1303	Same seal, paper with violet fibers and blue ends	27	38	100	210	260
1307	Smaller red seal (38 millimeters), paper with violet fibers and blue ends	27	38	110	160	215

FRACTIONAL CURRENCY

FOURTH ISSUE – FIFTY CENTS, TYPE 1

Face, black. Bust of Lincoln.

Back, green.

These were printed in sheets of 12 notes.

Friedberg No.	Description	F-12	VF-20	AU-50	Unc-60	Unc-63
1374	Large red seal (40 millimeters), watermarked paper with pink fibers	$120	$160	$365	$545	$680

FOURTH ISSUE – FIFTY CENTS, TYPE 2

Face, black. E.M. Stanton.

FRACTIONAL CURRENCY

FOURTH ISSUE – FIFTY CENTS, TYPE 2

Back, green.

These were printed in sheets of 12 notes. The bust of E.M. Stanton (1814–1869), secretary of War under Lincoln, appears on the face.

Friedberg No.	Description	F-12	VF-20	AU-50	Unc-60	Unc-63
1376	Small red seal, paper with violet fibers and blue ends	$40	$61	$130	$260	$275

FOURTH ISSUE – FIFTY CENTS, TYPE 3

Face, black. Samuel Dexter.

Bust of Samuel Dexter (born at Boston May 14, 1761, died May 4, 1816). Dexter served as secretary of War and secretary of the Treasury under President John Adams.

Back, green.

FRACTIONAL CURRENCY

FOURTH ISSUE – FIFTY CENTS, TYPE 3

These were printed in sheets of 12 notes.

Friedberg No.	Description	F-12	VF-20	AU-50	Unc-60	Unc-63
1379	Green seal, paper has violet fibers and blue ends. Some notes have a very light trace of blue on the ends. This seal comes in various shades of green	$34	$40	$100	$145	$195

FIFTH ISSUE—FEBRUARY 26, 1874, TO FEBRUARY 15, 1876

The fifth and last issue was short; it contained only three notes, each of a different design. The appropriations for printing Fractional Currency were exhausted with this issue. No new funds for this purpose were provided.

No Specimen notes were made of the Fifth Issue. Some notes were issued without seals, through error.

All notes of the Fifth Issue carry printed signatures. The 10-cent and 25-cent notes have John Allison, Register, and F.E. Spinner, Treasurer. The 5-cent notes have John C. New as Treasurer.

FIFTH ISSUE – TEN CENTS

Face, black. Long Key in seal.

Face, black. Short Key in seal.

Bust of William M. Meredith (1799–1873), secretary of the Treasury 1849–1850.

FRACTIONAL CURRENCY

FIFTH ISSUE – TEN CENTS

Back, green.

Friedberg No.	Description	F-12	VF-20	AU-50	Unc-60	Unc-63
1264	Green seal, printed on bank note paper. This note is always found with the long key	$27	$31	$68	$130	$180
1265	Red seal with long key, 5 millimeters	27	28	47	68	81
1266	Red seal with short key, 4 millimeters	27	28	47	68	81

FIFTH ISSUE – TWENTY-FIVE CENTS

Face, black.

Bust of Robert J. Walker (born at Northumberland, Pennsylvania, July 23, 1801, and died November 11, 1869). He was secretary of the Treasury under President Polk from 1845–1849.

Back, green.

FRACTIONAL CURRENCY

FIFTH ISSUE – TWENTY-FIVE CENTS

Friedberg No.	Description	F-12	VF-20	AU-50	Unc-60	Unc-63
1308	Red seal with long key, 5 millimeters	$27	$34	$54	$81	$120
1309	Red seal with short key, 4 millimeters	27	34	51	74	94

FIFTH ISSUE – FIFTY CENTS

Face, black.

Bust of William H. Crawford (1722–1834), secretary of War and Treasury Departments from 1815–1825.

Back, green.

Friedberg No.	Description	F-12	VF-20	AU-50	Unc-60	Unc-63
1380/1381	Red seal, white paper with silk fibers and blue ends. Some notes have a very slight trace of blue on the ends and some have a pink face	$34	$35	$68	$81	$130

The backs of this issue have various shades of green caused by yellow-green and blue-green ink. The seal is found in various shades of red, from an orange to a dark red color.

FRACTIONAL SHIELDS

The Fractional Shield was first issued in 1866 as an aid in the detection of counterfeits. It contains 39 Specimen notes of the first three issues of Postage and Fractional Currency, including the Grant and Sherman essays.

The Specimen notes were printed on one side and some were trimmed with very narrow margins before being pasted on the shields. Girls employed in the Treasury Department prepared these shields. They placed the notes on a cardboard back, size 20-5/8 inches by 24-5/8 inches. The shape of the shield with the eagle and stars above it was printed on this cardboard. Another piece of cardboard was placed behind this and both were then put under glass in a frame. The frame is a beautiful example of early wood moulding made of solid walnut.

The notes were not always placed in the same order, but the face value of the face Specimens was the same, $4.66. The Fourth and Fifth Issues were not included since the shields were completed before these were issued.

Shields were made available to banks and other institutions to show type sets of Fractional Currency which could be checked against those offered over their counters. In a letter written by the treasurer of the United States on May 28, 1868, he stated that the shields were "sent free of express charges for Four and 50/100 dollars each."

FRACTIONAL SHIELDS

The demand for the shields was not as great as anticipated; therefore, some were stored in Washington for a number of years. Most of the boards seen today are stained and seem to be water-damaged. Some shields remaining unsold reportedly were destroyed about 1869.

The 39 notes on the shield are composed of 20 faces and 19 backs. There are two faces of the 3¢ note, one with the light curtain and one with the dark curtain, but only one three-cent back.

An eagle and 13 stars appear at the top of the shield. The size of the actual shield is approximately 19-1/2 by 23-1/2 inches. The original frames were 24-1/2 by 28-1/4 inches. All these shields are rare, the gray background type being somewhat more available than the pink or green type.

Valentine, in his book *Fractional Currency of the United States,* gives this description of the shield:

> A "shield" is an assortment of 39 closely trimmed specimens that the government mounted on a mat of heavy paper on which was engraved a large shield, surmounted by an eagle standing on a shield, in the talons of the eagle, at the right is a number of arrows, and at the left is an olive branch with leaves and berries on it and a streamer on which is "E pluribus unum." Above the eagle are 13 stars in two curved rows, 9 in the upper and 4 in the lower. The engraved shield seems to have been spaced as for stars and bars, in the space where the stars would have been are 13 specimens in three rows, 4 in each of the upper two and 5 in the third row; in the space where the bars would have been are 26 specimens arranged in 6 rows of 4 in each row and below these under the second and third columns are the other 2, to fill out the space under the first and fourth columns is the Treasury seal. The assortment of 39 specimens were not all the same, on each shield, though the arrangement of denominations did not vary.

		VF
Shield with Gray Background	Rare	$4,000
Shield with Pink Background	Very Rare	6,500
Shield with Green Background	Very Rare	15,000

COUNTERFEIT FRACTIONAL CURRENCY

It did not take long for counterfeits of Fractional Currency to appear. The First Issue was counterfeited quickly and rather successfully; therefore, the Second Issue was prepared with a more intricate design. The paper was changed from regular bank note paper. Various types of fiber paper (or as it was called in that day, membrane paper) were tried. Each new issue employed other methods or new ideas, such as surcharges on the face and back, to discourage counterfeiters. Before the use of membrane and other special papers it was reported that about $350 of counterfeit Fractional Currency was uncovered daily.

Heath's Counterfeit Detector, issued at that time, pictured examples of Fractional Currency so that the originals could be distinguished. The following comment appeared in the second pocket-size edition:

> In presenting to the public two plates of Scrip, or Fractional Currency, we wish to say that the 50¢ Scrip (which is the first on the plates) is the best executed counterfeit ever issued. It was engraved by a man who was an expert in the art, as thousands who have been made dupes to his nefarious designs can testify. He was finally arrested by the Secret Service Division, convicted, his plates secured, and his illegal business broken up.

COUNTERFEIT FRACTIONAL CURRENCY

50-Cent Counterfeit.

25-Cent Counterfeit.

10-Cent Counterfeit.

50-Cent Counterfeit.

Side-by-side comparisons of a genuine example (left) and a counterfeit example (right) of the Third Issue, Type 2 Fifty-Cent Fractional Currency. The two impressions were printed one above the other on a single card and published in *Heath's Counterfeit Detector*, one of several resources banking officials used to detect fake notes.

COUNTERFEIT FRACTIONAL CURRENCY

In the December 1862 issue of the *Connecticut Bank Note List,* Hartford, Connecticut, the counterfeiting of Postage Currency was noted with the following article:

> There are counterfeit 50 cents of the Postage Currency in circulation, and as they are quite well executed, we desire to put the public on their guard against them. There are four distinct and easily noted marks by which they may be detected. 1st. The paper is thinner than the genuine. 2d. The five faces of Washington vary considerably from each other in the counterfeit—so much so, that two or three of them, if standing alone, would hardly be taken to be the portraits of Washington—while on the genuine they closely resemble each other. 3d. The linked letters "U.S." under the middle face of Washington in the counterfeit do not show the lower end of the "S" inside of the leg of the "U" while in the genuine they do. The mark is easily seen. 4th. The border around the lettering and "50" on the back of the counterfeit is dark, and the lines are crowded, while in the genuine the border is open which includes a line of light dots running though the middle. In the counterfeit the middle line is almost invisible, while in the genuine it is so distinct as to catch the eye at once. By these marks one will be enabled to detect the counterfeit.

Mr. Thomas Cunningham, Mohawk, New York, an intimate friend of Spinner, listed 13 counterfeit fractional notes in his article appearing in 1893 in the *American Journal of Numismatics,* Volume XXVII, No. 4. His actual collection as examined by the author contained 15 counterfeits.

A counterfeit is known of the 25¢ Fessenden, Third Issue, that is almost perfect to the last detail; but it did not have the bronze surcharges on the obverse, as this surcharge was hard to duplicate. Many rather crude counterfeits have been found in some of the old Fractional Currency still floating around. Most of these are of the various denominations of the First, Second, and Third Issues.

The United States Secret Service must take up all counterfeit U.S. currency, so naturally these counterfeits are non-collectible. However, they are mentioned because they explain why this series contains so many varieties, so many types of paper and so many designs. Much time and effort was spent on each new issue to prevent counterfeiting.

UNITED STATES SMALL-SIZE CURRENCY

Modern United States Currency, by Neil Shafer

GLOSSARY OF TERMS

The following diagram illustrates the respective positions of various characters and symbols found on modern U.S. currency issues. The nomenclature will be fully explained in succeeding sections of this book.

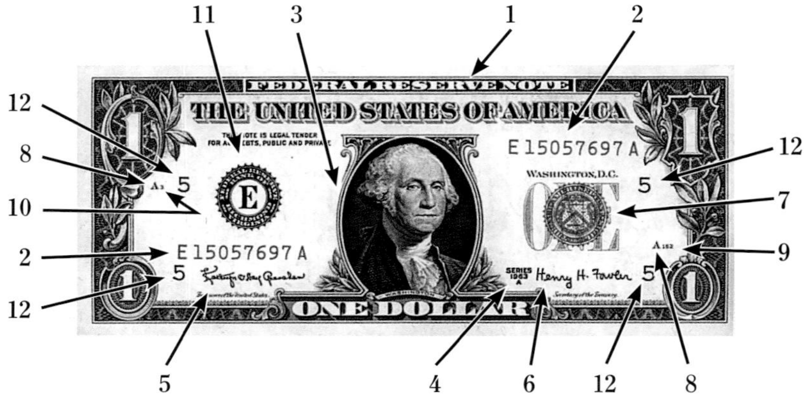

1. TYPE OF NOTE—Federal Reserve Note, Silver Certificate, United States Note, National Currency.*
2. SERIAL NUMBER—Every note has two identical serial numbers.
3. PORTRAIT—Each denomination carries a distinctive portrait. On notes of Series 1990 and later, the portrait has a security border of microprinting.
4. SERIES DATE—The indicated position is for notes of later issue. Earlier printings carry the series date two times on the face, and in varying positions.
5. SIGNATURE—Treasurer of the United States.
6. SIGNATURE—Secretary of the Treasury.
7. TREASURY SEAL—Blue, green, red, brown, gold or yellow.
8. CHECK LETTERS—Sheet-fed notes printed in Washington have two identical check letters which indicate the position on a full printed sheet. On sheet-fed notes printed at Fort Worth small letters FW are added before the check letter. Web-fed notes printed in Washington do not have a check letter.
9. FACE PLATE SERIAL NUMBER—On sheet-fed notes the plate number is positioned at the lower right adjacent to a check letter. It designates the specific plate from which the note was printed. The small number in this position on web-fed notes is a face check number used in place of a check letter.
10. QUADRANT NUMBER—Going from 1 to 4, this is found only on sheet-fed issues printed in sheets of 32 notes.
11. FEDERAL RESERVE BANK SEAL—Found only on Federal Reserve Notes.
12. FEDERAL RESERVE DISTRICT NUMBERS—Found only on Federal Reserve Notes.

* Gold Certificates do not have the type heading in the usual position at the top.

UNITED STATES SMALL-SIZE CURRENCY

TABLE OF PORTRAITS AND DESIGNS

Denomination	Portrait on Face	Design on Back
$1	George Washington	Great Seal
$2	Thomas Jefferson	Monticello
$5	Abraham Lincoln	Lincoln Memorial
$10	Alexander Hamilton	U.S. Treasury
$20	Andrew Jackson	White House
$50	Ulysses S. Grant	U.S. Capitol
$100	Benjamin Franklin	Independence Hall
$500	William McKinley	Value
$1,000	Grover Cleveland	Value
$5,000	James Madison	Value
$10,000	Salmon P. Chase	Value
$100,000	Woodrow Wilson	Value

Papers and Inks

To guard against counterfeiting, United States paper money is printed by engraved intaglio steel plates on distinctive paper. The currency paper for dry printing is made of 75 percent cotton and 25 percent linen, and contains small segments of red and blue fibers which are imbedded during manufacture. Strict government control is exercised during the preparation of this paper.

For 85 years (1879–1964) the firm of Crane and Company, Dalton, Massachusetts, was the sole producer of currency paper for the Bureau. From 1964 to 1969 the Bureau had contracts with the Gilbert Paper Company of Menasha, Wisconsin (a subsidiary of the Meade Paper Corporation of Dayton, Ohio) to furnish some of its paper needs. Since then Crane has been the exclusive supplier.

Until 1980, all inks used in plate and surface printing were manufactured in the Bureau by blending dry colors, oils, and extenders of the highest quality obtainable in huge mixers. The blended ink mixtures were ground under extreme pressure in large mills between water-cooled heavy steel rollers to ensure the proper texture. From 1980 to 1983, the Bureau withdrew from manufacturing its own ink. During that period SICPA of Lausanne, Switzerland, gradually undertook the supply of currency ink.

Plate Manufacture

To afford the best protection against counterfeiting, all United States paper money, as well as nearly all postage stamps and other evidences of a financial character issued by the United States government, are printed from plates made from steel engravings. This type of printing is known as intaglio. Of all the printing processes, intaglio is the most difficult to produce and to counterfeit. Other processes lack the fidelity of fine line engraving and the distinctive third dimensional effect of raised line on paper inherent in intaglio printing. Another outstanding element of protection is the portrait. The use of portraits in security design takes full advantage of the characteristics of intaglio printing since even a slight alteration in breadth, spacing, or depth of line on the part of a counterfeiter will cause a perceptible facial change.

In the intaglio-plate manufacturing process, the individual features of a chosen design are hand-tooled by highly skilled engravers who carve dots and lines of varying depths into soft pieces of steel with delicate steel-cutting instruments called gravers. With infinite care each feature, such as the portrait, the vignette, the numerals, the lettering, the script, and the scroll work is hand-engraved by a different master craftsman expertly trained in his own particular skill. The fine crosshatched lines in the background of the portrait are precisely etched from lines ruled in wax on a ruling machine. An unlimited number of intricate lacy patterns for use as borders and ornamentation are deftly cut by means of a geometric lathe. It takes years to acquire the skill of an engraver and it is impossible for him to exactly reproduce his own work, much less that of another engraver. It takes several engravers to prepare the hand-engraved pieces of steel, or dies, as they are called, that are used to make up a master roll or plate.

Currency Manufacture

The Bureau printed all currency by the wet intaglio process on sheet-fed flatbed presses until 1957. As part of an extensive modernization program which has been in progress since 1950, nine high-speed sheet-fed rotary intaglio printing presses, using one plate per press, were procured during the calendar year 1957 and one more in 1964 for printing currency by the dry intaglio process from plates bearing 32 notes (or subjects) to a sheet. These high-speed presses were first used to print one dollar Silver Certificates, Series 1957. Since new dies were adopted and new plates had to be made, these certificates were the first to include in the back design the motto "In God We Trust" in accordance with Public Law 140 of the 84th Congress. Early in 1965, four additional sheet-fed presses, having four plates each and capable of printing high-quality, 32-subject currency by the dry intaglio process at greatly increased production rates were purchased and placed in operation. By April of 1968, the transition to the dry process was completed.

The major components of these high-speed presses include an intaglio plate cylinder, an impression cylinder, an ink fountain and an automatic sheet-feeding device capable of holding 10,000 sheets in one loading. Each sheet of paper passes between the plate and impression cylinder, under extremely heavy pressure, forcing it down into the fine engraved lines of each plate to pick up the ink. The printed sheets are automatically delivered and deposited one on another in a well-aligned pile.

The backs of the notes are printed with green ink on one day and the faces are printed with black ink on the following day. After the intaglio printing operation, the stacks of 32-subject sheets are trimmed to a uniform dimension. The Treasury seal and serial numbers are then simultaneously overprinted on the face of each of the 32 notes on the sheet by the typographic process on two-color rotary presses.

For many years this overprinting also included the series date and the two signatures of Treasury officials, but with the complete conversion to the dry printing process in April of 1968, it was found more efficient to engrave these features once again on the plate itself. This was first accomplished on the $100 United States Note Series 1966 (issued in 1968). Next were the $1 Federal Reserve Notes Series 1963-B with Joseph W. Barr's signature as Secretary of the Treasury. All notes series dated 1969 and later have been made in a similar fashion.

A Federal Reserve district seal is also overprinted on the face of each Federal Reserve Note. The district seal and number are always overprinted in black ink. A detailed examination is then made in 16-subject form (1/2 of a full-size sheet) and the defective notes marked or identified for subsequent removal. When examined, the sheets are separated into stacks of individual notes on paper cutting machines. After a final note examination—in units of 100 each—for the removal of imperfect notes and the replacement with "star" notes, the currency is securely banded and wrapped for delivery to the vaults of the customer agencies. Each currency package or "brick" contains 40 units of 100 notes each, or 4,000 notes, and weighs about 8-1/2 pounds.

The COPE Process

During the past several years the Bureau has taken yet another giant step forward in its continuing program of modernization. A revolutionary new currency processing machine designed to automate the largely manual final steps in preparing paper money for issue has been activated for part of the Bureau's production. The Currency Overprinting and Processing Equipment (COPE), built to Bureau specifications by a German firm, is destined to save more than two million dollars a year in production costs. The machine starts with two stacks of 10,000 engraved 16-subject sheets which have been inspected for errors. This is the final human inspection, as COPE is designed to catch its own mistakes.

The sheets are fed simultaneously, one at a time, from each stack, into a letterpress overprinting unit which adds the seals and serial numbers. Sheets are accumulated into stacks of 100, then cut into two-subject units and finally into individual notes. Units of 100 notes each are banded and packaged into "bricks" containing 40 units. Each brick contains 4,000 notes and weighs approximately 8-1/2 pounds.

After the COPE operations and a final examination, the bricks are compressed and banded, then plastic shrink-wrapped and placed in pouches for shipment.

"Notes" From Test Plates

Several years ago some curious-looking items appeared, which at first glance seem to be some sort of United States paper money. This is because they are test prints from special 32-subject plates showing portions of design elements from various regular notes. The plates were made by the Bureau of Engraving and Printing and were sent to Germany for test runs on new Giori presses which were subsequently purchased for use by the Bureau.

This is a test "note" made in Germany.

Two color varieties are presently known: the first is printed in black on the face side and reddish brown on the back, and the second has a slate green face side and black printing on the back. All such special printings should have been destroyed, according to Bureau officials, even though they cannot be construed as obligations of the United States government. Thus, they may legally be held by collectors since they are test prints and not special notes. When available, which is very seldom, the green/black piece will bring more than $250. The rarer black/reddish brown piece has not been seen for sale publicly.

UNITED STATES SMALL-SIZE CURRENCY

Another similar test "note" believed to have been made in 1976 at Geneva, New York is being offered with increasing frequency on the market. Printed uniface and in 32-subject sheets, the design closely resembles the earlier version except for one portrait change (Washington for Jefferson) and some border elements which are different. Face and back designs are printed side by side on the sheets.

Miscellaneous Information

The cost of producing United States currency is less than 5¢ a note, regardless of denomination. Two-thirds of the currency notes produced are of the $1 denomination. The life of the dry-printed $1 Federal Reserve Note averages about 18 months. Other denominations remain in circulation longer. The size of a currency note is 2.61 inches by 6.14 inches, and the thickness is .0043 inch. There are 233 new notes to an inch (not compressed) and 490 to a pound. A million notes of any denomination weigh approximately 2,000 pounds and occupy approximately 42 cubic feet of space (with moderate pressure). Approximately 3,500 tons of paper and 1,000 tons of ink are used each year in producing the government securities.

THE SERIAL NUMBER SYSTEM FOR U.S. CURRENCY

The system of numbering paper money must be adequate to accommodate a large volume of notes. For security and accountability purposes, no two notes of any one type, denomination and series may have the same serial number. The serial numbers on each note have a full complement of eight digits and an alphabetical prefix and suffix letter. When necessary, ciphers are used at the left of the number to make a total of eight digits. Every note has two identical serial numbers.

This note is the 100 millionth in its run and should never have been released. It is probably unique in collectors' hands. For further information, see text below.

Whenever a new numbering sequence is used for United States Notes, Silver or Gold Certificates, the first note is numbered A00 000 001A; the second A00 000 002A, the hundredth A00 000 100A, the thousandth A00 001 000A, and so on through A99 999 999A.* The suffix letter "A" will remain the same until a total of 25 groups of 99,999,999 notes are numbered, each group having a different *prefix* letter from A to Z. The letter "O" is omitted, either as a prefix or as a suffix, because of its similarity to zero. The 100,000,000th note in each group will be a star note, since eight digits are the maximum practicable for the numbering machines.† Further testimony to

* Serial numbers start from the beginning when a completely new issue and series date is printed. For minor changes within a series date, the numbers usually continue undisturbed. This is not always the case; as an example, the $1 Silver Certificate Series 1957 has numbers starting from the beginning, and the same is true for the Series 1957-A notes as well. The 1957-B notes, however, do not start over but simply continue where the 1957-A notes leave off.

modern numbering machines' inability to produce the nine-digit number is seen in the late discovery of a note with a serial number of eight zeros.

At this point, the *suffix* letter changes to "B" for the next 25 groups of 99,999,999 notes, and numbering proceeds the same as with suffix letter "A." A total of 62,500,000,000 notes could be numbered before a duplication of serial numbers would occur. However, the Bureau has never been required to number that many notes of any one type, denomination and series.

The Federal Reserve Notes printed for the 12 districts are numbered the same way as United States Notes and Silver Certificates, except that the letter identifying each district is used as a *prefix* letter at the beginning of the two serial numbers, and it does not change. Only the suffix letter changes in the serial numbers on Federal Reserve currency.

The numbering system used for National Currency and Federal Reserve Bank Notes is illustrated and described in detail on pages 325 and 326.

STAR, OR REPLACEMENT NOTES

As mentioned previously on page 214, if during the course of examination a note is found to be imperfect, it is removed and replaced by a "star" note.

Typical star note.

Star notes are exactly the same as regular notes except that an independent series of serial numbers is assigned. Instead of the usual prefix letter, a star appears with the serial numbers on Gold Certificates, United States Notes and Silver Certificates; on Federal Reserve Notes and Federal Reserve Bank Notes the star appears in place of the suffix letter since the prefix letter is the Bank letter as well. No star notes were used in connection with the National Bank Note issues.

As explained above, the 100,000,000th note of any group will also be a star note because the numbering machines are not geared to print more than eight digits.†

Star Note Totals

A given total for any issue of star notes during the last few years refers only to the quantity of that series that was *printed,* not to the quantity issued. The practice has been to make star notes in anticipation of spoilage, with their actual issuance only as necessary. Thus they may or may not be released with their regular issue counterparts.

As cases in point, Fowler star notes were still available at the time the regular Barr series was issued, and were interspersed with them as required. Similarly, Barr star notes were mixed into early

† Apparently in earlier issues of modern-size notes, the 100,000,000th piece was prepared with nine digits. Such a note ($1 1928-A) was rediscovered and reported late in 1966 by Thomas B. Ross. The famed Grinnell sale of 1946 also contained one of these, as well as a specimen of the 1928-B series and two dated 1934.

releases of the Kennedy series. Another good example is the $100 U.S. Note Series 1966. There were 120,000 star notes printed but very few were released, as not many were needed. In any case, regular issue totals include all star notes (of whatever series) used to make up those totals, as no figures are available for the number of defective regular notes replaced by star notes in a given series. Occasionally whole decks (100) of star notes are "dumped" out when new notes have been printed.

Scarcity and Valuation

Recently a great deal of attention has been focused on star printings with demand centering chiefly on the better issues. Earlier issues of star notes are generally scarce, and certain ones are rare. The most popular of these are each listed in the catalog immediately after their regular issue counterparts. Selected later issues are also in demand; these are shown where possible. For example, ★28 on page 224 refers to the $1 star note for the Series of 1928.

BLOCK LETTERS

Many collectors are now seeking certain kinds of notes by their prefix-suffix letter combinations in serial numbers, such as A–A, A–B, A–C, and so on. This is called collecting by "block letters." Some combinations are obviously more difficult to find than others because of the varying amounts that might have been made. Scarcer combinations when sold may bring much more than the catalog valuations.

MULES

In modern United States paper money, the term "mule" indicates a note with face and back plate serial numbers (sometimes called check numbers) which differ in size. Mules came about because the size of the plate numbers was increased in the 1930s from 0.6 mm to 0.8 mm. Various issues dated 1934 and 1935 contain mule notes, and some are apparently very scarce.

COLLECTING "BY THE NUMBERS"

Many collectors are seeking notes with numbers which are special in some specific way. The most sought-after kinds of numbers include the following:

Solid Number—a number with numerals all the same, such as 22222222.

Low Number—the lower the better, with 00000001 being the ultimate. In United States issues, some of these may bring considerable premiums.

Radar Number or Palindrome—a number reading the same forward or backward, such as 25388352. (All solid numbers are, of course, radars too.)

Ladder—a number in unbroken order, such as 23456789 or 98765432.

Sequence—a recurring pattern in a number, such as 13243546 or 22556699.

Matched Beginning and Ending—this is a number such as 85000085.

Matching Digits and Sets—this is where the last one, two, three (or more) digits of more than one note are the same.

Even Notes—numbers in the tens (00000020), hundreds (00000500), thousands (00006000), and higher.

Poker Hand—number with three/two of a kind, four of a kind and other combinations.

At times a number contains elements of more than one peculiarity, such as 13243546 (sequence and ladder), 25526886 (sequence and radar), or 33445566 (ladder, sequence, solid). This kind of collecting is becoming more and more popular with a growing number of collectors. Star notes with unusual numbers are of added interest.

UNITED STATES SMALL-SIZE CURRENCY

THE SERIES YEAR ON U.S. CURRENCY

The series year which appears on the face of each note signifies the year in which the design was adopted. The series year does not change each calendar year; it changes when the basic design has a major revision. Beginning in 1974, the series year also changes when a new Treasury Secretary is appointed. The capital letter often found following the series year indicates that a minor change was authorized in a particular currency.

The series year appears twice on older printings of modern U.S. currency. More recent issues carry this designation only once.

THE TREASURY SEAL

The design of the Treasury seal now imprinted on the face of all U.S. currency is older than the Constitution. On September 25, 1778, the Continental Congress appointed a committee composed of John Witherspoon, Gouverneur Morris and Richard Henry Lee to design a seal. In the Journals of Congress of that date is a resolution providing "that the Comptroller shall keep the Treasury books and seal [and] shall draw bills under said seal." The resulting design was submitted and approved, and the seal is found on official documents dating back to 1782. It was retained after the ratification of the Constitution in 1788.

Through the years, the design of the seal has remained basically the same though minor changes were effected in 1849 when a new die was prepared. The third die made by the Bureau of Engraving in 1915 and in use until mid-1968 is described as follows: The design includes a shield on which appear a balance scale representing Justice and a key which symbolizes official authority. They are separated by a chevron bearing 13 stars for the 13 original colonies or states. The shield is surrounded by a spray of laurel in blossom. The following Latin legend surrounds the shield: THESAUR. • AMER. • SEPTENT. • SIGIL. Written out, this is "Thesauri Americae Septentrionalis Sigillum," meaning "The Seal of the Treasury of North America." There is no reverse to the Treasury seal.

As found on currency, the Treasury seal was originated by Spencer M. Clark, Chief Engineer of the Currency Bureau. It is imprinted on official Treasury documents and on the face side of U.S. currency beginning with the first issue of Legal Tender Notes authorized in 1862. The Demand Note Series 1861 and the first three issues of Fractional Currency constitute the only U.S. paper money issues that do not bear the Treasury seal.

REVISED SEAL ADOPTED

A new rendition of the seal was adopted during 1968 after its approval by Treasury Secretary Fowler in January of that year. While generally similar in appearance to previous designs, several major changes took place. English inscription "The Department of the Treasury 1789" replaced the Latin legend, and the surrounding laurel spray was removed.

The new seal was first used on the $100 United States Note Series 1966 (issued in 1968); it is also being used for all currency dated 1969 or later.

THE GREAT SEAL OF THE UNITED STATES

On August 15, 1935, the Treasury Department announced that production of a new $1 Silver Certificate had begun. The design chosen for the new back was the Great Seal of the United States. This was the first time both sides of the Great Seal were to appear on any U.S. money.

The obverse of the Great Seal is the familiar American eagle with a shield, holding an olive branch in one talon and arrows in the other. Above are 13 stars and the Latin motto "E Pluribus Unum."

The reverse of the Great Seal shows an unfinished pyramid, surmounted by an eye in a triangular glory. The pyramid bears in Roman numerals the year of the Declaration of Independence, 1776. Above the eye is the Latin motto "Annuit Coeptis," rendered as "He (God) favored our undertakings." The motto at the bottom is "Novus Ordo Seclorum" and is translated as "A new order of the ages." The eye and triangular glory represent an all-seeing Deity. The pyramid is the symbol of strength; its unfinished condition denotes the belief of the Great Seal's designers that there was yet work to be done. Both mottoes on the reverse are condensations of excerpts from Virgil's *Aeneid.*

The first committee on the Great Seal was formed on the afternoon of July 4, 1776, and consisted of Benjamin Franklin, Thomas Jefferson and John Adams. The Great Seal as finally adopted was largely the work of Charles Thomson, secretary of Congress, and William Barton, a private citizen of Philadelphia. The design was officially adopted on June 20, 1782, by Fundamental Law. The Great Seal was again ratified after the Constitution was adopted in 1789.

According to Treasury records, the only previous use of the reverse of the Great Seal was in 1882, when a centennial medal was issued by the United States Mint to celebrate the 100th anniversary of the Great Seal's adoption.

THE NATIONAL MOTTO ON U.S. CURRENCY

An Act of Congress approved by the president on July 11, 1955, authorized the appearance of the national motto on all U.S. currency. The first notes to bear the motto were $1 Silver Certificates Series 1935-G, which were released to circulation on October 1 of 1957.

The changeover was implemented gradually, as the Bureau installed new high-speed rotary presses using the dry-print method to produce sheets of 32 subjects. By April of 1968 the process of change was completed, and all currency now produced bears the motto.

UNITED STATES SMALL-SIZE CURRENCY

TREASURY OFFICIALS

Modern U.S. currency is very often collected by signature combination. These facsimile signatures appear on currency made either during the respective tenures of office of the Treasury officials or until one or both new officials are appointed. National Currency and Federal Reserve Bank Notes Series of 1929 used the Register-Treasurer signatures; all the rest from the first issue series dated 1928 to the present show the Treasurer-Secretary combination.

When the Treasurer or Secretary, or both, leave office and a new official is appointed, a letter is added after the series date and of course the signatures are changed. Originally these signatures were engraved on the face plates, which then had to be replaced upon the appearance of a new official. From the late 1930s until 1968, the signatures (along with other numbers and symbols) were overprinted.

As explained on page 214, the Bureau has again resumed the practice of engraving the signatures and series dates on the face plates. All notes printed since 1969 have been made from plates bearing engraved signatures and series dates.

Important: It should be clearly understood that the printing time of a particular issue does not generally coincide with the actual term of office of the officials whose names appear on the notes. Thus, while the length of joint tenancy of any two officials might serve as a rough indication of possible scarcity of notes containing their signatures, in actual practice it means little.

CHART OF CONCURRENT TERMS OF OFFICE

Following is a chart showing the length of time the various signatories of modern U.S. currency have held concurrent office:

Treasurer–Secretary	First Day	Last Day
H.T. Tate–A.W. Mellon	April 30, 1928	January 17, 1929
W.O. Woods–A.W. Mellon	January 18, 1929	February 12, 1932
W.O. Woods–Ogden L. Mills	February 13, 1932	March 3, 1933
W.O. Woods–W.H. Woodin	March 4, 1933	May 31, 1933
W.A. Julian–W.H. Woodin	June 1, 1933	December 31, 1933
W.A. Julian–Henry Morgenthau Jr.	January 1, 1934	July 22, 1945
W.A. Julian–Fred M. Vinson	July 23, 1945	July 23, 1946
W.A. Julian–John W. Snyder	July 25, 1946	May 29, 1949
Georgia Neese Clark–John W. Snyder	June 21, 1949	January 20, 1953
Ivy Baker Priest–G.M. Humphrey	January 28, 1953	July 28, 1957
Ivy Baker Priest–Robert B. Anderson	July 29, 1957	January 20, 1961
Elizabeth Rudel Smith–C. Douglas Dillon	January 30, 1961	April 13, 1962
Kathryn O'Hay Granahan–C. Douglas Dillon	January 3, 1963	March 31, 1965
*Kathryn O'Hay Granahan–Henry H. Fowler	April 1, 1965	October 13, 1966
Kathryn O'Hay Granahan–Joseph W. Barr	December 21, 1968	January 20, 1969
Dorothy Andrews Elston–David M. Kennedy	May 8, 1969	September 16, 1970
†Dorothy Andrews Kabis–David M. Kennedy	September 17, 1970	February 1, 1971
Dorothy Andrews Kabis–John B. Connally	February 8, 1971	July 3, 1971
Romana Acosta Bañuelos–John B. Connally	December 17, 1971	June 12, 1972
Romana Acosta Bañuelos–George P. Shultz	June 12, 1972	May 8, 1974

* Mrs. Granahan resigned as Treasurer on October 13, 1966, but no replacement was appointed for over 2-1/2 years. During this time her signature continued in use, explaining why her name is listed with Joseph W. Barr for his brief tenure of office.

† On September 17, 1970, the former Mrs. Elston became Mrs. Kabis. This is the first time the Treasurer's name was changed during tenure of office.

UNITED STATES SMALL-SIZE CURRENCY

Treasurer–Secretary	First Day	Last Day
Francine I. Neff–William E. Simon	June 21, 1974	January 20, 1977
Azie Taylor Morton–W. Michael Blumenthal	September 12, 1977	August 4, 1979
Azie Taylor Morton–G. William Miller	August 6, 1979	January 4, 1981
Angela M. Buchanan–Donald T. Regan	March 7, 1981	July 1, 1983
Katherine Davalos Ortega–Donald T. Regan	September 23, 1983	January 29, 1985
Katherine Davalos Ortega–James A. Baker II	January 29, 1985	August 17, 1988
Katherine Davalos Ortega–Nicholas F. Brady	September 15, 1988	June 30, 1989
Catalina Vasquez Villalpando–Nicholas F. Brady	December 11, 1989	October 29, 1992
Mary Ellen Withrow–Lloyd Bentsen	February 10, 1994	December 22, 1994
Mary Ellen Withrow–Robert Rubin	January 10, 1995	July 2, 1999
Mary Ellen Withrow–Lawrence H. Summers	July 2, 1999	January 20, 2001
Rosario Marin–Paul H. O'Neill	August 16, 2001	December 31, 2002
Rosario Marin–John W. Snow	February 3, 2003	June 30, 2003
Anna Escobedo Cabral–John W. Snow	December 13, 2003	June 29, 2006
Anna Escobedo Cabral–Henry M. Paulson	July 10, 2006	January 20, 2009
Rosa Gumatatao Rios–Timothy F. Geithner	August 6, 2009	January 25, 2013
Rosa Gumatatao Rios–Jack Lew	February 28, 2013	January 20, 2017
Jovita Carranza–Steven T. Mnuchin	February 13, 2017	—
Register–Treasurer		
E.E. Jones–W.O. Woods	January 22, 1929	May 31, 1933

Catalog Values

In compiling the average retail valuations as shown in this book, we have found that there is often a great deal of variation in pricing among the contributors. This is especially true with respect to the more popular issues, which often exhibit spurts of localized activity. We therefore wish to stress the idea that the values included here are meant only as a guide to general retail prices; the notes may be quoted at higher or lower prices depending on local supply and demand.

UNITED STATES NOTES—RED SEAL

United States Notes, also known as Legal Tender Notes or Greenbacks, were first authorized by the Act of Congress of February 25, 1862. Denominations for the large-size notes ranged from $1 to $10,000. Modern-size notes were printed in denominations of $1, $2, $5, and $100. Delivery of $2 notes was terminated in July of 1965 and $5 in November of 1967.* The $1 Series of 1928 was released mainly in Puerto Rico years after the notes were printed, but it is no longer in circulation.

When finished, United States Notes were delivered to a vault under custody of the treasurer of the United States. As required by the Act of May 31, 1878, and the Old Series Currency Adjustment Act, the amount outstanding was kept at $322,681,016. The Treasury holds a reserve in gold of $156,039,431 to back these notes. The seal and serial numbers are in red.

* $10 and $20 plates were made, as a specimen of each note (Series of 1928, Woods-Mills) was in the Treasury's currency exhibit at the Chicago World's Fair 1933–1934.

UNITED STATES NOTES—RED SEAL

Explanatory Notations for Various Series

Series of 1928—The legal tender clause on earlier issues of this type reads, "This Note Is A Legal Tender at its Face Value For All Debts Public and Private Except Duties on Imports and Interest on the Public Dept."

Series of 1928-B—The Act of May 12, 1933, removed legal tender restrictions from all U.S. money, and the clause on $5 notes of this type was changed as follows: "This Note Is A Legal Tender at its Face Value For All Debts Public and Private." For $2 notes, this change began with Series of 1928-C issues. All subsequent printings up to Series 1963 carry this same clause.

Series of 1928-C—For $5 notes, the face plate number appears in larger-size numerals on this and succeeding issues. For $2 notes this begins with Series of 1928-D. Lathework also added to frame of $2 notes, 1928-C.

Series 1953—Along with a general rearrangement of the face side, the following changes occurred on this and succeeding issues:

Series designation appears only once, and the word "OF" is deleted. The Treasury seal and serial numbers are reduced in size.

ONE DOLLAR

Face Design. Series 1928. Back Design on page 231.

Series 1963—The addition of the motto to the backs of United States Notes took place in 1963, along with the changeover in printing method from wet to dry and increase in number of subjects per sheet from 18 to 32. The new legal tender clause reads, "This Note is Legal Tender For All Debts, Public and Private." The "Will Pay" clause, near the bottom of the face side on previous issues no longer appears on the notes.

Series 1966—The $100 denomination was introduced late in 1968, but bearing the series date 1966. Signatures and series date were engraved in the plates for this issue. A new Treasury seal was also used for the first time. The series was discontinued in 1996, and all existing stocks destroyed.

UNITED STATES NOTES—RED SEAL

ONE DOLLAR

Friedberg No.	Series	Treasurer-Secretary	F-12	VF-20	AU-50	Unc-60	Unc-63
1500	1928	Woods-Woodin	$120	$145	$290	$390	$455
1500★	★28	(highest serial number seen 7643)	2,500	4,380	14,400	20,400	22,800

24,000 star notes reportedly assigned to be printed. BEP is unable to tell how many were actually made, or even to confirm the 24,000 assigned numbers.

* Value is for a well-centered note. These usually have serial numbers below 8000 (original April–May 1933 issue); those between 8001 and 1872000 were released in Puerto Rico in 1949 and most are imperfectly centered. Such notes are worth less than listed values.

TWO DOLLARS

Face Design. Series 1928 through 1928-G.

Friedberg No.	Series	Treasurer-Secretary		F-12	VF-20	AU-50	Unc-60
1501	1928	Tate-Mellon		$20.20	$38.00	$68	$130
1501★	★28			195.00	285.00	650	910
1502	1928-A	Woods-Mellon		35.00	54.00	130	230
1502★	★28-A			680.00	1,310.00	8,750	18,000
1503	1928-B	Woods-Mills		100.00	160.00	420	585
1503★	★28-B		Very Rare	12,000.00	24,000.00	—	—
1504	1928-C	Julian-Morgenthau		12.20	30.00	61	130
1504★	★28-C			175.00	290.00	910	1,250
1505	1928-D	Julian-Morgenthau		12.20	24.30	47	68
1505★	★28-D			74.00	94.00	235	325

Back Design. Series 1928 through 1953-C.

UNITED STATES NOTES—RED SEAL

TWO DOLLARS

Friedberg No.	Series	Treasurer-Secretary	F-12	VF-20	AU-50	Unc-60
1506	1928-E	Julian-Vinson	$12.20	$27.00	$68	$81
1506★	★28-E		2,500.00	2,880.00	6,250	10,000
1507	1928-F	Julian-Snyder	12.20	24.30	40	54
1507★	★28-F		74.00	110.00	230	325
1508	1928-G	Clark-Snyder	12.20	24.30	40	61
1508★	★28-G		54.00	74.00	195	260

Total star note printing for 1928 through 1928-G is 4,152,000.

Face Design. Series 1953 through 1953-C.

Friedberg No.	Series	Treasurer-Secretary	VF-20	EF-40	Unc-60	Unc-63
1509	1953	Priest-Humphrey	$10.80	$12.20	$14.80	$18.90
1509★	★53		27.00	38.00	54.00	68.00
1510	1953-A	Priest-Anderson	10.80	12.20	14.80	17.60
1510★	★53-A		27.00	34.00	54.00	68.00
1511	1953-B	Smith-Dillon	10.80	12.20	14.80	17.60
1511★	★53-B		27.00	34.00	47.00	54.00
1512	1953-C	Granahan-Dillon	10.80	12.20	14.80	17.60
1512★	★53-C		27.00	34.00	61.00	74.00

Face Design. Series 1963 and 1963-A.

UNITED STATES NOTES—RED SEAL

TWO DOLLARS

Back Design. Series 1963 and 1963-A.

Friedberg No.	Series	Treasurer-Secretary	VF-20	EF-40	Unc-60	Unc-63
1513	1963	Granahan-Dillon	$8.10	$9.50	$12.20	$16.20
1513★	★63		20.20	27.00	43.00	47.00
1514	1963-A	Granahan-Fowler	8.10	9.50	12.20	16.20
1514★	★63-A		24.30	34.00	61.00	68.00

FIVE DOLLARS

Face Design. Series 1928 through 1928-F.

Back Design. U.S. Notes Series 1928–1953-C, Silver Certificates, National Currency, Federal Reserve Bank Notes, Federal Reserve Notes Series 1928–1950-E.

UNITED STATES NOTES—RED SEAL

FIVE DOLLARS

Friedberg No.	Series	Treasurer-Secretary	VF-20	EF-40	Unc-60	Unc-63
1525	1928	Woods-Mellon	$18.90	$26.00	$74	$100
1525★	★28		195.00	390.00	1,150	1,620
1526	1928-A	Woods-Mills	21.60	35.00	94	150
1526★	★28-A		585.00	2,500.00	12,000	—
1527	1928-B	Julian-Morgenthau	27.00	40.00	61	94
1527★	★28-B		160.00	290.00	650	715
1528	1928-C	Julian-Morgenthau	16.20	20.20	54	68
1528★	★28-C		120.00	210.00	390	420
1529	1928-D	Julian-Vinson	40.00	62.00	130	155
1529★	★28-D		780.00	1,500.00	3,750	4,380
1530	1928-E	Julian-Snyder	16.20	20.20	54	61
1530★	★28-E		110.00	325.00	520	550
1531	1928-F	Clark-Snyder	16.20	20.20	54	68
1531★	★28-F		110.00	155.00	310	360

Total star note printing for 1928 through 1928-F is 9,744,000.

Face Design. Series 1953 through 1953-C and 1963.

Back Design. U.S. Notes Series 1963, Federal Reserve Notes Series 1963–present.

UNITED STATES NOTES—RED SEAL

FIVE DOLLARS

Friedberg No.	Series	Treasurer-Secretary	VF-20	EF-40	Unc-60	Unc-63
1532	1953	Priest-Humphrey	$13.50	$13.50	$32.00	$34
1532★	★53		68.00	81.00	115.00	130
1533	1953-A	Priest-Anderson	13.50	13.50	32.00	40
1533★	★53-A		34.00	61.00	110.00	130
1534	1953-B	Smith-Dillon	13.50	13.50	32.00	34
1534★	★53-B		34.00	54.00	94.00	110
1535	1953-C	Granahan-Dillon	13.50	13.50	32.00	34
1535★	★53-C		34.00	61.00	130.00	145
1536	1963	Granahan-Dillon	10.80	13.50	20.20	27
1536★	★63		24.30	30.00	61.00	81

ONE HUNDRED DOLLARS

Face Design. Series 1966 and 1966-A. Back Design on page 303.

Friedberg No.	Series	Treasurer-Secretary	EF-40	AU-50	Unc-60	Unc-63
1550	1966	Granahan-Fowler	$260	$290	$435	$490
1550★	★66		520	650	1,150	1,250
1551	1966-A	Elston-Kennedy	260	390	585	650

The remaining Treasury stocks of these notes were destroyed in 1996.

SILVER CERTIFICATES—BLUE SEAL

Certificates backed by silver dollars were first authorized by the Bland-Allison Act of February 28, 1878. Large-size notes were made in denominations from $1 to $1,000 at various intervals.

Modern-size Silver Certificates were made only in the $1, $5, and $10 denominations. Upon completion they were delivered to a vault under the custody of the treasurer of the United States. However, Silver Certificates are no longer being printed, as they were abolished by the Act of June 4, 1963 (at which time Federal Reserve $1 and $2 notes were authorized).

The seal and serial numbers are in blue.

SILVER CERTIFICATES—BLUE SEAL

Redemption and Catalog Value

Early issues of modern-size Silver Certificates were also backed by silver dollars; their wording referred to their redemption in "One Silver Dollar" as had all previous issues of Silver Certificates. All this was changed by the Silver Purchase Act of 1934, which allowed for such certificates to be issued against any standard silver dollars, silver or silver bullion held by the Treasury. Accordingly, the wording in the redemption clause was changed to read "One Dollar in Silver," allowing for the option of redemption in silver dollars or bullion.

On March 25, 1964, Treasury Secretary Dillon halted the outflow of silver dollars, stating that thenceforth silver bullion would be used for the redemption of Silver Certificates presented for that purpose.

On June 24, 1968, redemption in bullion was discontinued, but not before literally millions had been turned in. The initial effect on the collector market was a downward adjustment of catalog values.

$1 Note Varieties

Late issues of the $1 Silver Certificates present an unusual combination of significant technical and numismatic developments. The result of this is an array of different varieties created by the gradual changeover from wet to dry printing method and the addition of the motto "In God We Trust."

Notes Dated 1935

All notes with the date 1935 were produced by the old "wet-intaglio" method. These notes were made from 1935 through 1963. The motto was added to these notes in 1962 *during* the printing of the 1935-G issue; therefore, notes dated 1935-G come both without and with the motto. All 1935-H notes have the motto.

Notes Dated 1957

All notes dated 1957 were produced by the present "dry-intaglio" process. Three varieties are involved—1957, 1957-A, and 1957-B, made from 1957 through 1963. All such notes bear the motto on the back.

Order of Appearance

From the above, it may be seen that notes of both the wet-printed 1935 series and the dry-printed 1957 series were being produced and released concurrently from 1957 to 1963. According to delivery records, notes of both kinds were introduced in the following order: Series 1957, 1935-F, 1957-A, 1935-G (no motto), 1935-G (with motto), 1957-B, and 1935-H.

Explanatory Notations for Various Series

Series of 1928—The legal tender clause first read, "This Certificate is Receivable For All Public Dues and When So Received May Be Reissued."

Series of 1928-B—Those with prefix and suffix letters X/B, Y/B, and Z/B are experimental notes.

Series of 1928-E—See next page under Series of 1934.

SILVER CERTIFICATES—BLUE SEAL

Series of 1933—Pursuant to the Act of May 12, 1933, a new series of Silver Certificates was initiated. Issued only in the $10 denomination, this is one of the most desirable and unique notes in the modern U.S. currency series. It is in fact a "Silver Coin Note," so stated on the face side. Its legal tender clause is as follows: "This Certificate is Issued Pursuant to Section 16 of the Act of May 12, 1933, and is Legal Tender at its Face Value For All Debts Public and Private."

Series of 1934—The Act of June 19, 1934, necessitated further change in the legal tender clause; it was altered on the Series of 1928-E $1 notes, on all Series of 1934 notes and for the remainder of Silver Certificate issues, reading as follows: "This Certificate is Legal Tender For All Debts, Public and Private." On $1 notes of the 1934 series, the Treasury seal was moved to the right side and a large blue numeral 1 was added on the left.

Series of 1934-A—Numerals in the face plate serial number are larger on this and succeeding issues of $5 and $10 notes.

Series 1935—The word OF was deleted from the series designation on these $1 notes and succeeding series dates. "Series 1935" appears twice on the face. Also, the large word ONE at the right is removed, and the numeral 1 at the left is gray instead of blue.

There was an issue of experimental notes of this series in 1937.

Series 1935-A—The size of the numerals in the face plate serial number was made larger, and the series designation appears only once on this and succeeding issues of $1 notes.

Aside from issues for regular circulation, notes from this series were used as part of the special HAWAII overprint and Yellow Seal emissions of World War II.

Series 1935-G—For the first time the motto appears on U.S. currency, appearing on the $1 note. This series is not released to the public until 1957.

Series 1953—The following changes took place on the face side of this and succeeding issues of $5 and $10 notes:

Series designation appears only once, and the word OF is deleted.

Signatures are overprinted instead of engraved.

The Treasury seal and serial numbers are reduced in size.

The numeral at the left is gray instead of blue.

Series 1957—Printings of 32-subject sheets begin with this series.

ONE DOLLAR

Face Design. Series 1928 through 1928-E.

SILVER CERTIFICATES—BLUE SEAL

ONE DOLLAR

Back Design. U.S. Notes Series 1928, Silver Certificates Series 1928–1934.

Friedberg No.	Series	Treasurer-Secretary	VF-20	EF-40	Unc-60	Unc-63
1600	1928	Tate-Mellon	$34	$40	$68	$94
1600★	★28		130	210	290	420
1601	1928 A	Woods-Mellon	34	40	61	74
1601★	★28 A		88	130	285	360
1602	1928 B	Woods-Mills	31	40	81	94
1602★	★28 B		135	195	390	520
1603	1928 C	Woods-Woodin	145	275	420	490
1603★	★28 C		7,800	10,000	21,600	—
1604	1928 D	Julian-Woodin	88	145	235	275
1604★	★28 D		2,750	6,250	12,000	18,000
1605	1928 E	Julian-Morgenthau	415	940	1,220	1,250
1605★	★28 E		11,250	17,000	—	—

Face Design. Series 1934.

Friedberg No.	Series	Treasurer-Secretary	VF-20	EF-40	Unc-60	Unc-63
1606	1934	Julian-Morgenthau	$36.00	$38.00	$81.00	$94.00
1606★	★34		130.00	260.00	550.00	715.00
1607	1935	Julian-Morgenthau	6.80	8.10	13.50	40.00
1607★	★35		100.00	180.00	260.00	310.00
1608	1935 A*	Julian-Morgenthau	3.40	4.10	13.50	16.20
1608★	★35 A		21.60	47.00	88.00	100.00
1611	1935 B	Julian-Vinson	4.90	5.40	13.50	16.20
1611★	★35 B		54.00	88.00	115.00	130.00

* For HAWAII, yellow seal, and R & S notes, see World War II Issues.

SILVER CERTIFICATES—BLUE SEAL

ONE DOLLAR

Friedberg No.	Series	Treasurer-Secretary	VF-20	EF-40	Unc-60	Unc-63
1612	1935 C	Julian-Snyder	$3.40	$4.10	$8.10	$13.50
1612★	★35 C		24.30	32.00	68.00	88.00
1613W	1935 D†	Clark-Snyder, wide	3.40	4.10	8.10	13.50
1613W★	★35 D†	Wide	16.20	27.00	61.00	88.00
1613N	1935 D†	Clark-Snyder, narrow	3.40	4.10	8.40	13.50
1613N★	★35 D†	Narrow	16.20	27.00	61.00	94.00
1614	1935 E	Priest-Humphrey	3.40	4.10	8.10	13.50
1614★	★35 E		6.80	9.50	16.20	32.00
1615	1935 F	Priest-Anderson	3.40	4.10	8.10	13.50
1615★	★35 F		6.80	9.50	20.20	34.00
1616	1935 G	Smith-Dillon	5.10	5.40	9.80	13.50
1616★	★35 G	No motto	9.50	16.20	27.00	40.00

The 1935-D series was printed in sheets of 12 and 18 subjects:

4,510,024,000 in sheets of 12 notes
146,944,000 in sheets of 18 notes
4,656,968,000 Total 1935-D notes

† Wide and Narrow designs—See images below and explanation on following page.

Detail of the top border "Wide" style (F-1613W).

Detail of the top border "Narrow" style (F-1613N).

Face Design. Series 1935. General Face Design, Series 1935 through 1957-B.

Friedberg No.	Series	Treasurer-Secretary	VF-20	EF-40	Unc-60	Unc-63
1617	1935 G†	Smith-Dillon	$5.40	$5.40	$24.30	$30.00
1617★	★35 G	With motto	38.00	54.00	120.00	145.00
1618	1935 ★†	Granahan-Dillon	4.90	5.40	9.80	13.50
1618★	★35 ★		13.50	20.20	40.00	47.00
1619	1957	Priest-Anderson	2.60	3.40	6.80	8.40
1619★	★57		5.40	6.80	10.80	16.20
1620	1957 A	Smith-Dillon	2.60	3.40	7.40	8.40
1620★	★57 A		5.40	6.80	10.80	16.20
1621	1957 B	Granahan-Dillon	2.60	3.40	7.40	8.40
1621★	★57 B		5.40	6.80	10.80	13.50

† With motto "In God We Trust." 1935-G comes with and without the motto. See picture on page 233.

SILVER CERTIFICATES—BLUE SEAL

ONE DOLLAR

THE "GREAT SEAL" BACK DESIGN

Wide Back Design. Series 1935 through 1935-D.

There are two varieties of backs for Series 1935-D notes, designated as the Wide and Narrow designs. The Wide design is about 1/16 inch wider, easily recognized when compared with the Narrow design. The most obvious area for comparison is the lathe work border under ONE DOLLAR.

The Narrow design was used for subsequent issues of the 1935 series.

Back Design. Silver Certificates Series 1935-G, 1935-H, and Series 1957 through 1957-B. All Federal Reserve Notes.

FIVE DOLLARS

Face Design. Series 1934 through 1934-D. Back Design on page 226.

SILVER CERTIFICATES—BLUE SEAL

FIVE DOLLARS

Friedberg No.	Series	Treasurer-Secretary	VF-20	EF-40	Unc-60	Unc-63
1650	1934	Julian-Morgenthau	$14.80	$17.60	$47	$61
1650★	★34		74.00	100.00	275	305
1651	1934 A	Julian-Morgenthau	13.60	14.80	40	61
1651★	★34 A		61.00	88.00	195	220
1652	1934 B	Julian-Vinson	15.30	16.20	40	68
1652★	★34 B		145.00	255.00	715	780
1653	1934 C	Julian-Snyder	13.10	14.80	27	40
1653★	★34 C		54.00	81.00	155	195
1654	1934 D	Clark-Snyder	13.10	14.80	34	40
1654★	★34 D		40.00	61.00	130	210

Face Design. Series 1953 through 1953-C. Back Design on page 226.

Friedberg No.	Series	Treasurer-Secretary		VF-20	EF-40	Unc-60	Unc-63
1655	1953	Priest-Humphrey		$12.80	$13.50	$27	$40
1655★	★53			34.00	47.00	68	81
1656	1953 A	Priest-Anderson		12.80	13.50	27	40
1656★	★53 A			34.00	47.00	68	81
1657	1953 B	Smith-Dillon†		12.80	13.50	27	40
1657★	★53 B			605.00	1,340.00	7,500	8,050
1658	1953 C	Granahan-Dillon	Not released				

† Of the 1953-B issue only 14,196,000 notes were released because of the discontinuance of Silver Certificates. Apparently less than 400,000 star notes were released, according to O'Donnell's listings.

TEN DOLLARS

Face Design, Series 1933 and 1933-A.

SILVER CERTIFICATES—BLUE SEAL
TEN DOLLARS

Back Design. Silver Certificates, National Currency, Federal Reserve Bank Notes, Federal Reserve Notes Series 1928 through 1950-E, Gold Certificates.

The 1933 and 1933-A $10 Issues

The matter of just how many of the 1933 and 1933-A $10 notes were issued has never been cleared up satisfactorily. Bureau records show that 216,000 of the 1933 series and 336,000 of the 1933-A series were delivered; however, records of the Treasury Department Cash Division are at variance. Those records indicate 156,000 of the 1933 notes and 396,000 of the 1933-A notes as having been delivered. Further, their issue figures show that all 156,000 of the 1933 series and 28,000 of the 1933-A were released. The balance—368,000 of the 1933-A notes—were destroyed.

Though records show that one uncut sheet was released, no regular issue 1933-A notes are known today in collectors' hands; perhaps the only ones yet in existence are those of the single sheet of Specimen notes retained by the Bureau of Engraving and Printing.

As a matter of interest, the following letter written by former Bureau Director A.W. Hall on April 3, 1941 is included:

> In regard to the $10 silver certificates, series of 1933 and 1933-A, you are advised that a total of 552,000 of the two were delivered to the Treasurer of the United States in 1934. Of this number at least 300,000 were series 1933-A.
>
> Of the number delivered to the Treasurer, 184,000 were issued between January and August, 1934, and the remainder, 368,000, were destroyed in November, 1935. Whether any 1933-A's were among those issued apparently cannot be determined. However, as the 1933 plate was first at press, it is possible that all the certificates issued were from this plate.

This letter appeared in *The Numismatist,* June 1941, and was addressed to Mr. Robert H. Lloyd.

Friedberg No.	Series	Treasurer-Secretary		F-12	VF-20	AU-50	Unc-60
1700	1933	Julian-Woodin		$3,560	$5,250	$13,800	$16,800
1700★	★33		Unique				
1700a	1933 A	Julian-Morgenthau	None known in any collection.				

SILVER CERTIFICATES—BLUE SEAL

TEN DOLLARS

Face Design. Series 1934 through 1934-D.

Friedberg No.	Series	Treasurer-Secretary	VF-20	EF-40	Unc-60	Unc-63
1701	1934	Julian-Morgenthau	$43	$54	$120	$135
1701★	★34		130	220	600	680
1702	1934 A	Julian-Morgenthau	38	47	145	155
1702★	★34 A		145	310	520	780
1703	1934 B	Julian-Vinson	150	420	1,250	1,500
1703★	★34 B		1,560	2,620	10,000	12,000
1704	1934 C	Julian-Snyder	38	46	88	130
1704★	★34 C		94	210	275	290
1705	1934 D	Clark-Snyder	43	54	110	130
1705★	★34 D		160	420	1,220	3,000

Face Design. Series 1953 through 1953-B.

Friedberg No.	Series	Treasurer-Secretary	VF-20	EF-40	Unc-60	Unc-63
1706	1953	Priest-Humphrey	$68	$74	$100	$130
1706 ★	★53		100	215	360	390
1707	1953 A	Priest-Anderson	65	74	130	160
1707★	★53 A		145	260	370	390
1708	1953 B	Smith-Dillon	65	68	115	130
1708★	★53 B	None printed				

NATIONAL CURRENCY—BROWN SEAL

National Currency was first authorized by the National Banking Act of 1863, superseded by the National Currency Act of June 3, 1864. This Act provided for the establishment of national banks and the issuance of circulating notes. These notes were to be secured by United States interest-bearing registered bonds deposited with the Treasurer, upon which the banks could receive 90 percent of current market value in notes.

Modern-size National Currency was first issued on July 15, 1929. Unusual features of this issue include the use of the Register-Treasurer signature combination (instead of Secretary-Treasurer as found on most other modern-size notes) and the series date, 1929. The printing plates for the face side are also quite different from other modern-size types. The engraved borders are reduced in proportion and size to make room for the imprinting of bank names, locations, charter numbers and names of bank officials. All these details were printed by a logotype process onto the notes; since so many different banks issued such notes a great saving was thus made in the preparation of plates. The seal and serial numbers are in brown. The backs are uniform with other modern types. No star notes as such were made for the National Currency series.

There are two distinct types of modern-size National Currency. Type One, issued from July 1929 to May 1933, has the bank's charter number in two places, in black. National Currency was printed 12 notes to a sheet, then cut, overprinted, and delivered in vertical sheets of six. For Type One, each of these six notes had the same serial numbers and suffix letter but a different prefix letter, A through F, which served to denote its position on the vertical sheet.

Type Two notes were issued from May 1933 to May 1935. These bore consecutive serial numbers, the suffix letters were dropped and the charter number of the bank was added twice more, in thinner brown numerals. Thus, the charter number appears four times on Type Two notes—twice in black logotype and twice in brown as described. Type Two notes are much scarcer than those of Type One.

National currency is most often collected by states, cities or banks with odd names, places of historical interest, low charter numbers or low or unusual serial numbers. Recently there has been a surging interest in these notes, spurred by the publication of a specialized book sponsored by the Society of Paper Money Collectors.

Because of their high face value, $50 and $100 notes were not popularly collected until the last several years. None were issued from Alabama, Alaska, Arizona, Georgia, Maine, New Mexico, and South Carolina.

Throughout the years National Bank Notes were in use, various amendments were made affecting their circulation and redemption. Provisions were made for the transfer of redemption liability from the separate banks to the United States, which now cancels and retires any National Bank Notes that are turned in. National Currency became obsolete on May 20, 1935, as bonds matured or were otherwise declared ineligible for security purposes.

The redemption clause on these notes reads as follows: "Redeemable in Lawful Money of the United States at United States Treasury or at the Bank of Issue."

Valuations are at best a guide to general availability. Some states are very difficult to obtain, others may have one issue commonly available but very scarce otherwise.

The following table lists the states alphabetically with their respective rarity ratings. Values follow accordingly.

NATIONAL CURRENCY—BROWN SEAL

TABLE OF RARITY

Valuations following the Table of Rarity are based on this list:

State	Rarity	State	Rarity	State	Rarity
Alabama	4	Kentucky	3	North Dakota	4
Alaska	9	Louisiana	5	Ohio	1
Arizona	7	Maine	4	Oklahoma	4
Arkansas	5	Maryland	3	Oregon	5
California	2	Massachusetts	3	Pennsylvania	1
Colorado	4	Michigan	3	Rhode Island	6
Connecticut	4	Minnesota	3	South Carolina	4
Delaware	6	Mississippi	6	South Dakota	5
District of Columbia	4	Missouri	3	Tennessee	4
Florida	6	Montana	7	Texas	1
Georgia	6	Nebraska	3	Utah	6
Hawaii	7	Nevada	8	Vermont	5
Idaho	7	New Hampshire	6	Virginia	3
Illinois	1	New Jersey	3	Washington	5
Indiana	1	New Mexico	6	West Virginia	3
Iowa	2	New York	1	Wisconsin	2
Kansas	3	North Carolina	5	Wyoming	7

FIVE DOLLARS

Face Design, National Currency Type One. Back Design on page 226.

Face Design, National Currency Type Two. Back Design on page 226.

NATIONAL CURRENCY—BROWN SEAL

FIVE DOLLARS

$5 TYPE ONE (Friedberg F-1800-1)

Rarity	F-12	VF-20	EF-40	Unc-60
1	$50	$80	$110	$140
2	52	82	112	142
3	55	85	115	145
4	57	90	125	165
5	60	95	135	185
6	65	100	155	250
7	80	185	300	700
8	160	325	475	1,000
9	500	650	1,000	1,800

$5 TYPE TWO (Friedberg F-1800-2)

Rarity	F-12	VF-20	EF-40	Unc-60
1	$50	$80	$110	$145
2	52	85	115	150
3	55	87	120	155
4	57	92	130	175
5	65	95	140	200
6	70	105	165	275
7	85	210	340	825
8	170	340	500	1,200
9	550	700	1,200	2,000

TEN DOLLARS

Face Design, National Currency Type One. Back Design on page 235.

Face Design, National Currency Type Two. Back Design on page 235.

$10 TYPE ONE (Friedberg F-1801-1)

Rarity	F-12	VF-20	EF-40	Unc-60
1	$50	$80	$110	$150
2	52	82	115	155
3	55	85	120	160
4	60	87	130	170
5	63	90	140	190
6	75	100	160	235
7	85	175	310	400
8	200	410	600	1,250
9	800	1,200	1,800	2,800

$10 TYPE TWO (Friedberg F-1801-2)

Rarity	F-12	VF-20	EF-40	Unc-60
1	$50	$80	$115	$150
2	52	82	120	155
3	55	85	125	160
4	60	87	135	175
5	63	90	145	195
6	75	110	180	250
7	125	275	420	550
8	225	450	720	1,450
9	850	1,350	2,000	3,200

NATIONAL CURRENCY—BROWN SEAL

TWENTY DOLLARS

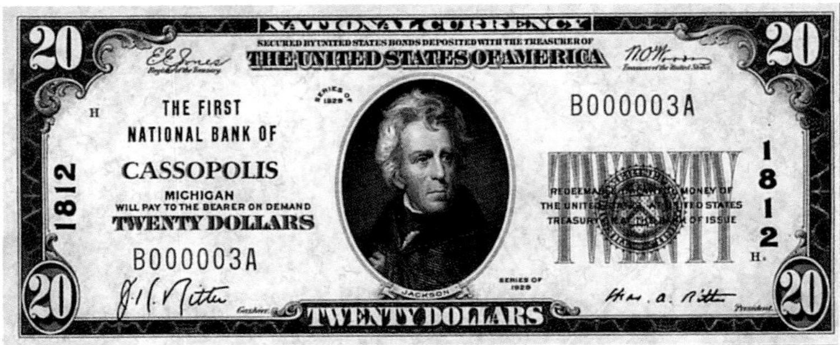

Face Design, National Currency Type One. Back Design on page 281.

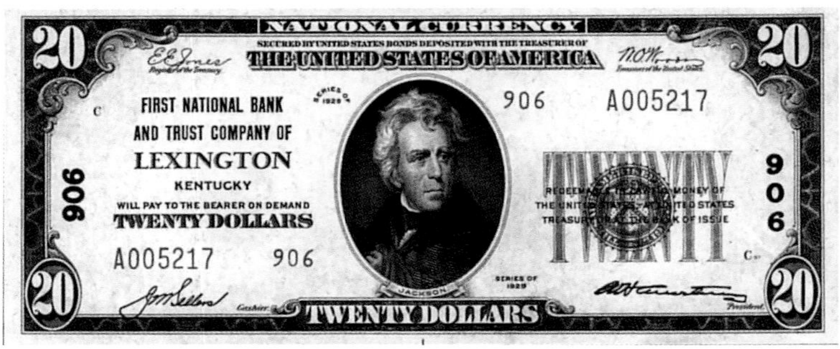

Face Design, National Currency Type Two. Back Design on page 281.

$20 TYPE ONE (Friedberg F-1802-1)

Rarity	F-12	VF-20	EF-40	Unc-60
1	$65	$90	$125	$190
2	70	95	130	200
3	75	100	135	210
4	80	105	145	220
5	90	110	155	255
6	100	130	175	350
7	300	375	475	700
8	400	675	950	1,800
9	900	1,325	2,000	3,000

$20 TYPE TWO (Friedberg F-1802-2)

Rarity	F-12	VF-20	EF-40	Unc-60
1	$70	$95	$130	$200
2	75	100	135	210
3	80	105	140	220
4	90	110	145	230
5	100	115	155	265
6	120	140	200	385
7	325	425	550	800
8	420	700	1,000	2,000
9	1,000	1,500	2,200	3,500

NATIONAL CURRENCY—BROWN SEAL

FIFTY DOLLARS

Face Design, National Currency Type One. Back Design on page 293.

Face Design, National Currency Type Two. Back Design on page 293.

$50 TYPE ONE (Friedberg F-1803-1)

Rarity	F-12	VF-20	EF-40	Unc-60
1	$150	$200	$275	$400
2	175	225	275	425
3	200	250	325	525
4	225	275	375	675
5	250	300	450	950
6	350	400	635	1,150
7	575	675	825	1,600
8	825	1,000	1,500	2,250
9	Not issued			

$50 TYPE TWO (Friedberg F-1803-2)

Rarity	F-12	VF-20	EF-40	Unc-60
1	$275	$350	$450	$650
2	300	400	475	750
3	325	450	525	900
4	365	575	675	1,150
5	400	685	825	1,500
6	500	790	1,150	2,000
7	725	1,150	1,600	2,500
8	950	1,325	2,000	3,500
9	Not issued			

NATIONAL CURRENCY—BROWN SEAL

ONE HUNDRED DOLLARS

Face Design, National Currency Type One. Back Design on page 303.

Face Design, National Currency Type Two. Back Design on page 303.

$100 TYPE ONE (Friedberg F-1804-1)

Rarity	F-12	VF-20	EF-40	Unc-60
1	$250	$300	$375	$600
2	275	325	400	650
3	300	350	450	725
4	325	375	500	850
5	350	400	575	1,250
6	450	500	775	1,400
7	675	785	1,125	2,000
8	925	1,150	1,400	2,750
9	Not issued			

$100 TYPE TWO (Friedberg F-1804-2)

Rarity	F-12	VF-20	EF-40	Unc-60
1	$325	$450	$550	$900
2	375	550	650	1,100
3	425	600	700	1,250
4	490	750	850	1,475
5	575	865	1,100	1,850
6	750	1,000	1,300	2,000
7	1,000	1,300	1,725	2,800
8	1,200	1,500	2,400	4,500
9	Not issued			

FEDERAL RESERVE BANK NOTES—BROWN SEAL

Federal Reserve Bank Notes were first authorized by the Act of December 23, 1913, which established the Federal Reserve System. Unlike Federal Reserve Notes, these Bank Notes were not obligations of the United States. Rather, they were obligations of the specific Federal Reserve Banks named on the face. The seal and serial numbers are in brown.

Modern-size Federal Reserve Bank Notes were authorized by the Act of March 9, 1933. This Act permitted Federal Reserve Banks to issue currency equal to 100 percent of the face value of United States bonds, or 90 percent of the estimated value of commercial paper used as collateral.

FEDERAL RESERVE BANK NOTES—BROWN SEAL

These Bank Notes were issued to relieve the emergency brought about by heavy withdrawals of Federal Reserve Notes in January and February of 1933.

Plates originally made for the Series of 1929 National Currency discussed on page 237 were hastily adapted and the Bank Notes were quickly prepared and issued. Naturally, these notes very closely resembled the National Currency issues: alterations were made only in the overprint on the face side. Instead of the local bank's Cashier and President signatures, there appeared the signatures of the Federal Reserve Bank's Cashier and Governor, with but three exceptions. The Cashier's signature was replaced by the Deputy Governor on New York district notes, the Assistant Deputy Governor on Chicago district notes, and the Controller on the St. Louis district notes. The designated letter of each Federal Reserve Bank and district was placed on the notes in four places. The brown seal was slightly larger than that used on the National Bank notes, and words OR BY LIKE DEPOSIT OF OTHER SECURITIES were logotyped near the top. The series date remained 1929 and the engraved signatures of Jones and Woods (Register and Treasurer) were also retained.

Serial numbers for each Federal Reserve Bank started with 00000001A, preceded by a District letter A to L. Star notes were made for these issues and are extremely scarce.

Federal Reserve Bank Notes were delivered in sheets of six notes, as were the National Currency issues. Denominations included $5, $10, $20, $50, and $100. Their issuance was discontinued in July 1935. However, during World War II (1942) and a temporary shortage of currency, additional supplies of these Bank Notes were released from storage and charged out as Federal Reserve Notes. In new condition FRBN's have become very scarce.

FIVE DOLLARS

Face Design. Federal Reserve Bank Notes. Back Design on page 226.

Friedberg No.	District	Federal Reserve Bank		VF-20	EF-40	Unc-60
1850A	A	Boston		$57	$61	$94
1850B	B	New York		57	61	94
1850C	C	Philadelphia		57	61	130
1850D	D	Cleveland		57	61	94
	E	Richmond	None printed			
1850F	F	Atlanta		57	61	120
1850G	G	Chicago		57	61	120
1850H	H	St. Louis		455	910	2,120
1850I	I	Minneapolis		110	390	940
1850J	J	Kansas City		57	61	94
1850K	K	Dallas		68	100	160
1850L	L	San Francisco		550	3,750	—

★ Star note values are at least twice as much for used; five times as much, or more, for New condition.

FEDERAL RESERVE BANK NOTES—BROWN SEAL

TEN DOLLARS

Face Design. Federal Reserve Bank Notes. Back Design on page 235.

Friedberg No.	District	Federal Reserve Bank	VF-20	EF-40	Unc-60
1860A	A	Boston	$57	$70	$118
1860B	B	New York	57	70	118
1860C	C	Philadelphia	57	70	118
1860D	D	Cleveland	57	70	118
1860E	E	Richmond	80	120	265
1860F	F	Atlanta	70	110	225
1860G	G	Chicago	57	70	94
1860H	H	St. Louis	57	70	94
1860I	I	Minneapolis	80	110	240
1860J	J	Kansas City	65	85	160
1860K	K	Dallas	375	725	1,850
1860L	L	San Francisco	125	400	1,200

★ For star notes, see chart note under $5 listing.

TWENTY DOLLARS

Face Design. Federal Reserve Bank Notes. Back Design on page 281.

FEDERAL RESERVE BANK NOTES—BROWN SEAL

TWENTY DOLLARS

Friedberg No.	District	Federal Reserve Bank	VF-20	EF-40	Unc-60
1870A	A	Boston	$70	$100	$220
1870B	B	New York	70	95	180
1870C	C	Philadelphia	70	95	180
1870D	D	Cleveland	70	95	180
1870E	E	Richmond	70	100	200
1870F	F	Atlanta	75	110	225
1870G	G	Chicago	70	95	180
1870H	H	St. Louis	70	100	180
1870I	I	Minneapolis	70	95	175
1870J	J	Kansas City	70	110	200
1870K	K	Dallas	350	650	1,800
1870L	L	San Francisco	70	100	325

FIFTY DOLLARS

Face Design. Federal Reserve Bank Notes. Back Design on page 293.

Friedberg No.	District	Federal Reserve Bank	VF-20	EF-40	Unc-60
	A	Boston	None issued	—	—
1880B	B	New York	$130	$145	$200
	C	Philadelphia	None issued	—	
1880D	D	Cleveland	130	145	200
	E	Richmond	None issued	—	—
	F	Atlanta	None issued	—	—
1880G	G	Chicago	130	160	370
	H	St. Louis	None issued	—	—
1880I	I	Minneapolis	130	150	325
1880J	J	Kansas City	130	145	200
1880K	K	Dallas	240	520	1,500
1880L	L	San Francisco	130	160	370

FEDERAL RESERVE BANK NOTES—BROWN SEAL

ONE HUNDRED DOLLARS

Face Design. Federal Reserve Bank Notes. Back Design on page 303.

Friedberg No.	District	Federal Reserve Bank	VF-20	EF-40	Unc-60
1890A	A	Boston	None issued	—	—
1890B	B	New York	$190	$235	$290
1890C	C	Philadelphia	None issued	—	—
1890D	D	Cleveland	180	215	260
1890E	E	Richmond	190	215	280
1890F	F	Atlanta	None issued	—	—
1890G	G	Chicago	190	240	370
1890H	H	St. Louis	None issued	—	—
1890I	I	Minneapolis	190	215	390
1890J	J	Kansas City	190	235	325
1890K	K	Dallas	305	550	1,250
1890L	L	San Francisco	None issued	—	—

FEDERAL RESERVE NOTES—GREEN SEAL

Federal Reserve Notes were first authorized by the Federal Reserve Act of December 23, 1913. Since then, the issues of these notes have increased to the point that today they comprise over 99 percent of the total volume of paper money in circulation. Federal Reserve Notes are obligations of the United States and until 1968 were secured by Gold Certificates or Gold Certificate credits to the amount of at least 25 percent of the notes in actual circulation. Government securities accounted for the other 75 percent of the backing for these notes.

Modern-size Federal Reserve Notes were first issued in 1929, series-dated 1928. Denominations range from $1 to $10,000. Those of $500 and higher were discontinued by action of the Board of Governors of the Federal Reserve System on June 26, 1946; on July 14, 1969, they were retired from circulation, but a few are still held in banks.

The twelve Federal Reserve Banks are organized and operate for public service as authorized by Congress. They are under supervision of the Board of Governors of the Federal Reserve System, an agency of the federal government. Members of this board are appointed by the president and confirmed by the Senate.

Each of the twelve banks has nine directors. Three of these, including the chairman, are appointed by the Board of Governors. The other six are elected by member banks.

FEDERAL RESERVE NOTES—GREEN SEAL

When Federal Reserve Notes are finished, they are delivered to the Federal Reserve vault, which is under supervision of the Comptroller of the Currency. They are then sent to the issuing banks as needed, which in turn distribute them to member banks and to the public.

Federal Reserve Banks release these notes according to the needs of their regions. One can easily tell which bank issued a particular note by examining its face side. A number and corresponding letter were assigned to each of the Federal Reserve Districts, and both have been used on the notes in various combinations. At present a bank seal to the left of the portrait carries the letter (and the name of the bank); this same letter serves as the prefix letter for every serial number on all notes issued by the respective bank. The district number is imprinted in four places, also on the face of the note. The Treasury seal and serial numbers are in green.

Explanatory Notations for Various Series

Series of 1928—The redemption clause on notes issued before 1934 reads as follows: "Redeemable in Gold on Demand at the United States Treasury, or in Gold or Lawful Money at Any Federal Reserve Bank."

Series of 1934—In 1933, Acts of Congress removed existing legal tender restrictions from all U.S. money, and in 1934 the Gold Reserve Act halted redemption of Federal Reserve Notes with gold. The redemption clause became a legal tender clause in accordance with these Acts, appearing on notes issued from 1934 to 1963 as follows: "This Note is Legal Tender For All Debts, Public and Private, and is Redeemable in Lawful Money at the United States Treasury, or at Any Federal Reserve Bank."

Series of 1934-A—The size of the numerals in the face plate serial number was made larger on this and succeeding issues.

Series 1950—The following changes are incorporated on the face side of the notes for this and succeeding issues until 1963-B:

Series designation appears only once, and the word "OF" is deleted.
The Treasury seal and serial numbers are reduced in size.
Signatures are overprinted instead of engraved.
The Bank seal is smaller and has a toothed edge.

Series 1950-E—Notes of this series date were released after the 1963 issue.

Series 1963—The change in printing method and increase in number of subjects per sheet took place with this issue. Also, this series marks the first appearance of $1 Federal Reserve Notes. The new legal tender clause is the same as that on United States Notes and reads, "This Note is Legal Tender For All Debts, Public and Private." The motto appears on the backs of denominations higher than $1, and the "Will Pay" clause near the bottom no longer appears on any of the notes. No $50 or $100 notes were printed series dated 1963.

The motto IN GOD WE TRUST was added to all bills printed hereafter.

Series 1963-A—This is the first issue of $50 and $100 notes bearing the motto. Vignettes are also slightly enlarged on the backs and show better detail.

Series 1963-B—Only $1 notes were made with this series date; these were the "Barr Notes" which caused so much publicity some years ago. Joseph W. Barr served as Treasury Secretary one month (December 21, 1968, to January 20, 1969) but notes with his signature were made into June of 1969. That, plus speculation that notes with Barr's signature would obviously be rarities, caused many to be saved. They remain easily available today.

This issue is also the first of the current $1 notes to have signatures and series date engraved in the plates (see page 214).

FEDERAL RESERVE NOTES—GREEN SEAL

Series 1969—A new rendition of the Treasury seal is introduced on all denominations.

Series 1969-A—This is the first time in a number of years that all notes of the same type and series do *not* bear the same signature combination. The $1 notes have the Kabis-Kennedy signatures and all higher denominations the Kabis-Connally signatures.

Printing of the Kabis-Kennedy $1 notes started October 26, 1970, and it was expected that higher denominations would follow soon afterwards. The announcement that Kennedy would resign effective February 1, 1971, caused a halt to preparations for all denominations higher than the $1. After Connally's name replaced Kennedy's, notes from $5 through $100 were made with the 1969-A designation but with the new Kabis-Connally combination.

Series 1969-B, C and D—Because of the signature changes which occurred on the previous issue, the succeeding three series also show a variance in the $1 from all the rest. Signatures appear as follows:

1969-B—$1, Kabis-Connally; $5–$50 Bañuelos-Connally.
1969-C—$1, Bañuelos-Connally; $5–$100 Bañuelos-Schultz.
1969-D—$1, Bañuelos-Shultz.

Series 1974—This is the first issue under the new policy that each time a different Treasury secretary is appointed there will be a new series date on the notes. All denominations thus carry the same date and signatures (Neff-Simon). Only the $1 notes have serial numbers starting over again from (A) 00 000 001A. Higher values continue the serial numbering from the previous issue.

Series 1976—This date marks the introduction of the $2 with the Bicentennial back design. Many consider this to be a commemorative issue, though the intention is to include the $2 as a regularly circulating note.

Series 1981-A and 1985—Some of the $1 notes of these series were printed with a unique back plate, number 129, which has the identification number placed at the lower left side of the back near the Great Seal. These are all scarce and generally valued at three to four times as much as the normal notes.

Series 1988-A—Operation of the government printing plant in Forth Worth, Texas, began in 1991. Since then $1 notes for the Dallas and San Francisco districts have been produced there. These have small letters FW preceding the face plate position number near the lower right side of the face design. Some of the notes in this series were printed on new web-fed equipment. These notes do not have the plate location or check number on the face. On the back of these notes the plate number has been moved from the bottom of E in ONE to the top.

Series 1988 and later—Incomplete information may be shown for some of the current issues where not all of the notes have been printed or released for circulation. Current notes with little or no premium value are listed as face value.

Series 1990—The first notes with advanced counterfeit deterrents were the Series 1990 $100 bills with signatures of Villalpando and Brady. Lower denominations, starting with the $50 notes, were introduced into circulation thereafter.

Series 1996—Notes of this and later issues are redesigned with larger numerals and portrait. Additional security devices are incorporated into the paper and printing. A watermark is used to show a duplicate of the central portrait.

Federal Reserve Banks and Their Letter Designations

There are 12 Federal Reserve Banks, and each has a specific letter designation on every note currently issued under its name. In this section either the bank name or its letter designation will be used for each note. Following is the listing of banks and their respective letters:

FEDERAL RESERVE NOTES—GREEN SEAL

A—Boston	E—Richmond	I—Minneapolis
B—New York	F—Atlanta	J—Kansas City, Missouri
C—Philadelphia	G—Chicago	K—Dallas
D—Cleveland	H—St. Louis	L—San Francisco

Note: There are some scarce block letters in various issues, which are of interest to collectors. See the Oakes/Schwartz book listed in the bibliography on page 339 for details.

ONE DOLLAR

Face Design. 1963 to present. Back Design on page 233.

$1 SERIES 1963—Signatures: *Granahan-Dillon*

Friedberg No.	Federal Reserve Bank		Unc-60	Unc-63
1900A	A	Boston	$4.70	$6.10
1900A★	A★	Boston	6.80	9.50
1900B	B	New York	4.70	6.10
1900B★	B★	New York	6.80	9.50
1900C	C	Philadelphia	4.70	6.10
1900C★	C★	Philadelphia	6.80	9.50
1900D	D	Cleveland	4.70	6.10
1900D★	D★	Cleveland	6.80	9.50
1900E	E	Richmond	4.70	6.10
1900E★	E★	Richmond	6.80	9.50
1900F	F	Atlanta	4.70	6.10
1900F★	F★	Atlanta	6.80	9.50

Friedberg No.	Federal Reserve Bank		Unc-60	Unc-63
1900G	G	Chicago	$4.70	$6.10
1900G★	G★	Chicago	6.80	9.50
1900★	H	St. Louis	4.70	6.10
1900H★	H★	St. Louis	6.80	9.50
1900I	I	Minneapolis	4.70	6.10
1900I★	I★	Minneapolis	6.80	9.50
1900J	J	Kansas City	4.70	6.10
1900J★	J★	Kansas City	6.80	9.50
1900K	K	Dallas	4.70	6.10
1900K★	K★	Dallas	6.80	9.50
1900L	L	San Francisco	4.70	6.10
1900L★	L★	San Francisco	6.80	9.50

$1 SERIES 1963-A—Signatures: *Granahan-Fowler*

Friedberg No.	Federal Reserve Bank		Unc-60	Unc-63
1901A	A	Boston	$4.10	$5.40
1901A★	A★	Boston	6.80	8.10
1901B	B	New York	4.10	5.40
1901B★	B★	New York	6.80	8.10
1901C	C	Philadelphia	4.10	5.40
1901C★	C★	Philadelphia	6.80	8.10
1901D	D	Cleveland	4.10	5.40
1901D★	D★	Cleveland	6.80	8.10
1901E	E	Richmond	4.10	5.40
1901E★	E★	Richmond	6.80	8.10
1901F	F	Atlanta	4.10	5.40
1901F★	F★	Atlanta	6.80	8.10

Friedberg No.	Federal Reserve Bank		Unc-60	Unc-63
1901G	G	Chicago	$4.10	$5.40
1901G★	G★	Chicago	6.80	8.10
1901★	H	St. Louis	4.10	5.40
1901H★	H★	St. Louis	6.80	8.10
1901I	I	Minneapolis	4.10	5.40
1901I★	I★	Minneapolis	9.50	10.80
1901J	J	Kansas City	4.10	5.40
1901J★	J★	Kansas City	6.80	8.10
1901K	K	Dallas	4.10	5.40
1901K★	K★	Dallas	9.50	10.80
1901L	L	San Francisco	4.10	5.40
1901L★	L★	San Francisco	6.80	8.10

FEDERAL RESERVE NOTES—GREEN SEAL

ONE DOLLAR

$1 SERIES 1963-B—Signatures: *Granahan-Barr*

Friedberg No.	Federal Reserve Bank		Unc-60	Unc-63
1902B	B	New York	$6.10	$7.40
1902B★	B★	New York	12.20	20.20
1902E	E	Richmond	6.10	7.40
1902E★	E★	Richmond	12.20	20.20
1902G	G	Chicago	6.10	7.40
1902G★	G★	Chicago	$12.20	$20.20
1902J	J	Kansas City	6.10	7.40
	J★	Kansas City	Not printed	
1902L	L	San Francisco	6.10	7.40
1902L★	L★	San Francisco	12.20	20.20

$1 SERIES 1969—Signatures: *Elston-Kennedy*

Friedberg No.	Federal Reserve Bank		Unc-60	Unc-63
1903A	A	Boston	$4.10	$5.40
1903A★	A★	Boston	6.80	8.80
1903B	B	New York	4.10	5.40
1903B★	B★	New York	6.80	8.80
1903C	C	Philadelphia	4.10	5.40
1903C★	C★	Philadelphia	6.80	8.80
1903D	D	Cleveland	4.10	5.40
1903D★	D★	Cleveland	6.80	8.80
1903E	E	Richmond	4.10	5.40
1903E★	E★	Richmond	6.80	8.80
1903F	F	Atlanta	4.10	5.40
1903F★	F★	Atlanta	4.10	6.80
1903G	G	Chicago	$4.10	$5.40
1903G★	G★	Chicago	6.80	8.80
1903H	H	St. Louis	4.10	5.40
1903H★	H★	St. Louis	6.80	8.80
1903I	I	Minneapolis	4.10	5.40
1903I★	I★	Minneapolis	15.00	22.00
1903J	J	Kansas City	4.10	5.40
1903J★	J★	Kansas City	6.80	8.80
1903K	K	Dallas	4.10	5.40
1903K★	K★	Dallas	6.80	8.80
1903L	L	San Francisco	4.10	5.40
1903L★	L★	San Francisco	4.10	6.80

$1 SERIES 1969-A—Signatures: *Kabis-Kennedy*

Friedberg No.	Federal Reserve Bank		Unc-60	Unc-63
1904A	A	Boston	$4.10	$5.40
1904A★	A★	Boston	6.80	8.80
1904B	B	New York	4.10	5.40
1904B★	B★	New York	6.80	8.80
1904C	C	Philadelphia	4.10	5.40
1904C★	C★	Philadelphia	6.80	8.80
1904D	D	Cleveland	4.10	5.40
1904D★	D★	Cleveland	6.80	8.80
1904E	E	Richmond	4.10	5.40
1904E★	E★	Richmond	6.80	8.80
1904F	F	Atlanta	4.10	5.40
1904F★	F★	Atlanta	6.80	8.80
1904G	G	Chicago	$4.10	$5.40
1904G★	G★	Chicago	6.80	8.80
1904★	H	St. Louis	4.10	5.40
1904H★	H★	St. Louis	8.10	12.20
1904I	I	Minneapolis	4.10	5.40
1904I★	I★	Minneapolis	24.30	35.00
1904J	J	Kansas City	4.10	5.40
1904J★	J★	Kansas City	6.80	8.80
1904K	K	Dallas	4.10	5.40
	K★	Dallas	Not printed	
1904L	L	San Francisco	6.80	8.80
1904L★	L★	San Francisco	4.10	5.40

FEDERAL RESERVE NOTES—GREEN SEAL

ONE DOLLAR

$1 SERIES 1969-B—Signatures: *Kabis-Connally*

Friedberg No.	Federal Reserve Bank		Unc-60	Unc-63
1905A	A	Boston	$4.10	$5.40
1905A★	A★	Boston	6.80	8.80
1905B	B	New York	4.10	5.40
1905B★	B★	New York	6.80	8.80
1905C	C	Philadelphia	4.10	5.40
1905C★	C★	Philadelphia	6.80	8.80
1905D	D	Cleveland	4.10	5.40
1905D★	D★	Cleveland	6.80	8.80
1905E	E	Richmond	4.10	5.40
1905E★	E★	Richmond	6.80	8.80
1905F	F	Atlanta	4.10	5.40
1905F★	F★	Atlanta	6.80	8.80
1905G	G	Chicago	$4.10	$5.40
1905G★	G★	Chicago	6.80	8.80
1905★	H	St. Louis	4.10	5.40
1905H★	H★	St. Louis	6.80	8.80
1905I	I	Minneapolis	4.10	5.40
1905I★	I★	Minneapolis	24.30	31.00
1905J	J	Kansas City	4.10	5.40
1905J★	J★	Kansas City	6.80	8.80
1905K	K	Dallas	4.10	5.40
1905K★	K★	Dallas	6.80	8.80
1905L	L	San Francisco	4.10	5.40
1905L★	L★	San Francisco	6.80	8.80

$1 SERIES 1969-C—Signatures: *Bañuelos-Connally*

Friedberg No.	Federal Reserve Bank		Unc-60	Unc-63
	A	Boston	Not printed	
	A★	Boston	Not printed	
1906B	B	New York	$5.10	$6.10
	B★	New York	Not printed	
	C	Philadelphia	Not printed	
	C★	Philadelphia	Not printed	
1906D	D	Cleveland	5.10	6.10
1906D★	D★	Cleveland	26.00	46.00
1906E	E	Richmond	5.10	6.10
1906E★	E★	Richmond	30.00	51.00
1906F	F	Atlanta	5.10	6.10
1906F★	F★	Atlanta	16.20	20.20
1906G	G	Chicago	$5.10	$6.10
1906G★	G★	Chicago	16.20	20.20
1906★	H	St. Louis	5.10	6.10
1906H★	H★	St. Louis	16.20	20.20
1906I	I	Minneapolis	5.10	6.10
1906I★	I★	Minneapolis	26.00	35.00
1906J	J	Kansas City	5.10	6.10
1906J★	J★	Kansas City	20.20	26.00
1906K	K	Dallas	5.10	6.10
1906K★	K★	Dallas	35.00	46.00
1906L	L	San Francisco	5.10	6.10
1906L★	L★	San Francisco	130.00	155.00

$1 SERIES 1969-D—Signatures: *Bañuelos-Schultz*

Friedberg No.	Federal Reserve Bank		Unc-60	Unc-63
1907A	A	Boston	$5.10	$6.10
1907A★	A★	Boston	12.20	18.20
1907B	B	New York	5.10	6.10
1907B★	B★	New York	7.40	10.10
1907C	C	Philadelphia	5.10	6.10
1907C★	C★	Philadelphia	7.40	10.10
1907D	D	Cleveland	5.10	6.10
1907D★	D★	Cleveland	7.40	10.10
1907E	E	Richmond	5.10	6.10
1907E★	E★	Richmond	7.40	10.10
1907F	F	Atlanta	5.10	6.10
1907F★	F★	Atlanta	7.40	10.10
1907G	G	Chicago	$5.10	$6.10
1907G★	G★	Chicago	7.40	10.10
1907★	H	St. Louis	5.10	6.10
1907H★	H★	St. Louis	7.40	10.10
1907I	I	Minneapolis	5.10	6.10
	I★	Minneapolis	Not printed	
1907J	J	Kansas City	5.10	6.10
1907J★	J★	Kansas City	7.40	10.10
1907K	K	Dallas	5.10	6.10
1907K★	K★	Dallas	7.40	10.10
1907L	L	San Francisco	5.10	6.10
1907L★	L★	San Francisco	7.40	10.10

FEDERAL RESERVE NOTES—GREEN SEAL

ONE DOLLAR

$1 SERIES 1974—Signatures: *Neff-Simon*

Friedberg No.	Federal Reserve Bank		Unc-60	Unc-63	Friedberg No.	Federal Reserve Bank		Unc-60	Unc-63
1908A	A	Boston	$3.70	$4.70	**1908G**	G	Chicago	$3.70	$4.70
1908A★	A★	Boston	6.10	8.10	**1908G★**	G★	Chicago	6.10	8.10
1908B	B	New York	3.70	4.70	**1908★**	H	St. Louis	3.70	4.70
1908B★	B★	New York	6.10	8.10	**1908H★**	H★	St. Louis	6.10	8.10
1908C	C	Philadelphia	3.70	4.70	**1908I**	I	Minneapolis	3.70	4.70
1908C★	C★	Philadelphia	6.10	8.10	**1908I★**	I★	Minneapolis	28.00	35.00
1908D	D	Cleveland	3.70	4.70	**1908J**	J	Kansas City	3.70	4.70
1908D★	D★	Cleveland	18.20	28.00	**1908J★**	J★	Kansas City	6.10	8.10
1908E	E	Richmond	3.70	4.70	**1908K**	K	Dallas	3.70	4.70
1908E★	E★	Richmond	6.10	8.10	**1908K★**	K★	Dallas	10.10	22.30
1908F	F	Atlanta	3.70	4.70	**1908L**	L	San Francisco	3.70	4.70
1908F★	F★	Atlanta	6.10	8.10	**1908L★**	L★	San Francisco	6.10	8.10

$1 SERIES 1977—Signatures: *Morton-Blumenthal*

Friedberg No.	Federal Reserve Bank		Unc-60	Unc-63	Friedberg No.	Federal Reserve Bank		Unc-60	Unc-63
1909A	A	Boston	$3.70	$4.70	**1909G**	G	Chicago	$3.70	$4.70
1909A★	A★	Boston	14.80	24.30	**1909G★**	G★	Chicago	6.10	8.10
1909B	B	New York	3.70	4.70	**1909★**	H	St. Louis	3.70	4.70
1909B★	B★	New York	6.10	8.10	**1909H★**	H★	St. Louis	6.10	8.10
1909C	C	Philadelphia	3.70	4.70	**1909I**	I	Minneapolis	3.70	4.70
1909C★	C★	Philadelphia	6.10	8.10	**1909I★**	I★	Minneapolis	6.10	8.10
1909D	D	Cleveland	3.70	4.70	**1909J**	J	Kansas City	3.70	4.70
1909D★	D★	Cleveland	6.10	8.10	**1909J★**	J★	Kansas City	6.10	8.10
1909E	E	Richmond	3.70	4.70	**1909K**	K	Dallas	3.70	4.70
1909E★	E★	Richmond	6.10	8.10	**1909K★**	K★	Dallas	6.10	8.10
1909F	F	Atlanta	3.70	4.70	**1909L**	L	San Francisco	3.70	4.70
1909F★	F★	Atlanta	6.10	8.10	**1909L★**	L★	San Francisco	6.10	8.10

$1 SERIES 1977-A—Signatures: *Morton-Miller*

Friedberg No.	Federal Reserve Bank		Unc-60	Unc-63	Friedberg No.	Federal Reserve Bank		Unc-60	Unc-63
1910A	A	Boston	$3.70	$4.70	**1910G**	G	Chicago	$3.70	$4.70
1910A★	A★	Boston	14.80	24.30	**1910G★**	G★	Chicago	6.10	8.10
1910B	B	New York	3.70	4.70	**1910★**	H	St. Louis	3.70	4.70
1910B★	B★	New York	6.10	8.10	**1910H★**	H★	St. Louis	6.10	8.10
1910C	C	Philadelphia	3.70	4.70	**1910I**	I	Minneapolis	3.70	4.70
1910C★	C★	Philadelphia	6.10	8.10	**1910I★**	I★	Minneapolis	6.10	8.10
1910D	D	Cleveland	3.70	4.70	**1910J**	J	Kansas City	3.70	4.70
1910D★	D★	Cleveland	6.10	8.10	**1910J★**	J★	Kansas City	6.10	8.10
1910E	E	Richmond	3.70	4.70	**1910K**	K	Dallas	3.70	4.70
1910E★	E★	Richmond	6.10	8.10	**1910K★**	K★	Dallas	6.10	8.10
1910F	F	Atlanta	3.70	4.70	**1910L**	L	San Francisco	3.70	4.70
1910F★	F★	Atlanta	6.10	8.10	**1910L★**	L★	San Francisco	6.10	8.10

FEDERAL RESERVE NOTES—GREEN SEAL

ONE DOLLAR

$1 SERIES 1981—Signatures: *Buchanan-Regan*

Friedberg No.	Federal Reserve Bank		Unc-60	Unc-63	Friedberg No.	Federal Reserve Bank		Unc-60	Unc-63
1911A	A	Boston	$3.70	$4.70	**1911G**	G	Chicago	$3.70	$4.70
1911A★	A★	Boston	8.10	10.10	**1911G★**	G★	Chicago	8.10	10.10
1911B	B	New York	3.70	4.70	**1911★**	H	St. Louis	3.70	4.70
1911B★	B★	New York	8.10	10.10	**1911H★**	H★	St. Louis	8.10	10.10
1911C	C	Philadelphia	3.70	4.70	**1911I**	I	Minneapolis	3.70	4.70
1911C★	C★	Philadelphia	26.00	43.00	**1911I★**	I★	Minneapolis	8.10	10.10
1911D	D	Cleveland	3.70	4.70	**1911J**	J	Kansas City	3.70	4.70
1911D★	D★	Cleveland	8.10	10.10	**1911J★**	J★	Kansas City	8.10	10.10
1911E	E	Richmond	3.70	4.70	**1911K**	K	Dallas	3.70	4.70
1911E★	E★	Richmond	8.10	10.10	**1911K★**	K★	Dallas	8.10	10.10
1911F	F	Atlanta	3.70	4.70	**1911L**	L	San Francisco	3.70	4.70
1911F★	F★	Atlanta	8.10	10.10	**1911L★**	L★	San Francisco	8.10	10.10

$1 SERIES 1981-A—Signatures: *Ortega-Regan*

Friedberg No.	Federal Reserve Bank		Unc-60	Unc-63	Friedberg No.	Federal Reserve Bank		Unc-60	Unc-63
1912A	A	Boston	$3.70	$4.70	**1912G★**	G★	Chicago	$13.50	$18.90
1912B	B	New York	3.70	4.70	**1912★**	H	St. Louis	3.70	4.70
1912B★	B★	New York	13.50	18.90	**1912I**	I	Minneapolis	3.70	4.70
1912C	C	Philadelphia	3.70	4.70	**1912J**	J	Kansas City	3.70	4.70
1912D	D	Cleveland	3.70	4.70	**1912K**	K	Dallas	3.70	4.70
1912E	E	Richmond	3.70	4.70	**1912K★**	K★	Dallas	490.00	585.00
1912E★	E★	Richmond	13.50	18.90	**1912L**	L	San Francisco	3.70	4.70
1912F	F	Atlanta	3.70	4.70	**1912L★**	L★	San Francisco	13.50	18.90
1912G	G	Chicago	3.70	4.70					

Notes with back plate number 129 at left are valued higher.

$1 SERIES 1985—Signatures: *Ortega-Baker*

Friedberg No.	Federal Reserve Bank		Unc-60	Unc-63	Friedberg No.	Federal Reserve Bank		Unc-60	Unc-63
1913A	A	Boston	$3.70	$4.70	**1913★**	H	St. Louis	$3.70	$4.70
1913B	B	New York	3.70	4.70	**1913H★**	H★	St. Louis	455.00	520.00
1913C	C	Philadelphia	3.70	4.70	**1913I**	I	Minneapolis	3.70	4.70
1913D	D	Cleveland	3.70	4.70	**1913I★**	I★	Minneapolis	8.10	10.10
1913E	E	Richmond	3.70	4.70	**1913J**	J	Kansas City	3.70	4.70
1913E★	E★	Richmond	8.10	10.10	**1913K**	K	Dallas	3.70	4.70
1913F	F	Atlanta	3.70	4.70	**1913K★**	K★	Dallas	8.10	10.10
1913G	G	Chicago	3.70	4.70	**1913L**	L	San Francisco	3.70	4.70
1913G★	G★	Chicago	8.10	10.10	**1913L★**	L★	San Francisco	8.10	10.10

Notes with back plate number 129 at left are valued higher.

FEDERAL RESERVE NOTES—GREEN SEAL

ONE DOLLAR

$1 SERIES 1988—Signatures: *Ortega-Brady*

Friedberg No.	Federal Reserve Bank		Unc-60	Unc-63
1914A	A	Boston	$4.70	$7.10
1914A★	A★	Boston	14.80	20.20
1914B	B	New York	4.70	7.10
1914B★	B★	New York	9.50	14.80
1914C	C	Philadelphia	4.70	7.10
1914D	D	Cleveland	4.70	7.10
1914E	E	Richmond	4.70	7.10
1914E★	E★	Richmond	9.50	14.80
1914F	F	Atlanta	4.70	7.10
1914F★	F★	Atlanta	715.00	1,020.00

Friedberg No.	Federal Reserve Bank		Unc-60	Unc-63
1914G	G	Chicago	$4.70	$7.10
1914★	H	St. Louis	4.70	7.10
1914I	I	Minneapolis	4.70	7.10
1914J	J	Kansas City	4.70	7.10
1914J★	J★	Kansas City	9.50	14.80
1914K	K	Dallas	4.70	7.10
1914K★	K★	Dallas	32.00	46.00
1914L	L	San Francisco	4.70	7.10
1914L★	L★	San Francisco	9.50	14.80

Sheet-fed, Washington facility. With normal face check letter/number.

$1 SERIES 1988-A—Signatures: *Vallalpando-Brady* — Sheet-Fed

Friedberg No., Washington: F-1915

Federal Reserve Bank		Unc-60	Unc-63
A	Boston	$3.70	$4.70
B	New York	3.70	4.70
B★	New York	6.10	8.10
C	Philadelphia	3.70	4.70
D	Cleveland	3.70	4.70
D★	Cleveland	6.10	8.10
E	Richmond	3.70	4.70
E★	Richmond	6.10	8.10
F	Atlanta W or FW	3.70	4.70
F★	Atlanta	6.10	8.10
G	Chicago W or FW	3.70	4.70

Friedberg No., Fort Worth: F-1916

Federal Reserve Bank		Unc-60	Unc-63
G★	Chicago W or FW	$6.10	$8.10
★	St. Louis W or FW	3.70	4.70
H★	St. Louis	14.80	22.30
I	Minneapolis W/FW	3.70	4.70
I★	Minneapolis W/FW	14.80	22.30
J	Kansas City W/FW	3.70	4.70
K	Dallas W or FW	3.70	4.70
K★	Dallas FW	3.70	4.70
L	San Francisco W/FW	3.50	4.50
L★	San Francisco FW	6.00	8.00

All sheet-fed: Washington (W), has normal face check letter/number. Fort Worth (FW) has check letter and number preceded by small letters FW.

$1 SERIES 1988-A—Signatures: *Vallalpando-Brady* — Web-Fed

Friedberg No.	Federal Reserve Bank		Unc-60	Unc-63
1917A	A	Boston	$40	$50
1917B	B	New York	455	620
1917C	C	Philadelphia	46	54
1917E	E	Richmond	40	50

Friedberg No.	Federal Reserve Bank		Unc-60	Unc-63
1917F	F	Atlanta	$40	$50
1917F★	F★	Atlanta	1,150	1,380
1917G	G	Chicago	100	130

Web-fed notes were printed in Washington, D.C. from 1992 to 1996 on an experimental press. They have only a face check number, and no letter in the lower right corner. The back check number is to the right of TRUST.

BEP Washington

Fort Worth

Web Press

FEDERAL RESERVE NOTES—GREEN SEAL

ONE DOLLAR

$1 SERIES 1993—Signatures: *Withrow-Bentsen* — Sheet-Fed

Friedberg No., Washington: F-1918

Federal Reserve Bank		Unc-60	Unc-63
A	Boston	$3.00	$4.10
B	New York	3.00	4.10
B★	New York	8.10	10.10
C	Philadelphia	3.00	4.10
C★	Philadelphia	160.00	210.00
D	Cleveland	3.00	4.10
E	Richmond	3.00	4.10
F	Atlanta	3.00	4.10

Friedberg No., Fort Worth: F-1919

Federal Reserve Bank		Unc-60	Unc-63
F★	Atlanta	$8.00	$10.00
G	Chicago W or FW	3.00	4.10
G★	Chicago FW	8.10	10.10
★	St. Louis W/FW	3.00	4.10
I	Minneapolis FW	115.00	155.00
K	Dallas FW	3.00	4.10
K★	Dallas FW	8.10	10.10
L	San Francisco W/FW	3.00	4.10

All sheet-fed: Washington (W), has normal face check letter/number. Fort Worth (FW) has check letter and number preceded by small letters FW.

$1 SERIES 1993—Signatures: *Withrow-Bentsen* — Web-Fed

Friedberg No.	Federal Reserve Bank		Unc-60	Unc-63
1920B	B	New York	$24.30	$32
1920C	C	Philadelphia	$24.30	$32

Web-fed notes were printed in Washington, D.C. from 1992 to 1996 on an experimental press. They have only a face check number, and no letter in the lower right corner. The back check number is to the right of TRUST.

$1 SERIES 1995—Signatures: *Withrow-Rubin* — Sheet-Fed

Friedberg No., Washington: F-1921

Federal Reserve Bank		Unc-60	Unc-63
A	Boston	$2.15	$3.00
A★	Boston	4.10	5.10
B	New York	2.15	3.00
B★	New York	8.10	12.20
C	Philadelphia	2.15	3.00
C★	Philadelphia	4.10	5.10
D	Cleveland	2.15	3.00
D★	Cleveland	4.10	5.10
E	Richmond	2.15	3.00
E★	Richmond	4.10	5.10
F	Atlanta	2.15	3.00
F★	Atlanta	4.10	5.10

Friedberg No., Fort Worth: F-1922

Federal Reserve Bank		Unc-60	Unc-63
G	Chicago	$2.15	$3.00
G★	Chicago	4.10	5.10
★	St. Louis	2.15	3.00
I	Minneapolis	2.15	3.00
I★	Minneapolis	4.10	5.10
J	Kansas City	2.15	3.00
J★	Kansas City	4.10	5.10
K	Dallas	2.15	3.00
K★	Dallas	18.20	24.30
L	San Francisco	2.15	3.00
L★	San Francisco	4.10	5.10

All sheet-fed. Washington (W), has normal face check letter/number. Fort Worth (FW) has check letter and number preceded by small letters FW.

$1 SERIES 1995—Signatures: *Withrow-Rubin* — Web-Fed

Friedberg No.	Federal Reserve Bank		Unc-60	Unc-63
1923A	A	Boston	$24.30	$32
1923B	B	New York	24.30	32
1923D	D	Cleveland	$24.30	$32
1923F	F	Atlanta	24.30	32

All $1 notes after 1995 are printed at both Washington, D.C. and the Western Facility in Fort Worth, Texas.

$1 SERIES 1999—Sigs.: *Withrow-Summers*
$1 SERIES 2001—Sigs.: *Marin-O'Neill*
$1 SERIES 2003—Sigs.: *Marin-Snow*
$1 SERIES 2003-A—Sigs.: *Cabral-Snow*
$1 SERIES 2006—Sigs.: *Cabral-Paulson*
$1 SERIES 2009—Sigs.: *Rios-Geithner*
$1 SERIES 2013—Sigs.: *Rios-Lew*
$1 SERIES 2017—Sigs.: *Carranza-Mnuchin*
$1 SERIES 2021—Sigs.: *Malerba-Yellen*

FEDERAL RESERVE NOTES—GREEN SEAL

TWO DOLLARS

Face Design. Series 1976 to present.

Back Design. Series 1976 to present.

$2 SERIES 1976—Signatures: *Neff-Simon*

Friedberg No.	Federal Reserve Bank		Unc-60	Unc-63
1935A	A	Boston	$3.40	$4.10
1935A★	A★	Boston	18.90	24.30
1935B	B	New York	3.40	4.10
1935B★	B★	New York	18.90	24.30
1935C	C	Philadelphia	3.40	4.10
1935C★	C★	Philadelphia	21.60	27.00
1935D	D	Cleveland	3.40	4.10
1935D★	D★	Cleveland	27.00	32.00
1935E	E	Richmond	3.40	4.10
1935E★	E★	Richmond	54.00	68.00
1935F	F	Atlanta	3.40	4.10
1935F★	F★	Atlanta	18.90	24.30
1935G	G	Chicago	$3.40	$4.10
1935G★	G★	Chicago	54.00	65.00
1935★	H	St. Louis	3.40	4.10
1935H★	H★	St. Louis	18.90	24.30
1935I	I	Minneapolis	3.40	4.10
1935I★	I★	Minneapolis	115.00	135.00
1935J	J	Kansas City	20.20	27.00
1935J★	J★	Kansas City	115.00	135.00
1935K	K	Dallas	3.40	4.10
1935K★	K★	Dallas	23.00	30.00
1935L	L	San Francisco	3.40	4.10
1935L★	L★	San Francisco	27.00	34.00

All $2 notes after 1995 are printed at the Western Facility in Fort Worth, Texas. Fort Worth (FW) printings have face check letter and number preceded by small letters FW.

$2 SERIES 2003—Signatures: *Marin-Snow*

$2 SERIES 2003-A—Signatures: *Cabral-Snow*

$2 SERIES 2009—Signatures: *Rios-Geithner*

$2 SERIES 2013—Signatures: *Rios-Lew*

$2 SERIES 2017-A—Signatures: *Carranza-Mnuchin*

FEDERAL RESERVE NOTES—GREEN SEAL

FIVE DOLLARS

Face Design. Series 1928 and 1928-A. Back Design on page 226.

$5 SERIES 1928—Signatures: *Tate-Mellon*

Large district numeral of bank at left.

Friedberg No.	Federal Reserve Bank		VF-20	EF-40	Unc-60	Unc-63
1950A	1	Boston	$68	$88	$145	$325
1950B	2	New York	68	88	145	155
1950C	3	Philadelphia	68	88	145	155
1950D	4	Cleveland	68	88	145	155
1950E	5	Richmond	215	360	1,250	2,120
1950F	6	Atlanta	68	88	145	155
1950G	7	Chicago	68	88	145	155
1950H	8	St. Louis	68	88	145	155
1950I	9	Minneapolis	215	340	960	1,250
1950J	10	Kansas City	120	180	260	325
1950K	11	Dallas	68	88	145	155
1950L	12	San Francisco	68	88	145	155

★ Star notes are worth about two to five times more than regular issues.

$5 SERIES 1928-A—Signatures: *Woods-Mellon*

Large district numeral at left, similar to Series of 1928 issues.

Friedberg No.	Federal Reserve Bank		VF-20	EF-40	Unc-60	Unc-63
1951A	1	Boston	$40	$120	$250	$350
1951B	2	New York	40	80	140	200
1951C	3	Philadelphia	45	90	160	225
1951D	4	Cleveland	40	80	140	200
1951E	5	Richmond	45	100	200	250
1951F	6	Atlanta	125	250	550	1,000
1951G	7	Chicago	40	80	140	200
1951H	8	St. Louis	45	90	180	250
1951I	9	Minneapolis	325	750	1,250	2,250
1951J	10	Kansas City	65	135	240	400
1951K	11	Dallas	75	125	275	450
1951L	12	San Francisco	40	100	220	275

FEDERAL RESERVE NOTES—GREEN SEAL

FIVE DOLLARS

$5 SERIES 1928-B—Signatures: *Woods-Mellon*

Large district letter replaces numeral in seal on this and succeeding issues.

Friedberg No.	Federal Reserve Bank		VF-20	EF-40	Unc-60	Unc-63
1952A	A	Boston	$25	$35	$65	$90
1952B	B	New York	25	35	65	90
1952C	C	Philadelphia	25	35	65	90
1952D	D	Cleveland	25	35	65	90
1952E	E	Richmond	25	35	65	90
1952F	F	Atlanta	30	40	90	125
1952G	G	Chicago	25	35	65	90
1952H	H	St. Louis	25	35	65	90
1952I	I	Minneapolis	55	80	160	275
1952J	J	Kansas City	30	40	90	125
1952K	K	Dallas	50	75	150	250
1952L	L	San Francisco	25	35	75	100

$5 SERIES 1928-C—Signatures: *Woods-Mills*

Friedberg No.	Federal Reserve Bank		VF-20	EF-40	Unc-60	Unc-63
1953D	D	Cleveland	—	—	—	—
1953F	F	Atlanta	$585	$1,020	$5,600	$7,500
1953L	L	San Francisco	—	—	—	—

$5 SERIES 1928-D—Signatures: *Woods-Woodin*

Friedberg No.	Federal Reserve Bank		VF-20	EF-40	Unc-60	Unc-63
1954F	F	Atlanta	$1,880	$2,500	$6,250	$10,600

Bureau records do not give any indication of the serial numbers for the Series of 1928-D $5. However, a fair number of them have been confirmed with serial numbers scattered from F26 282 729A to F28 617 186A. These were well interspersed with 1928-C notes*.

General Face Design. Series 1928-B through 1928-D.
Face Design. Series 1934 through 1934-D. Back Design on page 226.

* Robert H. Lloyd has also published the fact that nine plates are on record as having been used for the $5 Series of 1928-D notes.

FEDERAL RESERVE NOTES—GREEN SEAL

FIVE DOLLARS

$5 SERIES 1934—Signatures: *Julian-Morgenthau*

Light or dark green seal. Star notes exist for all districts.

Friedberg Nos., Light: F-1955; Dark: F-1956

Federal Reserve Bank		VF-20	EF-40	Unc-60	Unc-63
A	Boston	$17.60	$24.30	$54	$54
B	New York	17.60	24.30	54	54
C	Philadelphia	17.60	24.30	54	100
D	Cleveland	34.00	54.00	130	160
E	Richmond	68.00	94.00	650	910
F	Atlanta	17.60	54.00	155	195
G	Chicago	17.60	24.30	54	100
H	St. Louis	17.60	40.00	100	115
I	Minneapolis	20.20	43.00	115	130
J	Kansas City	34.00	47.00	115	155
K	Dallas	17.60	27.00	88	100
L	San Francisco	17.60	27.00	110	130

$5 SERIES 1934-A—Signatures: *Julian-Morgenthau*

Star notes exist for all issuing districts; they are scarce.†

Friedberg No.	Federal Reserve Bank		VF-20	EF-40	Unc-60	Unc-63
1957A	A	Boston	$17.60	$20.20	$34	$47
1957B	B	New York	17.60	20.20	34	47
1957C	C	Philadelphia	17.60	20.20	34	47
1957D	D	Cleveland	15.00	20.00	30	50
1957E	E	Richmond	15.00	20.00	30	50
1957F	F	Atlanta	30.00	60.00	125	220
1957G	G	Chicago	12.50	18.00	26	35
1957H	H	St. Louis	20.00	32.00	50	70
1957L	L	San Francisco	15.00	22.00	35	60

† Bureau records do not show any printings, regular or star, for $5 notes Series of 1934-A for Minneapolis, Kansas City, or Dallas.

$5 SERIES 1934-B—Signatures: *Julian-Vinson*

Friedberg No.	Federal Reserve Bank		VF-20	EF-40	Unc-60	Unc-63
1958A	A	Boston	$20	$40	$90	$125
1958B	B	New York	15	35	65	85
1958C	C	Philadelphia	15	35	65	85
1958D	D	Cleveland	15	35	65	85
1958E	E	Richmond	25	50	100	135
1958F	F	Atlanta	25	50	100	135
1958G	G	Chicago	20	40	80	110
1958H	H	St. Louis	20	40	80	110
1958I	I	Minneapolis	35	70	130	165
1958J	J	Kansas City	2,350	3,500	5,250	9,500
1958L	L	San Francisco	15	35	65	85

FEDERAL RESERVE NOTES—GREEN SEAL

FIVE DOLLARS

$5 SERIES 1934-C—Signatures: *Julian-Snyder*

Friedberg No.	Federal Reserve Bank		VF-20	EF-40	Unc-60	Unc-63
1959A	A	Boston	$20	$35	$70	$85
1959B	B	New York	15	30	50	75
1959C	C	Philadelphia	15	30	50	75
1959D	D	Cleveland	15	30	50	75
1959E	E	Richmond	15	30	50	75
1959F	F	Atlanta	15	30	50	75
1959G	G	Chicago	15	30	50	75
1959H	H	St. Louis	25	40	65	90
1959I	I	Minneapolis	30	50	85	120
1959J	J	Kansas City	25	40	65	90
1959K	K	Dallas	30	50	80	110
1959L	L	San Francisco	25	40	65	90

$5 SERIES 1934-D—Signatures: *Clark-Snyder*

Friedberg No.	Federal Reserve Bank		VF-20	EF-40	Unc-60	Unc-63
1960A	A	Boston	$18	$32	$55	$80
1960B	B	New York	15	30	50	75
1960C	C	Philadelphia	15	30	50	75
1960D	D	Cleveland	15	30	60	85
1960E	E	Richmond	25	40	70	90
1960F	F	Atlanta	125	225	350	575
1960G	G	Chicago	15	30	60	85
1960H	H	St. Louis	25	40	65	90
1960I	I	Minneapolis	95	200	325	575
1960J	J	Kansas City	25	40	70	90
1960K	K	Dallas	45	65	140	200
1960L	L	San Francisco	20	38	65	90

FIVE DOLLARS

Face Design. Series 1950 through 1950-E.
General Face Design. Series 1963 through 1995.
Back Design on page 226.

FEDERAL RESERVE NOTES—GREEN SEAL

FIVE DOLLARS

$5 SERIES 1950—Signatures: *Clark-Snyder*

Friedberg No.	Federal Reserve Bank		Unc-60	Unc-63
1961A	A	Boston	$46	$55
1961A★	A★	Boston	220	325
1961B	B	New York	46	55
1961B★	B★	New York	220	325
1960C	C	Philadelphia	46	55
1961C★	C★	Philadelphia	220	325
1961D	D	Cleveland	46	55
1961D★	D★	Cleveland	220	325
1961E	E	Richmond	46	55
1961E★	E★	Richmond	220	325
1961F	F	Atlanta	46	55
1961F★	F★	Atlanta	220	325
1961G	G	Chicago	$46	$55
1961G★	G★	Chicago	220	325
1961H	H	St. Louis	46	55
1961H★	H★	St. Louis	220	325
1961I	I	Minneapolis	46	55
1961I★	I★	Minneapolis	455	715
1961J	J	Kansas City	46	55
1961J★	J★	Kansas City	220	325
1961K	K	Dallas	46	55
1961K★	K★	Dallas	360	520
1961L	L	San Francisco	46	55
1961L★	L★	San Francisco	240	360

$5 SERIES 1950-A—Signatures: *Priest-Humphrey*

Friedberg No.	Federal Reserve Bank		Unc-60	Unc-63
1962A	A	Boston	$20.20	$30
1962A★	A★	Boston	61.00	74
1962B	B	New York	20.20	30
1962B★	B★	New York	61.00	74
1962C	C	Philadelphia	20.20	30
1962C★	C★	Philadelphia	61.00	74
1962D	D	Cleveland	20.20	30
1962D★	D★	Cleveland	61.00	74
1962E	E	Richmond	20.20	30
1962E★	E★	Richmond	81.00	100
1962F	F	Atlanta	20.20	30
1962F★	F★	Atlanta	61.00	74
1962G	G	Chicago	$20.20	$30
1962G★	G★	Chicago	54.00	68
1962H	H	St. Louis	20.20	30
1962H★	H★	St. Louis	61.00	74
1962I	I	Minneapolis	23.00	32
1962I★	I★	Minneapolis	260.00	325
1962J	J	Kansas City	20.20	30
1962J★	J★	Kansas City	81.00	100
1962K	K	Dallas	30.00	40
1962K★	K★	Dallas	88.00	120
1962L	L	San Francisco	20.20	30
1962L★	L★	San Francisco	61.00	74

$5 SERIES 1950-B—Signatures: *Priest-Anderson*

Friedberg No.	Federal Reserve Bank		Unc-60	Unc-63
1963A	A	Boston	$18.20	$26
1963A★	A★	Boston	51.00	65
1963B	B	New York	18.20	26
1963B★	B★	New York	40.00	54
1963C	C	Philadelphia	18.20	26
1963C★	C★	Philadelphia	51.00	65
1963D	D	Cleveland	18.20	26
1963D★	D★	Cleveland	51.00	65
1963E	E	Richmond	18.20	26
1963E★	E★	Richmond	51.00	65
1963F	F	Atlanta	18.20	26
1963F★	F★	Atlanta	51.00	65
1963G	G	Chicago	$18.20	$26
1963G★	G★	Chicago	40.00	54
1963H	H	St. Louis	18.20	26
1963H★	H★	St. Louis	51.00	65
1963I	I	Minneapolis	28.00	38
1963I★	I★	Minneapolis	115.00	155
1963J	J	Kansas City	18.20	26
1963J★	J★	Kansas City	51.00	65
1963K	K	Dallas	18.20	26
1963K★	K★	Dallas	51.00	65
1963L	L	San Francisco	18.20	26
1963L★	L★	San Francisco	51.00	65

FEDERAL RESERVE NOTES—GREEN SEAL

FIVE DOLLARS

$5 SERIES 1950-C—Signatures: *Smith-Dillon*

Friedberg No.	Federal Reserve Bank		Unc-60	Unc-63	Friedberg No.	Federal Reserve Bank		Unc-60	Unc-63
1964A	A	Boston	$16.20	$24.30	**1964G**	G	Chicago	$16.20	$24.30
1964A★	A★	Boston	130.00	180.00	**1964G★**	G★	Chicago	65.00	78.00
1964B	B	New York	16.20	24.30	**1964H**	H	St. Louis	22.30	30.00
1964B★	B★	New York	61.00	81.00	**1964H★**	H★	St. Louis	74.00	100.00
1964C	C	Philadelphia	16.20	24.30	**1964I**	I	Minneapolis	35.00	46.00
1964C★	C★	Philadelphia	61.00	81.00	**1964I★**	I★	Minneapolis	130.00	180.00
1964D	D	Cleveland	16.20	24.30	**1964J**	J	Kansas City	16.20	24.30
1964D★	D★	Cleveland	74.00	100.00	**1964J★**	J★	Kansas City	74.00	100.00
1964E	E	Richmond	16.20	24.30	**1964K**	K	Dallas	40.00	50.00
1964E★	E★	Richmond	84.00	120.00	**1964K★**	K★	Dallas	135.00	195.00
1964F	F	Atlanta	16.20	24.30	**1964L**	L	San Francisco	16.20	24.30
1964F★	F★	Atlanta	65.00	89.00	**1964L★**	L★	San Francisco	88.00	115.00

$5 SERIES 1950-D—Signatures: *Granahan-Dillon*

Friedberg No.	Federal Reserve Bank		Unc-60	Unc-63	Friedberg No.	Federal Reserve Bank		Unc-60	Unc-63
1965A	A	Boston	$16.20	$24.30	**1965G**	G	Chicago	$16.20	$24.30
1965A★	A★	Boston	81.00	100.00	**1965G★**	G★	Chicago	40.00	65.00
1965B	B	New York	16.20	24.30	**1965H**	H	St. Louis	16.20	24.30
1965B★	B★	New York	38.00	55.00	**1965H★**	H★	St. Louis	61.00	81.00
1965C	C	Philadelphia	20.20	30.00	**1965I**	I	Minneapolis	35.00	45.00
1965C★	C★	Philadelphia	55.00	70.00	**1965I★**	I★	Minneapolis	130.00	180.00
1965D	D	Cleveland	16.20	24.30	**1965J**	J	Kansas City	26.00	35.00
1965D★	D★	Cleveland	70.00	84.00	**1965J★**	J★	Kansas City	65.00	86.00
1965E	E	Richmond	16.20	24.30	**1965K**	K	Dallas	30.00	40.00
1965E★	E★	Richmond	76.00	94.00	**1965K★**	K★	Dallas	110.00	160.00
1965F	F	Atlanta	16.20	24.30	**1965L**	L	San Francisco	16.20	24.30
1965F★	F★	Atlanta	76.00	94.00	**1965L★**	L★	San Francisco	68.00	86.00

$5 SERIES 1950-E—Signatures: *Granahan-Fowler*

Friedberg No.	Federal Reserve Bank		Unc-60	Unc-63	Friedberg No.	Federal Reserve Bank		Unc-60	Unc-63
	A	Boston	Not printed		**1966G**	G	Chicago	$54	$68
	A★	Boston	Not printed		**1966G★**	G★	Chicago	195	245
1966B	B	New York	$30	$46		H	St. Louis	Not printed	
1966B★	B★	New York	68	94		H★	St. Louis	Not printed	
	C	Philadelphia	Not printed			I	Minneapolis	Not printed	
	C★	Philadelphia	Not printed			I★	Minneapolis	Not printed	
	D	Cleveland	Not printed			J	Kansas City	Not printed	
	D★	Cleveland	Not printed			J★	Kansas City	Not printed	
	E	Richmond	Not printed			K	Dallas	Not printed	
	E★	Richmond	Not printed			K★	Dallas	Not printed	
	F	Atlanta	Not printed		**1966L**	L	San Francisco	40	61
	F★	Atlanta	Not printed		**1966L★**	L★	San Francisco	130	215

Notes of the 1950-E series do not have the motto on the back. These were released *after* the 1963 series.

FEDERAL RESERVE NOTES—GREEN SEAL

FIVE DOLLARS

$5 SERIES 1963—Signatures: *Granahan-Dillon*

Motto "In God We Trust" added on the back. Back design on page 227.

Friedberg No.	Federal Reserve Bank		Unc-60	Unc-63
1967A	A	Boston	$25.00	$30
1967A★	A★	Boston	74.00	88
1967B	B	New York	20.20	26
1967B★	B★	New York	49.00	65
1967C	C	Philadelphia	20.20	26
1967C★	C★	Philadelphia	55.00	70
1967D	D	Cleveland	20.20	26
1967D★	D★	Cleveland	49.00	65
	E	Richmond	Not printed	
	E★	Richmond	Not printed	
1967F	F	Atlanta	20.20	26
1967F★	F★	Atlanta	40.00	50
1967G	G	Chicago	20.20	$26
1967G★	G★	Chicago	40.00	50
1967H	H	St. Louis	20.20	26
1967H★	H★	St. Louis	40.00	50
	I	Minneapolis	Not printed	
	I★	Minneapolis	Not printed	
1967J	J	Kansas City	20.20	26
1967J★	J★	Kansas City	50.00	65
1967K	K	Dallas	20.20	26
1967K★	K★	Dallas	61.00	84
1967L	L	San Francisco	20.20	26
1967L★	L★	San Francisco	45.00	55

$5 SERIES 1963-A—Signatures: *Granahan-Fowler*

Friedberg No.	Federal Reserve Bank		Unc-60	Unc-63
1968A	A	Boston	$14.80	$24.30
1968A★	A★	Boston	26.00	43.00
1968B	B	New York	14.80	24.30
1968B★	B★	New York	26.00	43.00
1968C	C	Philadelphia	14.80	24.30
1968C★	C★	Philadelphia	26.00	43.00
1968D	D	Cleveland	14.80	24.30
1968D★	D★	Cleveland	26.00	43.00
1968E	E	Richmond	14.80	24.30
1968E★	E★	Richmond	26.00	43.00
1968F	F	Atlanta	14.80	24.30
1968F★	F★	Atlanta	26.00	43.00
1968G	G	Chicago	$14.80	$24.30
1968G★	G★	Chicago	26.00	43.00
1968H	H	St. Louis	14.80	24.30
1968H★	H★	St. Louis	26.00	43.00
1968I	I	Minneapolis	14.80	24.30
1968I★	I★	Minneapolis	26.00	43.00
1968J	J	Kansas City	14.80	24.30
1968J★	J★	Kansas City	30.00	40.00
1968K	K	Dallas	14.80	24.30
1968K★	K★	Dallas	35.00	46.00
1968L	L	San Francisco	14.80	24.30
1968L★	L★	San Francisco	26.00	43.00

$5 SERIES 1969—Signatures: *Elston-Kennedy*

Friedberg No.	Federal Reserve Bank		Unc-60	Unc-63
1969A	A	Boston	$14.80	$24.30
1969A★	A★	Boston	35.00	46.00
1969B	B	New York	12.20	18.20
1969B★	B★	New York	22.30	30.00
1969C	C	Philadelphia	12.20	18.20
1969C★	C★	Philadelphia	22.30	30.00
1969D	D	Cleveland	12.20	18.20
1969D★	D★	Cleveland	22.30	30.00
1969E	E	Richmond	12.20	18.20
1969E★	E★	Richmond	22.30	30.00
1969F	F	Atlanta	12.20	18.20
1969F★	F★	Atlanta	22.30	30.00
1969G	G	Chicago	$12.20	$18.20
1969G★	G★	Chicago	22.30	30.00
1969H	H	St. Louis	12.20	18.20
1969H★	H★	St. Louis	35.00	49.00
1969I	I	Minneapolis	18.20	25.00
1969I★	I★	Minneapolis	49.00	68.00
1969J	J	Kansas City	12.20	18.20
1969J★	J★	Kansas City	22.30	30.00
1969K	K	Dallas	12.20	18.20
1969K★	K★	Dallas	30.00	40.00
1969L	L	San Francisco	12.20	18.20
1969L★	L★	San Francisco	24.30	32.00

FEDERAL RESERVE NOTES—GREEN SEAL

FIVE DOLLARS

$5 SERIES 1969-A—Signatures: *Kabis-Connally*

Friedberg No.	Federal Reserve Bank		Unc-60	Unc-63	Friedberg No.	Federal Reserve Bank		Unc-60	Unc-63
1970A	A	Boston	$14.80	$24.30	**1970G**	G	Chicago	$14.80	$24.30
1970A★	A★	Boston	46.00	61.00	**1970G★**	G★	Chicago	40.00	50.00
1970B	B	New York	14.80	24.30	**1970H**	H	St. Louis	14.80	24.30
1970B★	B★	New York	40.00	50.00	**1970H★**	H★	St. Louis	68.00	81.00
1970C	C	Philadelphia	14.80	24.30	**1970I**	I	Minneapolis	20.20	30.00
1970C★	C★	Philadelphia	40.00	50.00	**1970I★**	I★	Minneapolis	68.00	81.00
1970D	D	Cleveland	14.80	24.30	**1970J**	J	Kansas City	14.80	24.30
1970D★	D★	Cleveland	46.00	61.00	**1970J★**	J★	Kansas City	47.00	62.00
1970E	E	Richmond	14.80	24.30	**1970K**	K	Dallas	14.80	24.30
1970E★	E★	Richmond	46.00	61.00	**1970K★**	K★	Dallas	68.00	81.00
1970F	F	Atlanta	14.80	24.30	**1970L**	L	San Francisco	14.80	24.30
1970F★	F★	Atlanta	68.00	81.00	**1970L★**	L★	San Francisco	46.00	61.00

$5 SERIES 1969-B—Signatures: *Bañuelos-Connally*

Friedberg No.	Federal Reserve Bank		Unc-60	Unc-63	Friedberg No.	Federal Reserve Bank		Unc-60	Unc-63
1971A	A	Boston	$65	$76	**1971G**	G	Chicago	$61	$70
	A★	Boston	Not printed		**1971G★**	G★	Chicago	155	210
1971B	B	New York	61	70	**1971H**	H	St. Louis	61	70
1971B★	B★	New York	130	180		H★	St. Louis	Not printed	
1971C	C	Philadelphia	61	70	**1971I**	I	Minneapolis	61	70
	C★	Philadelphia	Not printed			I★	Minneapolis	Not printed	
1971D	D	Cleveland	61	70	**1971J**	J	Kansas City	61	70
	D★	Cleveland	Not printed		**1971J★**	J★	Kansas City	130	180
1971E	E	Richmond	61	70	**1971K**	K	Dallas	61	70
1971E★	E★	Richmond	130	180		K★	Dallas	Not printed	
1971F	F	Atlanta	61	70	**1971L**	L	San Francisco	61	70
1971F★	F★	Atlanta	130	180	**1971L★**	L★	San Francisco	130	180

$5 SERIES 1969-C—Signatures: *Bañuelos-Shultz*

Friedberg No.	Federal Reserve Bank		Unc-60	Unc-63	Friedberg No.	Federal Reserve Bank		Unc-60	Unc-63
1972A	A	Boston	$14.80	$24.30	**1972G**	G	Chicago	$14.80	$24.30
1972A★	A★	Boston	50.00	61.00		G★	Chicago	Not printed	
1972B	B	New York	14.80	24.30	**1972H**	H	St. Louis	14.80	24.30
1972B★	B★	New York	35.00	43.00	**1972H★**	H★	St. Louis	40.00	50.00
1972C	C	Philadelphia	14.80	24.30	**1972I**	I	Minneapolis	20.20	34.00
1972C★	C★	Philadelphia	40.00	50.00		I★	Minneapolis	Not printed	
1972D	D	Cleveland	14.80	24.30	**1972J**	J	Kansas City	14.80	24.30
1972D★	D★	Cleveland	65.00	73.00	**1972J★**	J★	Kansas City	35.00	43.00
1972E	E	Richmond	14.80	24.30	**1972K**	K	Dallas	14.80	24.30
1972E★	E★	Richmond	65.00	73.00	**1972K★**	K★	Dallas	43.00	54.00
1972F	F	Atlanta	14.80	24.30	**1972L**	L	San Francisco	14.80	24.30
1972F★	F★	Atlanta	40.00	50.00	**1972L★**	L★	San Francisco	40.00	50.00

FEDERAL RESERVE NOTES—GREEN SEAL

FIVE DOLLARS

$5 SERIES 1974—Signatures: *Neff-Simon*

Friedberg No.	Federal Reserve Bank		Unc-60	Unc-63
1973A	A	Boston	$12.20	$18.90
1973A★	A★	Boston	40.00	50.00
1973B	B	New York	12.20	18.90
1973B★	B★	New York	30.00	40.00
1973C	C	Philadelphia	12.20	18.90
1973C★	C★	Philadelphia	30.00	40.00
1973D	D	Cleveland	12.20	18.90
1973D★	D★	Cleveland	30.00	40.00
1973E	E	Richmond	12.20	18.90
1973E★	E★	Richmond	30.00	40.00
1973F	F	Atlanta	12.20	18.90
1973F★	F★	Atlanta	30.00	40.00
1973G	G	Chicago	$12.20	$18.90
1973G★	G★	Chicago	30.00	40.00
1973H	H	St. Louis	12.20	18.90
1973H★	H★	St. Louis	54.00	65.00
1973I	I	Minneapolis	12.20	18.90
1973I★	I★	Minneapolis	30.00	40.00
1973J	J	Kansas City	12.20	18.90
1973J★	J★	Kansas City	30.00	40.00
1973K	K	Dallas	12.20	18.90
1973K★	K★	Dallas	30.00	40.00
1973L	L	San Francisco	12.20	18.90
1973L★	L★	San Francisco	30.00	40.00

$5 SERIES 1977—Signatures: *Morton-Blumenthal*

Friedberg No.	Federal Reserve Bank		Unc-60	Unc-63
1974A	A	Boston	$12.20	$18.90
1974A★	A★	Boston	61.00	81.00
1974B	B	New York	12.20	18.90
1974B★	B★	New York	40.00	50.00
1974C	C	Philadelphia	12.20	18.90
1974C★	C★	Philadelphia	40.00	50.00
1974D	D	Cleveland	12.20	18.90
1974D★	D★	Cleveland	50.00	61.00
1974E	E	Richmond	12.20	18.90
1974E★	E★	Richmond	40.00	50.00
1974F	F	Atlanta	12.20	18.90
1974F★	F★	Atlanta	40.00	50.00
1974G	G	Chicago	$12.20	$18.90
1974G★	G★	Chicago	30.00	40.00
1974H	H	St. Louis	12.20	18.90
1974H★	H★	St. Louis	115.00	145.00
1974I	I	Minneapolis	14.80	20.20
	I★	Minneapolis	Not printed	
1974J	J	Kansas City	12.20	18.90
1974J★	J★	Kansas City	40.00	50.00
1974K	K	Dallas	12.20	18.90
1974K★	K★	Dallas	40.00	50.00
1974L	L	San Francisco	12.20	18.90
1974L★	L★	San Francisco	40.00	50.00

$5 SERIES 1977-A—Signatures: *Morton-Miller*

Friedberg No.	Federal Reserve Bank		Unc-60	Unc-63
1975A	A	Boston	$12.20	$18.90
1975A★	A★	Boston	74.00	88.00
1975B	B	New York	12.20	18.90
1975B★	B★	New York	40.00	50.00
1975C	C	Philadelphia	12.20	18.90
1975C★	C★	Philadelphia	61.00	74.00
1975D	D	Cleveland	12.20	18.90
1975D★	D★	Cleveland	62.00	81.00
1975E	E	Richmond	12.20	18.90
1975E★	E★	Richmond	145.00	195.00
1975F	F	Atlanta	12.20	18.90
1975F★	F★	Atlanta	74.00	88.00
1975G	G	Chicago	$12.20	$18.90
1975G★	G★	Chicago	62.00	81.00
1975H	H	St. Louis	12.20	18.90
1975H★	H★	St. Louis	50.00	61.00
1975I	I	Minneapolis	12.20	18.90
1975I★	I★	Minneapolis	130.00	150.00
1975J	J	Kansas City	12.20	18.90
1975J★	J★	Kansas City	74.00	88.00
1975K	K	Dallas	12.20	18.90
1975K★	K★	Dallas	62.00	81.00
1975L	L	San Francisco	12.20	18.90
1975L★	L★	San Francisco	74.00	88.00

FEDERAL RESERVE NOTES—GREEN SEAL

FIVE DOLLARS

$5 SERIES 1981—Signatures: *Buchanan-Regan*

Friedberg No.	Federal Reserve Bank		Unc-60	Unc-63
1976A	A	Boston	$20.20	$26
1976A★	A★	Boston	—	—
1976B	B	New York	20.20	26
1976B★	B★	New York	68.00	88
1976C	C	Philadelphia	20.20	26
1976C★	C★	Philadelphia	120.00	150
1976D	D	Cleveland	20.20	26
1976D★	D★	Cleveland	120.00	150
1976E	E	Richmond	20.20	26
1976E★	E★	Richmond	100.00	120
1976F	F	Atlanta	20.20	26
1976F★	F★	Atlanta	120.00	150
1976G	G	Chicago	$20.20	$26
1976G★	G★	Chicago	65.00	81
1976H	H	St. Louis	20.20	26
1976H★	H★	St. Louis	135.00	160
1976I	I	Minneapolis	20.20	26
1976I★	I★	Minneapolis	265.00	365
1976J	J	Kansas City	20.20	26
1976J★	J★	Kansas City	100.00	120
1976K	K	Dallas	20.20	26
1976K★	K★	Dallas	100.00	120
1976L	L	San Francisco	20.20	26
1976L★	L★	San Francisco	65.00	81

$5 SERIES 1981-A—Signatures: *Ortega-Regan*

Friedberg No.	Federal Reserve Bank		Unc-60	Unc-63
1977A	A	Boston	$40	$50
	A★	Boston	Not printed	
1977B	B	New York	35	40
1977B★	B★	New York	120	130
1977C	C	Philadelphia	35	40
	C★	Philadelphia	Not printed	
1977D	D	Cleveland	35	40
	D★	Cleveland	Not printed	
1977E	E	Richmond	35	40
	E★	Richmond	Not printed	
1977F	F	Atlanta	35	40
	F★	Atlanta	Not printed	
1977G	G	Chicago	$35	$40
	G★	Chicago	Not printed	
1977H	H	St. Louis	40	50
	H★	St. Louis	Not printed	
1977I	I	Minneapolis	40	50
	I★	Minneapolis	Not printed	
1977J	J	Kansas City	60	70
	J★	Kansas City	Not printed	
1977K	K	Dallas	40	50
	K★	Dallas	Not printed	
1977L	L	San Francisco	40	50
1977L★	L★	San Francisco	120	130

$5 SERIES 1985— Signatures: *Ortega-Baker*

Friedberg No.	Federal Reserve Bank		Unc-60	Unc-63
1978A	A	Boston	$14.80	$20.20
1978B	B	New York	14.80	20.20
1978B★	B★	New York	135.00	170.00
1978C	C	Philadelphia	14.80	20.20
1978C★	C★	Philadelphia	65.00	76.00
1978D	D	Cleveland	14.80	20.20
1978E	E	Richmond	14.80	20.20
1978E★	E★	Richmond	76.00	100.00
1978F	F	Atlanta	14.80	20.20
1978F★	F★	Atlanta	65.00	76.00
1978G	G	Chicago	$14.80	$20.20
1978G★	G★	Chicago	65.00	76.00
1978H	H	St. Louis	14.80	20.20
1978I	I	Minneapolis	14.80	20.20
1978J	J	Kansas City	14.80	20.20
1978K	K	Dallas	14.80	20.20
1978K★	K★	Dallas	76.00	100.00
1978L	L	San Francisco	14.80	20.20
1978L★	L★	San Francisco	76.00	100.00

$5 SERIES 1988—Signatures: *Ortega-Brady*

Issues from all 12 Federal Reserve Districts have nominal values and are commonly available in high grade condition. Star replacement notes have a 25 percent premium.

$5 SERIES 1988-A—Signatures: *Villalpando-Brady*

Issues from all 12 Federal Reserve Districts have nominal values and are commonly available in high grade condition. Star replacement notes have a 25 percent premium.

FEDERAL RESERVE NOTES—GREEN SEAL

FIVE DOLLARS

$5 SERIES 1988-A—Signatures: *Villalpando-Brady*

Sheet-fed, Fort Worth facility. Face check letter/number is preceded by small letters FW. Issues from most Federal Reserve Districts have nominal values and are commonly available in high grade condition. Star replacement notes have a 25 percent premium.

$5 SERIES 1993—Signatures: *Withrow-Bentsen*

Added security devices. Sheet-fed, Washington facility. With normal face check letter/number. Issues from Boston, New York, Philadelphia, Richmond, and Atlanta have nominal values and are commonly available in high grade condition. Star replacement notes have a 25 percent premium.

$5 SERIES 1993—Signatures: *Withrow-Bentsen*

Added security devices. Sheet-fed, Forth Worth facility. Face check letter/number is preceded by small letters FW. Issues from most Federal Reserve Districts have nominal values and are commonly available in high grade condition. Star replacement notes have a 25 percent premium.

$5 SERIES 1995—Signatures: *Withrow-Rubin*

Added security devices. Sheet-fed at both Washington and Fort Worth facilities. Issues from all Federal Reserve Districts have nominal values and are commonly available in high grade condition. Star replacement notes have a 25 percent premium.

REVISED LARGER PORTRAIT DESIGN

Face Design. Series 1999 through 2003-A.

Back Design. Series 1999 through 2003-A.

$5 SERIES 1999—Signatures: *Withrow-Summers*

Both sides redesigned. Sheet-fed at both Washington and Fort Worth facilities. Issues from all Federal Reserve Districts have nominal values and are commonly available in high grade condition. Star replacement notes have a 25 percent premium.

FEDERAL RESERVE NOTES—GREEN SEAL

FIVE DOLLARS

$5 SERIES 2001—Signatures: *Marin-O'Neil*

Added security devices. Sheet-fed at both Washington and Fort Worth facilities. Issues from all Federal Reserve Districts have nominal values and are commonly available in high grade condition. Star replacement notes have a 25 percent premium.

$5 SERIES 2003—Signatures: *Marin-Snow*

Added security devices. Sheet-fed at both Washington and Forth Worth facilities. Issues from all Federal Reserve Districts have nominal values and are commonly available in high grade condition. Star replacement notes have a 25 percent premium.

$5 SERIES 2003-A—Signatures: *Cabral-Snow*

Added security devices. Printed at the Fort Worth facility.

REVISED PORTRAIT AND COLORIZED DESIGN

Face Design. Series 2006 to present.

Back Design. Series 2006 to present.

$5 SERIES 2006—Signatures: *Cabral-Paulson*

Redesigned both sides, adding color elements. Printed at the Fort Worth facility.

$5 SERIES 2009—Signatures: *Rios-Geithner*

Added security devices. Printed at the Fort Worth facility.

$5 SERIES 2013—Signatures: *Rios-Lew*

Added security devices. Printed at the Washington and Fort Worth facilities.

$5 SERIES 2017-A—Signatures: *Carranza-Mnuchin*

Printed at the Fort Worth facility.

$5 SERIES 2021—Signatures: *Malerba-Yellen*

Printed at the Fort Worth facility.

FEDERAL RESERVE NOTES—GREEN SEAL

TEN DOLLARS

Face Design. Series 1928 and 1928-A. Back Design on page 235.

$10 SERIES 1928—Signatures: *Tate-Mellon*

Large district numeral of bank at left.

Friedberg No.	Federal Reserve Bank		VF-20	EF-40	Unc-60	Unc-63
2000A	1	Boston	$60	$100	$200	$350
2000B	2	New York	50	90	175	265
2000C	3	Philadelphia	55	95	175	275
2000D	4	Cleveland	50	90	200	350
2000E	5	Richmond	75	170	425	600
2000F	6	Atlanta	55	95	185	300
2000G	7	Chicago	50	90	175	250
2000H	8	St. Louis	55	95	175	265
2000I	9	Minneapolis	70	170	425	600
2000J	10	Kansas City	50	90	175	275
2000K	11	Dallas	60	145	375	600
2000L	12	San Francisco	55	95	175	250

$10 SERIES 1928-A—Signatures: *Woods-Mellon*

Large district numeral at left, similar to Series of 1928 issues.

Friedberg No.	Federal Reserve Bank		VF-20	EF-40	Unc-60	Unc-63
2001A	1	Boston	$75	$190	$450	$750
2001B	2	New York	50	90	200	275
2001C	3	Philadelphia	50	125	285	425
2001D	4	Cleveland	50	90	200	275
2001E	5	Richmond	100	275	725	1,000
2001F	6	Atlanta	50	125	300	425
2001G	7	Chicago	50	90	200	275
2001H	8	St. Louis	70	125	250	375
2001I	9	Minneapolis	600	1,350	3,750	5,500
2001J	10	Kansas City	435	1,100	2,400	3,250
2001K	11	Dallas	400	1,000	2,200	3,000
2001L	12	San Francisco	90	150	350	500

FEDERAL RESERVE NOTES—GREEN SEAL

TEN DOLLARS

General Face Design. Series 1928-B and 1928-C.
Face Design. Series 1934 through 1934-D. Back Design on page 235.

$10 SERIES 1928-B—Signatures: *Woods-Mellon*

Large district letter replaces numeral in seal on this and succeeding issues.

Friedberg No.	Federal Reserve Bank		VF-20	EF-40	Unc-60	Unc-63
2002A	A	Boston	$40	$55	$95	$115
2002B	B	New York	40	55	95	115
2002C	C	Philadelphia	40	55	95	115
2002D	D	Cleveland	40	55	95	115
2002E	E	Richmond	40	55	95	115
2002F	F	Atlanta	40	55	95	115
2002G	G	Chicago	40	55	95	115
2002H	H	St. Louis	40	55	95	115
2002I	I	Minneapolis	40	55	95	115
2002J	J	Kansas City	40	55	95	115
2002K	K	Dallas	75	100	140	250
2002L	L	San Francisco	40	55	95	115

$10 SERIES 1928-C—Signatures: *Woods-Mills*

Friedberg No.	Federal Reserve Bank		VF-20	EF-40	Unc-60	Unc-63
2003B	B	New York	$120	$180	$260	$360
2003D	D	Cleveland	130	390	900	1,550
2003E	E	Richmond	1,000	2,400	—	—
2003F	F	Atlanta	—	—	—	—
2003G	G	Chicago	120	180	260	360

$10 SERIES 1934—Signatures: *Julian-Morgenthau*

Friedberg No., Light: F-2004; Dark: F-2005

Federal Reserve Bank		VF-20	EF-40	Unc-60	Unc-63
A	Boston	$20	$35	$60	$75
B	New York	18	30	50	65
C	Philadelphia	20	35	60	75
D	Cleveland	20	35	60	75
E	Richmond	20	35	60	90
F	Atlanta	20	35	60	75
G	Chicago	18	30	50	65

Values are for dark seals. Light seals are valued somewhat higher.

FEDERAL RESERVE NOTES—GREEN SEAL

TEN DOLLARS

Friedberg No., Light: F-2004; Dark: F-2005

Federal Reserve Bank		VF-20	EF-40	Unc-60	Unc-63
H	St. Louis	$18.00	$35	$60	$90
I	Minneapolis	22.50	45	95	125
J	Kansas City	18.00	35	60	90
K	Dallas	20.00	42	75	100
L	San Francisco	18.00	35	60	90

Values are for dark seals. Light seals are valued somewhat higher.

$10 SERIES 1934-A—Signatures: *Julian-Morgenthau*

Friedberg No.	Federal Reserve Bank		Unc-60	Unc-63	Friedberg No.	Federal Reserve Bank		Unc-60	Unc-63
2006A	A	Boston	$30	$40	**2006G**	G	Chicago	$30	$40
2006B	B	New York	30	40	**2006H**	H	St. Louis	30	40
2006C	C	Philadelphia	30	40	**2006I**	I	Minneapolis	30	40
2006D	D	Cleveland	30	40	**2006J**	J	Kansas City	30	40
2006E	E	Richmond	30	40	**2006K**	K	Dallas	30	40
2006F	F	Atlanta	30	40	**2006L**	L	San Francisco	30	40

$10 SERIES 1934-B—Signatures: *Julian-Vinson*

Friedberg No.	Federal Reserve Bank		Unc-60	Unc-63	Friedberg No.	Federal Reserve Bank		Unc-60	Unc-63
2007A	A	Boston	$115	$140	**2007G**	G	Chicago	$50	$70
2007B	B	New York	65	80	**2007H**	H	St. Louis	85	110
2007C	C	Philadelphia	70	90	**2007I**	I	Minneapolis	115	150
2007D	D	Cleveland	115	150	**2007J**	J	Kansas City	90	115
2007E	E	Richmond	115	150	**2007K**	K	Dallas	135	175
2007F	F	Atlanta	75	100	**2007L**	L	San Francisco	80	100

$10 SERIES 1934-C—Signatures: *Julian-Snyder*

Friedberg No.	Federal Reserve Bank		Unc-60	Unc-63	Friedberg No.	Federal Reserve Bank		Unc-60	Unc-63
2008A	A	Boston	$40	$50	**2008G**	G	Chicago	$35	$40
2008B	B	New York	35	40	**2008H**	H	St. Louis	45	60
2008C	C	Philadelphia	35	40	**2008I**	I	Minneapolis	60	80
2008D	D	Cleveland	40	50	**2008J**	J	Kansas City	45	60
2008E	E	Richmond	40	50	**2008K**	K	Dallas	45	60
2008F	F	Atlanta	45	60	**2008L**	L	San Francisco	35	40

$10 SERIES 1934-D—Signatures: *Clark-Snyder*

Friedberg No.	Federal Reserve Bank		Unc-60	Unc-63	Friedberg No.	Federal Reserve Bank		Unc-60	Unc-63
2009A	A	Boston	$50	$65	**2009G**	G	Chicago	$50	$65
2009B	B	New York	50	65	**2009H**	H	St. Louis	55	70
2009C	C	Philadelphia	50	65	**2009I**	I	Minneapolis	65	85
2009D	D	Cleveland	50	65	**2009J**	J	Kansas City	60	75
2009E	E	Richmond	50	65	**2009K**	K	Dallas	60	75
2009F	F	Atlanta	50	65	**2009L**	L	San Francisco	55	70

FEDERAL RESERVE NOTES—GREEN SEAL

TEN DOLLARS

Face Design, 1950 through 1950-E. Back Design on page 235.

$10 SERIES 1950—Signatures: *Clark-Snyder*

Friedberg No.	Federal Reserve Bank		Unc-60	Unc-63
2010A	A	Boston	$60	$80
2010A★	A★	Boston	375	500
2010B	B	New York	55	70
2010B★	B★	New York	300	400
2010C	C	Philadelphia	60	80
2010C★	C★	Philadelphia	375	500
2010D	D	Cleveland	60	80
2010D★	D★	Cleveland	375	500
2010E	E	Richmond	60	80
2010E★	E★	Richmond	400	525
2010F	F	Atlanta	60	80
2010F★	F★	Atlanta	400	525
2010G	G	Chicago	$55	$70
2010G★	G★	Chicago	325	425
2010H	H	St. Louis	60	80
2010H★	H★	St. Louis	400	525
2010I	I	Minneapolis	70	90
2010I★	I★	Minneapolis	625	850
2010J	J	Kansas City	55	70
2010J★	J★	Kansas City	425	550
2010K	K	Dallas	60	80
2010★	K★	Dallas	425	550
2010L	L	San Francisco	60	80
2010L★	L★	San Francisco	400	525

$10 SERIES 1950-A—Signatures: *Priest-Humphrey*

Friedberg No.	Federal Reserve Bank		Unc-60	Unc-63
2011A	A	Boston	$60	$80
2011A★	A★	Boston	175	225
2011B	B	New York	55	70
2011B★	B★	New York	160	200
2011C	C	Philadelphia	60	80
2011C★	C★	Philadelphia	200	275
2011D	D	Cleveland	55	70
2011D★	D★	Cleveland	200	275
2011E	E	Richmond	60	80
2011E★	E★	Richmond	225	300
2011F	F	Atlanta	55	70
2011F★	F★	Atlanta	175	275
2011G	G	Chicago	$55	$70
2011G★	G★	Chicago	195	250
2011H	H	St. Louis	75	100
2011H★	H★	St. Louis	200	300
2011I	I	Minneapolis	60	80
2011I★	I★	Minneapolis	275	375
2011J	J	Kansas City	55	70
2011J★	J★	Kansas City	250	325
2011K	K	Dallas	60	80
2011K★	K★	Dallas	275	380
2011L	L	San Francisco	55	70
2011L★	L★	San Francisco	175	225

FEDERAL RESERVE NOTES
TEN DOLLARS

$10 SERIES 1950-B—Signatures: *Priest-Anderson*

Friedberg No.	Federal Reserve Bank		Unc-60	Unc-63
2012A	A	Boston	$30	$40
2012A★	A★	Boston	120	150
2012B	B	New York	30	40
2012B★	B★	New York	120	150
2012C	C	Philadelphia	30	40
2012C★	C★	Philadelphia	120	150
2012D	D	Cleveland	30	40
2012D★	D★	Cleveland	120	150
2012E	E	Richmond	30	40
2012E★	E★	Richmond	130	200
2012F	F	Atlanta	30	40
2012F★	F★	Atlanta	120	150

Friedberg No.	Federal Reserve Bank		Unc-60	Unc-63
2012G	G	Chicago	$30	$40
2012G★	G★	Chicago	120	150
2012H	H	St. Louis	30	40
2012H★	H★	St. Louis	150	200
2012I	I	Minneapolis	40	50
2012I★	I★	Minneapolis	225	300
2012J	J	Kansas City	40	50
2012J★	J★	Kansas City	125	160
2012K	K	Dallas	35	45
2012K★	K★	Dallas	200	250
2012L	L	San Francisco	35	45
2012L★	L★	San Francisco	125	160

$10 SERIES 1950-C—Signatures: *Smith-Dillon*

Friedberg No.	Federal Reserve Bank		Unc-60	Unc-63
2013A	A	Boston	$40	$50
2013A★	A★	Boston	240	320
2013B	B	New York	40	50
2013B★	B★	New York	140	175
2013C	C	Philadelphia	40	50
2013C★	C★	Philadelphia	200	300
2013D	D	Cleveland	55	60
2013D★	D★	Cleveland	200	275
2013E	E	Richmond	40	50
2013E★	E★	Richmond	225	350
2013F	F	Atlanta	40	50
2013F★	F★	Atlanta	200	300

Friedberg No.	Federal Reserve Bank		Unc-60	Unc-63
2013G	G	Chicago	$40	$50
2013G★	G★	Chicago	140	175
2013H	H	St. Louis	50	65
2013H★	H★	St. Louis	190	250
2013I	I	Minneapolis	55	75
2013I★	I★	Minneapolis	225	325
2013J	J	Kansas City	60	80
2013J★	J★	Kansas City	190	260
2013K	K	Dallas	60	80
2013K★	K★	Dallas	200	275
2013L	L	San Francisco	55	75
2013L★	L★	San Francisco	190	250

$10 SERIES 1950-D—Signatures: *Granahan-Dillon*

Friedberg No.	Federal Reserve Bank		Unc-60	Unc-63
2014A	A	Boston	$40	$50
2014A★	A★	Boston	125	200
2014B	B	New York	40	50
2014B★	B★	New York	100	165
2014C	C	Philadelphia	40	50
2014C★	C★	Philadelphia	125	200
2014D	D	Cleveland	40	50
2014D★	D★	Cleveland	125	200
2014E	E	Richmond	40	50
2014E★	E★	Richmond	175	250
2014F	F	Atlanta	40	50
2014F★	F★	Atlanta	175	250

Friedberg No.	Federal Reserve Bank		Unc-60	Unc-63
2014G	G	Chicago	$40	$50
2014G★	G★	Chicago	100	165
2014H	H	St. Louis	40	50
2014H★	H★	St. Louis	175	250
	I	Minneapolis	Not printed	
	I★	Minneapolis	Not printed	
2014J	J	Kansas City	40	50
2014J★	J★	Kansas City	150	225
2014K	K	Dallas	40	50
2014K★	K★	Dallas	175	250
2014L	L	San Francisco	40	50
2014L★	L★	San Francisco	165	225

FEDERAL RESERVE NOTES—GREEN SEAL

TEN DOLLARS

$10 SERIES 1950-E—Signatures: *Granahan-Fowler*

Friedberg No.	Federal Reserve Bank		Unc-60	Unc-63
	A	Boston	Not printed	
	A★	Boston	Not printed	
2015B	B	New York	$75	$100
2015B★	B★	New York	250	325
	C	Philadelphia	Not printed	
	C★	Philadelphia	Not printed	
	D	Cleveland	Not printed	
	D★	Cleveland	Not printed	
	E	Richmond	Not printed	
	E★	Richmond	Not printed	
	F	Atlanta	Not printed	
	F★	Atlanta	Not printed	
2015G	G	Chicago	$75	$100
2015G★	G★	Chicago	250	325
	H	St. Louis	Not printed	
	H★	St. Louis	Not printed	
	I	Minneapolis	Not printed	
	I★	Minneapolis	Not printed	
	J	Kansas City	Not printed	
	J★	Kansas City	Not printed	
	K	Dallas	Not printed	
	K★	Dallas	Not printed	
2015L	L	San Francisco	100	150
2015L★	L★	San Francisco	325	450

Notes of the 1950-E series do not have the motto on the back. These were released *after* the 1963 series.

Face Design. Series 1963 through 1995.

Back Design. Series 1963 through 1995.

FEDERAL RESERVE NOTES—GREEN SEAL

TEN DOLLARS

$10 SERIES 1963—Signatures: *Granahan-Dillon*

Friedberg No.	Federal Reserve Bank		Unc-60	Unc-63
2016A	A	Boston	$50	$60
2016A★	A★	Boston	100	125
2016B	B	New York	40	50
2016B★	B★	New York	80	100
2016C	C	Philadelphia	50	60
2016C★	C★	Philadelphia	80	100
2016D	D	Cleveland	50	60
2016D★	D★	Cleveland	100	125
2016E	E	Richmond	50	60
2016E★	E★	Richmond	100	125
2016F	F	Atlanta	50	60
2016F★	F★	Atlanta	80	100
2016G	G	Chicago	$40	$50
2016G★	G★	Chicago	80	100
2016H	H	St. Louis	50	60
2016H★	H★	St. Louis	80	100
	I	Minneapolis	Not printed	
	I★	Minneapolis	Not printed	
2016J	J	Kansas City	50	60
2016J★	J★	Kansas City	100	125
2016K	K	Dallas	50	60
2016K★	K★	Dallas	100	125
2016L	L	San Francisco	50	60
2016L★	L★	San Francisco	80	100

$10 SERIES 1963-A—Signatures: *Granahan-Fowler*

Friedberg No.	Federal Reserve Bank		Unc-60	Unc-63
2017A	A	Boston	$30	$40
2017A★	A★	Boston	60	75
2017B	B	New York	30	40
2017B★	B★	New York	55	70
2017C	C	Philadelphia	30	40
2017C★	C★	Philadelphia	55	70
2017D	D	Cleveland	30	40
2017D★	D★	Cleveland	55	70
2017E	E	Richmond	30	40
2017E★	E★	Richmond	55	70
2017F	F	Atlanta	30	40
2017F★	F★	Atlanta	60	75
2017G	G	Chicago	$30	$40
2017G★	G★	Chicago	55	70
2017H	H	St. Louis	30	40
2017H★	H★	St. Louis	55	70
2017I	I	Minneapolis	30	40
2017I★	I★	Minneapolis	70	90
2017J	J	Kansas City	30	40
2017J★	J★	Kansas City	60	75
2017K	K	Dallas	30	40
2017K★	K★	Dallas	60	75
2017L	L	San Francisco	30	40
2017L★	L★	San Francisco	55	70

$10 SERIES 1969—Signatures: *Elston-Kennedy*

Friedberg No.	Federal Reserve Bank		Unc-60	Unc-63
2018A	A	Boston	$30	$35
2018A★	A★	Boston	50	65
2018B	B	New York	30	35
2018B★	B★	New York	50	65
2018C	C	Philadelphia	30	35
2018C★	C★	Philadelphia	50	65
2018D	D	Cleveland	30	35
2018D★	D★	Cleveland	50	65
2018E	E	Richmond	30	35
2018E★	E★	Richmond	50	65
2018F	F	Atlanta	30	35
2018F★	F★	Atlanta	50	65
2018G	G	Chicago	$30	$35
2018G★	G★	Chicago	50	65
2018H	H	St. Louis	30	35
2018H★	H★	St. Louis	150	225
2018I	I	Minneapolis	30	35
2018I★	I★	Minneapolis	50	65
2018J	J	Kansas City	30	35
2018J★	J★	Kansas City	50	65
2018K	K	Dallas	30	35
2018K★	K★	Dallas	50	65
2018L	L	San Francisco	30	35
2018L★	L★	San Francisco	50	65

FEDERAL RESERVE NOTES—GREEN SEAL

TEN DOLLARS

$10 SERIES 1969-A—Signatures: *Kabis-Connally*

Friedberg No.	Federal Reserve Bank		Unc-60	Unc-63	Friedberg No.	Federal Reserve Bank		Unc-60	Unc-63
2019A	A	Boston	$30	$35	**2019G**	G	Chicago	$30	$35
2019A★	A★	Boston	50	70	**2019G★**	G★	Chicago	50	70
2019B	B	New York	30	35	**2019H**	H	St. Louis	30	35
2019B★	B★	New York	50	70	**2019H★**	H★	St. Louis	60	80
2019C	C	Philadelphia	30	35	**2019I**	I	Minneapolis	30	35
2019C★	C★	Philadelphia	50	70		I★	Minneapolis	Not printed	
2019D	D	Cleveland	30	35	**2019J**	J	Kansas City	30	35
2019D★	D★	Cleveland	50	70		J★	Kansas City	Not printed	
2019E	E	Richmond	30	35	**2019K**	K	Dallas	30	35
2019E★	E★	Richmond	75	120	**2019K★**	K★	Dallas	75	120
2019F	F	Atlanta	30	35	**2019L**	L	San Francisco	30	35
2019F★	F★	Atlanta	75	120	**2019L★**	L★	San Francisco	50	70

$10 SERIES 1969-B—Signatures: *Bañuelos-Connally*

Friedberg No.	Federal Reserve Bank		Unc-60	Unc-63	Friedberg No.	Federal Reserve Bank		Unc-60	Unc-63
2020A	A	Boston	$120	$150	**2020G**	G	Chicago	$120	$150
	A★	Boston	Not printed		**2020G★**	G★	Chicago	175	250
2020B	B	New York	100	125	**2020H**	H	St. Louis	120	150
2020B★	B★	New York	140	200	**2020H★**	H★	St. Louis	175	250
2020C	C	Philadelphia	120	150	**2020I**	I	Minneapolis	150	200
	C★	Philadelphia	Not printed			I★	Minneapolis	Not printed	
2020D	D	Cleveland	100	125	**2020J**	J	Kansas City	140	180
	D★	Cleveland	Not printed		**2020J★**	J★	Kansas City	250	375
2020E	E	Richmond	120	150	**2020K**	K	Dallas	120	150
2020E★	E★	Richmond	275	400		K★	Dallas	Not printed	
2020F	F	Atlanta	120	150	**2020L**	L	San Francisco	120	150
2020F★	F★	Atlanta	250	375	**2020L★**	L★	San Francisco	250	375

$10 SERIES 1969-C—Signatures: *Bañuelos-Shultz*

Friedberg No.	Federal Reserve Bank		Unc-60	Unc-63	Friedberg No.	Federal Reserve Bank		Unc-60	Unc-63
2021A	A	Boston	$30	$40	**2021G**	G	Chicago	$30	$40
2021A★	A★	Boston	80	125	**2021G★**	G★	Chicago	70	90
2021B	B	New York	30	40	**2021H**	H	St. Louis	30	40
2021B★	B★	New York	55	70	**2021H★**	H★	St. Louis	65	80
2021C	C	Philadelphia	30	40	**2021I**	I	Minneapolis	35	45
2021C★	C★	Philadelphia	65	80	**2021I★**	I★	Minneapolis	100	140
2021D	D	Cleveland	30	40	**2021J**	J	Kansas City	30	40
2021D★	D★	Cleveland	65	80	**2021J★**	J★	Kansas City	85	135
2021E	E	Richmond	30	40	**2021K**	K	Dallas	30	40
2021E★	E★	Richmond	70	90	**2021K★**	K★	Dallas	85	135
2021F	F	Atlanta	30	40	**2021L**	L	San Francisco	30	40
2021F★	F★	Atlanta	65	80	**2021L★**	L★	San Francisco	80	125

FEDERAL RESERVE NOTES—GREEN SEAL

TEN DOLLARS

$10 SERIES 1974—Signatures: *Neff-Simon*

Friedberg No.	Federal Reserve Bank		Unc-60	Unc-63	Friedberg No.	Federal Reserve Bank		Unc-60	Unc-63
2022A	A	Boston	$30	$35	**2022G**	G	Chicago	$30	$35
2022A★	A★	Boston	50	65	**2022G★**	G★	Chicago	50	65
2022B	B	New York	30	35	**2022H**	H	St. Louis	30	35
2022B★	B★	New York	50	65	**2022H★**	H★	St. Louis	50	65
2022C	C	Philadelphia	30	35	**2022I**	I	Minneapolis	35	45
2022C★	C★	Philadelphia	50	65	**2022I★**	I★	Minneapolis	75	85
2022D	D	Cleveland	30	35	**2022J**	J	Kansas City	30	35
2022D★	D★	Cleveland	50	65	**2022J★**	J★	Kansas City	50	65
2022E	E	Richmond	30	35	**2022K**	K	Dallas	30	35
2022E★	E★	Richmond	50	65	**2022K★**	K★	Dallas	50	65
2022F	F	Atlanta	30	35	**2022L**	L	San Francisco	30	35
2022F★	F★	Atlanta	50	65	**2022L★**	L★	San Francisco	50	65

$10 SERIES 1977—Signatures: *Morton-Blumenthal*

Friedberg No.	Federal Reserve Bank		Unc-60	Unc-63	Friedberg No.	Federal Reserve Bank		Unc-60	Unc-63
2023A	A	Boston	$30	$35	**2023G**	G	Chicago	$30	$35
2023A★	A★	Boston	65	80	**2023G★**	G★	Chicago	65	75
2023B	B	New York	30	35	**2023H**	H	St. Louis	30	35
2023B★	B★	New York	50	60	**2023H★**	H★	St. Louis	70	90
2023C	C	Philadelphia	30	35	**2023I**	I	Minneapolis	35	50
2023C★	C★	Philadelphia	75	95	**2023I★**	I★	Minneapolis	110	140
2023D	D	Cleveland	30	35	**2023J**	J	Kansas City	30	35
2023D★	D★	Cleveland	80	110	**2023J★**	J★	Kansas City	70	90
2023E	E	Richmond	30	35	**2023K**	K	Dallas	30	35
2023E★	E★	Richmond	75	95	**2023K★**	K★	Dallas	70	90
2023F	F	Atlanta	30	35	**2023L**	L	San Francisco	30	35
2023F★	F★	Atlanta	65	80	**2023L★**	L★	San Francisco	65	80

$10 SERIES 1977-A—Signatures: *Morton-Miller*

Friedberg No.	Federal Reserve Bank		Unc-60	Unc-63	Friedberg No.	Federal Reserve Bank		Unc-60	Unc-63
2024A	A	Boston	$30	$35	**2024G**	G	Chicago	$30	$35
2024A★	A★	Boston	75	100	**2024G★**	G★	Chicago	50	70
2024B	B	New York	30	35	**2024H**	H	St. Louis	30	35
2024B★	B★	New York	50	70	**2024H★**	H★	St. Louis	75	100
2024C	C	Philadelphia	30	35	**2024I**	I	Minneapolis	30	35
2024C★	C★	Philadelphia	50	70	**2024I★**	I★	Minneapolis	110	140
2024D	D	Cleveland	30	35	**2024J**	J	Kansas City	30	35
2024D★	D★	Cleveland	50	70	**2024J★**	J★	Kansas City	70	90
2024E	E	Richmond	30	35	**2024K**	K	Dallas	30	35
2024E★	E★	Richmond	60	80	**2024K★**	K★	Dallas	45	60
2024F	F	Atlanta	30	35	**2024L**	L	San Francisco	30	35
2024F★	F★	Atlanta	80	125	**2024L★**	L★	San Francisco	50	70

FEDERAL RESERVE NOTES—GREEN SEAL

TEN DOLLARS

$10 SERIES 1981—Signatures: *Buchanan-Regan*

Friedberg No.	Federal Reserve Bank		Unc-60	Unc-63
2025A	A	Boston	$30	$40
2025A★	A★	Boston	80	110
2025B	B	New York	30	40
2025B★	B★	New York	75	100
2025C	C	Philadelphia	30	40
2025C★	C★	Philadelphia	100	135
2025D	D	Cleveland	30	40
2025D★	D★	Cleveland	80	110
2025E	E	Richmond	30	40
2025E★	E★	Richmond	80	110
2025F	F	Atlanta	30	40
2025F★	F★	Atlanta	80	110
2025G	G	Chicago	$30	$40
2025G★	G★	Chicago	80	110
2025H	H	St. Louis	30	40
	H★	St. Louis	Not printed	
2025I	I	Minneapolis	30	40
2025I★	I★	Minneapolis	150	225
2025J	J	Kansas City	30	40
	J★	Kansas City	Not printed	
2025K	K	Dallas	30	40
	K★	Dallas	Not printed	
2025L	L	San Francisco	30	40
2025L★	L★	San Francisco	75	100

$10 1981-A—Signatures: *Ortega-Regan*

Friedberg No.	Federal Reserve Bank		Unc-60	Unc-63
2026A	A	Boston	$30	$40
2026B	B	New York	30	40
2026B★	B★	New York	225	300
2026C	C	Philadelphia	30	40
2026D	D	Cleveland	30	40
2026E	E	Richmond	30	40
2026E★	E★	Richmond	75	100
2026F	F	Atlanta	30	40
2026F★	F★	Atlanta	$75	$100
2026G	G	Chicago	30	40
2026H	H	St. Louis	30	40
2026I	I	Minneapolis	40	50
2026J	J	Kansas City	30	40
2026K	K	Dallas	30	40
2026L	L	San Francisco	30	40

$10 SERIES 1985—Signatures: *Ortega-Baker*

Friedberg No.	Federal Reserve Bank		Unc-60	Unc-63
2027A	A	Boston	$30	$35
2027A★	A★	Boston	50	60
2027B	B	New York	30	35
2027B★	B★	New York	55	70
2027C	C	Philadelphia	30	35
2027D	D	Cleveland	30	35
2027D★	D★	Cleveland	70	90
2027E	E	Richmond	30	35
2027F	F	Atlanta	30	35
2027F★	F★	Atlanta	100	140
2027G	G	Chicago	$30	$35
2027H	H	St. Louis	30	35
2027H★	H★	St. Louis	60	75
2027I	I	Minneapolis	30	35
2027J	J	Kansas City	30	35
2027K	K	Dallas	30	35
2027K★	K★	Dallas	65	80
2027L	L	San Francisco	30	35
2027L★	L★	San Francisco	65	80

$10 SERIES 1988-A—Signatures: *Villalpando-Brady*

Issues from all 12 Federal Reserve Districts have nominal values and are commonly available in high grade condition. Star replacement notes have a 25 percent premium.

$10 SERIES 1990—Signatures: *Villalpando-Brady*

Added security devices. Issues from all 12 Federal Reserve Districts have nominal values and are commonly available in high grade condition. Star replacement notes have a 25 percent premium.

FEDERAL RESERVE NOTES—GREEN SEAL

TEN DOLLARS

$10 SERIES 1993—Signatures: *Withrow-Bentsen*

Added security devices. Issued from most Federal Reserve Districts. All have nominal values and are commonly available in high grade condition. Star replacement notes from New York, Philadelphia and Chicago have a 25 percent premium. In circulation.

$10 SERIES 1995—Signatures: *Withrow-Rubin*

Added security devices. Sheet-fed at both Washington and Fort Worth facilities. Issues from all Federal Reserve Districts have nominal values and are commonly available in high grade condition. Star replacement notes have a 25 percent premium. In circulation.

REVISED LARGER PORTRAIT DESIGN

Face Design. Series 1999 through 2003.

Back Design. Series 1999 through 2003.

$10 SERIES 1999—Signatures: *Withrow-Summers*

Redesigned both sides. Sheet-fed at both Washington and Fort Worth facilities. Issues from all Federal Reserve Districts have nominal values and are commonly available in high grade condition. Star replacement notes have a 25 percent premium. In circulation.

$10 SERIES 2001—Signatures: *Marin-O'Neil*

Added security devices. Sheet-fed at both Washington and Fort Worth facilities. Issues from all Federal Reserve Districts have nominal values and are commonly available in high grade condition. Star replacement notes have a 25 percent premium. In circulation.

$10 SERIES 2003—Signatures: *Marin-Snow*

Added security devices. Sheet-fed at both Washington and Fort Worth facilities. Issues from all Federal Reserve Districts have nominal values and are commonly available in high grade condition. Star replacement notes have a 25 percent premium. In circulation.

FEDERAL RESERVE NOTES—GREEN SEAL

TEN DOLLARS

REVISED PORTRAIT AND COLORIZED DESIGN

Face Design. Series 2004-A to present.

Back Design. Series 2004-A to present.

$10 SERIES 2004-A—Signatures: *Cabral-Snow*
Redesigned both sides (only small changes to back), adding color elements. Printed at the Fort Worth facility. In circulation.

$10 SERIES 2006—Signatures: *Cabral-Paulson*
Added security devices with colorization. Printed at the Fort Worth facility. In circulation.

$10 SERIES 2009—Signatures: *Rios-Geithner*
Added security devices with colorization. Printed at the Fort Worth facility. In circulation.

$10 SERIES 2013— Signatures: *Rios-Lew*
Added security devices with colorization. Printed at the Fort Worth facility. In circulation.

$10 SERIES 2017— Signatures: *Carranza-Mnuchin*
Printed at the Washington and Fort Worth facilities. In circulation.

$10 SERIES 2017-A— Signatures: *Carranza-Mnuchin*
Printed at the Washington facility. In circulation.

FEDERAL RESERVE NOTES—GREEN SEAL

TWENTY DOLLARS

Face Design. Series 1928 and 1928-A.

Back Design. Federal Reserve Notes Series 1928 through 1934-C, National Currency, Federal Reserve Bank Notes, Gold Certificates.

$20 SERIES 1928—Signatures: *Tate-Mellon*

Large district numeral of bank at left.

Friedberg No.	Federal Reserve Bank		EF-40	Unc-60	Unc-63
2050A	1	Boston	$230	$2,000	$2,500
2050B	2	New York	80	175	250
2050C	3	Philadelphia	80	175	250
2050D	4	Cleveland	80	175	250
2050E	5	Richmond	100	200	275
2050F	6	Atlanta	110	225	300
2050G	7	Chicago	80	175	250
2050H	8	St. Louis	80	175	250
2050I	9	Minneapolis	125	240	300
2050J	10	Kansas City	80	175	250
2050K	11	Dallas	135	325	475
2050L	12	San Francisco	100	200	275

FEDERAL RESERVE NOTES—GREEN SEAL

TWENTY DOLLARS

$20 SERIES 1928-A—Signatures: *Woods-Mellon*

Large district numeral at left, similar to Series of 1928 issues.

Friedberg No.	Federal Reserve Bank		EF-40	Unc-60	Unc-63
2051A	1	Boston	$150	$365	$550
2051B	2	New York	125	325	450
2051C	3	Philadelphia	125	325	450
2051D	4	Cleveland	140	350	500
2051E	5	Richmond	125	325	450
2051F	6	Atlanta	125	325	450
2051G	7	Chicago	125	325	450
2051H	8	St. Louis	125	325	450
2051I	9	Minneapolis			
2051J	10	Kansas City	175	550	700
2051K	11	Dallas	125	325	450
2051L	12	San Francisco			

Face Design. Series 1928-B and 1928-C.
General Face Design. Series 1934 through 1934-D.

$20 SERIES 1928-B—Signatures: *Woods-Mellon*

Large district letter replaces numeral in seal on this and succeeding issues.

Friedberg No.	Federal Reserve Bank		EF-40	Unc-60	Unc-63
2052A	A	Boston	$55	$100	$125
2052B	B	New York	55	100	125
2052C	C	Philadelphia	55	100	125
2052D	D	Cleveland	55	100	125
2052E	E	Richmond	80	175	225
2052F	F	Atlanta	250	350	450
2052G	G	Chicago	55	100	125
2052H	H	St. Louis	60	110	160
2052I	I	Minneapolis	65	125	150
2052J	J	Kansas City	60	110	160
2052K	K	Dallas	60	125	200
2052L	L	San Francisco	60	110	160

FEDERAL RESERVE NOTES—GREEN SEAL

TWENTY DOLLARS

$20 SERIES 1928-C—Signatures: *Woods-Mills*

Friedberg No.	Federal Reserve Bank		EF-40	Unc-60	Unc-63
2053G	G	Chicago	$625	$1,200	$1,750
2053L	L	San Francisco	900	1,900	3,100

$20 SERIES 1934—Signatures: *Julian-Morgenthau*

Light or dark green seal.

Friedberg No.	Federal Reserve Bank		EF-40	Unc-60	Unc-63
2054A	A	Boston	$38	$47	$60
2054B	B	New York	38	47	60
2054C	C	Philadelphia	38	47	60
2054D	D	Cleveland	38	47	60
2054E	E	Richmond	38	47	60
2054F	F	Atlanta	38	47	60
2054G	G	Chicago	38	47	60
2054H	H	St. Louis	38	47	60
2054I	I	Minneapolis	38	47	60
2054J	J	Kansas City	38	47	60
2054K	K	Dallas	38	47	60
2054L	L	San Francisco	38	47	60

$20 SERIES 1934-A—Signatures: *Julian-Morgenthau*

Friedberg No.	Federal Reserve Bank		EF-40	Unc-60	Unc-63
2055A	A	Boston	$40	$60	$90
2055B	B	New York	35	55	70
2055C	C	Philadelphia	40	60	90
2055D	D	Cleveland	35	55	70
2055E	E	Richmond	40	60	80
2055F	F	Atlanta	40	60	80
2055G	G	Chicago	35	55	70
2055H	H	St. Louis	40	60	80
2055I	I	Minneapolis	45	65	90
2055J	J	Kansas City	45	65	90
2055K	K	Dallas	45	65	90
2055L	L	San Francisco	35	55	70

$20 SERIES 1934-B—Signatures: *Julian-Vinson*

Friedberg No.	Federal Reserve Bank		EF-40	Unc-60	Unc-63
2056A	A	Boston	$40	$75	$90
2056B	B	New York	40	75	90
2056C	C	Philadelphia	40	75	90
2056D	D	Cleveland	40	75	90
2056E	E	Richmond	40	75	90
2056F	F	Atlanta	40	75	90
2056G	G	Chicago	40	75	90
2056H	H	St. Louis	40	75	90
2056I	I	Minneapolis	45	90	100
2056J	J	Kansas City	40	75	90
2056K	K	Dallas	40	75	90
2056L	L	San Francisco	40	75	90

FEDERAL RESERVE NOTES—GREEN SEAL

TWENTY DOLLARS

New White House Vignette—Series 1934-C

On November 10, 1948, Treasury Secretary Snyder announced that the $20 note was to bear a new engraving of the White House on the back side. The "new look" was made from a photograph of the south front and grounds after the building was renovated. The design used until this time showed the south front as it appeared in 1929. The modified design was actually put to press for the first time on July 20, 1948.

Back Design. Series 1934-C through 1950-E (see old back on page 281).

Various structural modifications can be seen when the two designs are compared. These include a balcony at the second floor level and four chimneys instead of two. Other differences are also visible. Lettering beneath the building is changed from "White House" to "The White House."

The new White House vignette was first used during the issue of notes Series of 1934-C. Both the old and new back designs can be found with this same series date. Subsequent issues through 1950-E use the new design.

$20 SERIES 1934-C—Signatures: *Julian-Snyder*

Friedberg No.	Federal Reserve Bank		EF-40	Unc-60	Unc-63
2057A	A	Boston	$34	$50	$55
2057B	B	New York	34	50	55
2057C	C	Philadelphia	34	50	55
2057D	D	Cleveland	34	50	55
2057E	E	Richmond	34	50	55
2057F	F	Atlanta	34	50	55
2057G	G	Chicago	34	50	55
2057H	H	St. Louis	34	50	55
2057I	I	Minneapolis	34	50	55
2057J	J	Kansas City	34	50	55
2057K	K	Dallas	34	50	55
2057L	L	San Francisco	34	50	55

Above listing includes both the old or new back designs. At present there is no difference in value between them.

FEDERAL RESERVE NOTES—GREEN SEAL

TWENTY DOLLARS

$20 SERIES 1934-D—Signatures: *Clark-Snyder*

Friedberg No.	Federal Reserve Bank		EF-40	Unc-60	Unc-63
2058A	A	Boston	$35	$50	$60
2058B	B	New York	35	50	60
2058C	C	Philadelphia	35	50	60
2058D	D	Cleveland	35	50	60
2058E	E	Richmond	35	50	60
2058F	F	Atlanta	35	50	60
2058G	G	Chicago	35	50	60
2058H	H	St. Louis	35	50	60
2058I	I	Minneapolis	40	60	80
2058J	J	Kansas City	35	50	60
2058K	K	Dallas	35	50	60
2058L	L	San Francisco	35	50	60

Face Design. Series 1950 through 1950-E.
General Face Design. Series 1963 through 1995.

$20 SERIES 1950—Signatures: *Clark-Snyder*

Friedberg No.	Federal Reserve Bank		EF-40	Unc-60	Unc-63
2059A	A	Boston	$35	$50	$70
2059B	B	New York	25	45	60
2059C	C	Philadelphia	25	45	60
2059D	D	Cleveland	25	45	60
2059E	E	Richmond	25	45	60
2059F	F	Atlanta	35	50	70
2059G	G	Chicago	25	45	60
2059H	H	St. Louis	35	50	70
2059I	I	Minneapolis	40	80	100
2059J	J	Kansas City	35	50	70
2059K	K	Dallas	40	80	100
2059L	L	San Francisco	25	45	60

FEDERAL RESERVE NOTES—GREEN SEAL
TWENTY DOLLARS

$20 SERIES 1950-A—Signatures: *Priest-Humphrey*

Friedberg No.	Federal Reserve Bank		EF-40	Unc-60	Unc-63
2060A	A	Boston	$30	$60	$75
2060B	B	New York	25	40	65
2060C	C	Philadelphia	30	60	75
2060D	D	Cleveland	25	40	65
2060E	E	Richmond	25	40	65
2060F	F	Atlanta	30	55	70
2060G	G	Chicago	25	40	65
2060H	H	St. Louis	30	55	70
2060I	I	Minneapolis	35	70	85
2060J	J	Kansas City	25	40	65
2060K	K	Dallas	30	55	70
2060L	L	San Francisco	25	40	65

$20 SERIES 1950-B—Signatures: *Priest-Anderson*

Friedberg No.	Federal Reserve Bank		EF-40	Unc-60	Unc-63
2061A	A	Boston	$25	$40	$50
2061B	B	New York	25	40	50
2061C	C	Philadelphia	25	40	50
2061D	D	Cleveland	25	40	50
2061E	E	Richmond	25	40	50
2061F	F	Atlanta	25	40	50
2061G	G	Chicago	25	40	50
2061H	H	St. Louis	25	40	50
2061I	I	Minneapolis	25	40	50
2061J	J	Kansas City	25	40	50
2061K	K	Dallas	25	40	50
2061L	L	San Francisco	25	40	50

$20 SERIES 1950-C—Signatures: *Smith-Dillon*

Friedberg No.	Federal Reserve Bank		EF-40	Unc-60	Unc-63
2062A	A	Boston	$25	$40	$47
2062B	B	New York	25	40	47
2062C	C	Philadelphia	25	40	47
2062D	D	Cleveland	25	40	47
2062E	E	Richmond	25	40	47
2062F	F	Atlanta	25	40	47
2062G	G	Chicago	25	40	47
2065H	H	St. Louis	25	40	47
2062I	I	Minneapolis	25	40	47
2062J	J	Kansas City	25	40	47
2062K	K	Dallas	25	40	47
2062L	L	San Francisco	25	40	47

FEDERAL RESERVE NOTES—GREEN SEAL

TWENTY DOLLARS

$20 SERIES 1950-D—Signatures: *Granahan-Dillon*

Friedberg No.	Federal Reserve Bank		Unc-60	Unc-63	Friedberg No.	Federal Reserve Bank		Unc-60	Unc-63
2063A	A	Boston	$55	$75	**2063G**	G	Chicago	$55	$75
2063B	B	New York	55	75	**2063H**	H	St. Louis	55	80
2063C	C	Philadelphia	55	75	**2063I**	I	Minneapolis	55	85
2063D	D	Cleveland	55	75	**2063J**	J	Kansas City	55	80
2063E	E	Richmond	55	75	**2063K**	K	Dallas	55	80
2063F	F	Atlanta	55	75	**2063L**	L	San Francisco	55	80

$20 SERIES 1950-E—Signatures: *Granahan-Fowler*

Friedberg No.	Federal Reserve Bank		Unc-60	Unc-63	Friedberg No.	Federal Reserve Bank		Unc-60	Unc-63
2064B	B	New York	$120	$170	**2064L**	L	San Francisco	$145	$180
2064G	G	Chicago	120	170					

Back Design, Series 1963 through 1995.

$20 SERIES 1963—Signatures: *Granahan-Dillon*

Motto "In God We Trust" added.

Friedberg No.	Federal Reserve Bank		Unc-60	Unc-63	Friedberg No.	Federal Reserve Bank		Unc-60	Unc-63
2065A	A	Boston	$75	$90	**2065G**	G	Chicago	$75	$90
2065B	B	New York	75	90	**2065H**	H	St. Louis	75	90
	C	Philadelphia	Not printed			I	Minneapolis	Not printed	
2065D	D	Cleveland	75	90	**2065J**	J	Kansas City	100	120
2065E	E	Richmond	75	90	**2065K**	K	Dallas	75	90
2065F	F	Atlanta	95	110	**2065L**	L	San Francisco	75	90

FEDERAL RESERVE NOTES—GREEN SEAL

TWENTY DOLLARS

$20 SERIES 1963-A—Signatures: *Granahan-Fowler*

Friedberg No.	Federal Reserve Bank		Unc-60	Unc-63	Friedberg No.	Federal Reserve Bank		Unc-60	Unc-63
2066A	A	Boston	$50	$55	**2066G**	G	Chicago	$50	$55
2066A★	A★	Boston	115	145	**2066G★**	G★	Chicago	115	145
2066B	B	New York	50	55	**2066H**	H	St. Louis	50	55
2066B★	B★	New York	115	145	**2066H★**	H★	St. Louis	115	145
2066C	C	Philadelphia	50	55	**2066I**	I	Minneapolis	50	55
2066C★	C★	Philadelphia	115	145	**2066I★**	I★	Minneapolis	135	195
2066D	D	Cleveland	50	55	**2066J**	J	Kansas City	50	55
2066D★	D★	Cleveland	115	145	**2066J★**	J★	Kansas City	115	145
2066E	E	Richmond	50	55	**2066K**	K	Dallas	50	55
2066E★	E★	Richmond	115	145	**2066K★**	K★	Dallas	115	145
2066F	F	Atlanta	50	55	**2066L**	L	San Francisco	50	55
2066F★	F★	Atlanta	115	145	**2066L★**	L★	San Francisco	115	145

$20 SERIES 1969—Signatures: *Elston-Kennedy*

Friedberg No.	Federal Reserve Bank		Unc-60	Unc-63	Friedberg No.	Federal Reserve Bank		Unc-60	Unc-63
2067A	A	Boston	$46	$50	**2067G**	G	Chicago	$46	$50
2067A★	A★	Boston	125	145	**2067G★**	G★	Chicago	100	120
2067B	B	New York	46	50	**2067H**	H	St. Louis	46	50
2067B★	B★	New York	100	120	**2067H★**	H★	St. Louis	100	120
2067C	C	Philadelphia	46	50	**2067I**	I	Minneapolis	46	50
2067C★	C★	Philadelphia	125	145	**2067I★**	I★	Minneapolis	125	145
2067D	D	Cleveland	46	50	**2067J**	J	Kansas City	46	50
2067D★	D★	Cleveland	125	145	**2067J★**	J★	Kansas City	100	120
2067E	E	Richmond	46	50	**2067K**	K	Dallas	46	50
2067E★	E★	Richmond	100	120	**2067K★**	K★	Dallas	125	145
2067F	F	Atlanta	46	50	**2067L**	L	San Francisco	46	50
2067F★	F★	Atlanta	125	145	**2067L★**	L★	San Francisco	100	120

$20 1969-A—Signatures: *Kabis-Connally*

Friedberg No.	Federal Reserve Bank		Unc-60	Unc-63	Friedberg No.	Federal Reserve Bank		Unc-60	Unc-63
2068A	A	Boston	$50	$65	**2068G**	G	Chicago	$50	$65
	A★	Boston	Not printed		**2068G★**	G★	Chicago	100	120
2068B	B	New York	50	65	**2068H**	H	St. Louis	50	65
2068B★	B★	New York	100	120	**2068H★**	H★	St. Louis	130	145
2068C	C	Philadelphia	50	65	**2068I**	I	Minneapolis	50	65
	C★	Philadelphia	Not printed			I★	Minneapolis	Not printed	
2068D	D	Cleveland	50	65	**2068J**	J	Kansas City	50	65
2068D★	D★	Cleveland	130	145		J★	Kansas City	Not printed	
2068E	E	Richmond	50	65	**2068K**	K	Dallas	50	65
2068E★	E★	Richmond	130	145	**2068K★**	K★	Dallas	130	145
2068F	F	Atlanta	50	65	**2068L**	L	San Francisco	50	65
	F★	Atlanta	Not printed		**2068L★**	L★	San Francisco	100	120

FEDERAL RESERVE NOTES—GREEN SEAL

TWENTY DOLLARS

$20 SERIES 1969-B—Signatures: *Bañuelos-Connally*

Friedberg No.	Federal Reserve Bank		Unc-60	Unc-63	Friedberg No.	Federal Reserve Bank		Unc-60	Unc-63
	A	Boston	Not printed		**2069G**	G	Chicago	$155	$195
	A★	Boston	Not printed		**2069G★**	G★	Chicago	390	525
2069B	B	New York	$155	$195	**2069H**	H	St. Louis	170	235
2069B★	B★	New York	290	390		H★	St. Louis	Not printed	
	C	Philadelphia	Not printed		**2069I**	I	Minneapolis	290	370
	C★	Philadelphia	Not printed			I★	Minneapolis	Not printed	
2069D	D	Cleveland	155	195	**2069J**	J	Kansas City	155	195
	D★	Cleveland	Not printed		**2069J★**	J★	Kansas City	525	650
2069E	E	Richmond	155	195	**2069K**	K	Dallas	155	195
	E★	Richmond	Not printed			K★	Dallas	Not printed	
2069F	F	Atlanta	155	195	**2069L**	L	San Francisco	155	195
2069F★	F★	Atlanta	390	525	**2069L★**	L★	San Francisco	525	650

$20 SERIES 1969-C—Signatures: *Bañuelos-Shultz*

Friedberg No.	Federal Reserve Bank		Unc-60	Unc-63	Friedberg No.	Federal Reserve Bank		Unc-60	Unc-63
2070A	A	Boston	$46	$55	**2070G**	G	Chicago	$46	$55
2070A★	A★	Boston	100	120	**2070G★**	G★	Chicago	100	120
2070B	B	New York	46	55	**2070H**	H	St. Louis	46	55
2070B★	B★	New York	80	100	**2070H★**	H★	St. Louis	135	170
2070C	C	Philadelphia	46	55	**2070I**	I	Minneapolis	46	55
2070C★	C★	Philadelphia	100	120	**2070I★**	I★	Minneapolis	115	130
2070D	D	Cleveland	55	65	**2070J**	J	Kansas City	46	55
2070D★	D★	Cleveland	125	145	**2070J★**	J★	Kansas City	135	170
2070E	E	Richmond	46	55	**2070K**	K	Dallas	46	55
2070E★	E★	Richmond	100	120	**2070K★**	K★	Dallas	100	120
2070F	F	Atlanta	46	55	**2070L**	L	San Francisco	46	55
2070F★	F★	Atlanta	100	120	**2070L★**	L★	San Francisco	115	130

$20 SERIES 1974—Signatures: *Neff-Simon*

Friedberg No.	Federal Reserve Bank		Unc-60	Unc-63	Friedberg No.	Federal Reserve Bank		Unc-60	Unc-63
2071A	A	Boston	$49	$60	**2071G**	G	Chicago	$49	$60
2071A★	A★	Boston	100	120	**2071G★**	G★	Chicago	75	90
2071B	B	New York	49	60	**2071H**	H	St. Louis	49	60
2071B★	B★	New York	75	90	**2071H★**	H★	St. Louis	100	120
2071C	C	Philadelphia	49	60	**2071I**	I	Minneapolis	49	60
2071C★	C★	Philadelphia	100	120	**2071I★**	I★	Minneapolis	100	120
2071D	D	Cleveland	49	60	**2071J**	J	Kansas City	49	60
2071D★	D★	Cleveland	100	120	**2071J★**	J★	Kansas City	100	120
2071E	E	Richmond	49	60	**2071K**	K	Dallas	49	60
2071E★	E★	Richmond	100	120	**2071K★**	K★	Dallas	100	120
2071F	F	Atlanta	49	60	**2071L**	L	San Francisco	49	60
2071F★	F★	Atlanta	115	130	**2071L★**	L★	San Francisco	100	120

FEDERAL RESERVE NOTES—GREEN SEAL

TWENTY DOLLARS

$20 SERIES 1977—Signatures: *Morton-Blumenthal*

Friedberg No.	Federal Reserve Bank		Unc-60	Unc-63
2072A	A	Boston	$40	$50
2072A★	A★	Boston	80	95
2072B	B	New York	40	50
2072B★	B★	New York	80	95
2072C	C	Philadelphia	40	50
2072C★	C★	Philadelphia	80	95
2072D	D	Cleveland	40	50
2072D★	D★	Cleveland	80	95
2072E	E	Richmond	40	50
2072E★	E★	Richmond	80	95
2072F	F	Atlanta	40	50
2072F★	F★	Atlanta	80	95
2072G	G	Chicago	$40	$50
2072G★	G★	Chicago	80	95
2072H	H	St. Louis	40	50
2072H★	H★	St. Louis	80	95
2072I	I	Minneapolis	40	50
2072I★	I★	Minneapolis	110	130
2072J	J	Kansas City	40	50
2072J★	J★	Kansas City	80	95
2072K	K	Dallas	40	50
2072K★	K★	Dallas	80	95
2072L	L	San Francisco	40	50
2072L★	L★	San Francisco	80	95

$20 SERIES 1981—Signatures: *Buchanan-Regan*

Friedberg No.	Federal Reserve Bank		Unc-60	Unc-63
2073A	A	Boston	$50	$65
2073A★	A★	Boston	100	125
2073B	B	New York	50	65
2073B★	B★	New York	100	125
2073C	C	Philadelphia	50	65
2073C★	C★	Philadelphia	125	145
2073D	D	Cleveland	50	65
2073D★	D★	Cleveland	125	145
2073E	E	Richmond	50	65
2073E★	E★	Richmond	125	145
2073F	F	Atlanta	50	65
2073F★	F★	Atlanta	125	145
2073G	G	Chicago	$50	$65
2073G★	G★	Chicago	100	125
2073H	H	St. Louis	50	65
2073H★	H★	St. Louis	125	145
2073I	I	Minneapolis	70	80
2073I★	I★	Minneapolis	155	180
2073J	J	Kansas City	50	65
2073J★	J★	Kansas City	125	145
2073K	K	Dallas	50	65
2073K★	K★	Dallas	135	160
2073L	L	San Francisco	50	65
2073L★	L★	San Francisco	115	135

$20 SERIES 1981-A—Signatures: *Ortega-Regan*

Friedberg No.	Federal Reserve Bank		Unc-60	Unc-63
2074A	A	Boston	$40	$50
2074B	B	New York	40	50
2074C	C	Philadelphia	40	50
	C★	Philadelphia	Not printed	
2074D	D	Cleveland	40	50
2074D★	D★	Cleveland	80	115
2074E	E	Richmond	40	50
2074F	F	Atlanta	40	50
2074F★	F★	Atlanta	$80	$115
2074G	G	Chicago	40	50
2074H	H	St. Louis	40	50
2074J	J	Kansas City	40	50
2074K	K	Dallas	40	50
2074L	L	San Francisco	40	50
2074L★	L★	San Francisco	100	145

FEDERAL RESERVE NOTES—GREEN SEAL

TWENTY DOLLARS

$20 SERIES 1985—Signatures: *Ortega-Baker*

Friedberg No.	Federal Reserve Bank		Unc-60	Unc-63
2075A	A	Boston	$35	$45
2075A★	A★	Boston	75	90
2075B	B	New York	35	45
2075B★	B★	New York	75	90
2075C	C	Philadelphia	35	45
2075C★	C★	Philadelphia	75	90
2075D	D	Cleveland	35	45
2075D★	D★	Cleveland	75	90
2075E	E	Richmond	35	45
2075E★	E★	Richmond	75	90
2075F	F	Atlanta	35	45
2075G	G	Chicago	$35	$45
2075G★	G★	Chicago	75	90
2075H	H	St. Louis	35	45
2075I	I	Minneapolis	35	45
2075J	J	Kansas City	35	45
2075J★	J★	Kansas City	75	90
2075K	K	Dallas	35	45
2075K★	K★	Dallas	75	90
2075L	L	San Francisco	35	45
2075L★	L★	San Francisco	75	90

$20 SERIES 1988-A—Signatures: *Villalpando-Brady*

Issues from all 12 Federal Reserve Districts have nominal values and are commonly available in high grade condition. Star replacement notes have a 25 percent premium. In circulation.

$20 SERIES 1990—Signatures: *Villalpando-Brady*

Added security devices. Sheet-fed at both Washington and Fort Worth facilities. Fort Worth notes have a face check letter/number that is preceded by small letters FW. All of these notes have nominal values and are commonly available in high grade condition. Star replacement notes have a 25 percent premium. In circulation.

$20 SERIES 1993—Signatures: *Withrow-Bentsen*

Added security devices. Sheet-fed at both Washington and Fort Worth facilities. Fort Worth notes have a face check letter/number that is preceded by small letters FW. All of these notes have nominal values and are commonly available in high grade condition. None were issued from Minneapolis. Star replacement notes have a 25 percent premium. In circulation.

$20 SERIES 1995—Signatures: *Withrow-Rubin*

Added security devices. Sheet-fed at both Washington and Fort Worth facilities. All have nominal values and are commonly available in high grade condition. Star replacement notes have a 25 percent premium. In circulation.

REVISED LARGER PORTRAIT DESIGN

Face Design. Series 1996 through 2001.

FEDERAL RESERVE NOTES—GREEN SEAL

TWENTY DOLLARS

Back Design. Series 1996 through 2001.

$20 SERIES 1996—Signatures: ***Withrow-Rubin***
Both sides redesigned. In circulation.

$20 SERIES 1999—Signatures: ***Withrow-Summers***

$20 SERIES 2001—Signatures: ***Marin-O'Neill***
Added security devices. Sheet-fed at both Washington and Fort Worth facilities. Issues from all Federal Reserve Districts have nominal values and are commonly available in high grade condition. Star replacement notes have a 25 percent premium. In circulation.

REVISED PORTRAIT AND COLORIZED DESIGN

Face Design. Series 2004 to present.

Back Design. Series 2004 to present.

FEDERAL RESERVE NOTES—GREEN SEAL

TWENTY DOLLARS

$20 SERIES 2004—Signatures: ***Marin-Snow***
Redesigned both sides (only small changes to back), adding color elements. Sheet-fed at both Washington and Fort Worth facilities. Federal Reserve Districts have nominal values are commonly available in high grade. Star replacement notes have a 25 percent premium.

$20 SERIES 2004-A—Signatures: ***Cabral-Snow***
Added colorized security devices. Printed at both Washington and Fort Worth facilities. In circulation.

$20 SERIES 2006—Signatures: ***Cabral-Paulson***
Added colorized security devices. Printed at both Washington and Fort Worth facilities. In circulation.

$20 SERIES 2009—Signatures: ***Rios-Geithner***
Added colorized security devices. Printed at the Washington and Fort Worth facilities. In circulation.

$20 SERIES 2013—Signatures: ***Rios-Lew***
Added colorized security devices. Printed at the Washington and Fort Worth facilities. In circulation.

$20 SERIES 2017—Signatures: ***Carranza-Mnuchin***
Added colorized security devices. Printed at the Washington and Fort Worth facilities. In circulation.

$20 SERIES 2017-A—Signatures: ***Carranza-Mnuchin***
Printed at the Washington and Fort Worth facilities. In circulation.

FIFTY DOLLARS

Face Design. Series 1928.

Back Design. Federal Reserve Notes Series 1928 through 1950-E, National Currency, Federal Reserve Bank Notes, Gold Certificates.

FEDERAL RESERVE NOTES—GREEN SEAL

FIFTY DOLLARS

$50 SERIES 1928—Signatures: *Woods-Mellon*

Large district numeral of bank at left.

Friedberg No.	Federal Reserve Bank		EF-40	Unc-60	Unc-63
2100A	1	Boston	$600	$2,000	$3,200
2100B	2	New York	225	500	800
2100C	3	Philadelphia	225	500	800
2100D	4	Cleveland	220	400	625
2100E	5	Richmond	225	500	750
2100F	6	Atlanta	250	575	800
2100G	7	Chicago	220	400	625
2100H	8	St. Louis	225	425	650
2100I	9	Minneapolis	600	1,550	2,250
2100J	10	Kansas City	300	600	1,000
2100K	11	Dallas	400	1,400	1,800
2100L	12	San Francisco	235	425	650

$50 SERIES 1928-A—Signatures: *Woods-Mellon*

Large district letter replaces numeral in bank seal on this and succeeding issues.

Friedberg No.	Federal Reserve Bank		EF-40	Unc-60	Unc-63
2101A	A	Boston	$175	$275	$375
2101B	B	New York	175	275	375
2101C	C	Philadelphia	175	275	375
2101D	D	Cleveland	175	275	375
2101E	E	Richmond	175	275	375
2101F	F	Atlanta	200	325	450
2101G	G	Chicago	175	275	375
2101H	H	St. Louis	175	275	375
2101I	I	Minneapolis	175	275	375
2101J	J	Kansas City	175	275	375
2101K	K	Dallas	200	325	450
2101L	L	San Francisco	200	325	450

$50 SERIES 1934—Signatures: *Julian-Morgenthau*

Light or dark green seal.

Friedberg No.	Federal Reserve Bank		EF-40	Unc-60	Unc-63
2102A	A	Boston	$90	$130	$155
2102B	B	New York	90	130	155
2102C	C	Philadelphia	90	130	155
2102D	D	Cleveland	90	130	155
2102E	E	Richmond	90	130	155
2102F	F	Atlanta	90	130	155
2102G	G	Chicago	90	130	155
2102H	H	St. Louis	90	130	155
2102I	I	Minneapolis	100	175	250
2102J	J	Kansas City	90	130	155
2102K	K	Dallas	90	130	155
2102L	L	San Francisco	90	130	155

FEDERAL RESERVE NOTES—GREEN SEAL

FIFTY DOLLARS

$50 SERIES 1934-A—Signatures: *Julian-Morgenthau*

Friedberg No.	Federal Reserve Bank			EF-40	Unc-60	Unc-63
2103A	A	Boston		$110	$270	$400
2103B	B	New York		90	200	300
	C	Philadelphia	Not printed			
2103D	D	Cleveland		90	200	300
2103E	E	Richmond		90	200	300
2103F	F	Atlanta		100	225	375
2103G	G	Chicago		90	200	300
2103H	H	St. Louis		100	225	375
2103I	I	Minneapolis		125	350	500
2103J	J	Kansas City		125	350	500
2103K	K	Dallas		100	225	375
2103L	L	San Francisco		100	225	375

$50 SERIES 1934-B—Signatures: *Julian-Vinson*

Friedberg No.	Federal Reserve Bank			EF-40	Unc-60	Unc-63
	A	Boston	Not printed			
	B	New York	Not printed			
2104C	C	Philadelphia		$130	$365	$390
2104D	D	Cleveland		130	365	390
2104E	E	Richmond		130	365	390
2104F	F	Atlanta		130	365	390
2104G	G	Chicago		130	365	390
2104H	H	St. Louis		130	365	390
2104I	I	Minneapolis		130	365	450
2104J	J	Kansas City		130	365	390
2104K	K	Dallas		130	365	450
2104L	L	San Francisco		130	365	390

$50 SERIES 1934-C—Signatures: *Julian-Snyder*

Friedberg No.	Federal Reserve Bank			EF-40	Unc-60	Unc-63
2105A	A	Boston		$145	$235	$325
2105B	B	New York		100	185	250
2105C	C	Philadelphia		145	235	325
2105D	D	Cleveland		100	185	250
2105E	E	Richmond		100	185	250
2105F	F	Atlanta		200	325	500
2105G	G	Chicago		100	185	250
2105H	H	St. Louis		100	185	250
2105I	I	Minneapolis		150	260	350
2105J	J	Kansas City		100	185	250
2105K	K	Dallas		100	185	250
	L	San Francisco	Not printed			

FEDERAL RESERVE NOTES—GREEN SEAL

FIFTY DOLLARS

$50 SERIES 1934-D—Signatures: *Clark-Snyder*

Friedberg No.	Federal Reserve Bank			EF-40	Unc-60	Unc-63
2106A	A	Boston		$150	$275	$350
2106B	B	New York		110	195	235
2106C	C	Philadelphia		110	195	235
	D	Cleveland	Not printed			
2106E	E	Richmond		150	275	350
2106F	F	Atlanta		150	275	350
2106G	G	Chicago		110	195	235
	H	St. Louis	Not printed			
2106I	I	Minneapolis		600	—	—
	J	Kansas City	Not printed			
2106K	K	Dallas		125	250	320
	L	San Francisco	Not printed			

Face Design. Series 1950 through 1950-E.
General Face Design, Series 1963-A through 1993.

$50 SERIES 1950—Signatures: *Clark-Snyder*

Friedberg No.	Federal Reserve Bank		Unc-60	Unc-63
2107A	A	Boston	$150	$200
2107B	B	New York	150	200
2107C	C	Philadelphia	150	200
2107D	D	Cleveland	150	200
2107E	E	Richmond	150	200
2107F	F	Atlanta	150	200
2107G	G	Chicago	$150	$200
2107H	H	St. Louis	150	200
2107I	I	Minneapolis	350	500
2107J	J	Kansas City	150	200
2107K	K	Dallas	150	200
2107L	L	San Francisco	150	200

$50 SERIES 1950-A—Signatures: *Priest-Humphrey*

Friedberg No.	Federal Reserve Bank		Unc-60	Unc-63
2108A	A	Boston	$130	$170
2108B	B	New York	130	170
2108C	C	Philadelphia	130	170
2108D	D	Cleveland	130	170
2108E	E	Richmond	130	170
2108F	F	Atlanta	145	195
2108G	G	Chicago	$130	$170
2108H	H	St. Louis	145	195
	I	Minneapolis	Not printed	
2108J	J	Kansas City	180	265
2108K	K	Dallas	130	170
2108L	L	San Francisco	145	195

FEDERAL RESERVE NOTES—GREEN SEAL

FIFTY DOLLARS

$50 SERIES 1950-B—Signatures: *Priest-Anderson*

Friedberg No.	Federal Reserve Bank		Unc-60	Unc-63
2109A	A	Boston	$110	$145
2109B	B	New York	100	130
2109C	C	Philadelphia	100	130
2109D	D	Cleveland	100	130
2109E	E	Richmond	100	130
	F	Atlanta	Not printed	
2109G	G	Chicago	$100	$130
2109H	H	St. Louis	130	175
	I	Minneapolis	Not printed	
2109J	J	Kansas City	110	145
2109K	K	Dallas	125	170
2109L	L	San Francisco	100	130

$50 SERIES 1950-C—Signatures: *Smith-Dillon*

Friedberg No.	Federal Reserve Bank		Unc-60	Unc-63
2110A	A	Boston	$100	$125
2110B	B	New York	100	125
2110C	C	Philadelphia	100	125
2110D	D	Cleveland	100	125
2110E	E	Richmond	100	125
	F	Atlanta	Not printed	
2110G	G	Chicago	$110	$130
2110H	H	St. Louis	100	125
2110I	I	Minneapolis	155	235
2110J	J	Kansas City	155	235
2110K	K	Dallas	100	125
2110L	L	San Francisco	100	125

$50 SERIES 1950-D—Signatures: *Granahan-Dillon*

Friedberg No.	Federal Reserve Bank		Unc-60	Unc-63
2111A	A	Boston	$140	$195
2111B	B	New York	100	120
2111C	C	Philadelphia	100	120
2111D	D	Cleveland	100	120
2111E	E	Richmond	100	120
2111F	F	Atlanta	100	120
2111G	G	Chicago	$100	$120
2111H	H	St. Louis	100	120
2111I	I	Minneapolis	140	195
2111J	J	Kansas City	100	120
2111K	K	Dallas	195	290
2111L	L	San Francisco	140	195

$50 SERIES 1950-E—Signatures: *Granahan-Fowler*

Friedberg No.	Federal Reserve Bank		Unc-60	Unc-63
2112B	B	New York	$175	$215
2112G	G	Chicago	210	255
2112L	L	San Francisco	$175	$215

Back Design. Series 1963-A through 1993. Motto on back.

FEDERAL RESERVE NOTES—GREEN SEAL

FIFTY DOLLARS

$50 SERIES 1963-A—Signatures: *Granahan-Fowler*

Friedberg No.	Federal Reserve Bank		Unc-60	Unc-63
2113A	A	Boston	$90	$110
2113A★	A★	Boston	215	305
2113B	B	New York	90	110
2113B★	B★	New York	135	210
2113C	C	Philadelphia	100	125
2113C★	C★	Philadelphia	180	260
2113D	D	Cleveland	90	110
2113D★	D★	Cleveland	180	260
2113E	E	Richmond	100	125
2113E★	E★	Richmond	180	260
2113F	F	Atlanta	170	200
2113F★	F★	Atlanta	180	260
2113G	G	Chicago	$100	$125
2113G★	G★	Chicago	155	215
2113H	H	St. Louis	110	145
2113H★	H★	St. Louis	215	305
2113I	I	Minneapolis	155	195
2113I★	I★	Minneapolis	260	310
2113J	J	Kansas City	110	145
2113J★	J★	Kansas City	215	305
2113K	K	Dallas	90	110
2113K★	K★	Dallas	275	350
2113L	L	San Francisco	90	110
2113L★	L★	San Francisco	170	245

$50 SERIES 1969—Signatures: *Elston-Kennedy*

Friedberg No.	Federal Reserve Bank		Unc-60	Unc-63
2114A	A	Boston	$130	$175
	A★	Boston	Not printed	
2114B	B	New York	75	110
2114B★	B★	New York	145	195
2114C	C	Philadelphia	75	110
2114C★	C★	Philadelphia	160	230
2114D	D	Cleveland	90	125
2114D★	D★	Cleveland	145	195
2114E	E	Richmond	115	135
2114E★	E★	Richmond	220	305
2114F	F	Atlanta	130	170
	F★	Atlanta	Not printed	
2114G	G	Chicago	$75	$110
2114G★	G★	Chicago	145	195
2114H	H	St. Louis	130	180
	H★	St. Louis	Not printed	
2114I	I	Minneapolis	130	180
	I★	Minneapolis	Not printed	
2114J	J	Kansas City	115	135
2114J★	J★	Kansas City	260	350
2114K	K	Dallas	135	180
2114K★	K★	Dallas	260	325
2114L	L	San Francisco	75	110
2114L★	L★	San Francisco	170	230

$50 SERIES 1969-A— Signatures: *Kabis-Connally*

Friedberg No.	Federal Reserve Bank		Unc-60	Unc-63
2115A	A	Boston	$85	$125
2115A★	A★	Boston	180	215
2115B	B	New York	75	100
2115B★	B★	New York	180	215
2115C	C	Philadelphia	75	100
	C★	Philadelphia	Not printed	
2115D	D	Cleveland	75	100
	D★	Cleveland	Not printed	
2115E	E	Richmond	75	100
2115E★	E★	Richmond	325	455
2115F	F	Atlanta	130	170
2115F★	F★	Atlanta	325	490
2115G	G	Chicago	$75	$100
2115G★	G★	Chicago	180	215
2115H	H	St. Louis	145	170
	H★	St. Louis	Not printed	
2115I	I	Minneapolis	125	145
	I★	Minneapolis	Not printed	
2115J	J	Kansas City	145	170
	J★	Kansas City	Not printed	
2115K	K	Dallas	75	100
2115K★	K★	Dallas	345	455
2115L	L	San Francisco	75	100
2115L★	L★	San Francisco	215	285

FEDERAL RESERVE NOTES—GREEN SEAL

FIFTY DOLLARS

$50 SERIES 1969-B— Signatures: *Bañuelos-Connally*

Friedberg No.	Federal Reserve Bank		Unc-60	Unc-63	Friedberg No.	Federal Reserve Bank		Unc-60	Unc-63
2116A	A	Boston	$775	$1,000	**2116G**	G	Chicago	$290	$370
	A★	Boston	Not printed			G★	Chicago	Not printed	
2116B	B	New York	420	490		H	St. Louis	Not printed	
	B★	New York	Not printed			H★	St. Louis	Not printed	
	C	Philadelphia	Not printed			I	Minneapolis	Not printed	
	C★	Philadelphia	Not printed			I★	Minneapolis	Not printed	
	D	Cleveland	Not printed			J	Kansas City	Not printed	
	D★	Cleveland	Not printed			J★	Kansas City	Not printed	
2116E	E	Richmond	455	500	**2116K**	K	Dallas	525	650
	E★	Richmond	Not printed		**2116K★**	K★	Dallas	1,550	1,900
2116F	F	Atlanta	775	1,150		L	San Francisco	Not printed	
	F★	Atlanta	Not printed			L★	San Francisco	Not printed	

$50 SERIES 1969-C— Signatures: *Bañuelos-Shultz*

Friedberg No.	Federal Reserve Bank		Unc-60	Unc-63	Friedberg No.	Federal Reserve Bank		Unc-60	Unc-63
2117A	A	Boston	$70	$100	**2117G**	G	Chicago	$70	$100
2117A★	A★	Boston	195	290	**2117G★**	G★	Chicago	115	160
2117B	B	New York	70	100	**2117H**	H	St. Louis	70	100
2117B★	B★	New York	130	230	**2117H★**	H★	St. Louis	220	325
2117C	C	Philadelphia	70	100	**2117I**	I	Minneapolis	110	130
2117C★	C★	Philadelphia	130	230	**2117I★**	I★	Minneapolis	235	325
2117D	D	Cleveland	70	100	**2117J**	J	Kansas City	85	110
2117D★	D★	Cleveland	120	180	**2117J★**	J★	Kansas City	145	230
2117E	E	Richmond	70	100	**2117K**	K	Dallas	85	110
2117E★	E★	Richmond	170	260	**2117K★**	K★	Dallas	230	325
2117F	F	Atlanta	85	110	**2117L**	L	San Francisco	70	100
2117F★	F★	Atlanta	170	260	**2117L★**	L★	San Francisco	170	260

$50 SERIES 1974— Signatures: *Neff-Simon*

Friedberg No.	Federal Reserve Bank		Unc-60	Unc-63	Friedberg No.	Federal Reserve Bank		Unc-60	Unc-63
2118A	A	Boston	$85	$110	**2118G**	G	Chicago	$70	$100
2118A★	A★	Boston	115	135	**2118G★**	G★	Chicago	90	130
2118B	B	New York	70	100	**2118H**	H	St. Louis	125	145
2118B★	B★	New York	90	130	**2118H★**	H★	St. Louis	260	290
2118C	C	Philadelphia	85	110	**2118I**	I	Minneapolis	110	130
2118C★	C★	Philadelphia	155	210	**2118I★**	I★	Minneapolis	290	325
2118D	D	Cleveland	70	100	**2118J**	J	Kansas City	85	110
2118D★	D★	Cleveland	130	170	**2118J★**	J★	Kansas City	290	360
2118E	E	Richmond	85	110	**2118K**	K	Dallas	100	125
2118E★	E★	Richmond	130	170	**2118K★**	K★	Dallas	290	360
2118F	F	Atlanta	85	110	**2118L**	L	San Francisco	90	130
2118F★	F★	Atlanta	155	210	**2118L★**	L★	San Francisco	305	370

FEDERAL RESERVE NOTES—GREEN SEAL

FIFTY DOLLARS

$50 SERIES 1977— Signatures: *Morton-Blumenthal*

Friedberg No.	Federal Reserve Bank		Unc-60	Unc-63
2119A	A	Boston	$70	$100
2119A★	A★	Boston	110	130
2119B	B	New York	70	100
2119B★	B★	New York	90	110
2119C	C	Philadelphia	70	100
2119C★	C★	Philadelphia	160	215
2119D	D	Cleveland	70	100
2119D★	D★	Cleveland	130	195
2119E	E	Richmond	70	100
2119E★	E★	Richmond	130	195
2119F	F	Atlanta	70	100
2199F★	F★	Atlanta	120	145
2119G	G	Chicago	$70	$100
2119G★	G★	Chicago	110	130
2119H	H	St. Louis	70	100
2119H★	H★	St. Louis	145	195
2119I	I	Minneapolis	70	100
2119I★	I★	Minneapolis	215	260
2119J	J	Kansas City	75	120
2119J★	J★	Kansas City	215	260
2119K	K	Dallas	70	100
2119K★	K★	Dallas	155	195
2119L	L	San Francisco	70	100
2119L★	L★	San Francisco	120	170

$50 SERIES 1981— Signatures: *Buchanan-Regan*

Friedberg No.	Federal Reserve Bank		Unc-60	Unc-63
2120A	A	Boston	$100	$120
2120B	B	New York	100	120
2120B★	B★	New York	145	210
2120C	C	Philadelphia	100	120
2120D	D	Cleveland	100	120
2120D★	D★	Cleveland	145	210
2120E	E	Richmond	100	120
2120F	F	Atlanta	130	155
2120F★	F★	Atlanta	180	245
2120G	G	Chicago	100	120
2120G★	G★	Chicago	$145	$210
2120H	H	St. Louis	125	135
2120I	I	Minneapolis	125	135
2120I★	I★	Minneapolis	200	285
2120J	J	Kansas City	100	120
2120J★	J★	Kansas City	200	275
2120K	K	Dallas	100	120
2120L	L	San Francisco	100	120
2120L★	L★	San Francisco	155	215

$50 SERIES 1981-A— Signatures: *Ortega-Regan*

Friedberg No.	Federal Reserve Bank		Unc-60	Unc-63
2121A	A	Boston	$70	$100
2121B	B	New York	70	100
2121B★	B★	New York	160	230
2121D	D	Cleveland	70	100
2121E	E	Richmond	70	100
2121E★	E★	Richmond	230	260
2121F	F	Atlanta	70	100
2121G	G	Chicago	70	100
2121H	H	St. Louis	$70	$100
2121I	I	Minneapolis	70	100
2121J	J	Kansas City	70	100
	J★	Kansas City	Not printed	
2121K	K	Dallas	125	145
2121L	L	San Francisco	70	100
2121L★	L★	San Francisco	170	220

FEDERAL RESERVE NOTES—GREEN SEAL

FIFTY DOLLARS

$50 SERIES 1985—Signatures: *Ortega-Baker*

Issues from all 12 Federal Reserve Districts have nominal values and are commonly available in high grade condition. Star replacement notes have a 20 percent premium. In circulation.

$50 SERIES 1988—Signatures: *Ortega-Brady*

Issued from only seven districts. All are commonly available in high grade condition. Star notes were issued only from New York and have a 20 percent premium. In circulation.

$50 SERIES 1990—Signatures: *Villalpando-Brady*

Added security devices. Washington facility printings for all 12 Federal Reserve Districts. All are commonly available. Star notes have a 20 percent premium. In circulation.

$50 SERIES 1993—Signatures: *Withrow-Bentsen*

Added security devices. Produced only at Washington facility and not for all of the 12 Federal Reserve districts. All of these have nominal values and are commonly available in high grade condition. Star replacement notes have a 20 percent premium. In circulation.

REVISED LARGER PORTRAIT DESIGN

Face Design. Series 1996 through 2001.

Back Design. Series 1996 through 2001.

$50 SERIES 1996—Signatures: *Withrow-Rubin*

Redesigned both sides. All have nominal values and are commonly available in high grade condition. Star replacement notes have a 20 percent premium. In circulation.

FEDERAL RESERVE NOTES—GREEN SEAL
FIFTY DOLLARS

$50 SERIES 1999—Signatures: ***Withrow-Summers***

None printed.

$50 SERIES 2001—Signatures: ***Marin-O'Neill***

Printed at Washington facility. Star replacement notes have a 20 percent premium. In circulation.

REVISED PORTRAIT AND COLORIZED DESIGN

Face Design. Series 2004 to present.

Back Design. Series 2004 to present.

$50 SERIES 2004—Signatures: ***Marin-Snow***

Redesigned both sides (only small changes to back), adding color elements. Printed at the Fort Worth facility. In circulation.

$50 SERIES 2004-A—Signatures: ***Cabral-Snow***

Printed at the Fort Worth facility. In circulation.

$50 SERIES 2006—Signatures: ***Cabral-Paulson***

Printed at the Fort Worth facility. In circulation.

$50 SERIES 2009—Signatures: ***Rios-Geithner***

Added colorized security devices. Printed at the Fort Worth facility. In circulation.

$50 SERIES 2013—Signatures: ***Rios-Lew***

Added colorized security devices. Printed at the Fort Worth facility. In circulation.

$50 SERIES 2017-A—Signatures: *Carranza-Mnuchin*
Printed at the Fort Worth facility.

FEDERAL RESERVE NOTES—GREEN SEAL

ONE HUNDRED DOLLARS

Face Design. Series 1928.

Back Design. Federal Reserve Notes Series 1928 through 1950-E, U.S. Notes, National Currency, Federal Reserve Bank Notes, Gold Certificates.

$100 SERIES 1928—Signatures: *Woods-Mellon*

Large district numeral of bank at left.

Friedberg No.	Federal Reserve Bank		EF-40	Unc-60	Unc-63
2150A	1	Boston	$440	$1,200	$1,500
2150B	2	New York	350	900	2,200
2150C	3	Philadelphia	305	1,000	1,500
2150D	4	Cleveland	195	255	450
2150E	5	Richmond	235	650	1,000
2150F	6	Atlanta	245	525	650
2150G	7	Chicago	195	255	450
2150H	8	St. Louis	195	255	450
2150I	9	Minneapolis	650	1,500	3,100
2150J	10	Kansas City	260	575	950
2150K	11	Dallas	390	950	1,250
2150L	12	San Francisco	195	255	450

FEDERAL RESERVE NOTES—GREEN SEAL

ONE HUNDRED DOLLARS

Face Design. Series 1928-A. General Face Design. Series 1934 through 1934-D.

$100 SERIES 1928-A—Signatures: *Woods-Mellon*

Large district letter replaces numeral in bank seal on this and succeeding issues.

Friedberg No.	Federal Reserve Bank		EF-40	Unc-60	Unc-63
2151A	A	Boston	$235	$310	$350
2151B	B	New York	235	310	350
2151C	C	Philadelphia	235	310	350
2151D	D	Cleveland	235	310	350
2151E	E	Richmond	235	310	350
2151F	F	Atlanta	235	310	415
2151G	G	Chicago	235	310	350
2151H	H	St. Louis	235	310	350
2151I	I	Minneapolis	235	310	415
2151J	J	Kansas City	235	310	350
2151K	K	Dallas	235	1,000	1,950
2151L	L	San Francisco	235	310	350

$100 SERIES 1934—Signatures: *Julian-Morgenthau*

Light or dark green Treasury seal.

Friedberg No.	Federal Reserve Bank		EF-40	Unc-60	Unc-63
2152A	A	Boston	$170	$230	$255
2152B	B	New York	170	230	255
2152C	C	Philadelphia	170	230	255
2152D	D	Cleveland	170	230	255
2152E	E	Richmond	170	230	255
2152F	F	Atlanta	170	230	255
2152G	G	Chicago	170	230	255
2152H	H	St. Louis	170	230	255
2152I	I	Minneapolis	170	250	350
2152J	J	Kansas City	170	230	255
2152K	K	Dallas	170	230	255
2152L	L	San Francisco	170	230	255

FEDERAL RESERVE NOTES—GREEN SEAL

ONE HUNDRED DOLLARS

$100 SERIES 1934-A—Signatures: *Julian-Morgenthau*

Friedberg No.	Federal Reserve Bank			EF-40	Unc-60	Unc-63
2153A	A	Boston		$170	$215	$255
2153B	B	New York		170	215	255
2153C	C	Philadelphia		170	215	255
2153D	D	Cleveland		170	215	255
2153E	E	Richmond		170	215	255
2153F	F	Atlanta		170	215	255
2153G	G	Chicago		170	215	255
2153H	H	St. Louis		170	215	255
2153I	I	Minneapolis		170	215	255
2153J	J	Kansas City		170	215	255
2153K	K	Dallas		170	215	255
2153L	L	San Francisco		170	215	255

$100 SERIES 1934-B—Signatures: *Julian-Vinson*

Friedberg No.	Federal Reserve Bank			EF-40	Unc-60	Unc-63
2154A	A	Boston		$170	$235	$260
	B	New York	Not printed			
2154C	C	Philadelphia		170	235	260
2154D	D	Cleveland		170	235	260
2154E	E	Richmond		170	235	260
2154F	F	Atlanta		170	235	260
2154G	G	Chicago		170	235	260
2154H	H	St. Louis		170	235	260
2154I	I	Minneapolis		170	235	260
2154J	J	Kansas City		170	235	260
2154K	K	Dallas		170	235	260
	L	San Francisco	Not printed			

$100 SERIES 1934-C—Signatures: *Julian-Snyder*

Friedberg No.	Federal Reserve Bank			EF-40	Unc-60	Unc-63
2155A	A	Boston		$180	$260	$290
2155B	B	New York		180	260	290
2155C	C	Philadelphia		180	260	290
2155D	D	Cleveland		180	260	290
2155E	E	Richmond		180	260	290
2155F	F	Atlanta		180	260	290
2155G	G	Chicago		180	260	290
2155H	H	St. Louis		180	260	290
2155I	I	Minneapolis		180	260	290
2155J	J	Kansas City		180	260	290
2155K	K	Dallas		180	260	290
2155L	L	San Francisco		180	260	290

FEDERAL RESERVE NOTES—GREEN SEAL

ONE HUNDRED DOLLARS

$100 SERIES 1934-D—Signatures: *Clark-Snyder*

Friedberg No.	Federal Reserve Bank			EF-40	Unc-60	Unc-63
	A	Boston	Not printed			
2156B	B	New York	Rare	—	—	—
2156C	C	Philadelphia		$235	$490	$575
	D	Cleveland	Not printed			
	E	Richmond	Not printed			
2156F	F	Atlanta		235	490	575
2156G	G	Chicago		235	490	575
2156H	H	St. Louis		235	490	575
2156I	I	Minneapolis		—	—	—
2156J	J	Kansas City		—	—	—
2156K	K	Dallas		235	490	575
	L	San Francisco	Not printed			

Face Design. Series 1950 through 1950-E.
General Face Design. Series 1963-A through 1993.

$100 SERIES 1950—Signatures: *Clark-Snyder*

Friedberg No.	Federal Reserve Bank		Unc-60	Unc-63
2157A	A	Boston	$175	$265
2157B	B	New York	160	250
2157C	C	Philadelphia	160	250
2157D	D	Cleveland	160	250
2157E	E	Richmond	160	250
2157F	F	Atlanta	160	250
2157G	G	Chicago	$160	$250
2157H	H	St. Louis	160	250
2157I	I	Minneapolis	185	300
2157J	J	Kansas City	160	250
2157K	K	Dallas	175	265
2157L	L	San Francisco	160	250

$100 SERIES 1950-A—Signatures: *Priest-Humphrey*

Friedberg No.	Federal Reserve Bank		Unc-60	Unc-63
2158A	A	Boston	$155	$225
2158B	B	New York	155	225
2158C	C	Philadelphia	155	225
2158D	D	Cleveland	155	225
2158E	E	Richmond	155	225
2158F	F	Atlanta	155	225
2158G	G	Chicago	$155	$225
2158H	H	St. Louis	155	225
2158I	I	Minneapolis	155	225
2158J	J	Kansas City	155	225
2158K	K	Dallas	155	225
2158L	L	San Francisco	155	225

FEDERAL RESERVE NOTES—GREEN SEAL

ONE HUNDRED DOLLARS

$100 SERIES 1950-B—Signatures: *Priest-Anderson*

Friedberg No.	Federal Reserve Bank		Unc-60	Unc-63	Friedberg No.	Federal Reserve Bank		Unc-60	Unc-63
2159A	A	Boston	$170	$210	**2159G**	G	Chicago	$170	$210
2159B	B	New York	170	210	**2159H**	H	St. Louis	170	210
2159C	C	Philadelphia	170	210	**2159I**	I	Minneapolis	170	210
2159D	D	Cleveland	170	210	**2159J**	J	Kansas City	170	210
2159E	E	Richmond	170	210	**2159K**	K	Dallas	170	210
2159F	F	Atlanta	170	210	**2159L**	L	San Francisco	170	210

$100 SERIES 1950-C—Signatures: *Smith-Dillon*

Friedberg No.	Federal Reserve Bank		Unc-60	Unc-63	Friedberg No.	Federal Reserve Bank		Unc-60	Unc-63
2160A	A	Boston	$170	$210	**2160G**	G	Chicago	$170	$210
2160B	B	New York	170	210	**2160H**	H	St. Louis	170	210
2160C	C	Philadelphia	170	210	**2160I**	I	Minneapolis	170	210
2160D	D	Cleveland	170	210	**2160J**	J	Kansas City	170	210
2160E	E	Richmond	170	210	**2160K**	K	Dallas	170	210
2160F	F	Atlanta	170	210	**2160L**	L	San Francisco	170	210

$100 SERIES 1950-D—Signatures: *Granahan-Dillon*

Friedberg No.	Federal Reserve Bank		Unc-60	Unc-63	Friedberg No.	Federal Reserve Bank		Unc-60	Unc-63
2161A	A	Boston	$150	$175	**2161G**	G	Chicago	$150	$175
2161B	B	New York	150	175	**2161H**	H	St. Louis	150	175
2161C	C	Philadelphia	155	180	**2161I**	I	Minneapolis	170	215
2161D	D	Cleveland	155	180	**2161J**	J	Kansas City	155	180
2161E	E	Richmond	155	180	**2161K**	K	Dallas	170	215
2161F	F	Atlanta	150	175	**2161L**	L	San Francisco	155	180

$100 SERIES of 1950-E—Signatures: *Granahan-Fowler*

Friedberg No.	Federal Reserve Bank		Unc-60	Unc-63	Friedberg No.	Federal Reserve Bank		Unc-60	Unc-63
2162B	B	New York	$230	$260	**2162L**	L	San Francisco	$195	$230
2162G	G	Chicago	230	260					

Back Design. Federal Reserve Notes Series 1963-A through 1993 (motto on back), United States Notes.

FEDERAL RESERVE NOTES—GREEN SEAL
ONE HUNDRED DOLLARS

$100 SERIES 1963-A—Signatures: *Granahan-Fowler*

Friedberg No.	Federal Reserve Bank		Unc-60	Unc-63
2163A	A	Boston	$130	$170
2163A★	A★	Boston	170	285
2163B	B	New York	130	170
2163B★	B★	New York	170	285
2163C	C	Philadelphia	130	170
2163C★	C★	Philadelphia	170	285
2163D	D	Cleveland	130	170
2163D★	D★	Cleveland	170	285
2163E	E	Richmond	130	170
2163E★	E★	Richmond	210	305
2163F	F	Atlanta	130	170
2163F★	F★	Atlanta	235	325
2163G	G	Chicago	$130	$170
2163G★	G★	Chicago	170	285
2163H	H	St. Louis	130	170
2163H★	H★	St. Louis	170	285
2163I	I	Minneapolis	130	170
2163I★	I★	Minneapolis	170	285
2163J	J	Kansas City	130	170
2163J★	J★	Kansas City	240	310
2163K	K	Dallas	130	170
2163K★	K★	Dallas	170	285
2163L	L	San Francisco	130	170
2163L★	L★	San Francisco	170	285

$100 SERIES 1969—Signatures: *Elston-Kennedy*

Friedberg No.	Federal Reserve Bank		Unc-60	Unc-63
2164A	A	Boston	$130	$170
2164A★	A★	Boston	240	310
2164B	B	New York	130	170
2164B★	B★	New York	240	310
2164C	C	Philadelphia	130	170
2164C★	C★	Philadelphia	240	310
2164D	D	Cleveland	160	195
2164D★	D★	Cleveland	290	360
2164E	E	Richmond	130	170
2164E★	E★	Richmond	240	310
2164F	F	Atlanta	130	170
2164F★	F★	Atlanta	240	310
2164G	G	Chicago	$130	$170
2164G★	G★	Chicago	240	310
2164H	H	St. Louis	130	170
2164H★	H★	St. Louis	290	360
2164I	I	Minneapolis	145	260
2164I★	I★	Minneapolis	290	360
2164J	J	Kansas City	130	170
2164J★	J★	Kansas City	240	310
2164K	K	Dallas	130	170
2164K★	K★	Dallas	240	310
2164L	L	San Francisco	130	170
2164L★	L★	San Francisco	240	310

$100 SERIES 1969-A—Signatures: *Kabis-Connally*

Friedberg No.	Federal Reserve Bank		Unc-60	Unc-63
2165A	A	Boston	$130	$170
2165A★	A★	Boston	240	330
2165B	B	New York	130	170
2165B★	B★	New York	240	330
2165C	C	Philadelphia	130	170
2165C★	C★	Philadelphia	240	330
2165D	D	Cleveland	130	170
2165D★	D★	Cleveland	240	330
2165E	E	Richmond	130	170
2165E★	E★	Richmond	240	330
2165F	F	Atlanta	130	170
2165F★	F★	Atlanta	240	330
2165G	G	Chicago	$130	$170
2165G★	G★	Chicago	240	330
2165H	H	St. Louis	130	170
2165H★	H★	St. Louis	240	330
2165I	I	Minneapolis	130	170
	I★	Minneapolis	Not printed	
2165J	J	Kansas City	130	170
	J★	Kansas City	Not printed	
2165K	K	Dallas	130	170
2165K★	K★	Dallas	240	330
2165L	L	San Francisco	130	170
2165L★	L★	San Francisco	240	330

FEDERAL RESERVE NOTES—GREEN SEAL

ONE HUNDRED DOLLARS

$100 SERIES 1969-C—Signatures: *Bañuelos-Shultz*

Friedberg No.	Federal Reserve Bank		Unc-60	Unc-63	Friedberg No.	Federal Reserve Bank		Unc-60	Unc-63
2166A	A	Boston	$120	$150	**2166G**	G	Chicago	$120	$150
2166A★	A★	Boston	195	260	**2166G★**	G★	Chicago	170	235
2166B	B	New York	120	150	**2166H**	H	St. Louis	120	150
2166B★	B★	New York	170	235	**2166H★**	H★	St. Louis	215	360
2166C	C	Philadelphia	120	150	**2166I**	I	Minneapolis	145	215
2166C★	C★	Philadelphia	195	260	**2166I★**	I★	Minneapolis	215	360
2166D	D	Cleveland	120	150	**2166J**	J	Kansas City	120	150
2166D★	D★	Cleveland	195	260	**2166J★**	J★	Kansas City	215	360
2166E	E	Richmond	120	150	**2166K**	K	Dallas	120	150
2166E★	E★	Richmond	195	260	**2166K★**	K★	Dallas	215	360
2166F	F	Atlanta	120	150	**2166L**	L	San Francisco	120	150
2166F★	F★	Atlanta	195	260	**2166L★**	L★	San Francisco	215	360

$100 SERIES 1974—Signatures: *Neff-Simon*

Friedberg No.	Federal Reserve Bank		Unc-60	Unc-63	Friedberg No.	Federal Reserve Bank		Unc-60	Unc-63
2167A	A	Boston	$115	$145	**2167G**	G	Chicago	$115	$145
2167A★	A★	Boston	170	240	**2167G★**	G★	Chicago	170	240
2167B	B	New York	115	145	**2167H**	H	St. Louis	115	145
2167B★	B★	New York	170	240	**2167H★**	H★	St. Louis	170	240
2167C	C	Philadelphia	115	145	**2167I**	I	Minneapolis	115	145
2167C★	C★	Philadelphia	170	240	**2167I★**	I★	Minneapolis	195	290
2167D	D	Cleveland	115	145	**2167J**	J	Kansas City	115	145
2167D★	D★	Cleveland	170	240	**2167J★**	J★	Kansas City	175	265
2167E	E	Richmond	115	145	**2167K**	K	Dallas	115	145
2167E★	E★	Richmond	170	240	**2167K★**	K★	Dallas	195	290
2167F	F	Atlanta	115	145	**2167L**	L	San Francisco	115	145
2167F★	F★	Atlanta	170	240	**2167L★**	L★	San Francisco	175	265

$100 SERIES 1977—Signatures: *Morton-Blumenthal*

Friedberg No.	Federal Reserve Bank		Unc-60	Unc-63	Friedberg No.	Federal Reserve Bank		Unc-60	Unc-63
2168A	A	Boston	$115	$145	**2168G**	G	Chicago	$115	$145
2168A★	A★	Boston	145	200	**2168G★**	G★	Chicago	145	200
2168B	B	New York	115	145	**2168H**	H	St. Louis	115	145
2168B★	B★	New York	145	200	**2168H★**	H★	St. Louis	145	200
2168C	C	Philadelphia	115	145	**2168I**	I	Minneapolis	115	145
2168C★	C★	Philadelphia	145	200	**2168I★**	I★	Minneapolis	145	200
2168D	D	Cleveland	115	145	**2168J**	J	Kansas City	115	145
2168D★	D★	Cleveland	145	200	**2168J★**	J★	Kansas City	145	200
2168E	E	Richmond	115	145	**2168K**	K	Dallas	115	145
2168E★	E★	Richmond	145	200	**2168K★**	K★	Dallas	145	200
2168F	F	Atlanta	115	145	**2168L**	L	San Francisco	115	145
2168F★	F★	Atlanta	145	200	**2168L★**	L★	San Francisco	145	200

FEDERAL RESERVE NOTES—GREEN SEAL
ONE HUNDRED DOLLARS

$100 SERIES 1981—Signatures: *Buchanan-Regan*

Friedberg No.	Federal Reserve Bank		Unc-60	Unc-63
2169A	A	Boston	$130	$170
2169B	B	New York	130	155
2169C	C	Philadelphia	130	155
2169D	D	Cleveland	130	155
2169E	E	Richmond	130	155
2169E★	E★	Richmond	875	1,400
2169F	F	Atlanta	130	155
2169G	G	Chicago	$130	$155
2169H	H	St. Louis	130	155
2169I	I	Minneapolis	130	155
2169J	J	Kansas City	130	155
2169K	K	Dallas	130	155
2169L	L	San Francisco	130	155

$100 SERIES 1981-A—Signatures: *Ortega-Regan*

Friedberg No.	Federal Reserve Bank		Unc-60	Unc-63
2170A	A	Boston	$130	$155
2170B	B	New York	130	155
2170C	C	Philadelphia	130	155
2170D	D	Cleveland	130	155
2170E	E	Richmond	130	155
2170F	F	Atlanta	130	155
2170G	G	Chicago	$130	$155
2170H	H	St. Louis	130	155
2170I	I	Minneapolis	130	155
2170K	K	Dallas	130	155
2170L	L	San Francisco	130	155
2170L★	L★	San Francisco	575	850

$100 SERIES 1985—Signatures: *Ortega-Baker*

Issues from all 12 Federal Reserve Districts have nominal values and are commonly available in high grade condition. Star replacement notes have a 20 percent premium. In circulation.

$100 SERIES 1988—Signatures: *Ortega-Brady*

Issued from only nine districts. All are commonly available in high grade condition. Star notes were issued only from New York and have a 50 percent premium. In circulation.

$100 SERIES 1990—Signatures: *Villalpando-Brady*

Added security devices. Washington facility printings for each of the 12 Federal Reserve Districts. All are commonly available. Star notes have a 20 percent premium. In circulation.

$100 SERIES 1993—Signatures: *Withrow-Bentsen*

Added security devices. Produced for each of the 12 Federal Reserve Districts at the Washington facility. All are commonly available in high grade condition. Star replacement notes have a 10 percent premium. In circulation.

REVISED LARGER PORTRAIT DESIGN

Face Design. Series 1996 through 2006.

FEDERAL RESERVE NOTES—GREEN SEAL

ONE HUNDRED DOLLARS

$100 SERIES 1996—Signatures: *Withrow-Rubin*
Redesigned issue with larger portrait and new security devices. All have nominal values and are commonly available in high grade condition. Star replacement notes have a 10 percent premium. In circulation.

$100 SERIES 1999—Signatures: *Withrow-Summers*
Printed at Washington, D.C. All have nominal values and are commonly available in high grade condition. Star replacement notes have a 10 percent premium. In circulation.

$100 SERIES 2001—Signatures: *Marin-O'Neill*
Printed at Washington, D.C. All have nominal values and are commonly available in high grade condition. Star replacement notes have a 10 percent premium. In circulation.

$100 SERIES 2003—Signatures: *Marin-Snow*
Printed at Washington, D.C. All have nominal values and are commonly available in high grade condition. Star replacement notes have a 10 percent premium. In circulation.

$100 SERIES 2003-A—Signatures: *Cabral-Snow*
Printed at Washington, D.C. All have nominal values and are commonly available in high grade condition. Star replacement notes have a 10 percent premium. In circulation.

$100 SERIES 2006—Signatures: *Cabral-Paulson*
Printed at Washington, D.C., and the Fort Worth facility. All have nominal values and are commonly available in high grade condition. Star replacement notes have a 10 percent premium. In circulation.

REVISED PORTRAIT AND COLORIZED DESIGN

Face Design. Series 2009-A to date.

$100 SERIES 2009-A—Signatures: *Rios-Geithner*
Redesigned both sides, adding color elements and special security devices. Printed at Washington, D.C., and the Fort Worth facility. In circulation.

$100 SERIES 2013—Signatures: *Rios-Lew*
Printed at Washington, D.C.

$100 SERIES 2017-A—Signatures: *Carranza-Mnuchin*
Printed at Washington, D.C. and the Fort Worth facility. In circulation.

FEDERAL RESERVE NOTES—GREEN SEAL

FIVE HUNDRED DOLLARS

General Face Design. Federal Reserve Notes; resembles the Face Design of Gold Certificates.

Back Design. Federal Reserve Notes and Gold Certificates.

Friedberg No.	Series	Denomination	EF-40	AU-50	Unc-60
2200	1928	$500	$3,000	$3,750	$5,300
2201	1934	$500	3,000	3,750	5,300
2202	1934 A	$500	2,700	3,050	3,750

Issues of $500 Federal Reserve Notes have been recorded for the following series: *Series of 1928* (Woods-Mellon); *1934* (Julian-Morgenthau); *1934-A* (Julian-Morgenthau); *1934-B* (Julian-Vinson); *1934-C* (Julian-Snyder).

ONE THOUSAND DOLLARS

General Face Design. Federal Reserve Notes; resembles the Face Design of Gold Certificates.

FEDERAL RESERVE NOTES—GREEN SEAL

ONE THOUSAND DOLLARS

Back Design. Federal Reserve Notes and Gold Certificates.

Friedberg No.	Series	Denomination	EF-40	AU-50	Unc-60
2210	1928	$1,000	$4,700	$5,750	$7,500
2211	1934	$1,000	4,700	5,750	7,500
2212	1934 A	$1,000	4,700	5,750	7,500

Issues of $1,000 Federal Reserve Notes have been recorded for the following series: *Series of 1928* (Woods-Mellon); *1934* (Julian-Morgenthau); *1934-A* (Julian-Morgenthau); *1934-C* (Julian-Snyder).

FIVE THOUSAND DOLLARS

General Face Design. Federal Reserve Notes; resembles the Face Design of Gold Certificates.

Back Design. Federal Reserve Notes and Gold Certificates.

FEDERAL RESERVE NOTES—GREEN SEAL

FIVE THOUSAND DOLLARS

Friedberg No.	Series	Denomination	EF-40	AU-50	Unc-60
2220	1928	$5,000	$168,000	$180,000	—
2221	1934	$5,000	80,000	120,000	$156,000

TEN THOUSAND DOLLARS

General Face Design. Federal Reserve Notes;
resembles the Face Design of Gold Certificates.

Back Design. Federal Reserve Notes and Gold Certificates.

Friedberg No.	Series	Denomination	EF-40	AU-50	Unc-60
2230	1928	$10,000	$222,000	$240,000	—
2231	1934	$10,000	180,000	198,000	$234,000

Issues of both the $5,000 and $10,000 Federal Reserve Notes have been recorded for the following series: *1928* (Woods-Mellon); *1934* (Julian-Morgenthau); *1934-A* (Julian-Morgenthau); *1934-B* (Julian-Vinson).

GOLD CERTIFICATES—GOLD SEAL

Gold Certificates were not made for general circulation until 1882, though they first appeared in 1865. The first three issues were used for larger commercial transactions and were held mainly by banks and clearing houses. Denominations of large-size notes ranged from $10 to $10,000. These notes were often referred to as "gold backs" because of their orange or gold-colored backs.

Modern-size Gold Certificates were issued for general circulation from 1929 to 1933. Most were dated 1928 only, but it is possible that some 1928-A $10 notes were also released. There could not have been many, as the Emergency Bank Act of 1933 prevented further use of any Gold Certificates and required that they be turned in and exchanged for other currency. On December 28 of that year, Treasury Secretary Morgenthau issued an order prohibiting the holding of these notes by any private individual for any reason. Relatively few modern-size notes were thus saved, especially in new condition; if any could have been hidden, they would more likely have been the large-size pieces, which were naturally included in Morgenthau's order.

The Gold Reserve Act of January 31, 1934, immediately followed; this Act raised the value of gold from $20.67 to $35 per troy ounce, prohibited the circulation of gold coins and allowed Gold Certificates to be issued only to Federal Reserve Banks. A new series of Gold Certificates, Series of 1934, was made and released to the Federal Reserve Banks in exchange for gold coin or bullion. No specimen of any notes of this series was released outside the Federal Reserve System. The $100,000 note, the highest denomination printed, is included in the Series of 1934 issue.

On April 24, 1964, Treasury Secretary Dillon signed an order removing all restrictions from the holding or acquiring of Gold Certificates issued before passage of the Gold Reserve Act of 1934. This action made possible the entry of these notes into the numismatic market, and they are now openly collected and exhibited.

Modern-size Gold Certificates Series of 1928 and 1928-A are "Gold Coin" notes, so stated on the face. No heading is found in the usual place at the top; instead, it is to the left of the portrait near the Treasury seal. The color of the seal and serial numbers is gold.

Explanatory Notations for Various Series

Series of 1928—Notes of this series and Series of 1928-A carry the following legal tender clause: "This Certificate Is A Legal Tender in the Amount Thereof in Payment of All Debts and Dues Public and Private."

The backs of these notes are all uniform with other modern types of similar denominations, and are printed in green.

Series of 1928-A—Apparently a small quantity of $10 Gold Certificates of this series was in fact released. The following excerpts from a sworn and notarized statement dated Feb. 5, 1971, by Robert H. Lloyd are revealing:

> Robert H. Lloyd, of Silver Lake, Wyoming County, State of New York, being duly sworn, deposes, and says—
>
> 1. That during the year 1933, he was employed as a cashier in . . . Buffalo, New York, and
> 2. That on at least two occasions between April 1933 and July 1933 he received and paid out Gold Certificates, $10 denomination, Series of 1928-A (Woods-Mills) in circulated condition, and
> 3. That because the Certificates were soiled and wrinkled, he did not retain them for collection purposes, and
> 4. That he believes that the information supplied that none of these Certificates were issued is an oversight, and

5. That he believes that the early printings of the Series of 1928 A were shipped in packages bearing the label 'Series of 1928' and
6. That it is known that other types of notes were shipped in packages bearing 1928 designations, while the contents were Series of 1928-A or 1928-B, and
7. That it is unlikely that the Bureau had printed a supply of labels designating the Gold Certificates, Series of 1928-A."

Series of 1934—No notes of this series were released to circulation; therefore, they are not included in the catalog listings. The $100,000 note is illustrated, however, on page 319.

The backs of notes in this series are printed in gold, a radical departure from the green backs of all other types and series of modern notes. The "Gold Coin" clause is not used for this series, but the legal tender clause is the same as on earlier issues except for the deletion of the word "A."

TEN DOLLARS

Face Design. Series 1928 and 1928-A. Back Design on page 235.

Friedberg No.	Series	Treasurer-Secretary	F-12	VF-20	EF-40	Unc-60	Unc-63
2400	1928	Woods-Mellon	$145	$170	$370	$750	$910
2400★	★28		260	390	1,150	2,000	2,750
2401	1928 A	Woods-Mills	Unconfirmed in any collection				

GOLD CERTIFICATES—GOLD SEAL

TWENTY DOLLARS

Face Design. Series 1928 and 1928-A. Back Design on page 281.

Friedberg No.	Series	Treasurer-Secretary	F-12	VF-20	EF-40	Unc-60	Unc-63
2402	1928	Woods-Mellon	$145	$210	$455	$780	$910
2402★	★28		305	455	1,410	2,690	8,750
2403	1928 A	Woods-Mills			Not issued		

FIFTY DOLLARS

Face Design. Series 1928. Back Design on page 293.

Friedberg No.	Series	Treasurer-Secretary	F-12	VF-20	EF-40	Unc-60	Unc-63
2404	1928	Woods-Mellon	$290	$520	$1,500	$2,620	$3,190
2404★	★28		2,500	4,440	7,500	10,000	48,000

GOLD CERTIFICATES—GOLD SEAL

ONE HUNDRED DOLLARS

Face Design. Series 1928. Back Design on page 303.

Friedberg No.	Series	Treasurer-Secretary	F-12	VF-20	EF-40	Unc-60	Unc-63
2405	1928	Woods-Mellon	$455	$780	$2,750	$5,000	$9,400
2405★	★28		4,250	6,250	24,000	90,000	180,000

FIVE HUNDRED DOLLARS

PORTRAIT OF McKINLEY

See page 312 for resembling face and back designs.

Friedberg No.	Series	Treasurer-Secretary	F-12	VF-20	EF-40	Unc-60	Unc-63
2407	1928	Woods-Mellon	$6,900	$10,000	$18,600	$32,400	$48,000

ONE THOUSAND DOLLARS

PORTRAIT OF CLEVELAND

See pages 312 and 313 for resembling face and back designs.

Friedberg No.	Series	Treasurer-Secretary	F-12	VF-20	EF-40	Unc-60	Unc-63
2408	1928	Woods-Mellon	$9,400	$13,200	$28,800	$52,800	$78,000

FIVE THOUSAND DOLLARS

PORTRAIT OF MADISON

See page 313 for resembling face and back designs.

Friedberg No.	Series	Treasurer-Secretary	F-12	VF-20	EF-40	Unc-60
2410	1928	Woods-Mellon			Rare	

GOLD CERTIFICATES—GOLD SEAL

TEN THOUSAND DOLLARS

PORTRAIT OF CHASE

See page 314 for resembling face and back designs.

Friedberg No.	Series	Treasurer-Secretary		F-12	VF-20	EF-40	Unc-60
2411	1928	Woods-Mellon	Unknown	—	—	—	—

Gold Certificates were made in the Series of 1934 for use within the Federal Reserve System, and were not allowed into outside circulation. Denominations were $100, $1,000, $10,000, and $100,000. This last is the highest denomination of modern-size currency ever printed by the United States, and is shown below. The portrait is of Woodrow Wilson.

Face Design. $100,000 Gold Certificate, Series of 1934.

Back Design. $100,000 Gold Certificate, Series of 1934.

The order of April 24, 1964, legalizing the holding of Gold Certificates covered all such Certificates released to general circulation through January 30, 1934. Thus, no Gold Certificates Series of 1934 may be legally held, since they were all made and delivered after the January 30 cutoff date. For this reason, no Series of 1934 Gold Certificates are included in the listings.

WORLD WAR II ISSUES

THE YELLOW SEAL SILVER CERTIFICATES

These were issued in North Africa during operations there in 1942. Later they were issued briefly at the beginning of the Sicilian campaign.

All bear the Julian-Morgenthau signature combination. Though the Treasury seals were printed in yellow, the serial numbers retained their usual blue color.

Face Design. $1 North Africa Yellow Seal.

Friedberg No.	Denomination	Series		VF-20	EF-40	AU-50	Unc-60	Unc-63
2306	$1	1935 A		$74	$100	$130	$195	$230
2306★		★35 A		260	585	780	1,380	1,560
2307	$5	1934 A		94	120	160	220	245
2307★		★34 A		420	780	960	1,150	1,250
2308	$10	1934		2,250	5,000	7,500	11,250	12,600
2308★		★34	1 reported	36,000	—	—	—	—
2309	$10	1934 A		74	160	215	290	345
2309★		★34 A		230	455	550	1,150	1,620

The $5 1934 series was reported some years ago but has never been confirmed. Verification is welcomed.

THE HAWAII OVERPRINTS—BROWN SEAL

In July of 1942, specially marked U.S. currency was introduced in Hawaii as an economic defense measure against a possible Japanese invasion. If these notes had fallen into enemy hands, they could have been isolated easily and declared valueless. After August 15, 1942, no currency other than the "Hawaiian Series" was allowable without a license from the Territorial Governor. It was not until October 21, 1944, that all restrictions were revoked and normal monetary conditions returned to the area.

The notes are overprinted HAWAII face and back, as illustrated. They also contain brown seals and serial numbers. All bear the Julian-Morgenthau signature combination. The $1 notes are Silver Certificates; all the rest are San Francisco Federal Reserve notes.

It is significant that the HAWAII dollars were also used to redeem Japanese Military Yen on the liberated Central Pacific islands.

WORLD WAR II ISSUES

THE HAWAII OVERPRINTS—BROWN SEAL

Back Design. $10 HAWAII.

Face Design. $20 HAWAII.

Friedberg No.	Denomination	Series	VF-20	EF-40	AU-50	Unc-60	Unc-63
2300	$1	1935 A	$61	$100	$120	$135	$180
2300★		★35 A	260	490	715	1,380	1,620
2301	$5	1934	150	240	290	470	490
2301★		★34	2,120	4,380	6,250	12,000	14,400
2302	$5	1934 A	130	215	275	435	455
2302★		★34 A	3,120	6,000	10,000	—	—
2303	$10	1934 A	110	210	275	505	520
2303★		★34 A	910	2,250	3,000	10,000	13,800
2304	$20	1934	130	180	550	1,150	1,560
2304★		★34	3,120	5,000	12,000	—	—
2305	$20	1934 A	110	220	290	585	750
2305★		★34 A	1,020	3,000	4,500	8,500	9,400

EXPERIMENTAL "R" AND "S" $1 SILVER CERTIFICATES

These notes were made during World War II to test the wearing qualities of regular and special paper. Equal quantities were overprinted on the face with a red R or S, in the position shown. All bear signatures of Julian-Morgenthau and are dated Series 1935-A.

WORLD WAR II ISSUES

EXPERIMENTAL "R" AND "S" $1 SILVER CERTIFICATES

Face Design. "R" Note.

Face Design. "S" Note.

Friedberg No.	Denomination	F-12	VF-20	EF-40	Unc-60	Unc-63
1609	$1 with Red R	$115	$160	$260	$370	$430
1609★	R Star note	2,310	3,120	4,000	8,750	11,900
1610	$1 with Red S	115	145	195	310	360
1610★	S Star note	1,880	2,380	2,620	6,250	7,500

The "R" and "S" overprints were made to determine whether a special kind of paper might wear better in circulation than the regular paper normally used. The "R" represented those notes made of regular paper and the "S" was for those notes made of the special paper. Results of the experiment were inconclusive and no change was made in the kind of paper used for U.S. currency. About 12,000 star notes of each were printed, though the surviving number is very small.

UNCUT SHEETS OF CURRENCY

Subjects Per Sheet and Check Letters

Modern U.S. currency has been printed in sheets of 12, 18, and 32 notes. All issues up to April of 1953 were made in 12-subject sheets, with check letters from A to L (12 letters for 12 notes). Each note carries two identical check letters, which serve to indicate its particular position on the sheet when it was printed. These small capital letters are found in the upper left and lower right areas on the face side. The little number accompanying the lower right check letters is the face plate number; it has nothing to do with the sheet position of the note.

On April 2, 1953, the Treasury issued the first notes printed in 18-subject sheets. These carry check letters from A through R but are otherwise similar to earlier issues.

On July 25, 1957, the Bureau of Engraving began production of notes printed in sheets of 32 subjects. Each sheet consists of four quadrants of eight notes, as shown in the diagram on page 328. The upper left quadrant contains check letters and numbers A_1 through H_1, the lower left A_2 through H_2, the upper right A_3 through H_3, and the lower right A_4 through H_4. The letter indicates position and the number indicates the quadrant. As with earlier issues, each note bears two identical check letters, but there is an important difference. The quadrant number (1 to 4) appears only with the upper left check letters. The number found with the lower right check letters is the face plate serial number; while it may correspond at times with the quadrant number, it has no relationship to the position or quadrant of the note. (Backs also carry a back plate serial number; its position varies with the design or denomination.)

Serial Numbering for Different Sizes of Sheets

As the number of subjects per sheet was changed, so also was the system used for placing serial numbers on the notes. The following table shows which system was used for each size of sheet, and applies to all issues except National Currency Series of 1929 and Federal Reserve Bank Notes:

Size of Sheet	Check Letters	System of Numbering
12 Subjects	A through L	Consecutive numbering by half sheet, six down on the left and six down on the right.*
18 Subjects	A through R	Numbering advances by 8,000, six down on the left, six following in the middle and six down on the right.
32 Subjects	A_1–H_1 A_2–H_2 A_3–H_3 A_4–H_4	Numbering advances by 20,000 proceeding by quadrant from the upper left to the lower right.

* See next page for numbering of sheets released in uncut form.

UNCUT SHEETS OF CURRENCY

Sheet Sizes for Currency Issues 1929 to Date

		SHEET SIZE AND SERIES		
Type	**Denomination**	**12 Subjects**	**18 Subjects**	**32 Subjects**
United States Notes	$1	1928		
	$2	1928–1928-G	1953–1953-C	1963–1963-A
	$5	1928–1928-F	1953–1953-C	1963
	$100			1966–1966-A
Silver Certificates	$1	1928–1935-D	1935-D–1935-H	1957–1957-B
	$5	1934–1934-D	1953–1953-C	
	$10	1933–1934-D	1953–1953-B	
Federal Reserve Notes	$1			1963
	$2			1976
	$5, $10, $20	1928–1950	1950-A–1950-E	1963
	$50, $100	1928–1950	1950-A–1950-E	1963-A
	Above $100	All Series		

In addition, all small-size National Currency, Federal Reserve Bank Notes, and Gold Certificates were printed in 12-subject sheets, with the overprinting and serial numbering applied to 6-subject sheets.

Clarification of 12-Subject Numbering

Twelve-subject sheets exist both with consecutive serial numbers by half sheet as described above and with *all 12 notes* in full consecutive order. An example of this is illustrated on page 325. As explained by the Bureau, the general rule was that sheets intended for processing as regular issues for circulation were numbered by the half sheet according to the following example: Suppose that the total of a particular run was to be 1,200 notes, or 100 sheets. The first sheet would contain serial numbers from 1 to 6 on the left side and 601 to 606 on the right side, the second sheet would have numbers 7 to 12 and 607 to 612, and so on until the end of the run.

Sheets delivered to the Treasurer in uncut form, presumably for release upon request to collectors and others, often but not always bore consecutive numbers for all the notes on the sheet. In 1950, it was officially ordered that all uncut 12-subject sheets scheduled for delivery to the Treasurer should thenceforth bear serial numbers in fully consecutive order for the entire sheet.

Reconstructed Sheets and Consecutive Numbers

If a collector is able to locate all of the single notes originally printed as one unit or sheet, he will then be able to show them in the positions they formerly occupied before being cut apart. This group of notes comprises what is termed a "reconstructed sheet" of currency.

Reconstructed half-sheets of 12-subject printings could easily be assembled by obtaining six consecutively numbered notes from a new pack, making sure that check letters ran from A to F, or G to L. It would be extremely difficult to assemble all notes for a full 12-subject sheet as evidenced by the explanation of the numbering system (see above). Reconstruction of larger sheets is practically impossible, since the changes in the numbering system make a difference of 136,000 numbers on each 18-subject sheet and 640,000 numbers on each 32-subject sheet.

Consecutively numbered notes from the 18- or 32-subject sheets are readily available, but are of little consequence since *each note* comes from a *different* sheet. Easy proof of this fact can be seen on the notes themselves; they will all have the same check letters indicating identical positions on their respective sheets.

UNCUT SHEETS OF CURRENCY

12-subject sheet of currency with all notes consecutively numbered. Sheets with this kind of numbering were the ones generally made available to collectors during the early years when uncut sheets could be obtained.

National Currency and Federal Reserve Bank Notes

National Currency and Federal Reserve Bank Notes were printed in sheets of 12 subjects, then cut, overprinted, and delivered to the banks in vertical sheets of six subjects.

Type One National Currency used the same serial number and suffix letter for all six notes; however, each note had a different prefix letter (A through F) which also served to denote its position on that particular six-subject sheet.

Type Two National Currency notes were consecutively numbered and bore the same prefix letter, but the suffix letter was dropped. The only way to tell the sheet position of a Type Two note or a Federal Reserve Bank Note is by its check letters.

UNCUT SHEETS OF CURRENCY

Since National Currency and Federal Reserve Bank Notes were all printed in 12-subject sheets (even though delivered in six-subject sheets), check letters proceeded from A to L as on all other 12-subject printings. Thus, it is always possible to pinpoint the exact position of any note on the original 12-subject sheet. Check letters A through F indicate the left strip of six notes, and G through L indicate the right strip of six notes.

Each note also carries a face plate serial number in its normal position alongside the lower right check letter.

Numbering for Federal Reserve Bank Notes was also consecutive. Every serial number was preceded by the district letter as a prefix, and "A" as a suffix. No single issue was large enough to require the change of suffix letter to "B."

Valuations of Uncut Sheets

The most readily available uncut sheets of any U.S. currency are the six-subject sheets of National Currency which were delivered to issuing banks intact. It is easy to see why quantities of these sheets exist; the banks released the notes as they were needed, and many never used all that they had ordered. Also, quantities of sheets with low serial numbers were preserved for various reasons.

The following valuations apply to any sheet of these notes after the particular rarity rating of the issue as single notes has been ascertained from the listing on page 238.

National Currency Series of 1929

Six-subject Sheets

Denomination	Rarity 1 & 2	Rarity 3 & 4	Rarity 5	Rarity 6	Rarity 7	Rarity 8
$5	$1,100	$1,350	$1,500	$1,800	$2,500	$4,800
$10	1,200	1,400	1,550	1,900	2,600	6,250
$20	1,400	1,800	1,900	2,100	2,750	7,500
$50	4,500	5,200	6,300	9,000	11,000	18,000
$100	6,000	7,000	8,000	10,000	14,000	22,000

Until about 1954, limited quantities of certain uncut sheets of currency were available from the Bureau of Engraving for numismatic and educational purposes. Most sheets released in this manner were of 12 subjects, since the Bureau had only begun the printing of 18-subject sheets during 1953. Shortly thereafter, no more uncut sheets were made available to anyone until the new Series 1981 (and later) sheets were produced.

Apparently the two types generally released in sheets were United States Notes and Silver Certificates. Other types are known but are extremely rare.*

All uncut sheets are considered to be in new condition, even though the edges, corners or margins may have minor flaws. The following listing represents all sheets which may occasionally be available. Number of sheets issued is given where known. NR = Not Reported.

* One six-subject sheet of $10 New York Federal Reserve Bank Notes is recorded in the Grinnell Collection. Another, a 12-subject sheet of the same issue, was uncovered in the estate of a Federal Reserve Bank official in 1966. Both are possibly unique.

A few sheets of Federal Reserve Notes from $5 to $50, mostly dated Series 1928, were released probably for official use. They are rarely seen on the numismatic market.

UNITED STATES NOTES

ONE DOLLAR

Series	Issued	Sheet Size	Valuation
1928	11 (8 traced)	12 Subjects	$33,000

UNCUT SHEETS OF CURRENCY

UNITED STATES NOTES

TWO DOLLARS

Series	Issued	Sheet Size	Valuation
1928	5 (3 traced)	12 Subjects	Rare
1928C	25 (18 traced)	12 Subjects	$3,300
1928D	50	12 Subjects	—*
1928E	50 (21 traced)	12 Subjects	2,600
1928F	100	12 Subjects	1,900
1928G	100	12 Subjects	1,700
1953	100	18 Subjects	2,750

* At present there is no verification of any 1928-D $2 sheet. Confirmation is invited.

FIVE DOLLARS

Series	Issued	Sheet Size	Valuation
1928	5	12 Subjects	—
1928D	NR (15 traced)	12 Subjects	$4,200
1928E	100	12 Subjects	3,500
1953	100	18 Subjects	3,600

SILVER CERTIFICATES

ONE DOLLAR

Series	Issued	Sheet Size	Valuation
1928	80	12 Subjects	$4,500
1928B	6 (None verified)		—
1928C	11 (6 traced)	12 Subjects	Rare
1928D	60 (20 traced)	12 Subjects	Rare
1928E	25† (7 traced)	12 Subjects	Very Rare
1934	25 (9 traced)	12 Subjects	4,000
1935	100	12 Subjects	2,500
1935A	100	12 Subjects	1,750
1935B	100 (28 traced)	12 Subjects	2,300
1935C	100	12 Subjects	1,950
1935D	300	12 Subjects	1,500
1935D	102	18 Subjects	2,250
1935E	400?	18 Subjects	1,500

† Most were cut into single notes.

FIVE DOLLARS

Series	Issued	Sheet Size	Valuation
1934	25 (12 traced)	12 Subjects	$3,400
1934B	20? (10 traced)	12 Subjects	3,800
1934C	100	12 Subjects	2,600
1934D	100	12 Subjects	2,300
1953	100?	18 Subjects	2,900

TEN DOLLARS

Series	Issued	Sheet Size	Valuation
1933	1	12 Subjects	—
1933A	1	12 Subjects	Not located
1934	10 (7 traced)	12 Subjects	Rare
1953	100	18 Subjects	$5,250

UNCUT SHEETS OF CURRENCY

WORLD WAR II ISSUES

ONE DOLLAR
HAWAII OVERPRINT

Series	Issued	Sheet Size	Valuation
1935A	25	12 Subjects	$8,750

Serial numbers indicate a probable release of 60 sheets.

ONE DOLLAR
YELLOW SEAL

Series	Issued	Sheet Size	Valuation
1935A	25	12 Subjects	$10,000

Recent Issues of Uncut Sheets of U.S. Currency

The Bureau of Engraving and Printing began openly offering collectors uncut sheets of currency in October 1981. Series 1981 Buchanan-Regan notes were the first in the new series which has continued to be offered ever since, and includes issues of 1981-A, 1985, 1988, 1993, 1995, 1996, 1999, and 2001. Uncut sheets of Series 1976 $2 star notes were sold before the Bureau's current offering of 1995 $2 notes. Prior to that, in the 1950s, sheets had been available in only very limited quantities.

Current production consists of sheets of 32-, 16-, 8-, and 4-subject $1, $2, and $5 notes; and sheets of 16-, 8-, and 4-subject $10, $20, $50, and $100 notes. Some 16-subject sheets of $1 star notes (Series 1999) have also been printed.

Uncut sheets, which are priced at a premium over their face value, may be ordered directly from the Bureau of Engraving and Printing at www.moneyfactory.gov or via telephone (1-800-456-3408) or fax (1-888-891-7585).

A_1 A	E_1 E	A_3 A	E_3 E
B_1 B	F_1 F	B_3 B	F_3 F
C_1 C	G_1 G	C_3 C	G_3 G
D_1 D	H_1 H	D_3 D	H_3 H
A_2 A	E_2 E	A_4 A	E_4 E
B_2 B	F_2 F	B_4 B	F_4 F
C_2 C	G_2 G	C_4 C	G_4 G
D_2 D	H_2 H	D_4 D	H_4 H

Layout of 32 Subject Currency Sheet showing check letters and quadrant numbers.

ERROR NOTES

Though every effort is made to prevent error notes from slipping into circulation, some have occasionally been found by alert collectors. Error notes are those which show some irregularity from having gone incorrectly through one or more of the printing or cutting processes. Much collector interest has been focused on such notes, especially in recent years as a parallel to the spiraling demand for error coins.

There are many ways an error can occur in currency. Consider that the sheets must undergo separate processes for printing the faces, backs, and the overprint which for years consisted of seals, serial numbers, series, signatures (and district numbers where applicable). In addition, there are the trimming and cutting operations—and it is not difficult to imagine all sorts of errors or error combinations appearing on some notes.

Valuations of Error Notes

As a general rule, the prominence of the error directly affects its numismatic desirability. Valuations included here are thus to be considered as approximate premiums only, *in addition to the face value of any note.* Rare notes with a high catalog value may have an additional premium.

Caution: Collectors should be aware of contrived error notes which have recently been reported on the market.

On rare occasions a piece of paper will adhere to a currency sheet, take some of the imprint, go through the various processes and fall off at a later time. The above note carries a large blank space formerly occupied by just such a piece of paper, perhaps a marker or some sort of tab. On rarer occasions, such a note *with the stray piece of paper still adhering to it* has been found.

VF-20	EF-40	New
$110	$275	$400

ERROR NOTES

This note carries a double impression because the sheet on which it was printed went twice through the same overprinting process for its seals, signatures and serial numbers.

VF-20	EF-40	New
$1,750	$3,000	$9,000

The above note has an extra flap of paper on one corner, the result of an accidental folding of the sheet before it was face printed and cut. The flap is unfolded to show a corner of the face printing.

VF-20	EF-40	New
$150	$300	$450

ERROR NOTES

This note has a long white streak of unprinted paper through it, the result of an inner fold in the sheet before the face side was printed. This kind of note usually has one single white streak. Multiple streaking is rare. Values below are for the usually found single streak error.

VF-20	EF-40	New
$25	$40	$70

This note has the top of the next note showing, and a slice of its own top missing—resulting from the face of this note having been printed off-register.

Since notes are trimmed with faces showing, the faulty alignment went undetected.

VF-20	EF-40	New
$35	$45	$90

ERROR NOTES

A double denomination note, showing $5 on the face and $10 on the back. This is the result of a sheet printed on one side being inadvertently placed with sheets of another denomination which were also printed only on one side. Such notes are among the rarest and most desirable of all errors.

VF-20	EF-40	New
$15,000	$22,000	$35,000

A wet ink transfer, front printing on back. This was caused by the impression roller making contact with the plate, the plate transferring ink to the roller, then the roller placing the image in retrograde on the next sheet fed into the press.

	VF-20	EF-40	New
High denominations	$70	$110	$200
One Dollar bill	45	75	150

ERROR NOTES

Note with part of the overprinting on a corner of the face and some of the back is pictured with fold intact. Later the sheet became unfolded for cutting into individual notes.

VF-20	EF-40	New
$110	$155	$250

This note has its serial numbers mismatched on the last three digits.

VF-20	EF-40	New
$45	$75	$135

This Federal Reserve Note never received any of the usual overprinting features. Missing are the seal and serial numbers.

VF-20	EF-40	New
$200	$320	$500

ERROR NOTES

The seal and serial number on this Silver Certificate were overprinted too far to the right. It was caused by faulty alignment of sheets for the overprinting operation.

VF-20	EF-40	New
$125	$200	$350

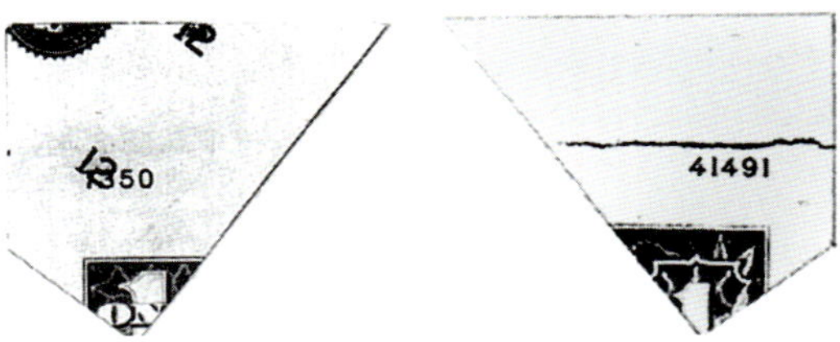

This extraordinary item is a fragment that went through the normal printing process as of a finished note. As such, it is an obvious rarity.

This misprint was caused by a large fold in the sheet prior to the overprint only, the back and face being normal. The fold remained intact through the cutting operation.

VF-20	EF-40	New
$175	$250	$450

ERROR NOTES

This note had a large portion of the sheet covered during the overprinting operation, thus deleting some features of the overprint, especially the seal.

VF-20	EF-40	New
$85	$110	$200

The above note received its overprint; however, the sheet was turned upside down as it was overprinted with seals, district numbers, series date, and serial numbers.

VF-20	EF-40	New
$125	$275	$500

The above note came from a sheet grossly out of alignment during the cutting process. Beware of such notes cut from Series 1981 or later sheets.

VF-20	EF-40	New
$225	$450	$700

ERROR NOTES

The note above received the overprinting of seals and serial numbers (third process) on the back instead of the face.

VF-20	EF-40	New
$100	$200	$375

Aside from those illustrated, some other errors are as follows:

a. Mis-matched type designation vs. overprint, such as a Silver Certificate frame with green seal, serial numbers, and a Federal Reserve Bank seal. This is truly an amazing error and obviously of extreme rarity.

VF-20	EF-40	New
$2,000	$3,000	$5,000

b. Completely missing face design, with only the third process overprinting (seal and serial numbers) on the blank face side.

VF-20	EF-40	New
$400	$600	$1,000

c. So-called inverted backs; in reality, inverted faces. This is because the backs are printed first and the sheet becomes rotated for the printing of its face side, the second operation.

VF-20	EF-40	New
$440	$880	$1,350

d. Uneven printing, where a section of the note may be lightly printed or practically missing.

VF-20	EF-40	New
$25	$60	$100

e. The "Red Dye Strip" note—this piece has a bright red strip diagonally across both the face and the back. The red strip on the paper meant the end of the roll was near. One example verified.

GLOSSARY

Charter number—Beginning in 1863, thousands of National Banks were chartered by the Treasury Department and were given Charter numbers, which were printed on the face of each note (beginning in the early 1870s, but not on the earlier National Bank Notes of the 1860s), in addition to the serial numbers. Charters for the earlier banks were for 19 years. Charters for later banks, 1864 to the early 1920s, were for 20 years and could be extended for a further 20 years, and extended again beyond that. Later, charters were made perpetual. Sometimes when a bank changed its name or even its geographical location, the same Charter number was retained.

Coin Note—Note from $1 to $1,000 issued in the Series of 1890 and 1891, redeemable in coins (silver or gold, at the option of the Treasury Department, but in practice the bearer could make the selection). These are called Treasury Notes or Coin Notes interchangeably.

Compound Interest Treasury Note—Note from $10 to $1,000 issued in the early 1860s yielding interest to the bearer. One of several distinct United States currency series.

Date Back—Describes certain Series of 1882 National Bank Notes with the dates 1882–1908 printed prominently on the back, or certain Blue Seal Series of 1902 National Bank Notes with the dates 1902 and 1908 printed on the back (in addition to other motifs).

Demand Note—Note of a denomination from $5 to $20 issued in 1861.

encased postage stamp—A regular federal postage stamp of a denomination from 1¢ to 90¢, enclosed within a brass frame with clear mica face. On the back of most, embossed in raised letters in brass, is the name of an advertiser. Patented by John Gault, and popular as a money substitute in 1862 and 1863. Often collected along with Fractional Currency.

Federal Reserve Bank Note—Note from $1 to $50 (Series of 1915 and 1918, large-size) and $5 to $100 (Series of 1929, small-size). Each bears the name of a Federal Reserve Bank (bolding imprinted across the center of the face on large-size notes) and a letter designating its district.

Federal Reserve Note—Note from $1 to $10,000 issued in large-size and small-size formats, Series of 1914 to the present day (the standard imprint on all of today's notes). Each bears the name of a Federal Reserve Bank and a letter designating its district.

Fractional Currency—Federal fractional bills made in denominations of 3¢, 5¢, 10¢, 15¢, 25¢, and 50¢, issued under the Act of March 3, 1863, succeeding Postage Currency notes.

Gold Certificate—Note from $10 to $10,000 issued in large-size and small-size formats, redeemable in gold coins.

greenback—Piece of paper money of $1 face value or higher with the back printed in green. Unofficial popular term for United States paper money in general, popularized by the Legal Tender Notes of the 1860s with their green backs (though these were not the first to be printed in this color), and widely used since.

Interest-Bearing Note—A note from $10 to $10,000 issued in the early 1860s, yielding interest to the bearer.

Legal Tender Note—Note from $1 to $10,000 issued in large-size and small-size formats. For a long time Legal Tender Notes were the basic mainstay of the federal paper-money system. Synonym: United States Note.

GLOSSARY

legal-tender status—A.k.a. obligation. Information given in the lettered inscriptions on a note, describing its exchangeability. As an example, certain early Legal Tender Notes have this inscription: "This note is a legal tender for all debts, public and private, except duties on imports and interest on the public debt, and is receivable in payment of all loans made to the United States."

National Bank Note—Note bearing the imprint of a specific National Bank and its location, plus the signature of bank officers, in addition to federal signatures and information. Original Series and Series of 1875 ("First Charter") issued in denominations from $1 to $1,000, large-size. Series of 1882 ("Second Charter") issued in denominations $5 to $100; large-size. Series of 1902 ("Third Charter"), issued in denominations $5 to $100, large-size. Series of 1929, issued in denominations $5 to $100, Type 1 and Type 2, small-size.

National Gold Bank Note—A note bearing the imprint of a specific National Bank and its location, plus the signature of bank officers, in addition to federal signatures and information. Issued in the early 1870s (in denominations of $5 to $100) by National Gold Banks located in the state of California. These notes were redeemable in gold coins.

pinhole—In the 19th century it was common practice to stitch several notes together for safekeeping, for hiding within a coat's lining, or storing in a small pile. Today, when certain notes are held to the light, tiny pinholes can be seen.

Plain Back—A description of certain blue-seal Series of 1902 National Bank Notes without the dates 1902 and 1908 printed on the back (such notes have other motifs, however).

Postage Currency—Federal fractional bills made in denominations of 5¢, 10¢, 25¢, and 50¢, and first issued in August 1862 to help alleviate a coin shortage. These were followed by Fractional Currency notes.

Refunding Certificate—Interest-bearing $10 certificate, not a currency note, issued in 1879.

Silver Certificate—A note from $1 to $1,000 issued in large-size and small-size formats, redeemable first in silver dollars, and later in silver bullion.

Specimen note—A Specimen note is an impression for test or other purposes, from a complete or partially complete plate, to illustrate its appearance. Such notes usually bear no serial numbers, or else just zeroes, and may be missing other elements, such as the Treasury seal and signatures. Specimen Fractional Currency note: general term for a Fractional Currency bill printed on one side only, face or back, and made for distribution to collectors, these being popular in the era in which they were made, the 1860s and 1870s. Usually capitalized, as Specimen.

star note—A large-size (beginning with silver certificates in 1910 and soon expanded to include all other series) or small-size note with a star next to the serial number is a replacement note, for one that was found to be defective and then destroyed. "Star notes" form a collecting specialty, especially for small-size notes. Stars added to serial numbers before 1910 are decorative and without meaning (examples including Series of 1890 Coin or Treasury Notes).

Value Back—Describes certain Series of 1882 National Bank Notes on which the denomination is printed in green on the back, spelled out, as FIVE DOLLARS, TEN DOLLARS, and so forth.

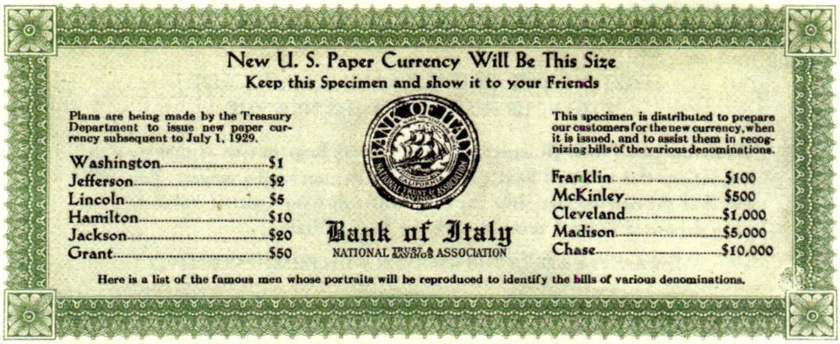

This is an example of a privately made circular describing the coming "reduced size" currency. Such circulars were distributed by various businessmen shortly before the new currency was placed into circulation in 1929. The back of the one shown contains an advertisement.

BIBLIOGRAPHY

Along with various smaller articles from a wide variety of sources, the following books and periodicals were consulted:

Bart, Dr. Frederich J., *United States Paper Money Errors,* Krause Publications, Iola, WI, 2003.

Bowers, Q. David. *Whitman Encyclopedia of U.S. Paper Money.* Whitman Publishing, LLC: Atlanta, GA, 2009.

DeLorey, Tom, and Fred Reed, *Price Guide For the Collector of Modern United States Paper Money Errors,* Amos Press, Inc., Sidney, Ohio, fourth ed., 1978.

Donlon, William P., *Donlon Price Catalog of United States Small Size Paper Money,* Hewitt Bros., Chicago, Illinois, various editions, 1964–1979.

Friedberg, Art. *A Guide Book of United States Paper Money*, fifth ed., Whitman Publishing, LLC: Pelham, Alabama, 2016.

Friedberg, Robert, *Paper Money of the United States,* Coin and Currency Institute, Inc., New York, various editions.

Gengerke, Martin, *United States Paper Money Records,* New York, ninth ed., 1998.

Hessler, Gene, *The Comprehensive Catalog of U.S. Paper Money,* BNR Press, 1997.

History of the Bureau of Engraving and Printing 1862–1962, Treasury Department, Washington, D.C., 1964.

Huntoon, P., and L. Van Belkum, *The National Bank Note Issues of 1929–1935,* ed. by M.O. Warns. Published by the Society of Paper Money Collectors, Hewitt Bros., Chicago, Illinois, 1970.

Kemm, Theodore, *Official Guide of United States Paper Money,* New York, various editions.

Lloyd, Robert, H., "National Bank Notes, Federal Reserve Bank Notes, Federal Reserve Notes 1928–1950," *Coin Collector's Journal,* Jan–Feb 1953, Wayte Raymond, Inc., 1953. Also other articles from this magazine.

Oakes, Dean and John Schwartz, *Standard Guide to Small-Size U.S. Paper Money 1928 to Date,* Krause Publications, Iola, WI, fourth ed., 2002.

O'Donnell et al., *Standard Handbook of Modern U.S. Paper Money,* sixth ed., 1977.

Petrov, Vladimir, *Money and Conquest—Allied Occupational Currencies in World War II,* The John Hopkins Press, Baltimore, Maryland, 1967.

Rundell, Walter, Jr., *Black Market Money,* Louisiana State University Press, 1964.

Shafer, Neil, *A Guide Book of Philippine Paper Money,* Whitman Publishing Co., Racine, Wisconsin, 1964.

Schwan, C.F., and Boling, J.E. *World War II Military Currency,* BNR Press, Portage, Ohio, 1978.

The Numismatist

Banknote Reporter

Numismatic News Weekly

Coin World weekly newspaper

Numismatic Scrapbook

Paper Money, published by the Society of Paper Money Collectors